THE AESTHETICS AND POLITICS OF THE CROWD IN AMERICAN LITERATURE

Mary Esteve provides a study of crowd representations in American literature from the antebellum era to the early twentieth century. As a central icon of political and cultural democracy, the crowd occupies a prominent place in the American literary and cultural landscape. Esteve examines a range of writing by Poe, Hawthorne, Lydia Maria Child, Du Bois, James, and Stephen Crane among others. These writers, she argues, distinguish between the aesthetics of immersion in a crowd and the mode of collectivity demanded of political-liberal subjects. In their representations of everyday crowds, ranging from streams of urban pedestrians to swarms of train travellers, from upper-class parties to lower-class revivalist meetings, such authors seize on the political problems facing a mass liberal democracy – problems such as the stipulations of citizenship, nation formation, mass immigration, and the emergence of mass media. Esteve examines both the aesthetic and political meanings of such urban crowd scenes.

MARY ESTEVE is Assistant Professor in the English Department at Concordia University, Montréal. Her work has appeared in *ELH*, *American Literary History*, and *Genre*.

CAMBRIDGE STUDIES IN AMERICAN LITERATURE AND CULTURE

Recent books in this series

THE AESTHETICS AND POLITICS OF THE CROWD IN AMERICAN LITERATURE

MARY ESTEVE

CAMBRIDGE
UNIVERSITY PRESS

PUBLISHED BY THE PRESS SYNDICATE OF THE UNIVERSITY OF CAMBRIDGE
The Pitt Building, Trumpington Street, Cambridge CB2 1RP, UK

CAMBRIDGE UNIVERSITY PRESS
The Edinburgh Building, Cambridge, CB2 2RU, UK
40 West 20th Street, New York, NY 10011-4211, USA
477 Williamstown Road, Port Melbourne, VIC 3207, Australia
Ruiz de Alarcón 13, 28014 Madrid, Spain
Dock House, The Waterfront, Cape Town 8001, South Africa

http://www.cambridge.org

First published 2003

Printed in the United Kingdom at the University Press, Cambridge

Typeface Adobe Garamond 11/12.5 pt   *System* LATEX 2$_\varepsilon$ [TB]

A catalogue record for this book is available from the British Library

ISBN 0 521 81488 X hardback

For Jeanie Gleason Esteve
my first, best, favorite word-farer

Contents

vii

Illustrations

Acknowledgments

So much of book-building depends on the generous contributions of others: their ideas, suggestions, objections, insights, anecdotes, enthusiasms. First and last I thank my dissertation director Ross Posnock for his relentless support at all stages of this project, for his magnanimous and, in the best sense of the word, bookish instruction. It is also a special pleasure to thank Frances Ferguson for her hospitality in Baltimore and for her sure-fire critical suggestions. Without the financial and intellectual infusion of a postdoctoral fellowship at Johns Hopkins's Center for Research on Culture and Literature, this book might never have seen the inside of a library. For his painstaking and incisive comments on the manuscript in its entirety, I am deeply grateful to Gregg Crane, ideal reader that he is. I am equally indebted to Walter Michaels for his exacting, refreshingly ruthless comments on this and previous work.

At an earlier stage of this project, the members of my dissertation committee at the University of Washington offered their wisdom and crucial advice: Bob Abrams, Mikkel Borch-Jacobsen, and Bob Markley. Since then readers of new or revised material have contributed much-needed criticisms and suggestions: Jason Frank, Neil Hertz, Cathy Jurca, Paul Kramer, Doug Mao, Sean McCann, John Plotz, Lisa Siraganian, Taylor Stoehr, Michael Szalay, Rochelle Tobias, and Michael Trask. Others, whose conversations, intelligence, and support I have greatly appreciated over the years, include Robin Blyn, Rick Bozorth, Tim Dean, Kevin Gustafson, Jayati Lal, Australia Tarver, and Steve Taubeneck. I am also very grateful for the input from those who took part in various works-in-progress forums: the Dallas Area Social History Group; the Colloquium on Women, Gender, and Sexuality at Hopkins, and the New York Americanist Group. More recently, the hospitality and remarkable sanity of my colleagues at Concordia, particularly the Chair, Terry Byrnes, have eased the transition to a new institution (and nation), thus making possible the completion of the manuscript. Ray Ryan and Nikki Burton at Cambridge University Press also deserve thanks for their patience and assistance.

For their abiding friendships and intellectual vitality I cannot thank sufficiently Jayati Lal (for the video-supper nights), Rochelle Tobias (for the midnight walks-talks), and Ross Posnock (for the 5-cents-a-minute conversational excursions). Finally, so much has depended upon the small, endearing crowd that has gathered more or less annually at the Oregon coast on the fourth Thursday of November: Alex, Ann, Donald, Doreen, Harry, Jeanie, Molly, Polly, Rachel, and Tracey.

Portions of this book have appeared previously: an earlier version of chapter 3 appeared in *ELH* in 1995; an earlier version of chapter 5 appeared in *American Literary History* in 1997. I am grateful to Johns Hopkins University Press and Oxford University Press for permission to reprint.

Introduction

The seventh section of George Oppen's poem *Of Being Numerous* (1968) appears as follows:

> Obsessed, bewildered
>
> By the shipwreck
> Of the singular
>
> We have chosen the meaning
> Of being numerous.[1]

The forty-part poem in its entirety can be read as a searching, speculative meditation on this particular section's concerns: crisis, singularity, choice, meaning, and above all numerosity. This section's syntax of narrative (the complete sentence, the present perfect verb tense), along with its testimonial collectivity (the first-person plural), gestures toward the historically persistent hold of these concerns on modern consciousness. The gesture is justifiable. In American literature, Edgar Allan Poe's "The Man of the Crowd" is often treated as the locus classicus of this inquiry into what being numerous entails. The story dramatizes one man's inexplicable attraction to crowds, an existential mystery that is compounded by the narrator-protagonist's inexplicable fascination with this one man. Oppen's lines could almost be taken as a latter-day ventriloquism of Poe's mute character, were it not for the fact that this man appears so obsessed and bewildered as to be incapable of choosing anything at all.

Choosing – or more simply exemplifying – the meaning of being numerous: this book offers a necessarily selective and truncated genealogy of this preoccupation. Its point of entry is the city crowd. Beginning with the antebellum era's incipient urban consciousness and concluding with what is commonly referred to as the nation's second great wave of mass immigration, I focus on the period during which Americans came to understand themselves as veritable veterans of numerosity, that is, as inhabiting a culture of crowds. By the end of the nineteenth century it was as commonplace to allude in passing, as William James did in his preface to *The Principles of Psychology*, to "this crowded age," as it was still inflammatory and melodramatic to pronounce it, as Gustave Le Bon and Friedrich Nietzsche respectively did, "the ERA OF CROWDS" and "the century of the crowd."[2] The aesthetic, political, psycho-physiological, and social scientific discursive currents that informed such comments comprise the material of my examination. My aim is to track the implications of this emerging imagination of the crowd as a ubiquitous, culturally saturating phenomenon for the era's concomitantly evolving political and aesthetic commitments. I undertake to demonstrate how a heightened awareness of inhabiting a crowd culture could contribute, perhaps ironically, to more resolute distinctions between political and aesthetic categories of experience.

Throughout Western history, crowd representations have been fraught with political meaning. In his book *The Crowd and the Mob* the historian J. S. McClelland suggests that since its inception political thought has practically revolved around the crowd: "It could almost be said that political theorizing was *invented* to show that democracy, the rule of men by themselves, necessarily turns into rule by the mob." McClelland goes on to sum up this preoccupation:

Plato's account in *The Republic* of democracy as mob rule degenerating into tyranny prepares the way for a host of crowd images: the crowd hounding Christ to death; the crowd bawling for blood in the circus; crowds of mutinous legionaries looking round for someone to raise to the purple; crowds led by wild men in from the desert in Late Antiquity; the Nika riots which nearly cost Justinian the Empire; later Roman mobs making trouble for popes; medieval crowds volatile at great festivals and fairs; peoples' crusades[;] ... the barbarism of crowds during the Wars of Religion; crowds at public executions; peasant revolts; Whilkite and Church and King mobs in London; liberty mobs in Boston; the crowd in the French Revolution; lynch mobs; the mobs of industrial discontent; the list is endless.[3]

In American literary history as well, the list of crowd representations verges on endlessness. The reader of this study may notice the absence of some of the more conspicuous crowd scenes: Hester Prynne enduring the punitive stare of the Puritan multitude; Ahab magnetizing his crew; Colonel Sherburn fending off the lynch mob after killing Boggs; Pudd'nhead Wilson alternately stirring and stilling the courtroom audience with his fingerprint evidence; Carrie Madenda generating male spectators' phantasmatic affection by frowning quaintly on stage; George Hurstwood being called a scab by trolley strikers; Lawrence Selden spotting the vivid Lily Bart amid the

Grand Central Station crowd; Tod Hackett finding himself caught up in the surges of the Hollywood premiere crowd. Rather than attempting a comprehensive account in which all these crowd scenes (and the multi-tudinous others going unmentioned) might be addressed, I have elected to dwell on a relatively small number of texts. While some of these are indeed obscure (such as Lydia Maria Child's *Letters from New York* and Henry James's "The Papers"), they have all been selected on the basis of their ways of representing, in particularly dramatic or crystallized form, certain aspects of the culture of crowds that I wish to highlight.

In the genealogy I trace, unmotivated city crowds turn out, similar to the motivated crowds McClelland cites, to register a fundamental incom-patibility with prevailing political practices. But they do so not so much by violating democracy as by abandoning liberalism, its principles and proce-dures of justice. Nevertheless, these crowds had a crucial discursive role to play, one that, for reasons elaborated below, can be termed aesthetic. Such figures of the crowd did ultimately bear political meaning, but it was a neg-ative meaning; it entailed the negation of their place at the political-liberal table. As opposed to politically motivated or purposeful crowds, urban crowds – the kind that Poe's character psychotically immerses himself in – became highly valuable for delineating the moral and psycho-physiological boundaries of liberalism, thus for rendering a political mode of "being numerous" distinct from other modes of being in the world.

In other words, because of the way urban crowds readily embodied a modern polity's democratic populace without, however, harboring any specific political contention, they, as discursive figures, made visible the idea of a categorically separate sphere, wherein this politically defined populace could be seen as engaged in distinctly non-political, but nevertheless deeply attractive and arguably humanly essential, activity. Such representations thus clarified the value of conceiving the political as *not* being everywhere, of conceiving it instead as a set of specific principles and procedures pertaining to a circumscribed sphere of social life. Even as an overarching conceptual structure of political liberalism would remain the enabling mechanism for such distinctions; even as certain non-trivial realms of life, such as the economic, would appear at once political and non-political; and even as certain features of non-political life, such as the Judeo-Christian tradition of the covenant, would overlap with central features of political liberalism, representations of urban crowds made visible the conceptual value and moral necessity of preserving such formally operative distinctions.

Broadly speaking, the central political task from the mid-nineteenth to the early twentieth centuries was to hammer out the formal meanings, the procedures, and the institutional formations of large-scale democratic liberalism, while confronting some of the nation's egregiously illiberal practices such as slavery and its aftermath of Jim Crow policies, gender discrimination, and the favoring of corporate power at the expense of the laboring poor. As Michael Schudson explains in his recent history of American civic life, "the politics of assent" characterizing the founding period of limited suffrage and largely uncontested elections "gave way early in the nineteenth century to a new mass democracy, the world's first." This expanded territory of politics required working out "basic rules of political practice, including formal constitutional provisions, statutory laws, and conventional patterns of public activity," all of which were destined to transform over the course of the century.[4]

But while this expansion of the political field would seem to require more, not less, political awareness and skill on the part of an increasingly enfranchised populace, the era also witnessed the rise of scientistic discourses, such as psycho-physiology and crowd psychology, that called into question the human being's capacity to function as an autonomous, self-determining, rational subject, that is, as a political-liberal agent. Literary representations that first flesh out the socio-political tensions arising from this prevailing set of phenomena and truths, of ambitions and misgivings, and second mediate these tensions through the articulation of a crowd aesthetics, constitute the focus of the present study. In order to clarify how these mediations took discursive shape, this study's key terms – the crowd, the public, the aesthetic, and the political – themselves need fleshing out, both historically and theoretically.

THE CROWD MIND

Crowd psychology derived its tools of analysis and explanatory authority from the era's medical research on hypnotic suggestibility and imitation, and advanced a set of "laws" which it saw as socially determining the actions and passions of all but the most self-controlled persons. Such premises were far-reaching. For while crowd psychologists built their cases on what had for centuries been stigmatized as undesirable mob behavior, they applied their arguments to widely divergent and largely normative social phenomena. Legislative bodies, electoral populations, juries, fashion crazes, religious movements, newspaper readerships, and urban street populations could all exhibit symptoms of a crowd mentality. Gabriel Tarde, for instance, warned against the city as such: its "animate environment" could function like "magnetic passes," thereby rendering its population "somnambulistic."[5]

Largely French and Italian, these analysts influenced the then burgeoning field of American sociology. "Imitation-suggestion," the historian of science Ruth Leys remarks, "became the unifying concept for a newly professionalizing American sociology committed to abandoning contractual, utilitarian, and biological models of society in order to place the study of the relation of self to other on a new, psychological foundation."[6] Committed as both American and European social scientists were to this overarching psychological theory, however, their own ideological stances betrayed a deep analytical inconsistency. Theorizing social suggestion and imitation, they exhorted individualism and innovation.[7] Indeed Le Bon's entire project aimed to explain how the best way to manage crowds was by becoming their savvy and manipulative leader. As the American sociologist Edward Ross argued in his 1897 essay, "The Mob Mind," in "a good democracy blind imitation can never take the place of individual effort to weigh and judge... We must hold always to a sage Emersonian individualism, that... shall brace men to stand against the rush of the mass."[8] Ross is best known as a theorist of social control who sought to mold individuals by means of suggestion, but clearly such means were not meant to apply to the molders themselves. Ross counts among the many nineteenth-century social scientists who retreated from their own theory of imitation-suggestion – and back into an essentialist individualism – at the point where it conflicted with their ideological desire to preserve the domain of innovation, leadership, and social progress.

In other words, crowd psychology undercuts its own oppositional structure, while the theorists of crowd psychology reactively back off from it. This double movement, as Mikkel Borch-Jacobsen has incisively shown, is especially prominent in Le Bon's work, in which the crowd is represented as verging on a sort of internal differentiation. "Profoundly 'anonymous,' even unnameable," Borch-Jacobsen writes, the crowd's unconscious "has no content [and no identity] of its own. The paradox of [Le Bon's] crowd is such that its homogenization is based not on a common ground but on the absence of any 'subjectal' ground." It is thus "impossible to define crowds except through their 'impulsiveness,' their 'mobility,' and their 'irritability'" – in other words, through "their *total lack of specificity*" or their "*noncharacteristics.*"[9] The crowd enters, in other words, what William James calls, in the preface to his former student Boris Sidis's work, *The Psychology of Suggestion* (1898), "the limits of the consciousness of a human being." Sidis himself will describe this hypnotic self (in reference to a schizophrenic patient) as a "[n]obody, nothing," "a reality [which] has no being." This self is "devoid of all personal character; it is both subpersonal and impersonal... [I]t is always roaming about, passing through the most fantastic metamorphoses." The final quarter of his book is devoted to applying imitation-suggestion theory to the analysis of crowd phenomena. He essentially reprises the arguments advanced in his 1895 article published in the *Atlantic Monthly*. There he describes the man who joins a mob as undergoing "the entire loss of his personal self."[10]

Long before crowd psychology emerged as a scientific discourse, conventional tropes registered this sense of a crowd's loss of personality. Rendered as oceans, streams, seas, swarms, and masses that press, jam, crush, flock, mob, throng, and pack their way into being, crowds were figured as inanimate, homogeneous, at best animalistic entities. In the crowdedness of the crowd thus obtains a pure, anonymous power or affect, what Borch-Jacobsen calls "unpower" – there no longer being present a subject, so to speak, to subject. In this sense the crowd is internally differentiated: it is constituted through the aggregation of persons, whereby the aggregation itself occasions the evacuation of these persons' personalities. Such is crowd psychology's key claim about the nature of human being.

But as Borch-Jacobsen goes on to clarify, this account of human being is effectively "blocked, in *The Crowd*, at the point where a leader, a *Führer*, is peremptorily assigned." Both Le Bon and Tarde are constrained by their "inability to think the group through to the very end: beyond the individual, beyond the subject... [E]verything came to freeze or fixate around the Hypnotist-Leader... [who] came out of nowhere, explained everything without explaining itself." Le Bon speaks of "the instinctive need of all beings forming a crowd to obey a leader." Similarly, Tarde asserts that "the magnetised subject imitates the magnetiser, but that the latter does not imitate the former," going on to insist that the "unilateral must have preceded the reciprocal. Without an age of authority... an age of comparative fraternity would never have existed."[11] Yet neither Tarde nor Le Bon explains how a hypnotic, affectively animated entity such as the crowd could produce an autonomous, self-willed individual such as a leader. Adhering nonetheless to this model of commanding hypnotist and obeying subject, crowd psychology thus forces itself to retreat from its radical conceptualization of the crowd as enacting what amounts to the pre-collective or pre-subjective "noncharacteristic" of human being.

To put it another, more schematic way, while late nineteenth-century social analysts muscled their way back into an ideological opposition of the one and the many, their own materialist theories of human psychophysiology posited the hypnotic limit of consciousness as something like a zero: hence Sidis's nobody, nothing, a reality without being. The zero, as

William James once suggested, is a sort of impossible actuality: "Half the ideas we make use of are impossible or problematic things – zeros, infinites, fourth dimensions, limits of ideal perfection, forces, relations sundered from their terms, or terms defined only conceptually."[12] The conception of zero also informs his idea of "pure experience." For the purposes of historical and theoretical contextualization, it is worth noting that when James endeavors to describe in *Essays on Radical Empiricism* the condition of pure experience, he does so by invoking an image that dramatically calls the crowd to mind: the mosaic. James jostles conventional empiricist expectations by having the mosaic illustrate something other than an atomistic, quantitative conception of manyness and diversity. He reconfigures it as an entity that coheres by virtue of impossibly real transitions – transitions which are both actual and absent:

In actual mosaics the pieces are held together by their bedding, for which bedding the substances, transcendental egos, or absolutes of other philosophies are taken to stand. In radical empiricism *there is no bedding*; it is as if the pieces clung together by their edges, the transitions experienced between them forming their cement . . . [E]xperience itself, taken at large, can grow by its edges. That one moment of it proliferates into the next by transitions, which, whether conjunctive or disjunctive, continue the experiential tissue, cannot, I contend, be denied. Life is in the transitions as much as in the terms connected.[13]

This passage illustrates how, without resorting to dialectical negation, "no bedding" paradoxically becomes bedding. Within James's radical empiricist or materialist reality, relations function as external yet immanent limits – as "edges." There is no negation but rather "proliferation," no nothingness but rather "life." In this configuration, as James writes elsewhere, "[n]o part *there* is so small as not to be a place of conflux. No part there is not really next its neighbors; which means that *there is literally nothing between*; which means again that no part goes exactly so far and no farther; that no part absolutely excludes another, but that they compenetrate and are cohesive; . . . that whatever is real is telescoped and diffused into other reals."[14] In pursuing this line of thought, James avoids the pitfalls of a conventional empiricism which reduces experience to sense-perception and ontology to atomistic humanism. He aims instead for a conception of reality that is "continuous yet novel," as he puts it in his notes, knowing full well that this "notion involves the whole paradox of an *it* whose modes are alternate and exclusive of each other [that is, internally differentiated], the same and not the same interpenetrating. Express it as you will, you can't get away from this *sort* of statement when you undertake to describe reality." Such "compenetration," he maintains, "admits better of the *con* and *ex* relation being simultaneous, [and] such simultaneity is the crux" of a radical empiricism.[15]

It is the crux as well, I want to suggest, of a revaluation of representations of urban modernity and its iconic topos, the crowd. For in his appropriation and redescription of the mosaic as an exemplum of "pure experience," James effectively affirms crowd psychology's logic of internal differentiation while eliminating crowd psychology's self-contradictory assertion of a crowd leader. In James's system there is no place for leaderly management of pure experience. Emblematic of a psycho-physiological or ontological condition, the mosaic marks the originary novelty of being, the emergence of something out of nothing, of persons and consciousness out of an impersonal, non-conscious state.[16] Though usually formulated in far less philosophical or scientistic terms, the crowd representations to which I attend in this study incorporate crucial elements of this psycho-physiological or what I would call hyper-materialist ontology. In the nineteenth and early twentieth centuries, the urban crowd became the material, socio-political site on which to elaborate this ontology's conditions and ramifications.

Some literary and cultural historians, enjoined by a causation-oriented methodology, might regard skeptically this study's scant attention to historical sequence. I do not squarely address, for instance, whether crowd phenomena gave rise to the very idea of internal differentiation or vice versa. For me, however, of far more compelling interest than the issue of historical causation are the broader political and aesthetic implications of such highly charged crowd representations. For during this time period, the crowd, as an icon of American democracy, of "the people," already bore considerable discursive weight. What I hope to demonstrate over the course of this study was the viability of accepting, as an aesthetic mode of being, the hyper-materialist logic of the crowd, in which the crowd or hypnotic subject embodied the limit – the mosaic's "edge" – of consciousness, while simultaneously maintaining a commitment to the political requirements of liberal republicanism, whose presupposed citizen possessed self-conscious reason.[17]

Most of the writers featured in this study perform this u-turn by subscribing, if only implicitly, to a Kantian dualism between the sensible and the intelligible (or supersensible), between affect and reason. Kant's political-moral thought entered the American scene primarily by way of the Transcendentalist movement of the 1830s and 1840s. The movement's resident Kant authority, Frederic Henry Hedge, saw in his system of distinctions (between subject and object, phenomena and noumena, reason and understanding) a proclamation of "moral liberty...as it had never been proclaimed before."[18] As an alternative to Locke's sensationalism and Hume's instrumentalist claim of reason's enslavement to the passions, Kant offered, according to the committed democrat, German scholar, and semi-Transcendentalist George Bancroft, "the categorical rule of practical morality, the motive to disinterested virtue"; he goes on to suggest that "therefore [Kant's] philosophy claims for humanity the right of ever renewed progress and reform."[19] Where the Calvinist theologians at Princeton, J. W. Alexander, Albert Dod, and Charles Hodge, criticized the Transcendentalists for mistakenly using Kant to support their claims to reason's "divine and active powers," they also (disparagingly) clarified Kant's work:

[Kant] meant to attribute to pure reason the power of directing the cognitive energy beyond its nearer objects, and to extend its research indefinitely; but by no means to challenge for this power the direct intuition of the absolute, as the veritable object of infallible insight... The system of Kant led to skepticism... that all the laws of thought are altogether subjective, and the evil consequence was remedied only by assigning an illogical office to the Practical Reason.[20]

However murkily and even mistakenly understood, and however unappealing to devout theologians, Kant's thought contributed to the on-going engagement in the United States with Enlightenment ideas and ideals.

In his anti-slavery writings, William Ellery Channing perhaps stated most succinctly the political-moral dimension of this engagement:

Such a being [the enslaved man] was plainly made for an End in Himself. He is a Person, not a Thing. He is an End, not a mere Instrument or Means...Such a being was plainly made to obey a law within Himself. This is the essence of a moral being. He possesses as a part of his nature, and the most essential part, a sense of Duty, which he is to reverence and follow, in opposition to all pleasure and pain, to all interfering human wills. The great purpose of all good education and discipline is, to make a man Master of Himself, to excite him to act from a principle in his own mind.[21]

In this system of personal autonomy and non-sensible Duty, "excite[ment]" serves merely to activate the moral will; it is what John Rawls designates a conception-dependent desire, in contradistinction to object-dependent desires, which comprise our bodily impulses and socially internalized inclinations.[22] Thus intentions and motives, rather than rational self-interest or prudence, serve as the basis for moral reasoning. The confidence that, as Bancroft put it, "reason is a universal faculty," made possible in turn the confidence in the political-moral rectitude of "the common mind," "the multitude," hence in the viability of mass democracy.[23]

Where the widely influential Scottish moral sense philosophy underwrote alternately sentiment-based and reason-based moral structures, with Kant, such equivocation disappeared. Common sense or the *sensus communis* entailed for him not simply knowing innately moral truth, but being capable of justifying it through reason. It is "a *public* sense, i.e. a critical faculty which in its reflective act takes account (*a priori*) of the mode of representation of every one else, in order, *as it were*, to weigh its judgement with the collective reason of mankind."[24] Universal reason, of course, informs the "categorical rule of practical morality" invoked by Bancroft and recorded by Emerson in "Civilization" (1862):

The evolution of a highly destined society must be moral[.] ... It must be catholic in its aims. What is moral? It is the respecting in action catholic or universal ends. Hear the definition which Kant gives of moral conduct: "Act always so that the immediate motive of thy will may become a universal rule for all intelligent beings."[25]

Even the Harvard professor, Unitarian theologian, and *North American Review* editor Francis Bowen, who in his *Principles of Metaphysical and Ethical Science Applied to the Evidences of Religion* (1852/1855) eschewed Kant's a priori categories and considered the moral faculty "above reason" (282), tilted far more toward Kant's ethical system than toward the sympathy-driven rational benevolence and outcomes-driven instrumentalism articulated by various Scottish Enlightenment philosophers.[26] Apart from Kant's claim of a priori reason as the limit of human capacity, which disabled Bowen's proving God's existence by way of reasoning from effect back to the "infinite Cause," Bowen's ethical conceptions accorded fully with Kant's. He argued that the conscience or moral obligation is innate, that it is distinct from sense or sympathy, from desire or compulsion, that it is not subject to a system of punishment and reward, that it is grounded in motives and intentions, not in prudence or consequences, and that it has no prior cause, not even divine command: "We do not do right because God commands it, but God commands it because it is right."[27] Altogether Bowen's moral universe shares remarkably much with Kant's.

What is primarily absent from Bowen's moral universe is the element of universal reason. Besides serving as a legitimizing mechanism, universal reason functions in Kant's system to link individual morality to a political justice grounded in equality. It also functions to endow ethical reason with what Rawls terms its own "court of appeal." Reason "is always free to reconsider its prior decisions; no case is ever shut for good." By contrast, Bowen maintains that a characteristic of conscience is "the absolute certainty of its decisions."[28] Such substantive (as opposed to formal) absolutism proved highly problematic for the nineteenth century. As Gregg Crane has recently shown in his important work, *Race, Citizenship, and Law in American Literature*, a political-moral system capable of flexibility and change, yet also grounded in principles of conscience and consent, was crucial to the antebellum abolitionist movement. Adducing the confluence of natural rights discourse and higher law doctrine in abolitionist texts, Crane sheds valuable light on the key role Enlightenment universalism – as opposed to coercive ideology – played in shaping the political and cultural landscape of the nineteenth century.[29]

By appealing to evidence of the concomitant emergence of Kantian ethics, I endeavor to broaden the view of the Enlightenment project's historical presence in American literature and culture. My focus is specifically on the signs of investment in secular ethical reason as the basis of judgment and justice. However spotty the evidence of Kant's direct impact on nineteenth-century (particularly antebellum) American views, it is clear that Kantian thought was, as Foucault might say, *thinkable* at this time and place. It may be helpful to flag, once again, my methodological commitments. I am less motivated by the idea of developing a positivist reception history of Kant's work than by the ambition of tracking the effects of a Kantian way of thinking in American literature and culture. Analogous to the way, as Rawls puts it, Kant "believes that our everyday understanding is implicitly aware of the requirements of practical reason, both pure and empirical," I adhere to the historicist claim that discursive venues implicitly convey a political-ethical logic along with its consequent values.[30] Oddly enough, or so it may seem at first glance, nineteenth-century fictional representations involving intensely affecting crowds formed a crucial venue for registering and affirming the features and implications of a Kantian political-ethical logic.

In the chapters that follow, I examine texts with an eye for the way they build dramatic tension and social meaning not around American crowd culture's skirmishes between the one and the many (the leaders and the led), nor, conversely, around skirmishes between the dominant bourgeois many and the marginalized few (the conformist middle-class consumer-spectators and their excluded but desired rebel-objects of consumption). Nor do I look for how texts figure the crowd merely to celebrate the heterogeneous give-and-take, rough-and-tumble world of Whitmanesque democracy. Certain elements of these critical approaches do, of course, factor into my discussion – for instance, where I argue that Poe dramatizes the categorical exclusion of the psychotic man of the crowd from the political-liberal domain. Nevertheless, my analytical orientation in general has little to do with the ideology critique of power. Rather, it is framed by the question of how crowd representations make visible the reciprocally defining contours of a broadly existing culture of affect and a more narrowly existing, yet (as discussed above) conceptually overarching, sphere of political-liberal reason. In short, the anonymous, hypnotic persons entering the crowd mind by affective compulsion and the abstract, self-conscious persons entering the public square by reasoning consent constitute the *dramatis personae* of this study. As literary representations tend to set in motion constellations of persons rather than swaths of aggregate populations, much of my analysis dwells on persons who I adduce embody various permutations of the crowd or public states of being. The state of being numerous turns out to have much to do with the state of being singular.

In the antebellum era, as in other times, "crowd" and "public" were often used interchangeably. But however discursively interchanged these *words* were, the *ideas* of the crowd and the public registered two fundamentally distinct meanings of being numerous. In the next section of this introduction I survey some of the central features of the contemporary debate revolving around the theorization of the public sphere.

THE PUBLIC SQUARE

Recent debates stimulated by Jürgen Habermas's *The Structural Transformation of the Public Sphere* have done much to clarify the political theoretical issues at stake in conceptualizing the status and function of the public sphere. His endorsement of bourgeois modernity's commitment to a public sphere based on abstract universalism has been aggressively critiqued on both historical and theoretical grounds. In his book Habermas makes the historical-descriptive and theoretical-prescriptive claim that in the eighteenth century "abstract universality afforded the sole guarantee that the individuals subsumed under it in an equally abstract fashion... were set free in their subjectivity precisely by this parity."[31] The historical accuracy of his description of the liberal bourgeois public's rise and fall can be legitimately disputed, as Habermas himself readily concedes – in that, for instance, it fails to consider substantially the bourgeois public's exclusionary dimensions, failing as well to take into account the role of the working class in its formation.[32] But confusions arise when critics attempt to use evidence of the bourgeois public's historical shortcomings to critique its theoretical legitimacy.

For instance, Nancy Fraser and Michael Warner argue independently that the bourgeois public's deployment of abstraction excludes in principle (not simply in malpractice) from public forums the sociopolitically marginalized, whose identities as such are determined by bourgeois standards of race, class, gender, and so forth. In "Rethinking the Public Sphere" Fraser contends that "the bourgeois conception of the public sphere was [not] simply an unrealized utopian ideal; it was also a masculinist ideological notion that functioned to legitimate an emergent form of class rule" and to enforce "exclusionary norms."[33] Similarly, Warner in "The Mass Public and the Mass Subject" argues that the "bourgeois public sphere has been structured from the outset by a logic of abstraction that provides a privilege for unmarked identities: the male, the white, the middle class, the normal... As the bourgeois public sphere paraded the spectacle of its disincorporation, it brought into being this minoritizing logic of domination." While reiterating historical commonplaces, these arguments are logically adrift. To be sure, historically "the ability to abstract oneself has always been an unequally available resource," one most readily available to white, literate, propertied males; further, this class of people proved functionally equipped to mask their identities, unmarking themselves by equating themselves with the abstract individual, and thereby preserving their privileges and power.[34] But it makes no sense to attribute the abusive practices carried out in the name of self-abstraction to the principle of self-abstraction, that is, to cite the principle as the logical premise ("the masculinist ideological notion," "the minoritizing logic," the "logic of domination") of such practices. Historians have shown that the identification, domination, and abuse of the socially marginalized indeed coincided with the rise of the bourgeois public; and there can be little doubt that the coincidence was not accidental but genetic. But the genesis has surely to do with situational (that is, material) asymmetries, not with logical, abstract principles. Social inequality cannot even become phenomenologically significant until the abstract, universal principle of equality is conceptually installed and culturally naturalized.[35] A crucial point about abstract equality is that it is abstract, which is to say non-empirical, and thus unavailable for co-optation by a particular subset of persons. Where Warner contends that "the very mechanism designed to end domination is a form of domination," he mistakenly reads form as content, principle as practice.[36] As a normative ideal, political-theoretical universalism does not signify some utopian place to be attained in the future; rather, it signifies the reasoning principles with which a liberal polity operates as it proposes to structure itself according to such moral values as justice as fairness, legislative openness, due process, and so forth.

In the current climate of literary and cultural studies it has become increasingly difficult to make or defend arguments based on liberal principles such as reason, abstract individualism, and universalism without coming across as a conservative authoritarian or worse. The postmodern suspicion of the Enlightenment has inspired this general assault on reason; it has also inspired a romanticization of the socially marginalized or the politically oppressed as "the other of reason," to borrow Jürgen Habermas's phrase, while neglecting to account for the fact that the integration of abstract reason – which informs modern conceptions of justice as fairness, of agreement to the norms of public law, and equality before it – as a political value both defined modern oppression as such and over the course of modern history has helped to eliminate much of it. Consequently the celebration of concrete, local difference, of dynamic instability, of contradiction, transition, change and contingency has become ipso facto the mark of a privileged political radicalism or resistance to what one critic calls (with no compulsion to justify or explain) "the heavy thumb of the normative."[37] Certain preferred theoretical models have legitimized this trend. Bakhtinian dialogism, for instance, aims to show how a double-voicedness inhabits monologic discourse, the assumption being that the now-revealed heteroglossia serves to disrupt or subvert totalitarian monologism. Similarly, deconstruction is often deployed to demonstrate the constitutive instability of a linguistic, social, psychological, or political system. Locating the heretofore hidden otherness in such systems is also asserted, or presumed, to be politically salutary because disruptive and transformative.

Closer to this study's thematics of collectivity, the Bakhtinian model has inspired recent critics to make distinctions between what they see as elitist (hence conservative) and populist (hence progressive) representations of crowds. Philip Gould, for instance, in *Covenant and Republic*, an analysis of early nineteenth-century American historical romance and the politics of Puritanism, applies Bakhtin "to show the unintended presence of dual voices, which...reveals...the cultural tensions inhabiting a conservative elite faced with the rise of modern capitalism." More specifically, he turns to nineteenth-century representations of the seventeenth-century crowd hysteria occasioned by the Puritan witch hunts to show how "Harvard-centered liberals" with their "conservative republican ideology" express their "class-driven fears of popular democracy," and how as "status quo groups" they "further shored up their power by assailing the social margins."[38] In this account, writers who represent crowds as impassioned and unreasoning register their conservative, reactionary fear that a democratic populace threatens to destroy their stable world of reason, hierarchy, and privilege. Implicit in Gould's account, then, is the dubious view that to defend reason is anti-democratic and authoritarian, while crowd passion is essentially democratic and thereby of positive political value.

Another critic, Jonathan Elmer, in his study of Edgar Allan Poe, *Reading at the Social Limit*, understands the democratic *socius* to be not so much managed and policed by elites as itself totalitarian. He follows the political philosopher Claude Lefort's deconstructive theorization of democracy as a mode of social power which, propped up by the symbolic ideal of popular sovereignty, always threatens to become totalitarian, but whose totality is also constitutively incoherent or incomplete. The net effect, then, is "a destabilization of the transcendent categories of justice and reason, submitting law and science alike to a generalized interpretive uncertainty."[39] Poe's crowd representations in Elmer's account thus reveal antebellum America's totalitarian tendencies and self-undermining ruptures. His argument relies heavily on the conflation of political and social modes of power and being. As suggested earlier, this conflation is by no means a conceptual necessity. In the next section I endeavor to clarify how representations of social propensities and powers can be read as aesthetic rather than political, thereby undoing this conflation.

THE AESTHETIC BEHOLDER

The following chapters feature writers who exhibit a supple understanding of liberal democracy's presuppositions and values while also registering the era's aesthetic fascination with crowds. In W. E. B. Du Bois's narrative "Of the Coming of John," for instance, the crowd, in the form of a lynch mob, is redescribed by the victim as an irresistibly sublime feature of both the New York street crowds and Wagnerian opera. In this manner Du Bois importantly if also disturbingly empties the lynch mob of its political meaning. Figuring sublime absorption or involvement, which, by virtue of its extreme demands on consciousness, is fundamentally incompatible with political liberalism, the crowd functions to mark out an experiential category apart from the political.

This is not to say, however, that all modes of aesthetic experience or all elements of aesthetic discourse are at odds with political-liberal principles. Indeed, as Steven Knapp has importantly shown, most are not. He argues that literary art objects serve to validate liberal agency by constructing for the reader an occasion to oscillate between typicality and particularity, wherein the literary artifact's communicability is predicated on the typical or public quality of the reader's affective response to it.[40] In addition to this structural commensurability, one might consider aesthetic terms of evaluation, such as symmetry and balance, which readily find political-liberal counterparts. Sublime absorption, however, eludes these predications. Within the representational frame, the crowd instantiates the incommunicable, the radically asymmetrical and incommensurable. Of course, "I" as critical analyst am situated in the liberal world outside the text's representational frame, as is the text's author.

In adducing this link between the crowd mind and the sublime aesthetic and this disarticulation of the aesthetic from the political, I am both drawing on and re-aligning particular aspects of Kantian aesthetic theory and current deconstruction-inspired political theory. Kant's *Critique of Judgement* revolutionized aesthetic theory by locating in the beholder rather than the art object the source of meaning. According to this theory aesthetic pleasure remains essentially a matter of unarguable, private taste; aesthetic reflection, on the other hand, is provoked by the senses but then travels to its antinomy, to the disinterested realm of the supersensible where it lays down a judgment "ostensibly of general validity (public)." It is thus predicated on the idea of common sense – an indeterminate norm of agreement that implies a non-empirical or intelligible relation to the aesthetic object.[41] As Anthony Cascardi has noted, Kant importantly distinguishes between a *sensus communis aestheticus* and a *sensus communis logicus*. The latter pertains to determinate political matters because it engages concepts such as moral rules, whereas the former pertains to indeterminate aesthetic matters because it engages purely subjective feeling. Still, both aesthetic-reflective and political-critical modes of judgment are necessarily conditioned by a non-empirical public orientation: "the assertion is not that everyone *will* fall in with our judgement, but rather that everyone *ought* to agree with it."[42]

In crowd representations, the beholder is also the source of aesthetic meaning. But in contrast to Kant's aesthetic and political judgment, the aesthetic relation elicited by the crowd begins in the realm of sense and then, provoking absorption, travels not to the realm of non-empirical supersensibility but as it were to the realm of non-empirical insensibility – non-empirical because the beholder-subject is no longer aware of itself as an organizing receiver of experience. Thus a wholly different mode of disinterest obtains. As mentioned, the aesthetic relation to the crowd is more akin to the sublime than the beautiful in that the crowd takes on qualities of startlingly powerful nature, through its inanimacy, impersonality, and size.[43] But here, too, the same conceptual differences from Kant's account apply. Where Kant understands the sublime to be an occasion for apprehending "what is absolutely great" – beyond all comparison – thus for eliciting reflective feelings of respect, the crowd elicits mimetic identification.[44] The beholder enters, as it were, rather than apprehends the sublime object, that is, that which occasions sublimity in the beholder.

Hawthorne's description in *The House of Seven Gables* of Clifford Pyncheon's encounter of a crowd in the form of a parade marching past the house captures the operative distinction between the Kantian and the mimetic sublime:

As a mere object of sight, nothing is more deficient in picturesque features than a procession, seen in its passage through narrow streets. The spectator feels it to be fool's play, when he can distinguish the tedious common-place of each man's visage . . . and the dust on the back of his coat. In order to become majestic, it should be viewed from some vantage-point, as it rolls its slow and long array through the centre of a wide plain, or the stateliest public square of a city; for then by its remoteness, it melts all the petty personalities, of which is made up, into one broad mass of existence – one great life – one collected body of mankind, with a vast, homogeneous spirit animating it. But, on the other hand, if an impressible person, standing alone over the brink of one of these processions, should behold it, not in its atoms, but in its aggregate – as a mighty river of life, massive in its tide, and black with mystery, and, out of its depths, calling to the kindred depth within him – then the contiguity would add to the effect. It might so fascinate him, that he would hardly be restrained from plunging into the surging stream of human sympathies . . . Had Clifford attained the balcony, he would probably have leaped into the street.[45]

Hawthorne's explication in this passage of how distance from the crowd contributes to its majesty at first works to establish a Kantian sublime, much as Kant stressed that a "safe" distance from sublime nature's dangers enabled "this soul-stirring delight."[46] But Hawthorne takes a significantly different turn when speculating on an "impressible" person's relation to the crowd. With him, distance or no, the crowd would prove overpowering in its fascination, appealing to "kindred depths." This person's mimetic compulsion would land him in the "blackness" of the crowd's "homogeneous spirit."

To be sure, Clifford, who incarnates this impressible person, is the town's resident oddball. But as Hawthorne intimates elsewhere in the novel "almost everybody is" to some extent like Clifford.[47] In their manner of making available the imagination of a subjectivity radically devoid of identity or value, this and other figures of the crowd contributed importantly to a redescription of pluralism. This redescription takes diversity to be not a matter of multi-cultural or multi-positional identity but of formally distinct spheres of value and human propensity. Rawls explains how liberal democratic society builds itself on the fact of reasonable pluralism, that is, on the fact that a diversity of non-political religious, moral, and philosophical doctrines animates reasonable persons' affirmation of political liberalism. This political conception is nevertheless "free-standing and expounded apart from, or without reference to, any such wider background." Rawls is careful to distinguish reasonable pluralism from pluralism as such, so as to disallow the inclusion of "doctrines that are not only irrational but mad and aggressive." An absorptive crowd aesthetics would count as one of these disallowed doctrines, which Rawls assumes "always exist" but do not endanger democratic society so long as they "do not gain enough currency to undermine society's essential justice."[48] Foregrounding the human subject's affective propensity to overstimulate itself to the point of self-evacuation, crowd figurations drive home the point that not everything need or should be political. The aesthetic, as dramatized by absorptive fascination with crowds, divides itself off from the political.

THE POLITICAL CITIZEN

This book's argument hinges on the fact that, in addition to figuring extremely impressible persons, crowd representations also supplied abundant if more subtle indications of an unimpressible political consciousness, that is, of a prevailing commitment to the a priori principles underwriting political liberalism. The quoted passage from *The House of Seven Gables* can also serve to illustrate this sort of awareness. At first glance the fact that Hawthorne names the beheld street crowd a "political procession" might suggest that he conflates conceptions of the crowd and the public. Indeed he notes further that such a procession's usual movement is through the "stateliest public square." But deeper consideration reveals that for Hawthorne the crowd and the public, as modes of collectivity, remain distinct, even when embodied by the same aggregation. For one thing, what makes the procession political is not so much that it passes through the public square but that its "flaunting banners, and drums, fifes, clarions, and cymbals" along with the "multitude" produce a spectacle of celebration.[49] Hawthorne supplies no specifics, but the obvious assumption is that the parade is indeed celebrating something specific, be it a candidate, an election day, a legislative success, or something more general and symbolic like Constitution Day. The point is that the procession functions to validate the polity. Its political significance derives from its ceremonial and symbolic referentiality; and the spectacle relies on the townspeople's pre-existing political consciousness and values to endow it with relevance.

What the procession offers as an aesthetic experience is entirely different. Political self-consciousness gives way to the attractions of self-immersion in the "mighty river of life"; as the crowd "melts all the petty personalities," surfacing in their stead is "one broad mass of existence." After Hepzibah and Phoebe restrain Clifford from plunging into the crowd, Hawthorne (as narrator) speculates with obvious irony that it might have done Clifford some good to "take a deep, deep plunge into the ocean of human life... and then to emerge, sobered, invigorated, restored to the world and to himself." That is, Clifford, whom Hawthorne later describes as "too inert to operate morally on his fellow-creatures," might thereby have regained his political-moral consciousness.[50]

The relation between the aesthetic and the political has informed much recent political-theoretical analysis and debate. As Martin Jay notes in his concluding survey of the essays in a volume devoted to the political thought of Hannah Arendt, "[i]f the book as a whole has had any center of gravity, it has been the vexed issue of the relationship between politics, aesthetics, and ethics."[51] Several contributors to this volume, *Hannah Arendt and the Meaning of Politics*, illustrate how political theory inspired by deconstruction takes as one of its central projects the reinstatement of the aesthetic within the political sphere. Kimberly Curtis, for instance, argues that the aesthetic foundation of Arendt's theory "deepens and stimulates our ethical imaginations toward radical democratic practices." It does this by transforming the aesthetic judge into a spectator of myriad dramas and stories, thus non-cognitively rekindling "our feeling for human particularity," our recognition of others and difference. But as Jay points out, Curtis's focus on Arendt's theory of ontological plurality offers only a description: "You can't get so easily from an ontological description of what is to an ethical command of what should be."[52] (After all, the Nazi regime recognized the existence of differences; but that did not engender an ethical imperative to preserve the ones it disliked.)

Conversely, Anthony Cascardi faults Arendt for failing to preserve the potential of "radical transformation" offered by Kantian aesthetics because she too quickly aligns aesthetic reflection with political judgment.[53] Whereas aesthetic reflection moves outward from the radically new and free particular (that is, artistic geniuses create new works whose universal laws are only retrospectively discoverable), political judgment moves inward from the universal (that is, the categorical imperative finds application). Cascardi's argument thus turns on the privileging of radical newness (a privileging with which Arendt is usually associated). As aesthetically attractive as this notion of the transformative sublime is, especially in conceiving particularity as not subordinate to universal rule, Cascardi offers no justification for it as a political precept: he does not explain why newness in politics is better than the old, or why political transformation must be "radical" to be interesting and significant. As Kant noted, genius is best applied to aesthetic matters only: "But, for a person to hold forth and pass sentence like a genius in matters that fall to the province of the most patient rational investigation, is ridiculous in the extreme." It also remains unclear, as Martin Jay suggests, how such a conception of the political maintains a distinction from anarchic or fascist violence.[54]

If the broader ambition of this study is to map out urban modernity's articulations of two incompatible forms of consciousness – the public's self-consciousness and the crowd's limit of consciousness – its narrower aim is to neutralize the appeal of such claims as Cascardi's and Curtis's. This is not because I do not share their appreciation for radical transformation or ontological particularity, but because I fail to see the specifically political value of privileging such concepts. Like Wai Chee Dimock's *Residues of Justice*, which argues for the integration of luck, grace, and an "ethics of preference" into a theory of justice, further suggesting that an ethics apart from "the morality of reason" is "perhaps more genuinely humane," these arguments reflect a puzzling and highly problematic willingness to re-theologize the political.[55]

The authors featured in the following chapters certainly do seize on particularized and affecting scenes of American life – such as a solitary peddler serving the train station crowds; a young woman ensconced in domestic gentility replete with engagement party crowds; an educated black man facing a Southern lynch mob; and New York slum dwellers and immigrants on anaesthetized sprees. They thereby register their deep appreciation for diverse histories and contingencies, for obscure and fleeting modes of social assemblage, and for the powerful affections informing urban subjectivity. But as they also seize on the specific public-political problems facing a mass liberal democracy – such as the stipulations of citizenship; socio-economic justice; nation formation; mass immigration; and the mass media – they make equally clear their appreciation for abstract, disinterested, secular reason as the most viable and readily justifiable political-moral principle. To cite Rawls once again, all political power is coercive, but constitutional liberalism differs from others in a crucial way:

In a constitutional regime the special feature of the political relation is that political power is ultimately the power of the public, that is, the power of free and equal citizens as a collective body.[56]

As deeply intimate as the following chapters show the illiberal crowd mind and the liberal public square to be, they also disclose the implications of mistaking one for the other.

CHAPTER I

When travelers swarm forth: antebellum urban aesthetics and the contours of the political

When Walt Whitman, democratic crowd champion bar none, salutes the people of the polity, he looks to the masses crossing Brooklyn Ferry, the crowds milling about Manhattan's commercial district, the tides flowing through Broadway. In other words, he does not look to explicitly political crowds, such as those in Baltimore rioting against rampant bank faults in the late 1830s, or those in upstate New York rebelling against rents on long term leases in the 1830s and 1840s, or even those widely admired Dorrites demanding suffrage expansion and forming an extra-legal People's Convention to protest the elected state government in Rhode Island in 1842. Similarly, when Hawthorne scrutinizes what it means to be a "naturalized citizen," he turns to an everyday crowd scene: a train-station peddler selling his goods to the "travellers [who] swarm forth."[1] Such literary enterprises testify to the trend, begun in the antebellum period, to displace revolutionary crowds with urban crowds in representations of the fledgling democracy's populace. They accord with Tocqueville's observation in 1838 that "[a]t this moment perhaps there is no country in the world harboring fewer germs of revolution than America."[2] Indeed such crowd representations bear the mark of a polity preoccupied less with self-installation than self-maintenance.

This is not to say that those writing in the antebellum period lost all interest in representing revolutionary crowds, but that their support for such crowd action was at best ambivalent. To take only one well-known example, when Hawthorne describes Robin in "My Kinsman, Major Molineux" (1832) as "seized" by the "contagion" of brutal, mocking, anti-Royalist laughter that "was spreading among the multitude" who have tarred and feathered his uncle (*TS* 86), he reminds his readers of the nation's brutalizing past. But as Nicolaus Mills contends in *The Crowd in American Literature*, "Hawthorne will not let us forget that what is going on is controlled political violence."[3] That is, even when the revolutionary mob, a "mighty stream," has succumbed, like Robin, to "mental inebriety," Hawthorne

22

acknowledges – and gives qualified support to – its pre-political relevance (*TS* 84–85). The mob is implicitly acknowledged as an effective, almost supernaturally unifying force that helps to install democratic republicanism. However, Hawthorne's skeptical and ambivalent account of what led up to the "temporary inflammation of the popular mind" – that is, the townspeople's suspiciousness and secrecy, the passwords and masks, the night-time intrigue and conspiratorial activity – suggests that the affair is not to be confused with bona fide democratic procedure (*TS* 68). A mob's pre-political relevance or even historical necessity, in other words, does not for Hawthorne legitimize it as a constitutive feature of liberal-democratic collectivity.

In his valuable study, Mills examines novelists' depictions of politically motivated crowds, disputing the claims of Lionel Trilling, Richard Chase, Henry Nash Smith, and others that American writers are either attuned primarily to the pastoral features of American life or socially and politically disengaged from it altogether. He illuminates the parallels between nineteenth-century "classic American novel[s]" and Tocqueville's well-known concern about the tyranny of the majority. "In the midst of an era of nationalism and expansion," Mills writes, these novels reflect "an abiding fear that in America democratic men are the enemy of democratic man." Depictions of mobs in the shape of overly demanding farmers (Cooper), overly rigid Puritans (Hawthorne), overly duplicitous anti-royalists (Hawthorne), overly compliant sailors (Melville), and overly rabid slave hunters (Twain) all display the "belief that in the America they [the writers] knew, democratic men acting as a crowd were time and again a danger to the freedom and independence of democratic man."[4] Mills thereby suggests that the central conflict made visible by crowd representations is between the individual and the group.

While many of Mills's specific interpretive claims are insightful, his general analytic opposition of man and men tends to imply, mistakenly I think, that democracy is at odds with itself.[5] The danger of crowds that tyrannically hunt slaves or slavishly succumb to charismatic captains is not that they're "antidemocratic" per se as Mills suggests, but that they violate the republican or liberal virtues by means of which the polity legitimizes its democratic structure.[6] Members of such crowds have abandoned the ethical principles of propriety, public reason, and justice as fairness that render popular sovereignty an acceptable form of governance. When Tocqueville warns against the tyrannous capacity of a majority, he aims his criticism at that which embodies interests and opinions, which is to say, a body politic distinctly unmoored from liberal justice. For Tocqueville, "justice" is the "one law which has been made, or at least adopted, not by the majority of this or that people, but by the majority of all men." Significantly, he goes on to quote Madison on the subject: "Justice is the end of government. It is the end of civil society." Thus implying the legitimacy of justice as modernity's dominant *and universally acceptable* political ethos, Tocqueville shows that the trouble with majorities is not that they embody democratic man multiplied, but that, in his view, there are few "guarantee[s]" built into the American form of government to ward off those occasions when the majority will abandons justice.[7] The crowd representations cited by Mills do indeed dramatize the tyranny of the majority, but not simply by positioning the many against the one, but by positioning those with a diminished capacity to reason justly against others (a character, a narrator, an implied reader) who possess the faculty of reflective, ethical judgment. Writers such as Hawthorne, Melville, and Twain are deeply invested in portraying the human frailties and psychic susceptibilities that weaken liberal democratic governance, but they do not for all that imply an internal contradiction within democracy itself.

While features of the tyranny of the majority discourse also appear in some of the everyday urban crowd representations on which I focus, one core reason for focusing on them is that the cultural work they perform extends beyond this specific and familiar political problem. As icons of implicitly rather than explicitly political collectivity, everyday urban crowd scenes allowed antebellum writers to keep attention locked on the *demos* of the American landscape while also bringing into focus the nation's emerging socio-economic realities. Such crowds effectively embodied the incipient mass phenomena – immigration, urbanization, industrialization, and technological innovations in transportation and communications – that indeed brought dense populations into being and to which municipal, state, and national polities prepared to respond. For instance, urban crowds attracted the attention of those concerned with suffrage expansion, that is, with the moral and civic competency of voting citizens. Tocqueville, for one, considered the "lowest classes in these vast cities [New York and Philadelphia]" to be "a real danger threatening the future of democratic republics of the New World."[8] His was not an isolated view. In *Urban Masses and Moral Order in America, 1820–1920*, the historian Paul Boyer has pointed out that religious reformers from the early part of the century, such as Lyman Beecher, warned "that without vigorous countermeasures hordes of urban poor would soon 'swarm your streets, and prowl your dwellings.'" This attitude had changed little by the middle of the century, as evidenced by another reformer, John Todd, who "unleashed a vehement attack on cities as 'gangrenes on the body politic,' 'greenhouse[s] of crime,' and centers of 'all that demoralizes and pollutes.'"[9]

The volatile ambivalence with which the new nation's new masses were received is illustrated by the singular case of author-editor Orestes Brownson. One-time staunch defender of both democracy and Transcendentalism, and equally staunch supporter of the laboring classes, Brownson initially declared in no uncertain terms his confidence in the crowds: "the masses are not so poor and destitute as... [is] suppose[d]. They are not so dependent on *us*, the enlightened few, as we sometimes think them. We need not feel that, if we should die, all wisdom would die with us, and that there would be henceforth no means by which the millions would be able to come at truth and virtue."[10] But a few years later, in 1840, after these masses were, as Brownson saw it, duped into electing the Whig candidate Benjamin Harrison, Brownson "commenced to regard the 'people' as an inchoate mass which would probably follow the side of the loudest songs and biggest torchlight procession."[11] Subsequently and infamously Brownson converted to Roman Catholicism and authoritarian politics.

Complicating the socio-political valence of the antebellum urban crowd was its by no means unique but nonetheless not inconsiderable aesthetic power – be this power negatively or positively charged. Hence, for instance, Lydia Maria Child's supreme pleasure in a "multitude of doves" encountered on Broadway, but also her profound aversion to a "hopeless mass" of beggars encountered on her doorstep.[12] Similarly, as discussed more fully in the introduction, it is the parade crowd's aesthetic appeal that nearly lures Hawthorne's Clifford Pyncheon from his second-story window, just as it is the aesthetic intrigue of a man of the crowd that lures Poe's protagonist from the café. As Dana Brand has shown in *The Spectator and the City*, there emerged not only in early nineteenth-century Europe but also in the antebellum United States a "creative and consuming" modern consciousness. It was embodied by the *flâneur*, and effected an aestheticization of everyday urban life, including its crowds.[13] As early as Book Seven of Wordsworth's *Prelude*, literature in English began to depict the urban street crowd as deeply attractive to modernity's aestheticizing consciousness, even as that attraction was often fraught with disturbing, alienating apprehensions.

It is fair to say, then, that the antebellum figure of the everyday urban crowd garnered formidable political and aesthetic interest. In my view it is precisely because of, not despite, the urban crowd's double duty as democratic icon and aesthetic object that it became so prominent a discursive touchstone for the modern era. As outlined in the introduction, modernity's central aesthetic and political models shared the structural feature of entailing one or another conception of common sense. Whether in the mode of rational intuitionism's perception-based common sense (or good taste) or Kant's non-empirical, reason-based universal public, the available logics underpinning modern political and aesthetic theory applied equally to the one and the many, to the subject and the socius. At stake in this and ensuing chapters, then, is not so much an opposition between the one and the many (man and men), nor for that matter between the political and the aesthetic (even if this latter situation is what the crowd representations I examine so often imply); rather, the point I develop is that certain writers, as they stage the relation between the beholder and the crowd, make visible modernity's available political and aesthetic logics and their varying commitments to them. In doing so, they participate in the era's imagination of the foundational structure of the democratic-republic polity and, concomitantly, the incumbencies and potentialities of this polity's citizens. Such crowd figures yielded insight, in other words, into what it meant to be or not to be a liberal democratic entity, whether subject or socius, while simultaneously yielding insight into the implications of absorptive and reflective modes of aesthetic experience.

For even if antebellum Americans were now focused more on political maintenance than installation, there were many issues pertaining to democratic–republican life, to the consequences of its principles and practices, that remained unsettled. One important issue before the new nation was the polity's very capacity to change. As the antebellum era witnessed such phenomena as the rise of the party system, Jacksonian populism, the institutional strengthening of the presidency, the influx of immigrants from non-democratic countries, and increasing tensions between the North and South, concerns as to how the polity was or, equally important, was not changing animated political and literary discourses. After the British visitor Charles Joseph Latrobe observed Georgia's State Convention in 1835, he commented that "[i]t is not merely because their government is a democratic republic that I think it is liable to change, or to pass away – but because it is one of human institution, and as such the seeds of mutability are within its bosom."[14] In other words, he suggests (even if without conviction himself) the possibility of political "change" occurring without incurring the "pass[ing] away" of republican democracy. I hope to clarify over the course of this chapter what kind of democracy – popular or constitutional, radical or liberal, material or formal – underwrote what kind of change.

Rather than following a strict chronology, I begin this chapter with a discussion of Whitman, given his reputation as the most enthusiastic champion of democracy and its crowds. I point out the stresses and limitations marking his poetic-political project, especially where he aspires to reach beyond his envisioned fact-world of flux and force and into the realm of value and truth claims. As contrasts I examine Child's *Letters from New York* (1843), Poe's "The Man of the Crowd" (1840), and Hawthorne's "The Old Apple-Dealer" (1843). While these texts exhibit a similar receptivity to the notion that flux and force inform human experience, they also understand the relation of these material conditions to the political sphere to be causal rather than constitutive. That is, implicit in their various representations of urban crowds is the argument that empirical phenomena and human dispositions may well contribute to the very desire for a politically structured society, but that these material causes do not determine the ethical form or constitutional principles underlying their preferred political structure. To the contrary, their preferred principles turn out to be ideational, not material, grounded in ethical reason, not sentiment. All of these writers' crowd representations, I argue, disclose much about the prevailing conceptions of political democracy in the antebellum era. Articulating the socio-political conditions of everyday life, they also importantly foreground the structural relation between these conditions and the subject-citizen who experiences them.

PHYSIOLOGY FROM TOP TO TOE

When Walt Whitman champions "the word Democratic, the word En-Masse," he declares his allegiance not simply to democracy but to democracy of a particular kind: radical, embodied, affective. In "One's-Self I Sing" (1867) the word democratic holds out the promise of a political "physiology from top to toe," a "Life immense in passion, pulse, and power."[15] This poem of nine lines emblematizes in miniature Whitman's decades-long poetic project of envisioning democracy as something thoroughly to relish more than to recommend, to adore more than to respect. But however unequivocally affirmative, Whitman's celebratory embrace of crowds, of the entire culture of crowds, reveals the difficulty radical democracy faces when it endeavors to move beyond the world of fact and to make claims of value. Critical or reflective judgment, the constitutive disposition of a political and aesthetic reasoning being within a liberal polity, is supplanted by universal physiological affection. In *Song of Myself*, the body politic maps perfectly onto an urban body: "This is the city... and I am one of the citizens; / Whatever interests the rest interests me" (*LG* 76, ellipsis in original). This ubiquity of interest makes everyone eligible for reciprocal affection, the ambition that he famously proclaims at the end of the 1855 *Preface*: "The proof of a poet is that his country absorbs him as affectionately as he has absorbed it" (*LG* 26).

Further, every*thing* warrants and reciprocally promises affection. Crowds play a central role in merging persons and things so as to envision democratic affection as radically ubiquitous. In the opening stanza of "Crossing Brooklyn Ferry" (1856), for instance, Whitman salutes "face to face" flood-tides and clouds in the first two lines before proceeding in the third to their human counterparts, the "Crowds of men and women" (*LG* 307–308). In "Out of the Rolling Ocean the Crowd" (1865), "ocean" and "crowd" are no longer separated by line, but only by definite article: "Out of the rolling ocean the crowd came a drop gently to me, / Whispering *I love you, before long I die*" (*LG* 263). As objects of a prepositional phrase, "ocean" and "crowd" grammatically occupy the same place: seemingly indistinguishable, one or the other bears a "drop" capable of human speech. As the poem thematizes separation and union ("I too am part of that ocean my love, we are not so much separated"; "the irresistible sea is to separate us"), it becomes clear that such formal components as line breaks and definite articles do not serve to reinforce the separation of persons and things, but to occasion separation itself so as indeed to dramatize the ontological union (or undifferentiation) of persons and things.

As everyone and everything, indeed every notorious atom in the Whitmanian universe, avail themselves of exchange and attraction, of transformation and reversal, the ethical toothlessness of a political metaphysics of "passion, pulse, and power" comes to the fore. Whitman's commitment to the embodied and the interested tends to sweep into the sensible realm words and phrases that might otherwise evince a reflective, abstractly universalizing disinterest, and thereby offer political-liberal anchorage. Such is the case, for instance, when he writes in *Song of Myself*, "[I] peruse manifold objects, no two alike, and every one good, / The earth good, and the stars good, and their adjuncts all good" (*LG* 32). Here, goodness's ubiquity and the speaker's unflagging agreeableness combine to suggest that the designation of goodness is less a demonstration of the speaker's reasoned or moral evaluation of the object at hand than it is a registration of something like the object's talent for being what it is. And from this affirmation of all that is, as is, the author derives sensible pleasure, much as he does when he joins the crew of a Yankee clipper: "I tucked my trowser-ends in my boots and went and had a good time" (*LG* 35). In Whitman's hands, then, the good drives out the bad entirely; the good brooks, in effect, no opposition.

Which is to say, it loses its relevance as a term of ethical judgment, of critical discrimination.

Whitman's aesthetics of democratic goodness, in which reflective judgment is elided and replaced by all-encompassing affect, delivers to radical democratic theory its nearest poetic correlative. The self-proclaimed "poet of commonsense" (*LG* 48), Whitman renders the *sensus communis* a site of "arduous struggle," as Kerry Larson puts it in *Whitman's Drama of Consensus*, "to secure consent." In other words, rather than making, as in Kant's theory (to which Larson refers), the *abstract possibility* of everyone's agreement the basis for reflective judgment, which in turn assumes the non-negotiable separation of the poem or poet-object from the beholder or reader-subject, Whitman imagines an *empirical* agreement wherein everybody simply feels the same way. He aspires, as Larson observes, "to erase all boundaries, to overcome all distance, to create, in effect, a space in which reader and poem are one."[16]

As Allen Grossman also explains, "Whitman devised a 'song' that would reconcile variety and order, equality and constitution, one and many without compromising either term... [He] situates his new American organic law and true sovereign... at the zero point of unanimity."[17] His, then, is a project which works to make agreement synonymous with physiological rapport – with being "face to face" and seeing eye to eye. No wonder the historian George Frederickson counts Whitman among the Northern radicals whose politics takes the form of a "nonpolitical, noninstitutional theory of mass democracy [that affirms] the anarchist's faith that formal government can be replaced by the spontaneous action of the people."[18] In short, Whitman contributes importantly to the radical democratic project of rendering essentially indistinguishable objects and representations, particulars and universals, things and persons, sentiments and reasons, causes and effects, poetry and policy.[19]

What this drama of consensus achieves, then, is the elimination of the space for argument. As Whitman remarks about the democratic poet in the *Preface*, "He is no arguer... he is judgment. He judges not as the judge judges but as the sun falling around a helpless thing" (*LG* 9, ellipsis in original). This statement may have appeared refreshingly open-minded to a mid-nineteenth-century liberal oppressed by the era's narrow moralism. But as a political-theoretical claim, it is devastating for the political agent of any era who "aims," as even the contemporary, self-described radical democrat Chantal Mouffe does, to "challeng[e] a wide range of relations of subordination," to "assert... equal liberty for all," and "to constitute forms of power that are compatible with democratic values." In *Bodies That Matter*

Judith Butler similarly envisions a politics that effects a "radical rearticulation of what qualifies as bodies that matter,... lives worth protecting, lives
worth saving, lives worth grieving" [*sic*].[20] Yet such moral yearnings are
rendered simply irrelevant by a materialist metaphysics of "passion, pulse,
and power" because, as Whitman discloses, everyone and everything under
the sun are transformed into helpless things. Without the a priori, non-
empirical idea of justice as fairness (the ethical correlative of disinterested
reason), there is no possible way to evaluate one set of experiences or treat-
ments over and against another. Disturbingly, then, radical democracy's
negation of reason as the source of moral deliberation leaves "abjected and
delegitimated bodies" rather high and dry.[21]

In other words, with no ethical grounds for arguing what might constitute a democratic value or how a specific helplessness might benefit
from "rearticulation," radical democracy's plurality of "lives" dissolves into
what Mouffe calls (and Whitman exemplifies) "total pluralism." As she acknowledges, "extreme pluralism" culminates in "a multiplicity of identities
without any common denominator, and it is impossible to distinguish between differences that exist but should not exist and differences that do not
exist but should exist." She acknowledges as well that this total pluralism
amounts to a "pluralism without antagonism." What she fails to acknowledge, however, is that her own brand of democratic theory produces this
culminant condition, and that to block its arrival, she must capitulate to an
arbitrary imperative: "such a view [radical, pluralist democracy] does not
allow a total pluralism."[22] Which is to say, she deploys a moral universal
after all.

In Whitman's own time, the Whigs and even the Jacksonian populists
understood the significance of mediating democracy through liberal ethical
principles, embedded as these principles were in the discourse of republican
virtue. Invocations of the crowd often served to drive home the point. In
one of his *Junius Tracts* (1844), for instance, the Whig spokesperson and
Henry Clay supporter Calvin Colton stated in no uncertain terms that what
was wrong with Jackson was his mob appeal. The problem with him was
not so much his popularity, but that under his "new 'Democracy'" politics
meant "servility in the masses and despotism in the leaders." Jackson's
mobocracy, according to Colton, "is as remote from grammatical, historical,
and philosophical democracy, and from *any* democracy ever recognized as
such, as Monarchy itself."[23]

In his concomitant effort to show that Whigs were democrats, not
elitists, Colton reclaimed Jefferson as the party ideal: "Jeffersonian democracy...was the power of the PEOPLE. Jackson 'Democracy' was the

ascendant star of one MAN. The first grew out of an alarm for the safety of popular rights; the last sprung from an obsequious regard for a Military Chieftain." Colton clearly hoped to redirect party politics away from the "property versus people" debate (in which Whigs looked like privileged aristocrats) and toward one about the conditions of liberal democracy as revolving around rights and popular civility. Thus he also insisted that for Whigs, democracy "is not MEN, but PRINCIPLES," by which he meant the natural rights principles "of the Constitution, [which is] the organ and instrument of the democracy of the country."[24] For Colton, then, political democracy signified something other than the passion, pulse, and power of the masses. Similarly, many of those who supported the substantive goals of the Dorrites balked at their revolutionary, extra-constitutional means of achieving them. "Dorrism," as Arthur Schlesinger, Jr. has noted, "threatened all constitutional guarantees. If a majority out of power could overturn the constitution at will, then a majority in power could plainly do so, 'and thus, all constitutional right is merged with the will of the strongest.'"[25]

The Jacksonians, too, made their arguments in the name of the common man's *virtue*. While rhetorically emphasizing their ability to represent and better protect the commoners' *interests* (by way, for example, of extending the franchise and establishing direct elections of party candidates), the Jacksonians championed their constituents' capacity to make reasoned, prudent decisions that accorded with democratic republican premises of natural rights and justice. As Russell Hanson explains in *The Democratic Imagination*, Jackson's "Democracy was the organized expression of 'the democracy;' it was the party that might serve as the governing agent of 'the democracy' and its allies. The Democracy would restore virtuous men to their rightful place in the republic, and in so doing, restore virtue to the republic polity."[26] While the parties may have harbored differing levels of trust vis-à-vis the virtue of common citizens, the necessity of virtue was recognized on both sides. It was this basic socio-political agreement that enabled terms such as "King Andrew" and "mobocracy" to circulate so easily as pejorative epithets.

But the overt political logic most resembling Whitman's is neither the Whigs' nor the Jacksonians'. Despite his Free-Soiler credentials, Whitman's political-poetic commitments to affection and embodied power have much in common with the political logic espoused by Southerners such as John Calhoun and the monomaniacal George Fitzhugh (for whom virtue pertained to Christian obedience and destiny, not to liberal-republican self-legitimation). Not unlike Tocqueville, but with considerably more at stake personally and politically, Calhoun was concerned with the way a numerical majority could drown out the voices of a minority faction. Thus he devised a theory of "concurrent majorities" whereby a dissenting region such as the South would have "the power of preventing or arresting the action of government, be it called by what term it may, veto, interposition, nullification, check or balance of power."[27]

Resonating with Whitman's politics of affection and "arduous struggle," Calhoun built his political philosophy upon a psychology, in his words, of "feeling and affection," adding to it a "great law of self-preservation which pervades all that feels" and "which makes us feel more intensely what affects us directly than what affects us indirectly." This law "necessarily leads to conflict between individuals" – hence "the tendency to a universal state of conflict between individual and individual," in which "government has its origin."[28] Thus adhering to Hobbesian modes of psychology and social contract, Calhoun argued for a constitution that would protect minority interests and secure a state's or region's material improvement. But as Hanson remarks, "Calhoun's attempt to provide a constitutional accommodation for diverse and competing interests undermined the traditional republican idea of commonwealth politics."[29] In effect Calhoun dismissed what Tocqueville saw as the danger, indeed the inevitable self-destructiveness, of a "mixed government, that is to say, one equally shared between contrary principles." Where Calhoun was prepared to build conflicts of interest into the polity's foundation, Tocqueville insisted on underlying agreement: "in any society one finds in the end some principle of action that dominates all others." Moreover, such a unifying (liberal) principle must be adopted by means of political legitimation, not force: "Force is never more than a passing element in success; the idea of right follows immediately after it. Any government which could only reach its enemies on a battlefield would soon be destroyed."[30]

Calhoun's efforts to redraw the federal polity as one based on competing state interests rather than on nationally unifying principles of justice and equality were amplified by the South's most diligent pro-slavery propagandist, George Fitzhugh, who took radical political theory to its logical and distinctly anti-democratic conclusion. His writings comprise perhaps the most illuminating antebellum account of the implications of a politics of power. One might say that he stands as the nineteenth century's paragon of localist, situationalist, anti-legalist, anti-abstractionist virtue. In line with his argument in *Cannibals All!* (1857) that governments are always established by force, never by consent, and are always "continued by force," is his claim that "[a]ll platforms, resolutions, bills of rights and constitutions are true in the particular, false in the general. Hence all legislation should be repealable, and those instruments are but laws" – not, then, "fundamental principles" meant to endure.[31]

Finding, moreover, the theories of eighteenth-century British writers such as Adam Smith and John Locke too "abstract" if not downright "here[tical]," Fitzhugh maintains in *Sociology for the South* (1854) that American slavery has been misunderstood because critics have ignored its specificity.[32] Only the Southerners who "see every day around them the peculiarities and characteristics of slave society" can assess its positive value. He elaborates in the later text: "the wisest and best of men are sure to deduce, as general principles, what is only true as to themselves and their peculiar circumstances." Apart from the logical absurdity of Fitzhugh's particularism and Calhoun's regionalism – absurd because ever smaller particulars and regions can always contest the status quo by claiming to know what is "true as to themselves" – there are also the subtler but in some ways more crucial problems having to do with presupposed relations between cause and effect. Most remarkable is Fitzhugh's presumption that a government "originated in force" must needs be "continued by force."[33] He thereby elides the distinction between installation (where force may be required to ward off external adversaries) and maintenance (where agreement and civil debate among internal constituents may well take the place of force). He eliminates the possibility of replacing force with agreed-upon principles and procedures (such as are mandated by a constitution). In his world there is no such thing as a reasoning, consenting political public.

If Fitzhugh could be seen as merely supplying an immanent description (with however many revisionist twists) from within American history and politics, then his account would be simply one among many, to be accepted or rejected. It would be intelligible to those who see history and politics as he does, and unintelligible to those who do not. But Fitzhugh breaks his compact with his vision of a particularist, force-driven politics of transformation when he stops describing and starts endorsing (as he does throughout both texts) his brand of authoritarianism. Which he does, moreover, "simply [to] point out what is natural and universal, and humbly [to] try to justify the ways of God to man." Authoritarianism is clearly for him of universal moral value: "Good men obey superior authority, the laws of God, [and] of morality."[34]

Bearing ideological as well as testimonial weight, Fitzhugh's defensive-aggressive account thus contains an ineradicable universalist moment – one, however, that precludes argument by locating that universalism in God the Object, God the Interested Father. This convergence of a politics of power and faith is what enables Fitzhugh to hate Jefferson's sins – the

Declaration of Independence and the Virginia Bill of Rights – but love the sinner: "The true greatness of Mr. Jefferson was his fitness for revolution. He was the genius of innovation, the architect of ruin, the inaugurator of anarchy."[35]

What becomes clear through the example of Fitzhugh is how a commitment to particularist politics recuperates a universalist element as soon as it makes any value claim for itself. Where Fitzhugh grounds his universalism explicitly in "God," contemporary secular theorists more often invoke a seemingly more material but for all that no less divinely motivated conception of power. "Power's condition of possibility," Foucault contends, "is the moving substrate of force relations which, by virtue of their inequality, constantly engender states of power, but the latter are always local and unstable." A politics emanating from a materialist metaphysics of immanent power has no grounds, say, for making policy because it has no grounds for distinguishing materializations or identifications worth preserving from those worth eradicating. Its own commitment to immanence limits it to descriptions of, in Foucault's words, "the process which, through ceaseless struggles and confrontations, transforms, strengthens, or reverses them [multiple force relations]."[36] A metaphysics of force and transformation, in other words, must make much of force and transformation.

In *Democratic Vistas* (1871) Whitman indicates just how close radical democratic ideology is to an objective naturalism. Claiming "variety and freedom" to be the "greatest lessons of Nature," he goes on to liken these qualities of "general humanity" to "the influences that make up, in their limitless field, that perennial health-action of the air we call the weather – an infinite number of currents and forces, and contributions, and temperatures, and cross purposes, whose ceaseless play of counterpart upon counterpart brings constant restoration and vitality."[37] If fluxes in the social field assume the same significance as fluxes in the atmosphere, then the situation, say, of getting struck by a mob of anti-abolitionists would be equivalent to getting struck by lightning.[38] Cosmologically appealing perhaps, such equivalence – which is the upshot of radical democracy – offers little in the way of social justice.

ORGANS OF JUSTICE

Lydia Maria Child was one who recognized the limitations of a politics of feeling and force; and she mobilized representations of crowds to dramatize these limitations. In *Letters from New York* (1843) she records parenthetically a phrenologist's prognosis: her "organ of justice" is "unusually developed in

[her] head" (*LNY* 189). She thus confirms what her weekly reader would have by that letter already surmised, namely, that her recorded impressions are invariably filtered not only through a Christian-reformist but also a democratic-republican lens. Indeed, there may be no significant evaluation or judgment in the series of letters that is not guided by a procedure of critical reflection and by principles of equality and justice as fairness. Child's gravitation toward this liberal ideology strengthens her explicitly made claim of distinction from the numerous antebellum Christian doctrinaires and authoritarians who contend, as she puts it, that "God has sanctioned" such unjust practices as slavery and the slave trade (*LNY* 148). In *Letters from New York*, which is a compilation of her columns published in the *National Anti-Slavery Standard* during her tenure as editor, and offers a panoramic yet also highly detailed account of New York life, Child demonstrates that liberal ethical reason, rather than either personal sentiment or Christianity's command morality, animates her political sensibility. Where she enters public debate on such current issues as capital punishment, slavery, the city's routine and brutal dog-killing, and laissez-faire capitalism's effects of urban poverty, she exhibits her capacity to deliberate and to form judgments according to "fixed principles of right and wrong" (*LNY* 146). And when she examines the banes of American society, she finds theological sects, political parties, and local prejudice at the source of selfish, blind, and whimsical public opinion. Public opinion of this stripe constitutes in her view a social dysfunction, hobbling the effort to legislate out of existence such national crimes as slavery.

Over and against such public opinion stands the "lamp" of "reason and conscience in each individual," which, she maintains, "never goes out, though it may shine dimly through a foggy atmosphere" (*LNY* 149).[39] Succumbing fully to the forces of partisan politics or local prejudices, Child implies, amounts to blowing out the lamp. This is not to say, however, that she eliminates all sentiment from her sensibility, only that she does not attempt to legitimize her political positions through sentiment or particular attachments. For example, while "sad and troubled" by the "savage custom" of capital punishment (*LNY* 207), Child condemns the practice not on account of these "surging sympathies," but on account of its being "legalized murder." As such capital punishment would serve as a public-destroying symbol, provoking "the very spirit of murder... among the dense crowd which throng[s] the place of execution" (*LNY* 208–209). Here the imagined bloodthirsty spectator crowd attending an execution, "throng[ing]" in its physicality, functions rhetorically as the antithesis of a reasoning and just political public.

However grounded in reason her political ethics may be, Child's aesthetic disposition is decidedly sentimental. Yet perhaps because, like so many nineteenth-century persons, harmony matters to her, she manages to square this sentimental aesthetics with her political-moral organ of justice. Whatever is good is beautiful, by her lights, and vice versa. Where she is "charm[ed]" by the Battery's natural beauty (*LNY* 109) and uplifted when a "multitude of doves [goes] careering before [her]" on Broadway (*LNY* 104), she exhibits her belief that "beauty alone is immortal and divine" (*LNY* 157). Conversely, she despairs over New York's "bloated disease, and black gutters, and pigs uglier than their ugly kind," and finds "oppressive" the visual effect of brick walls painted their own color, "like the shining face of a heated cook" (*LNY* 11–12). In line with her conviction "that it is wisest and best to fix our attention on the beautiful and the good, and dwell as little as possible on the evil and false" (*LNY* 218), Child concludes she would not like her memory to work like a daguerreotype machine, "taking likenesses of whatsoever the light of imagination happens to rest upon," given the world's abundance of "disagreeable" material (*LNY* 76–77).

Child's aesthetics, in sum, is a matter of personal, sentimental preference, which happens also to be calibrated to her organ of justice. In terms of *content* her aesthetics can be seen as an almost redundant extension of her moral and political faculty; but in terms of *form* it operates according to her personal disposition. Thus for Child, the personal is not the political. Her reader is not invited to debate her dislike of red paint on brick walls as he or she is her position on capital punishment. Though restricted on account of her sex from participating fully in political processes, Child thus demonstrates that her person answers to the minimum daily requirements of liberal democratic citizenship. This demonstration turns less on the content of her political and aesthetic assessments (such as opposing slavery and favoring flocks of doves) than on the means through which she comes to those assessments, specifically, the means of separating out the political from the personal.

Child's representations of her relation to urban crowds underscore this double maneuver, which allows for the possibility of being oppressed aesthetically while remaining politically reasonable and responsive. One scene involves her encounter at her door of yet "[a]nother group" of impoverished "suffering wretches" (peddlers and beggars), to which she responds by "turn[ing] away again, with the feeling that there was no use in attending to the hopeless mass of misery around [her]" (*LNY* 181–182). As one of those aesthetically "disagreeable" moments, Child's excessive sentiment prompts her to imagine this "group" as a "mass" from which she first recoils but finally "yield[s]," returning as she does to her more characteristic "generous impulse" and buying up all their (to her useless) wares, as well as donating her remaining change (*LNY* 182). The emotionally fraught encounter also triggers moral-political analysis, leading her to argue that the desperation of the "hopeless mass" has its source not in the lower classes' genetic immorality or criminality but in material "[h]ardship, privation, and perchance severity." This set of conditions has transformed the "gladsome thoughtlessness" gracing unfettered childhood into one particular mass-child's "grasping sensuality" (*LNY* 182). In such analyses, Child exhibits her command of ethical judgment, applying it to the socio-economic realities of antebellum New York.

At the same time the quotidian ordeal of facing a mass of beggars inspires in Child a moment of self-witnessing: "At times I almost fancy I can feel myself turning to stone by inches" (*LNY* 182). In other words, she imagines herself transforming into an inhuman mass, not unlike the beggars and peddlers themselves. In this metaphor of turning to stone Child reveals much about the kinds of transformation that are and are not available within a liberal democracy's political sphere. Turning to stone plainly is not. Now, insofar as she remains, through "feel[ing]" keyed to reason, aware of her increasing stoniness (which amounts to an increasing disincorporation, to a divestment of specific, contingent interests), one might say that her organ of justice becomes ever more "developed," purifying itself of excess sentiment. In this metaphorical scenario she increasingly assumes the form of the abstract, equalized, disinterested yet still nominally sympathetic citizen-subject undergirding liberal justice.[40] If, however, stone creep were indeed to traverse all available "inches," overtaking her completely, she would be not only bodiless but mindless. Where the organ of justice once was, would now be inert mass.

In contrast to the middle classes' more widely received view of the urban masses as criminal and immoral, for Child, becoming a hopeless mass, like turning to stone, means having no moral faculty at all. That she views such a state as beyond the justice principle rather than a transformation of it becomes clearer elsewhere in the *Letters*, namely, where she associates the extra-moral disposition specifically with urban crowds. Having encountered in the "public square" – that is, the marketplace – the busy auction of "piles" of "ready-made coffins," she describes the disconcerting effect on her of this "business transaction":

There is something impressive, even to painfulness, in this dense crowding of human existence, this mercantile familiarity with death. It has sometimes forced upon me, for a few moments, an appalling night-mare sensation of vanishing identity; as if I were but an unknown, unnoticed, and unseparated drop in the great ocean of human existence. (*LNY* 57)

Taken together, these passages make evident that for Child, affective and physical crowdedness or amassment, whether of the wretchedly impoverished or the middle-class kind, amounts to subjective death, to a vanishing of identity, even as it obtains within the realm of "human existence." Whereas moral turpitude might threaten because it corrupts liberal democracy, the extra-moral threatens because it could wipe out the polity altogether. In her nightmare vision of economic populism, the evacuation of ethical (as opposed to calculative) reason implies the utter elimination of moral, political, and aesthetic life as she knows it. Some forms of change are viable; others clearly are not.

While she acknowledges the multiple force relations acting upon and within the world, such as are materialized in New York's mercantile crowds and the "nightmare sensation" "forced upon" her, Child relies on a resilient reflective capacity to separate her moral and political "identity" from these forces. That is, her organ of justice, bound as it is to principles of equality and fairness, and articulated through critical judgment, enables her to distinguish the morally unjust such as hopeless poverty from the extra-morally unjust such as the sensation of unseparation from a crowd. Discriminating between the worlds of empirical force and formal justice, Child articulates a system which is governed by a conceptual separation of cause and effect. Moreover, this separation enables Child, once her flash-flood of sentiment recedes, to mount a persuasive – which is to say arguable – indictment of laissez-faire capitalism's socially crippling effects. In contrast to those who see politics as war by other means, as Fitzhugh and Foucault the Machiavellian would have it, for Child liberal-democratic politics begins where power ends, where coercion is replaced by consent.[41]

In Child's and Whitman's work we begin to see how crowd representations contribute to the articulation of political and aesthetic modalities. For Child, the crowd embodies the end of the political – the end of justice, of reason, of autonomous identity – and the beginning of "grasping sensuality," of oceanic feelings. The crowd likewise embodies the end of the aesthetic, a foreclosure on the possibility of conceptually determining a correspondence between an object of beauty and moral goodness. Whether troped as liquid or solid, massification functions in Child's prose to mark the outside limit of the ethically human self, to mark the vanishing of identity. For Whitman, crowds signify the birth of the political: masses, both human and non-human, receive affirmation as organic, affectively consensual entities. As figures of "passion, pulse, and power," Whitman's crowds similarly give rise to the aesthetic, to the sensual attractions of everyday life. Decades later William James will comment, in "On a Certain Blindness in Human Beings" (1899), that Whitman, embodying "a sort of ideal tramp, a rider on omnibus-tops and ferry boats... felt the human crowd as rapturously as Wordsworth felt the mountains, felt it as an overpoweringly significant presence, simply to absorb one's mind." James recognized that, in contrast to Schopenhauer's "emotional anaesthesia" and Carlyle's reprobation, Whitman finds "beauty" in everyday urban life, obtaining from it "mystic satisfaction."[42]

In sum, Child and Whitman elaborate formally (though not substantively) similar modes of sentimental aesthetics, but two different relations between sentiment and democracy. In Child's version, sentiment stimulates awareness of the need for political deliberation but does not extend into the polity's fundamental principles. In Whitman's version, sentiment and democracy are inseparable, hence the interminably "arduous struggle." This is a struggle not so much to come into accord with presupposed political-moral principles as to bring into accord new sentiments and new principles.

Poe and Hawthorne, on the other hand, differ both from Child's sentimental aesthetics, which wishes all aesthetic objects to be good and beautiful, and from Whitman's sentimental politics, which wishes all objects and subjects to feel their rapport. Contributing importantly to their reconfigurations of aesthetics and politics are their representations of anonymous urban crowds. With Poe's putative contempt for American politics and Hawthorne's putative conservatism, one might expect them to harbor deep doubts about the value of liberal democracy in the manner, say, of Joel Headley who recounted in his 1873 history, *The Great Riots of New York, 1712–1873*, the election riots of 1834. He held that these riots were incited by party antagonisms, as well as by the immigration of (and automatic extension of suffrage to) a "mass of [human] material wholly unfit for any political structure," that is, "men, the greater part of whom could neither read nor write, who were ignorant of the first principles of true civil liberty, who could be [politically] bought and sold like sheep in the shambles."[43] If believed to be predominant, such "masses" might well throw into question the viability of political liberalism.

However much it may appear that Poe and Hawthorne generally share Headley's skepticism, in their depictions of urban crowds they both register (in various ways) rather firm commitments to the principles of reason and autonomy that underwrite liberalism.

SHOCK AESTHETICS

In considering the political and aesthetic implications of "The Man of the Crowd," it is important to keep in mind that its drama depends on two characterological relations. The one usually receiving attention by critics is between the old man and his beholder, who, when in feverish pursuit of the old man through the crowd, resembles him. The relation often overlooked is between the beholder-protagonist's slightly more distant past acting self – when he follows the old man – and his nearer past acting self – when he does not. Also worth mentioning is the difference between the protagonist's acting and narrating self. In his essay "On Some Motifs in Baudelaire" Walter Benjamin works out an analysis of urban aesthetic experience that helps to explicate the first relation. He makes a case for Baudelaire's innovative aesthetics, engendered by urban capitalism and inspired in part by the *flânerie* exhibited in Poe's story. Baudelaire's anti-academic theory of beauty is well known for celebrating modernity's "*particular* beauty, the beauty of circumstance," by which he means "the ephemeral, the fugitive, the contingent."[44] Benjamin sees in this feature of contingency the ideas for an aesthetics no longer grounded in what he calls aura. Aura, he explains, is a specific mode of "perceptibility":

Experience of the aura thus rests on the transposition of a response common in human relationships to the relationship between the inanimate or natural object and man. The person we look at, or who feels he is being looked at, looks at us in turn. To perceive the aura of an object we look at means to invest it with the ability to look at us in return.[45]

Baudelaire develops, in contrast to this auratic aesthetics, one grounded in shock, one which Benjamin likens to photography "since the camera records our likeness without returning our gaze." While it is possible to dispute this particular claim about photography (and to argue, say, for photography's auratic status), it is more important to understand what Benjamin means by a shock aesthetics derived from urban experience. This has to do with Baudelaire's self-referential gestures of the "poet at work," where he is engaged in "fantastic combat," stumbling over words, and colliding with verses: "it is the phantom crowd of words, the fragments, the beginnings of lines from which the poet, in the deserted streets, wrests the poetic booty." These are instances of the poet in shock: the returned gaze is replaced by a "mirrorlike blankness" which has its own aesthetic "charm."[46]

"The Man of the Crowd" provides the blueprint for this mode of urban aesthetics. The story's protagonist twice undergoes shock: first, when he suddenly catches sight of the old man through the window of the cafe; and second, when, after following the old man through the crowd for twenty-four hours, he "stop[ped] fully in front of the wanderer, [and] gazed at him steadfastly in the face. He noticed [him] not, but resumed his solemn walk, while [the protagonist], ceasing to follow, remained absorbed in contemplation."[47] Granted, there is little in this second moment to indicate the protagonist's physiological experience of a shock of non-recognition; but it is telling that he explains to himself why he "ceas[ed] to follow" only *after* the fact of being face to face with the old man's mirrorlike blankness: "I said at length,... 'It will be vain to follow; for I shall learn no more of him, nor of his deeds'" (*PT* 396). This act of suddenly ceasing to follow can be understood as a shock effect in that it replicates in reverse the moment in which the pursuit is initiated, when the protagonist is evidently quite shocked: "suddenly there came into view a countenance...which at once arrested and absorbed my whole attention" (*PT* 392). The combination of being both "arrested" and "absorbed" by an object of attention establishes an urban aesthetic situation of radical detachment from the environs. The arresting shock by definition severs the protagonist-beholder from his self-consciousness. It renders him incapable of being further excited by external stimuli, leaving him, as common locution has it, beside himself. It thus transforms him into a perceiving but impassive, self-enclosed fragment – a fragment which is its own totality. Like another figure whom Benjamin regards as constituted through shock, the gambler, he has no past. For the person who plays the game of chance, each game is its own totality; "no game is dependent on the preceding one."[48] This is what it means for Poe's protagonist's "whole attention" to be given over to the old man: in being wholly attentive he is also wholly disconnected, just as a mirror is both reflective and blank. It thus makes a certain kind of sense that a few lines later he records how "[t]hen came a craving desire to keep the man in view" (*PT* 392). Such intensely consuming desire may be understood as the temporal and psychical extension of the shocked, essentially unself-conscious state.

This account of Poe's shock aesthetics differs from Dana Brand's. He argues that Poe "exploits the aesthetic appeal of shock" for the same reason that he "exploit[s] the aesthetic appeal of urban anxiety," namely, in order to develop a sensationalist "aesthetic capable of embracing the phenomenological qualities of urban experience."[49] While there is certainly no disputing Poe's sensationalist streak, I want to suggest that shock in Poe, at least as it is staged in "The Man of the Crowd," contributes to a wholly different aesthetic situation. Whereas sensationalism involves a conventional kind of transaction between shocking object and titillated viewer, Poe charts out an essentially non-transactional situation of perception, whereby the viewer is himself so extremely affected as also to embody a mirrorlike blankness. In these moments he does indeed become the old man's doppelgänger, an anonymous figure in and of the mass. No longer returning the human gaze while in this state of absorption or shock, he and the old man construct a sort of wall-to-wall blankness.

Of course, it is possible to argue that as long as art objects or human beings possess empirical presence, they are also culturally embedded. Consequently they would bear the inscriptions of their birth-culture's ideological structure and content, walking that culture's walk, and talking its talk. But still the question remains as to whether or not they speak that culture's speech – whether or not those inscriptions signify. Almost too succinctly, "The Man of the Crowd" shows what is required to answer this question, which at bottom has to do with the determining of intention, with the determining of whether or not the participants in the scene of perception possess self-awareness.[50] And the process of determining intention maps onto the process of determining who should and should not count as active members of a liberal polity.

First of all, the story shows that there must be someone with sufficient presence of mind to pose the question of intention and to answer it. The fact that the protagonist ultimately ceases to follow the old man, leaving the crowd to record and evaluate his experiences, indicates his reacquired faculty of reflection. Even within the temporal frame of the narrative's action, the protagonist exhibits his regained reflective faculty when, after encountering the old man face to face, he is as it were shocked out of his state of shock. For directly on the heels of this encounter the protagonist famously likens the old man to a book that "*lasst sich nicht lesen*" [*sic*], that "does not permit itself to be read" (*PT* 396, 388). No longer subject to "craving desire," the protagonist once again engages in the activity of distanced analysis, interpretation, and judgment.

Second and yet more to the point, the story shows that inscribed marks signify or are readable only when they too are backed by a presence of mind. If "The Man of the Crowd" counts among Poe's detective stories, it must be understood that while the protagonist's collection of evidence might have initially pertained to discovering *what kind* of person the old man is – hence the mystery of the diamond and dagger – it ultimately pertains to *whether* he is an interpretable person, a man with intentional consciousness. At first it seems that the protagonist indeed detects such mindfulness in the old man. After remarking on his "absolute idiosyncracy [*sic*] of expression," he goes on to detail the old man's motley array of personal characteristics which give rise to "the ideas of vast mental power, of caution, of penuriousness, of avarice, of coolness, of malice, of blood-thirstiness, of triumph, of merriment, of excessive terror, of intense – of supreme despair" (*PT* 392). But later, after embarking on his pursuit of the man through the crowd, the protagonist's view begins to reverse itself. He describes how, when "the press was still so thick that... [he] was obliged to follow him closely," the old man "[c]rossed and re-crossed the way repeatedly *without apparent aim*" (*PT* 393, emphasis added). Just as it makes sense to call a book unreadable only if extra-textual evidence demonstrates that what looks like words or speech turns out really to be mimed or mindless talk (or the equivalent of accidental marks), the protagonist must gather sufficient evidence to determine beyond a reasonable doubt that the old man is not a mysteriously complex "mental power" but a psychotically *aimless* hence unreadable figure. This is why he observes him closely for twenty-four hours before delivering his verdict: the old man indeed turns out to be a live version of Child's unfeeling stone, a mass unto himself. He is not only in but of the crowd.

What is Child's worst aesthetic nightmare is for Poe's narrator "fascinat[ing]"; the old man represents for him "the type and genius of deep crime" (*PT* 392, 396). Convicting the old man of the really deep crime of unreadability, the capital crime against humanity, the narrator effectively banishes him from the political domain, though only to re-install him as an aesthetic agent, a carrier of deeply attractive, mirrorlike blankness. He becomes the embodiment of urban aestheticism, a figure that is permitted to be in but not entirely of a liberal democracy. And the narrator's assessment of him as such indicates, in turn, his own capacity for reflective judgment, which is to say, his own potential for possessing liberal agency.

To elaborate further, Poe's story lays out what a liberal democracy entails and what it by historical and theoretical definition cannot assimilate (but might well tolerate: the narrator-protagonist, after all, does not hail the police). Textually, much hinges, as suggested above, on the word "apparent" – on the old man's actions' being "without apparent aim." Culturally and politically, much hinges on the formal conditions of the antebellum public sphere. The historian David Henkin takes up this issue in his recent work, *City Reading*. He examines the importance of literal signs – street signs, theater bills, political broadsides, commercial advertisements, and so forth – for the development of an antebellum urban public, that is, for the carving out of democratic, impersonal spaces. He includes Poe's narrator as one who "seeks to make sense of the changing city by finding meaning in the signs of everyday life."[51] But for the old man to count as one of these signs, his actions would have to appear aimless without truly being so; his aimlessness would have to be casual, rather than exceptional or psychotic. Designating the old man the latter, the narrator does not "read" him as one reads a sign; rather, he identifies him as unreadable, as outside the domain of signification, hence, outside the public sphere.[52]

There is another point regarding the formation of the antebellum public sphere on which it is important to be clear. Henkin convincingly suggests that antebellum sign culture contributed to "democratic inclusiveness" by addressing "impersonally and indifferently...an unprecedentedly broad range of strangers and residents" whereby "city dwellers became public subjects stripped of their particular identities." He calls this development a "new kind of public." But it is crucial to understand what can and cannot be meant this statement. To be sure, the public is new in the historical sense that the unpropertied or working-class persons who read these signs could thereby demonstrate their worthiness of inclusion within the democratic and impersonal polity. But this newness does not amount to a structurally new kind of public; it cannot mean, as Henkin claims, that "[i]nstead of creating a neutral, detached site for rational deliberation, city reading blurred the lines between politics and commerce, interested and disinterested authority, information and exhortation, judgment and promotion."[53] Public sign reading and consequent street gathering may well have created a realm in which all this happened simultaneously, perhaps even confusedly so; but such historical facts do not warrant the claim that such activities, or faculties giving rise to them, were themselves constitutively blurred. Democratic liberalism's fundamental distinctions between them still held sway, as Child's and Poe's crowd representations indicate. Indeed, Henkin's own account of the growing pervasiveness of an impersonal public-street environment suggests as much.

Both Henkin's and my analyses of Poe's participation in the representation of democratic liberalism's entailments run counter to Jonathan Elmer's recent study of Poe, *Reading at the Social Limit*. Following Claude Lefort's lead, he draws on Tocqueville, whose insight, according to Lefort, was to understand political democracy as a regime of power relations. For Elmer the key passage is one in which Tocqueville observes the democratic citizen to be egocentric, to be one who only sees an "immense form of society at large" whenever he "raises his looks higher" than himself. Elmer provides the gloss:

There where we should find gradations of social forms, a network of institutions, social hierarchizations, all serving to mediate between the individual and social totality, we find nothing – a void. Tocqueville is not arguing that there really is in the American democracy of the 1830's such a complete absence of mediating social structures, but rather that there might as well not be such structures, for all the hold they have on the social imagination.[54]

Elmer's reliance on Tocqueville's description of the vacuousness of the American social imagination is puzzling, given the abundance of historical evidence to the contrary. In addition to Henkin's history of antebellum sign-reading, Mary Ryan's account, for example, of the era's construction of public spaces for the purposes specifically of *political* deliberation, reveals a rather different social imagination at work. She documents the spaces in which "citizens [could] assemble to discuss a wide range of special issues, like the public school, relief during a severe winter, erecting a public building, providing a public service, or organizing a public celebration." The "homespun democratic theorists" who organized and participated in these assemblies, Ryan goes on to explain, "were also careful to prescribe the procedures for maintaining public sovereignty. Invitations to public assemblies were regularly rescinded when it was discovered that a private, vested interest had contrived them."[55] "Public sovereignty," she shows, might have overlapped with, but was not equivalent to, popular interest.

Still, one needs to take seriously Elmer's claim to find in Poe "figurative crystallizations of social totality," such as in the futuristic satire "Mellonta Tauta" (1849). In this story Poe's epistle-writing narrator describes democracy's demise, one thousand years past, on account of "a fellow by the name of *Mob*, who took everything into his own hands and set up a despotism" (*PT* 880). Once having identified the monstrousness of democratic social totality, Elmer endeavors to show that Poe's work ambivalently represents that totality; Poe shows the totality's limit to be opaque as well as encounters of it to be destabilizing, which in turn renders the totality incoherent, constitutively disjoined as it is from itself. The empty place of democracy's limit thus amounts, according to Elmer, to "a destabilization of the transcendent categories of justice and reason, submitting law and science alike to a generalized interpretive uncertainty."[56] It is important to note, however, that in "Mellonta Tauta," Mob-democracy isn't so much destabilized as entirely wiped out; for the narrator informs his correspondent that "He died, at length, by dint of his own energies, which exhausted him" (*PT* 880).

In "The Man of the Crowd," moreover, Poe explicitly represents "gradations of social forms" that mediate between the egocentric individual and the social totality. At first the narrator-protagonist, sitting comfortably in a café, seems indeed to play the role of ego, identifying the totality as such when he references the "tides of population," the "tumultuous sea of human heads" emerging during the evening rush hour (*PT* 388–389). But his subsequent taxonomy of the "innumerable varieties" of individuals passing by goes far to register the firm structural hold of a liberal society in which civil and private individualities are respected. He attends largely to occupational or economic identities, from the upper-middle and "decent" classes to the criminal and beggarly (*PT* 389–391); among these he also spots attorneys and military men, suggesting the interdependent (but not, for all that, blurred) relations between economic and political dimensions of the liberal polity.[57] Poe's emphasis on the public intermingling of classes and identities, along with his attention to sartorial details and deceptive costume, enhances the sense of urban modernity's social heterogeneity. Although public-political institutions are not named in the story, the individuals' ostensive economic sufficiency implies the presence of some such infrastructure. It is not until a singular old man emerges as aimless and unreadable that the socio-political totality encounters its limit. And as explained above, this figure by no means destabilizes the totality. Quite the contrary: he reveals how the totality's immanent yet transcendent limit bears no destabilizing function. In his sublime anonymity and quantitative marginality (he is the only unreadable man in the crowd), the old man figures an aesthetic, rather than a political, attraction or power. As a figure of mirrorlike blankness he does not so much submit reason and justice to interpretive uncertainty as blot them out. In turn, the protagonist-narrator blots him out when he deems him unreadable and himself returns to the world of reflection and deliberation.

Evidence of the actuality and viability of a deliberative polity would doubtless have offered Poe little consolation. Just as he notoriously distrusted democracy's ability to withstand the threat of popular sovereignty's devolution into "mobocracy," he doubted its capacity to cultivate imaginative, artistic expression.[58] What I have attempted to show, however, is how Poe himself provides the antidote to his personal aversions and doubts: first, by showing that it requires someone's (the narrator's) critical or reflective judgment to assess the political danger and aesthetic fascination of men of the crowd; and second, by himself exemplifying magnificently the way in which imaginative expression survives as a by-product of a liberal democratic polity.

FLUTTERING CORPSES AND CITIZENS

In "The Old Apple-Dealer" (1843), Hawthorne both reduces the dramatic situation of Poe's "The Man of the Crowd" to the salient elements of a face-to-face urban encounter and amplifies the specifically aesthetic and political implications of this encounter. The circumstantial details comprising the two narratives of course differ. The setting is not the streets of London but a crowded train station in New England. The old man scrutinized by Hawthorne, an "utter stranger," is obviously employed and possesses not a hint of criminality (*TS* 714). There are no moments of shock or high drama to match Poe's protagonist's first sighting of and final departure from his old man. In fact, Hawthorne is never intimately face to face with his object of interest. He has, however, "studied" him carefully and "often," "while [himself] awaiting the departure of the cars." And now he elects to represent him by "word-painting" (*TS* 714). Thus one finds the same situation of an anonymous male beholder in a crowded environment attempting to make sense both of an extraordinarily peculiar person and of his own fascination with that person.

In the opening paragraph of "The Old Apple-Dealer" Hawthorne frames this urban encounter with distinctly aesthetic and political categories of being. In the very first sentence he identifies himself as a "lover of the moral picturesque." A few lines later he identifies the old man as one who, after Hawthorne's prolonged study, "has become a naturalized citizen of [his] inner world" (*TS* 714). Much of the text, I argue below, wrestles with and at certain points even undercuts both the aesthetic and the political frames erected here, before ultimately confirming their validity. In this process of erecting, undercutting, and eventually re-erecting, Hawthorne packs this sketch with a sort of Socratic lesson in the science of political morality. To a certain degree Darrel Abel is surely right when he asserts in *The Moral Picturesque* that, regarding Hawthorne's larger *oeuvre*, the *moral* in his moral picturesque may be broadly construed; it need not "refer merely to right and wrong behavior, but to all underlying human reality – vital, spiritual, and psychological."[59] Nevertheless, in the text in which the phrase so conspicuously appears there is evidence to suggest that Hawthorne brings it to bear on the specifically political morality of citizenship, dwelling as the beholder does on the elemental features of a man whom he (retroactively) designates a citizen.

Hawthorne's campaign biography of Franklin Pierce from 1852 is but one, if also the most full-blown, indication of his attention to the constituent features of liberal-democratic citizenship. Undertaking to produce a "representation of the principles and acts of a public man, and identifying Pierce as a "brave, faithful, and able citizen," Hawthorne goes on to spell out the qualities Pierce possesses.[60] Besides praising Pierce's general gifts in leadership, his generosity, kindness, integrity, and so forth, Hawthorne zeroes in on what makes him, like his father, a "public-spirited" and "most decided democrat" (*CE* 23: 277). Not only does Pierce exhibit "perfect calmness, full self-possession, and the power of action," especially in the face of crisis (*CE* 23: 288). He also appreciates the distinction between private feeling and public decision: "The whole speech [of Pierce's, before the U.S. Senate] is a good exponent of his character; full of the truest sympathy, but, above all things, just, and not to be misled, on the public behalf, by those impulses that would be most apt to sway the private man" (*CE* 23: 297).

At stake in "The Old Apple-Dealer," as we shall see, are the political-moral identities of both the beholder-aesthete interested in a moral picturesque and the beheld-laborer admitted as citizen, as is the very relation between these aesthetic and political frames of reference. Further, in disclosing the elemental conditions that enable the beholder's moral picturesque and the peddler's citizenship, the sketch also delineates the antitheses of these conditions, namely, the states of unconsciousness and of a non-moral or non-political consciousness. Both beholder and beheld seem to be powerfully influenced by one or another of these antithetical states. Just how powerfully influenced they are is what the lesson-purveying Hawthorne asks his reader to consider.

To begin with Hawthorne himself, as both narrator and beholder: at the outset he may well declare himself a "lover of the moral picturesque," but he also suggests that the mode of fascination that has drawn him to the apple-dealer eludes the moral-aesthetic consciousness necessary to locate such features in a beheld object. He explains (again, retroactively) that he has been studying the peddler "unconsciously," that his "observation...has often settled insensibly upon" him, and that "[i]t is a strange witchcraft, whereby this faded and featureless old apple-dealer has gained a settlement in [his] memory!" (*TS* 714). In other words, as beholder, Hawthorne possesses little in the way of moral consciousness. With the narrating Hawthorne (who loves the moral picturesque) at such a remove from the beholding Hawthorne (who succumbs to bewitchery), Hawthorne the author will reveal, over the course of the sketch, the means of re-aligning these entities.

Such re-alignment will involve the calibration of what Hawthorne refers to as his "inner world" to what the sketch shows is the outer world of antebellum modernity, replete with small trade, public conveyance, and liberal-democratic citizenship. By itself, the sketch's introduction leaves open the possibility that Hawthorne intends to grant his citizen-laborer something like voting rights within his "inner" republic only (having discovered this "settl[er]" already squatting there); he has yet to delineate the degree of overlap between his inner and outer worlds.

The sketch's introduction, then, appears to avow and disavow the creation of a morally picturesque "word-painting" in practically the same breath.[61] Moreover, its principal subject matter practically demands this treatment. According to Hawthorne, at any rate, the peddler is an "almost hueless object," a "character" who is "of too negative a description to be seized upon, and represented to the imaginative vision by word-painting" (*TS* 714). An object that defies representation, however unwittingly, can hardly be called picturesque, let alone moral. Yet here too Hawthorne withdraws what he offers, though in this case reversing the direction: having announced at the outset that the apple-dealer cannot be "seized upon" and "represented," the balance of the sketch does in effect seize upon and represent this "faded and featureless" old man (*TS* 714). If it did not, there would be no sketch. Indeed Hawthorne eventually seizes him with a kind of clinical satisfaction. Near the end of the sketch he declares, after having found the appropriate contrasting context in which to scrutinize and decipher this "specimen," "I have him now" (*TS* 717, 719). Between the ending's firm grip and the beginning's disavowal of any grip at all, the sketch works out the relation between this clinical mode and a morally picturesque mode of representation.

Hawthorne's mode of apprehending and representing the train-station peddler can be seen to follow from the sketch's original status as a notebook entry. The published version differs little from this entry, apart from, significantly, the opening and closing paragraphs in which he erects the aesthetic and political frames. Henry James, in his biographical study of Hawthorne, offers an astute account of this notebook-keeping practice:

It [the chronicle] is in a very partial degree a register of impressions, and in a still smaller sense a record of emotions. Outward objects play much the larger part in it; opinions, convictions, ideas pure and simple, are almost absent... [T]he simplest way to describe the tone of these *extremely objective journals* is to say that they read like a series of very pleasant, though rather dullish and decidedly formal letters, addressed to himself by a man who... [has] determined to insert nothing compromising.[62]

There is no contradiction in James's declaration that Hawthorne's note-books are both "pleasant" and "extremely objective." As "an inveterate observer of small things," Hawthorne the note-taker resembles the scientific naturalist who likes his job.[63] And this mode of naturalist inquiry was understood in the antebellum era to apply both to nature – its animals and its inanimate objects – and to humans (such as is on view in *Uncle Tom's Cabin*, where Stowe describes a "stranger" who encounters Simon Legree at a slave auction, as "looking upon him with the curiosity of a naturalist studying some out-of-the-way specimen").[64]

The more specific scientific-naturalist orientation that Hawthorne adopts is psycho-physiology (which, in the antebellum era included such pseudosciences as phrenology and physiognomy).[65] This is what encourages him to examine first the visible surfaces of the man, such as his "thin, withered, furrowed" face, which reveals a "frost-bitten aspect." But where the "slight observer" might stop at this "patient, long-suffering, quiet, hopeless, shivering aspect," and "speak of the old man's quietude" only, Hawthorne pursues more obscure phenomena. "[O]n closer scrutiny" the old man's physiology reveals a markedly different quality: "you discover that there is a continual unrest within him, which somewhat resembles the fluttering action of the nerves, in a corpse from which life has recently departed" (*TS* 714–715). Though he "might appear to be sitting quite still," Hawthorne goes on to remark, "yet you perceive, when his minuter peculiarities begin to be detected, that he is always making some little movement or other" (*TS* 715). This figurative likeness to a fresh corpse recalls the actual situation over which Hawthorne ponders in his 1837 notebook entry, where he records the account given by a ship captain of a man he witnessed walking "pretty briskly" for about twenty feet after his head had been shot off by a cannon, "with two jets of blood gushing from his headless trunk" (*CE* 8: 73).[66] In both cases Hawthorne seems as interested in whether the respectively unfeeling and decapitated men have consciousness as in whether they have sensation.

The apple-dealer's "unrest" also resembles what in the mid-nineteenth century was known as the *maladie des mécaniciens* which affected railroad train personnel. As Wolfgang Schivelbusch explains in *The Railway Journey*, this affliction was the result of the locomotive's "condition of continuous vibration." In addition to descriptions from 1838 he cites one from 1860 that is particularly apposite:

[This article] gives a more exact account of the way in which the vibration affects the body: "In the locomotive personnel *these shocks express themselves as a continuous tremor* in all the joints of the body that is only interrupted by sudden vertical jolts or sideways motions: this tremor is so intense and rapid that if the engine-driver or fireman were to attempt to rest his body on its bone structure in a rigid fashion by planting his feet firmly on the floor, it would be impossible for him to stand even for a short time."[67]

Exhibiting something like durational shock, the train personnel seem only physically affected. Hawthorne, in his dispassionate observations of a despondent, morbidly "fluttering" peddler who works only near, not on, the trains, probes for possible mental correlatives.

In these preoccupations, Hawthorne resembles the early nineteenth-century neuro-physiologists who, experimenting primarily on newly decapitated frogs, sought to determine just what their movements might mean. In *From Sympathy to Reflex* the historian of science Ruth Leys provides a most fascinating and informative account of the era's neuro-physiological research and experimentation on the nervous system, particularly the discovery of the spinal reflex arc's independence from the brain. This scientific pursuit involved efforts to distinguish between mechanistic and mental actions, and to identify the physical location of the source of these actions. It therefore also involved scientists' making metaphysical determinations, such as whether sensations were states of body or of mind; whether the spinal cord possessed sensations, thence a soul; whether the cries and struggles of provoked animals (with their heads still attached) indicated their feeling pain; indeed, whether even the oral testimony of human paralytics evidently capable of introspection and communication could be considered applicable to non-pathological cases and thus verify, say, the distinction between the reflex function and sensation or volition.[68] Such determinations would carry significant implications for understanding and defining the mental and moral capacities of the human being.

By the 1830s and 1840s, medical jurisprudence began to develop what Taylor Stoehr, in *Hawthorne's Mad Scientists*, has called a "new category" of mania, namely, "the inability to distinguish between good and evil."[69] The 1834 American edition of *Observations on Mental Derangement* by Scottish phrenologist Andrew Combe, brother of the better-known medical authority George Combe (Hawthorne had read works by both), described not only the medical practitioner's role in separating out the legally sane from the insane, but also the necessary assistance of the "intelligent jury":

The point of difficulty...is to determine, not the mere existence of a mental affection, but *the limit at which that affection begins to deprive the individual of the power of proper self-direction, and at which therefore, it becomes the duty of the law, and of the friends, to step in for his protection.* The right solution of this problem is no easy task; for it requires in the jurors not only clearness of perception, and soundness of judgment, but a knowledge of human nature, and an acquaintance with the general functions of the body, and with the p[r]evious habits and constitution of the suspected lunatic, which unhappily, under our imperfect systems of general education, very few persons are found to possess.[70]

Although having enrolled at Bowdoin in courses in anatomy and physiology, and having classmates who later participated in the development of medical jurisprudence, Hawthorne himself was of course no trained practitioner of medicine.[71] In "The Old Apple-Dealer" he figures himself as the next best thing, the intelligent juror. As such, he takes upon himself the project of determining how best to comprehend the old peddler.

Thus when Hawthorne describes the apple-dealer's likely "nerveless boyhood," and his current "expression of frost-bitten, patient despondency," he is building toward his speculation that the old man "can never suffer the extreme of misery, because *the tone of his whole being* is too much subdued for him to feel anything acutely" (*TS* 716–717 emphasis added). Such speculation frames his inquiry into both the mental and moral conditions of the peddler. Might this man be so "susceptible of morbid action," to quote Combe again, or so "deficient" in "organic endowment" as to produce "mental derangement"?[72] Is he so fully enclosed in a "moral frost, which no physical warmth or comfortableness could counteract" (*TS* 714), as to warrant medical or legal intervention? Combe notes that "the true problem to be resolved, where the rights of liberty and property are concerned, is not so much whether mental derangement exist [*sic*], but *whether it has extended so far as to deprive the individual of the power of sound judgment in his own affairs, or of regulating his own moral conduct, so that he shall not endanger the welfare either of others or of himself*."[73] In "The Old Apple-Dealer" the drama is located in Hawthorne's determining just how "far" the "moral frost" of his corpse-like, fluttering peddler has "extended."

Hawthorne is concerned in this sketch to minimize psychologizing, that is, to limit conjecture about the peddler's specific motives or thoughts; but he does observe that the man appears to harbor none of the resentment or even frustration that might be expected from one so easily deemed a social failure. "As all his past life, probably, offers no spots of brightness to his memory, so he takes his present poverty and discomfort as entirely a matter of course" (*TS* 714–715). What he thus detects in the apple-dealer is someone utterly devoid of the need for social recognition. The peddler is thus the distinct contrast to one of Hawthorne's other urban figures, Wakefield, who all too humanly relinquishes the cover of the crowd and returns to his wife because he cannot endure the lack of recognition: "It was Wakefield's unprecedented fate, to retain his original share of human sympathies, and to be still involved in human interests, while he had lost his reciprocal influence on them" (*TS* 297). What the sentimental and morally conventional Wakefield cannot abide, namely, "expos[ing] himself to the fearful risk of losing his place [in society's systems] forever" (*TS* 297), the apple-dealer takes as "entirely a matter of course." Though he engages in his slim way in conventional market practices, he has radically disengaged himself from bourgeois culture's pretense of cheerful industry. Hawthorne writes: "The old apple-dealer never speaks an unnecessary word; not that he is sullen and morose; but there is none of the cheeriness and briskness in him, that stirs up people to talk." Even when greeted by a familiar customer, he "presumes not on any past acquaintance; he makes the briefest possible response to all general remarks, and shrinks quietly into himself again" (*TS* 717).

Shrinking into himself and his frozen yet nervous patience, the apple-dealer figures a rejection of the sentimental conception of subjectivity, which is dependent on sympathetic communication, fellow feeling, and reciprocal recognition. When Hawthorne invokes the peddler's "subdued" "tone" (in the passage cited earlier), he draws on popular nineteenth-century parlance for the state of physiological and moral health. Mary Gove (later Nichols), in her 1842 *Lectures to Ladies on Anatomy and Physiology*, quotes the Philadelphian doctor Francis Condie who deems it "proper to lay down a definition of *tone* – which is that state of the nervous system, when it responds with sufficient promptitude, vigor and regularity, to the healthful and natural stimuli." In this same extract Condie goes on to describe two kinds of "want of tone," namely "deficient excitability," leading to "a state of torpor," and an "excess of excitability." Such wants of tone were thought to carry moral consequences, because, as Gove quotes Condie further, "Every physiological propensity, appetite or passion, is implanted in the human organism by its Almighty Author, for a wise purpose, and hence . . . [proper indulgence is] necessary for the well being of the individual, and for the preservation of the species . . . The great hygienic law . . . is, carefully to guard against every thing which has a tendency to cause any of [these passions] to become so excessive, as to control the action of the organism . . . destroying by their tyranny our individual happiness, and depriving us of the power to do good."[74] Being and well-being, in this ideological frame, were essentially identical.

However nearly Hawthorne comes in "The Old Apple-Dealer" to rein-scribing this middle-class tauto-ontology of the physically and morally well-balanced being, he ultimately rejects it. Observing the way the peddler's "eyelids droop," the way he "shivers, perhaps, folds his lean arms around his lean body, and resumes [his] life-long frozen patience," Hawthorne documents the physical symptoms of the old man's "almost passive disposition" – "in which consists his *strength*" (*TS* 716, emphasis added). In transforming passivity into a "strength," Hawthorne reverses conventional nineteenth-century value judgments of character. Yet interestingly enough, he effects this reversal not by abandoning the antebellum era's psychophysiological paradigm but by embracing it all the more firmly. That is, his intense scrutiny of the peddler's being enables him to assess the peddler's mental and moral condition in a manner consistent with contemporaneous faculty psychology, which understood the human psychical apparatus to be pluralistic. According to Andrew Combe, for instance, in his account of the "fundamental principles of the new physiology," the brain was "an aggregate of parts, each serving for the reception of particular sensations, or for the manifestation of a primitive mental power":

It [phrenology] proves that one or more of these [distinct] organs may be injured or diseased, and their functions impeded or altered, without necessarily affecting the remainder; and thus explains how a man may be insane on one feeling or faculty, and sound on all the rest.[75]

In Hawthorne's text, the brain in question fits this description. To recall, the peddler appears simultaneously "quite still" and "always making some little movement or other." He is both "frozen" and "fluttering", filled both with "patience" and "unrest." In other words, Hawthorne represents the appledealer as a bundle of discontinuous perceptions, cognitions, spasmodic and reflex actions, who also engages in voluntary and involuntary spontaneous movements. Chiefly lacking in this man is a conventional set of affections, social sympathies, and recognitive memories.

As such the man resembles nothing so much as the swarm of insects Hawthorne describes in yet another journal entry on the topic of yet another deadish thing, this time the "grim and grisly corpse" of a newly crushed mosquito:

In truth, the whole insect tribe, so far as we can judge, are made more for themselves, and less for man, than any other portion of creation. With such reflection, we look at a swarm of them, peopling, indeed, the whole air, but only visible when they flash into the sunshine; and annihilated out of visible existence, when they dart into a region of shadow, to be again re-produced as suddenly. (*CE* 8: 248)

In this word-painting insects become a "swarm" or a "tribe" only because they belong to the same quasi-universal animal class and physically "people" the same air, and because sufficient numbers of them are visibly present, rather than "annihilated," from the perspective of the beholder. None of the swarm's members bears a pre-collected collective identity, apart from its humanly designated species status as an insect. In other words, while physically several, only formally do they constitute a plurality or a collectivity.

While not physically several, the apple-dealer appears to possess autonomously active and inactive ("annihilated" in Hawthorne's terminology) faculties. This mode of plurality forces Hawthorne to consider the man's *overall* functionality. Clearly constituting a formation, a physical unit, the apple-dealer's swarming faculties invite the question as to whether he functions well enough to count as a liberal-democratic human form or, rather like the insect tribe, is made for himself and not "for man." Again, questions arise as to whether Hawthorne has granted the peddler citizenship to his inner world merely, and whether Hawthorne's inner world squares with the liberal-democratic outer world in which he lives.

According to Hawthorne's observations, the peddler functions with perfect competence as an economic being. He exchanges goods for money; he rearranges his wares; he makes change; he even takes discreet precautions against fraud: "If he have received a silver coin, he waits till the purchaser is out of sight, then examines it closely, and tries to bend it with his finger and thumb" (*TS* 717). Such evidence of cognitive competence, moral alertness, and overall self-sufficiency in the economic realm goes far to confirm this impoverished laborer's likely competence as a political "citizen" as well. He is the psychological contrast to a better-heeled merchant imagined in an entry in Hawthorne's lost notebook: "A dealer in women's black worsted stockings was so in love with the article, that when it was going out of fashion, he still continued to buy large quantities, and invested his whole property in them, so that, by the reduction of the price, he was totally ruined" (*CE* 23: 131). In an era of widespread and enduring skepticism about the extension of suffrage to the lower classes – especially immigrants – Hawthorne offers something like a formal profile of lower-class consciousness. He suggests that even if not empirically provable, a reasoning and morally sound consciousness is typically evinced by even the most corpse-like male members of the human species.

Hawthorne finds that he is best able to capture the old man's "decided sense of reality... [by] look[ing] at him in the very moment of intensest bustle, on the arrival of the cars," when the "travelers swarm forth" (*TS* 719). Hawthorne seeks a "contrast" (*TS* 718) so as better to discern the old man's character, and he finds it in the crowd, which is "full of the momentum which they have caught from their mode of conveyance." He associates this crowd with all that is "both morally and physically... detached from its old standfasts, and set in motion." Meanwhile, the old man "sits" and "folds his lean arms around his lean figure, with that quiet sigh, and that scarcely perceptible shiver, which are the tokens of his inward state" (*TS* 719). Hawthorne finally seizes his man: the gesture of relegating all other humans in their traveling, swarming crowdedness to the state of moral and physical detachment enables him to reclaim the old man, by contrast, as physically fast and morally fit.

Moreover, in the sketch's last paragraph, Hawthorne makes clear that the apple-dealer's citizenship has currency not only within his inner but also the outer liberal-democratic world. Here he defends this one man against the "[m]any" in the world who "would say that you [the apple-dealer] have hardly individuality enough to be the object of your own self-love" (*TS* 719). With autonomy and self-love (in the sense of self-respect) being preconditions of a liberal democracy, Hawthorne's assertion of the apple-dealer's possession of these qualities stands as the end result of his careful and frequent study of this "specimen" (*TS* 717). In this spirit of inclusion Hawthorne concludes that the peddler's individuality is unfathomably deep, like "a volume of deeper and more comprehensive import than all that the wisest mortals have given to the world" (*TS* 719). Unlike Poe's human text of the crowd, Hawthorne's remains readable.

In "The Old Apple-Dealer" it is by playing the naturalist card of detachment while fingering, but only barely, the moral card of relation, that Hawthorne recovers his hold on the picturesque. Darrel Abel explains that nature and morality have essentially nothing to do with each other in Hawthorne's scheme of things. Where nature has its own "impersonal laws" and remains "unfeeling," morality "has reference to a higher, distinctively human level of being." The picturesque, on the other hand, may apply both to natural scenes and human character or behavior. Moreover, as it registers "strikingly graphic and extraordinary" phenomena, the picturesque may refer either to "intense typicality" or "irregularity" and "eccentricity."[76] By adopting a naturalist orientation, Hawthorne first scrutinizes the old apple-dealer as an extraordinary human specimen, one whose picturesqueness has to do with his psycho-physiological, which is to say, his animal rather than his moral presence. By the sketch's conclusion, however, Hawthorne's observations lead him to assertions about the peddler's "picturesque, and even sublime" qualities, about his "depths of the human soul," indicating his mental and moral "strength" (*TS* 719, 716).

For Dana Brand this sketch reveals Hawthorne's abiding ethical disposition in the way it "reaffirms the opacity of the world by showing how little an honest flaneur or panoramic spectator would actually accomplish" in attempting to represent urban realities. It exhibits "Hawthorne's evident respect for the privacy and the rights of individuals to be opaque, complex, and mysterious." In Brand's view the (unethical and dishonest) *flâneur*, with his pretentious bid for "epistemological control," reduces everything in the urban environment to a "legible, accessible, and non-threatening version of itself."[77] What Brand fails to acknowledge, however, is the way Hawthorne renders the apple-dealer legible and accessible – and even non-threatening, at least to the extent that "he never exhibits any violent action" (*TS* 715). While allowing the apple-dealer more than a modicum of opacity and complexity, Hawthorne's ethical strength, in my view, is in his willingness to peg the apple-dealer as *not* opaque all the way down, but rather, as, at bottom, *one of us*. Indeed, having cast him as public-politically one of us, Hawthorne is then able to contemplate the apple-dealer's more subjective and weirdly expressive mysteries.

Furthermore, I would suggest that Hawthorne, in "naturalizing" the apple-dealer as a citizen, reveals the lengths to which antebellum liberal-democratic society might go in accepting that which could possibly be threatening. The naturalist-juror's judgment may well be wrong; the apple-dealer may well be severely deranged. Where Poe's dismissal of the man of the crowd effectively eliminates him as an internal political threat, Hawthorne's naturalization of the apple-dealer represents antebellum America's liberal-democratic risk-taking. In contrast to Joel Headley, cited earlier in the chapter, who viewed the immigrant lower class as a "mass of material wholly unfit for any political structure," Hawthorne's political liberalism encourages his giving the benefit of the doubt.[78] Discerning something of this disposition was likely the grounds for Henry James's speculation that Hawthorne "must in the nature of things have been more or less of a consenting democrat."[79] Hawthorne's drama of scrutiny turns out to acknowledge the viability, under liberal democracy, of a pluralistic, incommensurate self. The peddler's constitution, with its autonomously operating faculties – emotional inanimation and economic animation – parallels Hawthorne's own, with his autonomously operating political and aesthetic faculties. While ethical reason is clearly not what motivates his fascination with the fluttering corpse, it just as clearly is what motivates his political decision to retain the peddler as a "naturalized citizen" of both his inner and outer worlds.

Apart from *Leaves of Grass*, this chapter has dwelt on arguably marginal literary works: a compilation of newspaper columns, a short story, and a sketch. Their slightness testifies, I would suggest, to the still-incipient state of urban consciousness in the antebellum United States. Of course more prominent and in some cases more popular urban works appeared in this period – for instance, Melville's "Bartleby, the Scrivener" and *Pierre*, Fanny Fern's *Ruth Hall*, and George Foster's *New York by Gas-Light*. But the widespread self-evidence of an American crowd culture did not take hold until the post-Reconstruction period. Another forty or fifty years would pass before "White City," as the name for the Columbian Exposition's fairgrounds, made cultural sense, resonating with a national identity.

In the next chapter, Henry James's *Washington Square* serves as a bridge of sorts between the antebellum and post-Reconstruction eras. Published in the early 1880s, but with an antebellum fictional time frame, James imports into this earlier period certain concerns about urban modernity that might seem more intelligible to, or at least more widely apprehended by, people of the later period. The background culture that he depicts, of being ever on the uptown move, of desiring to possess the very latest in home fixtures, belongs rather to Dreiser's world than to Hawthorne's or Melville's.

On the other hand, James's Dr. Sloper can be viewed as a somewhat more imperious version of Bartleby's decidedly pre-war, problematically urban employer. Bartleby himself exhibits a distinct aversion to the emerging crowd culture – taking offense as he does when the co-workers crowd about him behind his screen, as well as registering what Gillian Brown so astutely sees as symptoms of agoraphobia.[80] Whereas James's main character, Catherine, though not unlike Bartleby in her uncanny steadfastness and awkwardness, exhibits little uneasiness with New York's urban conditions. James points toward what antebellum writers perhaps realistically could not: the culture of crowd's environmental pervasiveness and permanence.

CHAPTER 2

In "the thick of the stream": Henry James and the public sphere

This chapter examines Henry James's representation of the intricate links between crowds and publics, between private and public life. While critics have attended to James's many portrayals of modern publicity's invasions of privacy and its constructions of visibility, I focus on two narratives, *Washington Square* (1880) and "The Papers" (1903), in which public and private are differently configured. In these texts the public-private dyad turns less on ideologically structured spatial or institutional differences (between, say, marketplace and domicile, work and family) than on formal differences between two spheres of modern experience: the rational, in which debate (and consent) is the operative mode, and the sentimental, in which force is. Both *Washington Square* and "The Papers" thematize urban modernity's trends toward mass culture and consumerism. But more is at stake than the commercial public's invasion of domestic relations. To be sure, *Washington Square* depicts New York gentility's obsessive conformism, disclosing with acerbic irony the way its members hang on consumerist values of upward mobility and treat intimate relations – marital prospects – either as melodramatic spectacle or commercial transaction, that is, either as emotional entertainment or calculated investment. In "The Papers" James turns to London's mass-circulation newspaper industry, portraying what one of the two main characters Harold Bight calls "the laws – so mysterious, so curious, so interesting – that govern the great currents of public attention."[1] But more significant, in my view, is how James in both narratives draws out the implications for intimate relations of having – or not having – in place an operative Kantian public sphere.

For Kant, public reason takes place in an interest-free, dutiful zone, where the categorical imperative of universalizable maxims and a critical-rational method of argument prevail. In "What Is Enlightenment?" Kant proffers the "man of learning addressing the entire reading public" as the exemplary public person.[2] As opposed to the civil servant who must obey incumbent directives, the university scholar's use of reason is unencumbered and his claims are open to argument. As Habermas stresses, Kant's point is not that only university scholars should count as public reasoners, but that the formal conditions scholars enjoy should also obtain in the public sphere: "The public sphere was not realized in the republic of scholars alone but in the public use of reason by all who were adept at it."[3] Adding to Kant's model public person, Habermas identifies several modern institutions that he contends contributed importantly to the making and maintaining of the liberal public sphere, including the coffee house, the newspaper, art criticism, and the bourgeois family. His remarks regarding the latter are instructive:

The public's understanding of the public use of reason was guided by such private experiences as grew out of the *audience-oriented* [emphasis added] subjectivity of the conjugal family's intimate domain ... The status of private man combined the role of owner of commodities with that of head of the family, that of property owner with that of "human being" *per se* ... [B]efore the public sphere explicitly assumed political functions in the tension-charged field of state-society relations, the subjectivity originating in the intimate sphere of the conjugal family created, so to speak, its own public.

The bourgeois family, then, with its audience orientation, was in Habermas's view as central to the development of the liberal public sphere as the more recognizably public realm of print media. Even such seemingly private practices as aesthetic judgment and psychological self-examination could thus be seen as "training ground" for critical, public analysis.[4]

Habermas goes on to argue that over the course of the nineteenth century the transformation of both the bourgeois family and the newspaper industry severely diminished its public capacity. The family's expanding function as the locus of private consumption and leisure, along with its illusion of freedom from the marketplace and delusion of intimate, love-inspired autonomy, eclipsed its relation to public discourse. Likewise, the commercialization of the press, its commodification of social knowledge, and its promotion of the "sham-private world of culture consumption," transformed a critical public forum into a manipulative one.[5] While mass media expanded the market of readers, it yielded to capitalism's profit-maximizing, self-interested logic, and thereby lost its political-liberal relevance.

While Henry James has long been understood as harboring an animated disdain for vulgar commercialization and for modern journalism's invasive disregard for privacy, recent critics have convincingly demonstrated James's keen attunement to urban modernity's vicissitudes, such disdain notwithstanding.[6] Concurring with these recent critical approaches, I hope to show that James exemplifies, but also psychodramatically intensifies, and thus resignifies, the Habermasian account of the fall of the public sphere. James represents in *Washington Square*'s Sloper family the ways in which the commercialization of the domestic sphere might indeed diminish the urban family's role in rational-critical discourse; but he also dramatizes how one member of this family, Catherine Sloper, as though taking her cue from the impersonal urban crowd, remains herself psychically undetermined both by commercial modernity's rational operations of contract and exchange and its sentimental operations of self-interest. In "The Papers" James shows how the mass media industry engenders simultaneously a consumerist (private) sphere of celebrity spectacle and a Kantian-liberal public sphere of ethical reflection. Yet here, too, James figures the crowd effect as an alternative to both. If consumerism can be said to be coded by grammatical norms of subjectivity – "I want" – James puts into narrative circulation a female character, Maud Blandy, who cracks this code by embodying what he suggests is a quasi-Darwinian mode of mutation in which the subject as such plays no directing part in the transformation of her desire. She whom James describes as being "one of the stages of an evolution" is enlightened by Howard in this matter: "You've played, you see, a most unusual game. The code allows for everything *but* that" (*CT* 12: 15, 110). Howard refers here specifically to journalism's professional code of conduct; but I aim to show that the idea of code also has larger implications vis-à-vis this narrative's representation of mass-mediated public culture. As we shall see in both texts, crowds of one variety or another, and the absorptive aesthetic state they entail, play an important role in representing these alternatives.

But before turning to the two narratives themselves, it is worth noting that one of James's lexical favorites (judging by his frequent and various application of the term) appears to be "swarm." Like many other writers, he uses the word to describe the kinetic circulation of urban crowds. In *A Small Boy and Others*, for instance, he recalls from his childhood looking onto London streets from the refuge of a carriage, and witnessing the "swarming crowds" that refuse to remain picturesque and instead appear to him as "the bigger brutality of life, which pressed upon the cab." In *The American Scene* he similarly describes the Lower East Side's "quality of appealing, surrounding life" as one "of a great swarming, a swarming that had begun to thicken, infinitely, as soon as we had crossed to the East side."[7] Such passages register James's aesthetic fascination with the "life" of crowds. At other moments he refers to swarms more vaguely, such as in his late short story "Crapy Cornelia," where the nostalgic protagonist White-Mason feels somewhat threatened by his consummately modern, potential fiancée Mrs. Worthingham's capacious response to New York life: "Her outlook took form to him suddenly as a great square sunny window that hung in assured fashion over the immensity of life. There rose toward it as from a vast swarming *plaza* a high tide of motion and sound" (*CT* 12: 343). Grammatically employing the term to qualify a material place, that is, eliding the difference between the aggregation of persons in the square and the square itself, James verges on the surreal.

With similar figurative license, James refuses the opposition between conceptions of memory as an indivisible unity and as a swarm of fragments, when describing his own recollective experience. "The truth is," he writes in *A Small Boy and Others*, "much less in the wealth of my experience than in the tenacity of my impression, the fact that I have lost nothing of what I saw and that though I can't now quite divide the total into separate occasions the various items surprisingly swarm for me." Elsewhere in the same text James suggests that the swarm, or the condition of swarming, applies not simply to personal but, more intimately, to familial experience. He tropes his "cousinship" as "swarming," just as in *The American Scene* he refers to the "old Cambridge ghosts" "sight[ed]" during his visit to the family plot in the Mount Auburn cemetery as having "swarmed all the while too thick" for him "to name."[8] Swarming too thick to name: James introduces the most impersonal of urban conditions, the unnameable crowd, into the sphere of private, solitary recollection, of remembering family members and close friends. The trope thus serves to knit together without synthesizing modes of experience that are conventionally viewed as antithetical: the anonymity of the crowd and the intimacy of the family. James suggests that at a certain degree of density, intimacy itself will shade into the impersonal. More than mere literary license, then, the swarming crowd images for James that which cannot be empirically imaged but nonetheless beguiles his imagination: modernity's formal conditions of human experience.

DOMESTIC CROWDEDNESS

In *Washington Square* the binding together of intimacy and impersonality factors into James's representation of Catherine Sloper and her relationship to her father. The first time James presents daughter and father together they are in a crowd. The scene is the engagement party for her cousin, and she has been dancing. "Just when the dance was over, she found herself in the crowd face to face with her father."[9] With their physical bodies "face to face" in this manner, James recapitulates one of the most common scenarios in urban literature, one that as often as not registers a shock of non-recognition.[10] James's dramatic twist on the scenario is to bring it indoors, indicating the nuclear family's susceptibility to urban anonymity. Dr. Sloper's mock failure to recognize his daughter and his surprise at meeting her thus – "Is it possible that this magnificent person is my child?" (*WS* 46) – prefigures his very real failure to recognize the significance of her actions throughout the entire affair with Morris Townsend, which is to say, throughout the rest of his life. Adding to this episode's circumstances of anonymity (in the sense of epistemological uncertainty) is Dr. Sloper's and his sister Mrs. Penniman's failure to obtain Morris Townsend's name (whom they see showing interest in Catherine) and Catherine's willingness in the carriage ride home to feign ignorance of it (*WS* 48). That Dr. Sloper's own daughter, for all his protective gentility, is romantically accosted by "a perfect stranger" (*WS* 53), signals the stress that the urban environment exerts upon the nineteenth-century bourgeois ideal of domestic familiarity and shelter. His Washington Square domicile, "the ideal of quiet and of genteel retirement" (*WS* 39), is no match for the transactional anonymity upon which the commercial structure of urban modernity depends.

But not only does this face-to-face confrontation bear the markings of the anonymous urban encounter; it also calls to mind another, more extreme mode of non-recognition, namely, the mesmeric or hypnotic scenario, in which the operator, physically close to the subject, initiates the trance. The entranced subject is by definition incapable of recognition; whatever the means of inducement (which could well depend on the pre-hypnotic subject's recognition of the operator's power), the entranced state itself disables recognitive capacities. As discussed in the Introduction, it entails an absorbed, mimetic identification with, not a recognition of, the operator. Catherine's prominent features – James renders her characteristically "motionless," "inanimate," "unnaturally passive," "silent," and "patient" – make her the perfect mesmeric match for her medically trained and characteristically forceful father.[11] James draws on contemporaneous images of the hypnotic operation in his representation of her response to Dr. Sloper's and Mrs. Penniman's disagreement over Morris's recent first visit. While the doctor stabs his sister with verbal retorts and she simpers, Catherine listens in the posture of a hypnotic subject: "with her forehead touching the window-panes, [she] listened to this exchange of epigrams as reservedly as if they had not each been a pin-prick in her own destiny" (*WS* 55). Pressure on the forehead was known to be one of the means of inducing hypnosis.[12] Like Bartleby with his walls, Catherine against the glass impersonally removes herself from her relatives' vituperations to the point of affective anaesthesia – no longer feeling their "pin-pricks," the method commonly applied to measure a hypnotic subject's unawareness of physical sensation. She might well hear their verbal exchanges but her "reserve" prevents her from recognizing them as applying to her.

These seemingly minor details – the engagement party crowd, the accoutrements of hypnosis discourse – point toward James's larger concerns in this novel. Critic Ian Bell persuasively argues that *Washington Square* is "about the ways in which economic and commercial practices structure human relationships." As another critic Andrew Scheiber claims, the novel counts among several of James's works that are "informed by the language and method of evolutionary biology, ethnology, and other nascent human sciences of the era."[13] For both critics James's novelistic achievement is the exposure of the damaging effects of modernity's rationalist practices, be they commercial or scientific. Bell goes on more specifically to analyze, among other aspects, how the novel registers the imposing and debilitating structures of authoritarian rationalism, the ideologies of money-mediated, hence quantified, exchange and balance, and the adjudications of possession, all inscribed within nineteenth-century bourgeois systems of value. As Dr. Sloper's and Morris Townsend's competing claims on Catherine Sloper intensify, she "is victimized as the commodity in human form, paralyzed within the instability of the marketplace." According to Bell, in other words, she is victimized "by domestic versions of institutions." Concurring with Millicent Bell's analysis, that Catherine eventually triumphs over the two men, Ian Bell nevertheless maintains that Catherine suffers from the immobility of commodification; she displays "the alienation of the self that is customarily associated with the effects of developing industrialism."[14]

Scheiber in turn argues that James depicts the anti-humanism of Dr. Sloper's Darwinistic methodology. "[S]ee[ing] reason and logic as the benchmarks of evolutionary superiority," Dr. Sloper exemplifies the authoritarian abuses of "standard medicine [which] shifted emphasis from the patient as an *individual* to his or her function as a representative instance of uniform laws." Dr. Sloper commits the crime of converting human beings into "actuarial constructs" and of making assessments based on "anthrometric odds." Thus "the novel's greatest pathos derives from Sloper's application of this methodology to his own daughter."[15]

Important as Bell's and Scheiber's relevant and illuminating contexts are, their interpretations of the novel in relation to these contexts require, in my view, some revision. Embedded in both their arguments is something akin to moral indignation, which the critics imply they and James share, over Dr. Sloper's importation of modernity's rationalist practices into the home, as though his treating Catherine as a commodity or a statistic intrinsically violates her dignity as a person, violating as well the venerable distinction between public rationality and private affection. By contrast, I argue that James refuses to rehearse this standard critique of urban capitalism's alienating, dehumanizing, dispiriting effect on persons of diverse classes. Instead, I hope to suggest that Dr. Sloper's violation consists in his abandonment of reason when he most needs it, in his assumption that he is motivated by rational judgment when he is not, and consequently in his severance of the domestic sphere from its audience-oriented, political-liberal capacities. In Catherine, moreover, James represents a character who is not so easily damaged by urban modernity's economic and scientific structures.

The engagement party and the encounter there between father and daughter crystallize in domestic form the crowd mentality that is poised to move in once this audience-oriented principle is driven out. James's allusions in the novel to New York's "tide of fashion" and "great hum of traffic" indicate the crowd's ubiquitous proximity (*WS* 39). He depicts New York as motivated not only by economic self-interest but by the inhuman tides and hums of a crowd mentality. Moreover, James distinctly associates this crowd culture with an aesthetic propensity. In the same passage in which he diagnoses in New York's northward expansion an attraction *en masse* to fashion for its own sake, he goes on to describe this "commercial development" – once a "murmur" but now a "mighty uproar" – as being "music in the ears of all good citizens interested in [it]" (*WS* 39). James's compounding into a single sentence the terms of political liberalism ("citizens") and aesthetic delight ("music") conveys succinctly the antinomy inhering in liberal democracy's economic sphere. On the one hand, a liberal democratic polity develops public terms of contract and a public currency to facilitate commercial transactions in a manner that conforms to its idea of justice as fairness. On the other hand, the privatization of property and commerce opens up the economic sphere to the vicissitudes of a non-reflective, hence unarguable, aesthetic attachment. These aesthetic vicissitudes fluctuate between personal taste and impersonal absorption.

In *Washington Square* the drama between father and daughter turns on the manners in which they accept or reject this antinomy. Dr. Sloper, in my view, delusively presumes to have succeeded in rejecting it by operating solely in accordance with enlightened self-interest. Hence his annoyance when Catherine appears at the engagement party in what he calls her "sumptuous, opulent, expensive" attire, "look[ing] as if [she] had eighty thousand a year" (*WS* 46). Dr. Sloper deems aesthetically appropriate only the "look" that is commensurate with a person's financial worth and, Catherine's dowry being more modest, he is offended by her extravagance.

(Even taking into account what the reader learns is his habitual ironic if not satiric attitude toward Catherine, the aesthetic offense still holds. For while it may well be the case that he does not really think Catherine looks as though she were worth eighty thousand a year – because homely, clumsy Catherine, with none of the graces and virtues expected of a high-society female prize, could never be worth so much on the marriage market – he nevertheless remains annoyed with her for not squaring her looks with her marriage market value.)

Despite this use of market rationality to devise a moral aesthetics, Dr. Sloper's deeper affliction has to do, as mentioned above, with his rejection, when most needed, of rationalist principles. More precisely, it has to do with his success at masking sentimental attachments as reasonable judgments. That Dr. Sloper married into wealth and that his renowned medical expertise failed him in times of family crisis (when first his three-year old son and later his wife lay dying) testifies to the contingencies of the one, wealth, and the fallibility of the other, expertise. His disavowals of the roles contingency and error play signal his overweening, indeed, unreasonable commitment to rationalization. That is, these disavowals cloud his very ability to reason publicly – to deliberate and to argue. In the first pages of the novel, James notes that Dr. Sloper "walked under the weight of [a] very private censure for the rest of his days, and bore forever the scars of a [self-] castigation" for having not prevented the deaths of his wife and son (*WS* 29). Yet more significant for the present discussion than this clue to the probable cause of Dr. Sloper's abnegation of audience-oriented reason are James's insights into how the doctor's modes of rationalization assume the guise of public reason without, however, adhering to its core principles.

It is in Dr. Sloper's treatment of Morris Townsend that he exhibits distinctly both his unwillingness to acknowledge contingency and his ability to mask sentiment as rationality. Despite his own "modest patrimony," a circumstance which James suggests could have rendered him a dubious suitor of a wealthy "young woman of high fashion" (*WS* 28), Dr. Sloper insists that a suitor of his own daughter match her fair market value. What makes his position obnoxious is less that he is so calculating – financial considerations would be in keeping with the customary evaluation of spousal suitability – than that he determines the variables of a potential spouse according to his own deeply idiosyncratic social calculus. Getting wind of Morris's lack of wealth, he sets out to fix him as a fortune hunter and nothing but. To be sure, in coming to this conclusion, Dr. Sloper relies on his trained powers of observation: "He had passed his life in estimating people (it was part of the medical trade), and in nineteen cases out of twenty he was right" (*WS* 94). Further, he "give[s Morris] the benefit of the doubt" (*WS* 94), at least until he collects substantial evidence from the young man's widowed sister that points conclusively to his mercenary ambitions. But once having established Morris's identity as a fortune hunter, Dr. Sloper considers the case, the marriage suit, closed. "[Y]ou belong to the wrong category," he says to Morris, decorously pretending to allude to his "absence of means, of a profession, of visible resources or prospects" (*WS* 89–90). As the dialogue ensues it becomes clear to Morris that Dr. Sloper's accusations actually stem from his ascertainment of Morris's duplicity. What Morris lacks is moral transparency – "the word of a gentleman" (*WS* 90). While Dr. Sloper turns out to be correct in this assessment, as Catherine must traumatically discover for herself some months later, it is the manner in which he makes this correctness substitute for the hard work of deliberation that reveals his evasion of audience-oriented reason. More than financial or occupational status, the contingency of duplicity – one of urban modernity's emergent conditions – is what Dr. Sloper, "thoroughly honest" as he deems himself (*WS* 28), cannot abide. Emotionally intolerant of discrepancies between appearance and reality, as evidenced by his market-rationalist aesthetics, Dr. Sloper converts even the slightest hint of duplicity into a sign of moral vacuity. Role playing is a variable he excludes *in toto* from his social calculus.

This peremptory exclusion, not his over-rationalizing, is what renders Dr. Sloper unfit to take a deliberative part in urban modernity's domestic trials. James suggests as much by contrasting the doctor's mode of calculation with his sister Mrs. Almond's. More so than he, she readily acknowledges the variables both of fortune hunting and role playing, and factors them into her judgments. In the face of her brother's early suspicions about Morris's interest in Catherine, Mrs. Almond counters, "'I don't see why you should be incredulous[.] . . . It seems to me that you have never done Catherine justice. You must remember that she has the prospect of thirty thousand a year'" (*WS* 60). By contrast, Mrs. Almond is capable of doing Catherine justice. First, she is not rigidly beholden to normative measures of feminine value, and thus appraises Catherine as having "a style all her own" – unlike her own daughter who "has no style at all." Second, she does not assume marital negotiations to be matters purely of the heart. Indeed she veritably laments the fact that people marry so young, "at the age of innocence and sincerity," wishing instead that they would "only wait . . . a little" until they reach "the age of calculation." Catherine, she reasons, would "fare better" if men were more "intelligent" (*WS* 60–61). This view contrasts to Dr. Sloper's: he "was very curious to see whether Catherine might really be loved [by Morris] for her moral worth" (*WS* 62).

Later, Mrs. Almond goes so far as to offer a defense of Morris Townsend as a husband; without denying his likely duplicity, she reasons that it may not be the hindrance Dr. Sloper envisions: "'I don't believe in lovely husbands [...] I only believe in good ones. If he marries her, and she comes into Austin's money, they may get on. He will be an idle, amiable, selfish, and, doubtless tolerably good-natured fellow'" (*WS* 151). In *Washington Square* Mrs. Almond is the one close family member who is not emotionally hinged to Catherine's marital fate. She harbors neither the rivalrous antipathy of Dr. Sloper nor the prurient sentimentality of Mrs. Penniman. While nowhere in the novel does James explicitly confirm the correctness of Mrs. Almond's judgments, her clear-headed method of reasoning, her open-minded, pragmatic adjustment to modernity's social conditions, and her disinterested sympathy make her into the novel's exemplar of public-oriented reason. Above all, in recognizing Catherine's own style, Mrs. Almond confirms Catherine's claim to be treated as an autonomous, self-respecting person. In this recognition, more than in the specific endorsement of Townsend as a husband, resides Mrs. Almond's sense of justice.

Mrs. Almond's marginal effect on the central decisions and events in the novel reflects the considerable extent to which Dr. Sloper has succeeded in driving audience-oriented reason out of his domestic sphere. The rivalrous antipathy that motivates his rejection of Morris evolves into acute rage upon his discovery that Catherine has no intention of giving up her beau. It is during this process of discovery that the father abandons his rational faculties when he needs them most. In the early stages of the domestic problem of Catherine's being in love with Morris, James writes that Dr. Sloper "was more than anything else amused with the whole situation... [H]e went so far as to promise himself some entertainment from the little drama" (*WS* 62). Entertainment by his lights merges seamlessly into scientific curiosity. Rather delighted to find himself in the position of wondering whether or not Catherine will "stick" to him and break off her engagement, Dr. Sloper imagines himself as "cold-blooded" and "relent[less]" as a "geometrical proposition" (*WS* 137). Catherine becomes for him a study in human behavior.

To Mrs. Almond's warning that he is joking with Catherine's adoration, he responds, "'It is the point where the adoration stops that I find it interesting to fix.'" Similar is his response to her further warning that hatred might start once adoration stops:

Not at all[.] ... The two things are extremely mixed up, and the mixture is extremely odd. It will produce some third element, and that's what I'm waiting to see. I wait with suspense – with positive excitement; and that is a sort of emotion that I didn't suppose Catherine would ever provide for me. I am really very much obliged to her. (*WS* 138)

The excitement that he here allows is of a scientific "sort"; he presumes to remain disinterested regarding the outcome of the experiment. This is how he can imagine himself at once cold-blooded and positively excited.

But precisely this stance of disinterested curiosity is what Dr. Sloper fails to maintain, once he discovers that Catherine chooses to "stick" to Morris rather than to him; for he is willing to accept only the result he favors. Thus scientific disinterest gives way to his ultimate admission that he is "at bottom very passionate... very hard," and "very angry" (*WS* 154). Such anger results in his "hav[ing] passed," as he later tells Mrs. Almond "into the exasperated stage," thence to his decision still later, after Catherine refuses to promise never to marry Morris, greatly to reduce her share of inheritance. With such imperious and sentiment-driven judgments, it is no wonder that Catherine finds "something hopeless and oppressive in having to argue with her father" (*WS* 86). In his household, argument is effectively annulled by the privatization of rationality; that is, as science- and market-oriented as Dr. Sloper imagines himself to be, he has severed this rationality from public reason and tethered it to the "bottom" of himself – to unarguable affect.

What remains to be addressed is how Catherine herself functions in the face of her father's exposure of his bottommost passion, in the face of a domestic sphere severed from reason. I want to suggest that rather than either being "victimized as the commodity in human form" or having internalized her father's "sternly judging gaze," as Ian Bell and Andrew Scheiber respectively claim, James portrays Catherine as remaining in crucial ways outside the dialectics of exchange and internalization by virtue of her own mode of passional being: her passive patience.[16] Her "unnaturally passive" disposition, her "unaggressive obstinacy" (*WS* 105, 146), renders her constitutively non-assimilable to Dr. Sloper's scientific and economic order. Through the etymological interplay among passivity, patience, and passion – stemming as these words all do from *pati*, meaning "to suffer" – James builds his constellation of family members upon a linguistic family whose members, though related, are made to perform markedly different functions. Specifically, where Dr. Sloper's passion emanates from and reinforces his self-interest and self-identity, Catherine's passive patience emanates from an essential anonymity, which James articulates through the discourse of hypnotic subjectivity. Try as her physician father might to prevent her from "suffering" on Morris Townsend's account, as Morris's own sister has, as well as to make her "patien[ce]" *his* by taking her to Europe, Catherine's "unimpassioned manner" skirts his prescription (*WS* 101, 105).

In contrast to Bell's argument that Catherine's passivity is analogous to a commodity's immobility, thus marking a self-alienation derived from her father's and suitor's maltreatment, in my view James represents her thing-like quality as an a priori disposition that in fact provokes their defensive reactions. From the outset – from the moment she is born and inherits none of those "amiable, graceful, accomplished, [and] elegant" ways that had made her mother the coveted item of "a dozen suitors" (*WS* 28), Catherine functions as a wrench in the domestic machine and its art of reproduction. As Dr. Sloper's only surviving child who herself will bear no children, Catherine derails the nineteenth-century domestic ideal of patriarchal self-extension through progeny. Having been the circumstantial "fault" (*WS* 166) of Dr. Sloper's beloved spouse's death, and veritably draining her matronymic of all its familial glory and social value, Catherine in effect castrates her father, who notably does not remarry.

In addition to the scenes cited earlier in which Catherine exhibits hypnotic propensities, in one of the novel's dramatic turning points she does so as well. This occurs when Catherine confronts her father about the engagement and her wish to wait for his consent. Here too a face-to-face encounter takes place, when Dr. Sloper, upon opening the door of his library, discovers Catherine "standing there like a ghost" (*WS* 120).[17] During the ensuing conversation between them, Catherine performs simultaneously her most submissive and her most spontaneously disruptive parts. In hearing him assert that engaging herself to Morris is tantamount to waiting for his death, she responds first by retreating from his terminal "point": "It came to [her] with the force – or rather with the vague impressiveness – of a logical axiom which it was not in her province to controvert; and yet, though it was a scientific truth, she felt wholly unable to accept it" (*WS* 124). Lacking the "beauty of reason" that we learn her mother possessed, Catherine's only recourse at first is to "turn . . . away, feeling sick and faint" (*WS* 38, 124).

Yet this intimidation provokes Catherine to succumb not to her father's will but to her own hypnotic mode of being. At first, contemplating her father's point, she seems self-divided, as though recognizing her own hypnotic state: she "turned it over – her father's words had such an authority for her that her very thoughts were capable of obeying him." But in the next moment James has his heroine act most abruptly and with no more justification than "inspiration." She thus fulfills what was considered by some hypnosis researchers to be the ultimate psycho-physiological consequence of hypnosis, namely, *spontaneous* action and thought. The medical doctor James Esdaile, for instance, in *Mesmerism in India* (published first in London in 1846, and the next and subsequent years in Hartford, Connecticut, as well as again in 1902 by the Psychic Research Society in Chicago), took note of the subject's "obeying constitutional laws we do not understand" (rather than obeying the operator), laws which prompt the subject to "act" "spontaneously." He describes patients who, in the very act of carrying out a command, abruptly alter their behavior. One case involves a visitor, Mr. Blyth:

Mr. B. begged to see the imitative stage of somnambulism... Mr. B. was sitting on a table a few yards in front of the man, and made all kinds of noises, which he echoed back. Wishing to examine him more closely, Mr. B. jumped off the table, and came running forward with his body bent, and singing. The man did exactly the same, but a sudden fit of rigidity passed through him and he plunged head foremost against the floor.

Esdaile goes on to caution that frequent mesmerizing is especially problematic in this respect, for then "the excitement of the nervous system... takes on an independent diseased action, obeying constitutional laws we do not understand: we, in fact, have inoculated the system with a nervous disease which often acts *spontaneously*."[18] What emerges from these comments is a remarkable reconfiguration of the hypnotic scenario: while the subject indeed succumbs to the trance, thus to the operator's commands, he also pursues a course of action entirely independent of that operator-subject relation. That is, even when self-consciousness seems wholly expunged, something like "spontaneity" or self-interruption obtains.

These observations and analyses accorded with other neuro-scientific projects of the mid-nineteenth century whose ambition it was to account for the seeming capacity of the brain to function without consciousness. The British researcher Thomas Laycock, for instance, developed by 1845 his theory of "the reflex function of the brain," which originated in his work in the late 1830s on women's nervous diseases and experiments with magnetism. Where other researchers had limited the concept of reflex action to the spinal cord, Laycock claimed that it also pertained to the brain. Soon a host of terms such as unconscious cerebration, the cerebral reflex function, cerebral dynamics, and psychic automatism evolved. What emerged, in other words, was the possibility of conceptualizing consciousness, as the historian Marcel Gauchet explains, as not antecedent to, but coincident with, an individual's will and action. "Consciousness is an *accompaniment*, a *more*. It is not a *source*."[19] This hypothesis called into question the presumed metaphysical correlation of consciousness, will, and self-determination; it thus led to reconceptualizations of the self-conscious self as an entity never entirely whole, as always interrupted. Gauchet quotes the physiologist Moritz Schiff from an 1871 publication: "It is not consciousness that serves as the basis of thought; to the contrary, it is always thought that evokes consciousness... The consciousness of the self is therefore not continuous but *interrupted* ... The *self* at a given moment is always incomplete."[20]

In short, as a product of impersonal brain activity, a self's self-consciousness would be embedded within but discontinuous with its other cerebral activity. From this perspective the human mind would look like a slightly more sophisticated version of the animal brain. It would possess the additional feature of self-consciousness, but even that was a dubious distinction, susceptible as it was to hypnotic submersion. Still, many practitioners agreed that the subject's consent to hypnotize was, if not always and absolutely necessary, then highly desirable and usually required. Moreover, they were aware of the hypnotized subject's power over the hypnotist. An 1870 report describes an 1844 case in which a physician attempts to cure his servant of "fits": "Although Dr. Larkin was unable precisely to determine what were the best conditions for the prosecution of his magnetic researches with this clairvoyant, there were certain results growing out of them which were to him – at that time – as unaccountable as they were *spontaneous* and unlooked for."[21]

In Catherine's case, her constitution prompts her not only to have a spontaneous inspiration, but also to commit herself to a "logical axiom" as reasonable – more precisely, as unreasonable – as her father's: "Suddenly, however, she had an inspiration – she almost knew it to be an inspiration. 'If I don't marry before your death, I will not after,' she said" (*WS* 124). With such an abrupt shift in affect and decision, Catherine oddly both affirms and unconditionally undermines his axiom by carrying it out to its family-stunting conclusion. To be sure, on one level Catherine must be understood as responding to, hence as recognizing, her father; her contributions to their dialogue reflect this fact. I am arguing, however, that on another level her responses emanate from a self-transcendence, which James figures as sudden inspiration, and which is bound up with her hypnotic, non-recognizing mode of being. Where some critics see Catherine as a tragic victim, in that her father effectively consigns her to spinsterhood, others see her as ultimately autonomous and self-possessed, as evidenced by her refusals later of Mr. Macalister's and John Ludlow's marriage proposals. On my view, however, Catherine's spinsterhood stems from her adherence to this sudden, unreasoned inspiration – her own logical axiom. Such adherence does indeed register her autonomy, but of the absorptive and dispossessed, rather than the self-possessed, kind.

It is with this view in mind of Catherine's hypnotic, anonymous subjectivity that we can assess more clearly what she does, rather than what she does not do, as a passive human being. One of the things she does with very little fanfare but with remarkable effect, it turns out, is aestheticize. In part what makes her aesthetics remarkable is her fluid alternation between a reflective and an absorptive relation to the artifact at hand. Morris Townsend is perhaps her most frequent but not her only target. During their initial conversation at the engagement party, "with her eyes fixed on him," Catherine contemplates the young man as one might an *objet d'art*: "He had the features like young men in pictures; Catherine had never seen such features – so delicate, so chiseled and finished – among the young New Yorkers whom she passed in the streets[.] . . . Catherine thought he looked like a statue" (*WS* 43–44). After the relationship has grown more complicated and strained, and upon receiving him after some absence, she is still taken with his beauty: "the first thing that she was conscious of was that he was even more beautiful to look at than fond recollection had painted him" (*WS* 131).

If Morris is thus victimized, as it were, by reverse sexism, it is a victimization with a difference. The difference has to do with *how* Catherine aestheticizes. For one thing, she does not devise as her father does a moral aesthetics based on congruence between apparent and real market value. This is evident from the comments exchanged pertaining to her party dress:

"You are sumptuous, opulent, expensive," her father rejoined. "You look as if you had eighty thousand a year."
"Well, so long as I haven't – " said Catherine, illogically. Her conception of her prospective wealth was as yet very indefinite.
"So long as you haven't you shouldn't look as if you had." (*WS* 46)

In this scene Catherine's "illogical" view derives from her "indefinite" relation to her prospects. In other words, Catherine does not reflect on her present state in a prospectively determinate manner. She does not define her future. We see this mode of reflective but still indefinite aestheticization distinctly at work in the scene in which she contemplates Morris's phrase "some other time" during one of their initial tête-à-têtes:

"I sing a little myself," he said; "some day I will show you. Not to-day, but some other time."
And then he got up to go. He had omitted, by accident, to say that he would sing to her if she would play to him...Catherine had not noticed the lapse. She was thinking only that "some other time" had a delightful sound; it seemed to spread itself over the future. (*WS* 57)

To be sure, Catherine in this scene has some idea of a "future"; yet as the phrase "spreads," this future itself assumes a liquid, shapeless, infinite quality. It remains unspecified, functioning solely for Catherine's *present* contemplation, not for prospective self-determination.

For another thing, Catherine separates both her reflection on and absorptive pleasure in aesthetic artifacts from what the reader sees are the morally compromised circumstances out of which these artifacts arise. In the above scene, Catherine is so captivated by her aestheticization that she fails even to "notice" Morris's "lapse" in genteel courtesy. Yet more striking, even when aware of being unjustifiably abused, Catherine sustains her aesthetic sensibility. Such is the case when she discerns, as mentioned previously, "something hopeless and oppressive" in her father's arguments. For as James also remarks, "strangely enough – I hardly know how to tell it – even when she felt that what he said went so terribly against her, she admired his neatness and nobleness of expression" (*WS* 86). That James's narrative persona himself has difficulty describing Catherine's aesthetic sensibility testifies to its estranging significance; it does not sit well with nineteenth-century modes of feminine domesticity and submission.

Catherine's capacity for aesthetic indefinition and separation factors into what can be seen as her aestheticizing self-regard. This emerges most prominently when she is forced to confront her father's aggressive disapproval of her matrimonial wishes, which effects in her the "entirely new feeling" of "suspense." Traces of the hypnotic state also enter into James's representation of this scene:

Catherine meanwhile had made a discovery of a very different sort...She had an entirely new feeling, which may be described as a state of expectant suspense about her own actions. She watched herself as she would have watched another person, and wondered what she would do. It was as if this person, who was both herself and not herself, had suddenly sprung into being, inspiring her with a natural curiosity as to the performance of untested functions. (*WS* 106)

Whereas Ian Bell interprets this scene as an illustration of Catherine's internalization of the market culture's reifying ideologies, thus prompting her self-alienation, in my view nearly the opposite is the case.[22] It is through self-suspension that Catherine, in fact, avoids reducing herself to Dr. Sloper's and Morris Townsend's rationalist, market aesthetics. Sustaining this suspense not by specific ambition but by wonderment and "natural curiosity," Catherine reveals a more tenacious capacity than does her scientist father for "inspired" but dispassionate observation – all the more striking because it is directed at herself.

With the figuration of a sudden spring into being of a second self, of being out of non-being, James recalls the hypothesis of hypnotic discourse that an impersonal self, inhabiting the limit of consciousness, co-extends with the conscious self. James's recourse in the passage cited above to the "as if" formulation illustrates the difficulty inhering in hypnosis discourse – as well as, more generally, in ontological philosophy – of finding an idiom adequate to describe the originary leap from the hypnotic state to consciousness, from matter to mind. That psycho-physiological spontaneity factors so importantly in the novel's domestic plot also indicates the distance Dr. Sloper's family is from public reason and reflective judgment. In contrast to Kant's idea of spontaneity, whose non-empirical but intelligible status "links the problem of our free will to the problem of describing existence of our self-consciousness," the psycho-physiological spontaneity represented in James's text serves to throw doubt on the enduring, consistent, ubiquitous presence of self-consciousness.[23]

Further, it is telling that Catherine has "no talent for sketching" herself, neither verbally nor visually, as Morris soon learns (*WS* 56). A sketched self-portrait would presume coherence, an ability to adhere to a particular description. Her positive lack of this talent is on display when Morris kisses her for the first time. Here too James alludes to her peculiar mode of imagining a future (of marriage, which would permit the kiss) yet also not projecting into it any prepossessive specificity. And here too we see Catherine in her suspensive, disjoined mode of subjectivity. "It may even be doubted whether she had ever definitely expected to possess it [the kiss]; she had not been waiting for it . . . she took what was given her from day to day" (*WS* 79). If Catherine abides in a sort of eternal but always passing present, this presentness itself is marked by discontinuity: after Morris's kissing spree "she begged him to go away, to leave her alone, to let her think . . . But Catherine's meditations had *lacked a certain coherence*. She felt his kisses on her lips and cheeks a long time afterward; the sensation was *rather an obstacle than an aid to reflection*" (*WS* 79, emphasis added). Her short-term memory of sensation is so absorbing that it blocks reflective thought. With her organs of sense-perception functioning as obstacles to conscious thought, Catherine enacts a self-estrangement that departs from the conventional mechanics of alienation through internalization of a commodifying ideology.

Indeed, Catherine's self-estrangement is joined not to ideology but to what she tells Morris is her "secret passion for the theatre" (*WS* 56). We see this passion in the very moment of her declaration to Morris that she does not "make scenes," which he insists "all women do" (*WS* 181). In making this declaration she repeats what the reader has already learned, when Dr. Sloper comments to Mrs. Almond much earlier in the narrative that Catherine "is not scenic" (*WS* 95). The father's statement is more significant than he knows. In *Washington Square* James reveals the social and ontological complexity of not being scenic. Catherine is obviously not included in James's indictment of both the melodramatic and sentimental sensibility – as acted out most explicitly by Mrs. Penniman but also by Dr. Sloper (despite his pretended disapproval of role playing) and Morris Townsend in their manipulative rivalries and feuding attitudes. Such performances require the "histrionic talent" that Catherine lacks (*WS* 105).

For beyond merely distancing his odd heroine from the affected theatrics of those surrounding her, James reveals in her the distinction between two modes of theatricality: one defensively possessive and the other vulnerably passional. Etymologically *scene* stems from the Greek word *skene*, meaning a covered, sheltered place. Within such protected environments conventional, scripted theater takes place. In not being scenic, then, Catherine is constitutively at odds with the standard script belonging to bourgeois womanhood, which would shelter her from the vagaries of modern life. But this does not mean that she refuses to perform. Rather, it means that where those surrounding her rehearse, she acts. Where they stick acquisitively and protectively to their roles, she improvises – at times incoherently and indeed vulnerably. To put it in contemporary theoretical terms, where they reify a description of human reality as always constructed, represented and simulated, consequently redeploying it as a prescription for action, Catherine in her hypnotic ghostliness, her self-suspension, performs the evanescent, "outside" limit of representation. Her mode of theatricality thus resembles what Walter Benjamin discovers in Kafka's Nature Theater:

Kafka's world is a world theater. For him, man is on stage from the very beginning... [E]veryone is accepted by the Nature Theater of Oklahoma. What the standards for admission are cannot be determined. Dramatic talent, the most obvious criterion, seems to be of no importance. But this can be expressed in another way: all that is expected of the applicants is the ability to play themselves.[24]

For all the sincerity and naturalness that characters and critics alike ascribe to Catherine, it is this unself-conscious theatricality, this ability to play herself, that marks her as "really too perverse" according to her aunt, and "unnaturally passive" according to her father (*WS* 190, 105). It is this theatricality that Morris attempts to suppress in her – not insignificantly by kissing her on the forehead, as though hoping to cast his own hypnotic spell on her – when he wants to stage a graceful exit from her life, but which her agitation botches. "'When you are quiet, you are perfection,' he said; 'but when you are violent, you are not in character.'" He is wrong, of course – she is entirely "in character" – and the force of her theatricality succeeds in throwing him out of his: "He tried a frown at one moment, a smile at another; he was at his wit's end" (*WS* 183).

Perhaps most important, Catherine's ability to play herself manifests itself psychologically as her acceptance of her fear of her father. James tells us early in the narrative that she "was extremely fond of her father, and very much afraid of him." He goes on to explain, however, that such fear as hers is by no means debilitating: "the little tremor of fear that mixed itself with her filial passion gave the thing an extra relish rather than blunted its edge" (*WS* 34). Even her explicit lack of courage is not to be taken as a sign of weakness. Though "she had not the courage to turn the latch" and enter Dr. Sloper's library (hence forcing him to get up and open the door himself), Catherine "had no sense of weakness, [meaning] that she was not afraid of herself" (*WS* 121). Similarly, when Morris imputes that she is "terribly afraid of him [her father]," Catherine "felt no impulse to deny it, because she had no shame in it" (*WS* 133). Having indeed "no aptitude for organized resentment," Catherine is able to maintain a fondness for her father despite her suspicion that he "is not very fond of [her]" (*WS* 193, 166). Accepting as she does the obviously unjust and legally contestable terms of her father's will because she "like[s] it very much" (*WS* 208), she appears to have little sense of justice as fairness. She adheres in its stead to a patriarchal calculus of retribution. These attitudes and their consequent actions pose serious risks. They leave her financially worsened; they expose yet cannot extinguish the patriarchal abuse upon which her nuclear family is based; and they halt, in her celibate solitude, Catherine's procreative potential, thus her family's continuing self-extension.

Passive though she may appear, Catherine's mode of acceptance can be distinguished from the more conventional and ultimately self-protective stance of resignation. With no organization for resentment, Catherine remains, in her own fashion, face to face before her would-be operators – as James remarks in the novel's final line, "for life, as it were" (*WS* 220).

He implies in this comment both her lifetime endurance (for *life*) and her lifetime affirmation (*for* life) of her fate. No wonder Dr. Sloper looks at her at one point when they are at home "as if she had been a stranger" (*WS* 144). While in a sense James shows her lack of resentment to trump her father's fury, he also illuminates in this novel how such a triumph – if it may even be called such – takes place entirely outside the sphere of reason and justice. Instead, it takes place within the sphere of force – her patience against his passion. Catherine, in becoming like a "stranger," has brought the world of the urban crowd, not the political-liberal public, indoors.

GREAT FORCES OF PUBLICITY

In "The Papers" James tests the public air outdoors. Appearing in 1903, by which time evolutionary theories, mass technologies, and laissez-faire capitalism provoked some social analysts to doubt the viability of sustaining public reason anywhere, much less in the mass circulation press, "The Papers" explores the seeming impossibility of driving reason out entirely. Habermas describes how even several decades earlier analysts such as Mill and Tocqueville believed that democratization's broadening of the public sphere, bringing on as it did a flood of unreconciled interests, had "turned public opinion (in the form of the currently dominant opinion) into a coercive force, whereas it had once been supposed to dissolve any kind of coercion into the compulsion of reason."[25] As newspapers came to be seen as speaking in the name of the public or "the people," they too contributed to the tyrannical force of public opinion. Such views were only reinforced at the turn of the century by social psychologists who saw society as governed by laws of imitation and hypnotic influence rather than by political-liberal laws of contract or even economic-liberal laws of utility.

In a 1901 essay entitled "The White Peril," the British historian G. M. Trevelyan cited "the uniform modern man," spawned by "the great cities" and subject to the "uprooting of taste and reason by the printing press," as civilization's greatest threat:

Journals, magazines, and the continued spawn of bad novels, constitute our national culture, for it is on these that the vast majority of all classes employ their power of reading. How does it concern our culture that Shakespeare, Milton, Ruskin, in times gone by wrote in our language, if for all the countless weary ages to come the hordes that we breed and send out to swamp the world shall browse with ever-increasing appetite on the thin swollen stuff that commerce has now learnt to supply for England's spiritual and mental food?[26]

At first glance "The Papers" might well look as though it recapitulates this criticism of urban modernity's mass media. In his recent book *Henry James and the Culture of Publicity* Richard Salmon argues as much, though from a leftist perspective. He sees in "The Papers" a Marxist critique (along the lines of Adorno and Horkheimer) of the mass print industry's complicity in the elimination of the critical public sphere; the narrative stages a "nightmare scenario" in which commercial publicity's "totalization" means that "there is no longer any historical trace of an organized community of speech[.] . . . Instead, James presents an apocalyptic, if grotesquely comic, vision of publicity as a well-nigh universal ontological condition[.] . . . Within this phantasmagorical world, publicity is conceived to be the sole source of desire and meaning." As illuminating as Salmon's interpretation is, it does not consider elements of the narrative that are not subsumed by the totalizing, "autotelic force" of publicity.[27]

To be sure, towards the end of his discussion of "The Papers" Salmon concedes "that Maud and Howard remain capable, in some measure, of articulating resistance to the Papers," and goes on to identify James's authorial stance with the two journalists. What demands examination, however, is the form such "resistance" takes. Salmon appears to understand resistance in terms of negative affection, hence in his discussion of *The Reverberator* resistance is manifest in the scandalized shock felt by the Probert family members when George Flack publishes stories on their private affairs. Similarly, but more ambiguously, "a moment of resistance" occurs when James "questions the desire for publicity by transforming it into a nightmare of exposure and where, conversely, he elevates the anguish of anonymity into a place of refuge."[28] By contrast, I argue that the faculty of reason forms the basis of resistance to the forces of publicity.

In the discussion that follows I hope to demonstrate that for James public reason is not so easily swamped by the commercialization of print media. For one thing, reason permeates implicitly his own commercialized print artifact, that is, in the narrative at hand, by way of such farcical elements as the "Principal Public Person's" name, Sir A. B. C. Beadel-Muffet, KCB, MP. Such distancing gestures lend the narrative a satirical, hence critical, edge. For another thing, reason enters explicitly by way of the two central characters' consciousness. Howard's and Maud's capacity to reason and reflectively to judge the roles they themselves play in the newspaper industry points toward their enduring capacity indeed to organize "a community of speech" based on intelligible agreement. Through these characters James suggests that publicity is by no means the "sole source of desire and meaning." Though obsessed with the Papers to the degree that the industry is, as James puts it, "all the furniture of their consciousness" (*CT* 12: 14), the two journalists embody a *form* of consciousness – the "furniture" being the content – that is immune to "the great forces of publicity," as Howard calls them. Hoping to "get *at*" "the laws – so mysterious, so curious, so interesting – that govern the great currents of public attention," Howard is certain that such laws are "not wholly whimsical – wayward and wild"; yet he admits that "they have their strange logic, their obscure reason" (*CT* 12: 86). By the end of the narrative Howard has still not obtained the knowledge he seeks, but neither has his person been entirely subsumed by publicity's obscure laws.

In the same vein, we shall see that in addition to deflating the nightmare vision of publicity's ominous, totalizing hold on modern consciousness, James in this story deflates evolutionary naturalism's conception of the human being as fully conditioned by biological and utilitarian drives. He explores in "The Papers" the epistemological and ontological reach of the sciences of force and evolution, seeking as he does to identify the modes and significance of transformation within the human sphere. The narrative positively bristles with the scientistic idiom. Most prominently, besides Howard Bight's quest for publicity's laws, is James's description of the journalists themselves. As an occupational group they are subject to Darwinian struggle, which James figures as a scramble for positions on a "ladder" resting "against the great stony wall of public attention – a sustaining mass which apparently wore somewhere, in the upper air, a big, thankless, expressionless face[.] ... The ladder groaned meanwhile, swayed and shook with the weight of the close-pressed climbers, tier upon tier, occupying the upper, the middle, the nethermost rounds and quite preventing, for young persons placed as our young friends were placed, any view of the summit" (*CT* 12: 17).

As an individual pursuing this occupation, Maud Blandy is endowed with scarcely more distinction:

She was fairly a product of the day – so fairly that she might have been born afresh each morning, to serve, after the fashion of certain agitated ephemeral insects, only till the morrow. It was as if a past had been wasted on her and a future were not to be fitted; she was really herself ... an edition, an "extra-special," coming out at the loud hours and living its life, amid the roar of vehicles, the hustle of pavements, the shriek of newsboys, according to the quantity of shock to be proclaimed and distributed ... thanks to the varying temper of Fleet Street, to the nerves of the nation. (*CT* 12: 14–15)

Living in "an age of 'emancipations,'" and resembling an "extra-special" edition in her ephemerality, Maud has "naturally so much of the young bachelor" in her that the "straddling or elbowing" demanded of her "struggle for life, the competition with men," does not mark her with "disfigurement"; rather, she has "the effect of one of the stages of an evolution" (*CT* 12: 15–16). Thus circulating in the endless flow of publicity's shocks, the city's uproarious traffic, and the nation's temperamental nerves, Maud Blandy is as forgettable as both her surname and the misnomer, the "extra-special" newspaper edition, imply. Even within the familial sphere, she is indifferently named and gendered: "she had recognised that there had been eleven of them at home, with herself as youngest, and distinctions by that time so blurred in her that she might as easily have been christened John" (*CT* 12: 17). Further, Maud has a certain mannishness about her: she drinks beer and smokes cigarettes; she is "long-limbed" and "angular" (*CT* 12: 47); Howard habitually addresses her as "my dear chap" or "my dear fellow."

For his part, Howard is feminized. He is "not so fiercely or so freshly a male as to distance Maud in the show"; rather than caring about the "cultivation of a bold front," he is in fact "so passive that it almost made him graceful" (*CT* 12: 16). Altogether, then, James treats these modern occupational and gender types as evolutionary phenomena. The two journalists belong to the species of human being that makes logistically possible the communicative flow between publisher and public, insofar as they locate newsworthy objects and write stories about them in a manner that is sensational enough to print. With these two struggling freelancers occupying the pressurized space between the capitalized, looming "Papers" – the "Daily Press" – and the ostensibly reading "crowd" – otherwise designated "the flood of the Strand," "the roaring Strand," "the thick of the uproar," the "dense thoroughfare," the "thick of the stream that stared and passed and left" (*CT* 12: 52, 65–68, 93) – James without question drives hard toward a representation of the world of publicity as a totality of ominous forces.

Further contributing to this effect is the narrative's focus on mass media's prize human commodity, the celebrity, with Sir A. B. C. Beadel-Muffet, KCB, MP being the man of the quarter-hour. His constitutive talent, of course, is continually to make conspicuous waves. He moves, by strategic manipulation, from simply appearing daily – inspiring Howard Bight to play "a thrilling little game" of "catch[ing] him once out" – to being "universal and ubiquitous, commemorated, under some rank rubric, on every page of every public print every day in every year," and ultimately to the point where, after his alleged disappearance and the subsequent shock of his announced suicide, the "gentleman seemed, with a continuance, with indeed an enhancement, of his fine old knack, to have the successive editions *all* to himself" (*CT* 12: 23, 18, 103). When he suddenly reappears alive, the Papers, as Howard remarks, being in a "chronic state of rabies," can do no more than "howl" out the news (*CT* 12: 64, 118).

Significantly, James neither describes this man's physical features nor even presents him directly. Sir A. B. C. Beadel-Muffet KCB, MP's name alone announces a social status worth celebrating as the "Principal Public Person" (*CT* 12: 53). Regarding the general phenomenon of the celebrity at the turn of the century, Philip Fisher has pointed out that public conspicuousness produces an economy of social desire structured by lack: "Everyday reality comes to be 'merely' so, once a higher dimension of conspicuous and performed reality has been added, like a new economy of being, on top. The star and... [the] 'mere' man, are created at the same moment."[29] Similarly, in "The Papers" Beadel-Muffet's success defines the failure of Mortimer Marshal, the unpublicized playwright whose profile Maud has been trying without success to place and who desires nothing so much as to see his name in the papers, to be "[l]oved by the great heart of the public." "He wants to be," Maud remarks to Howard, "well, where Beadel-Muffet is" (*CT* 12: 32). The desperation with which Mortimer Marshal pursues Maud the journalist – to the extent of desiring to make their relationship not merely professional but marital – renders him one of those "starving fish," as Howard calls them, who would "almost rather be jabbered about unpleasantly than not be jabbered about at all." They "leap straight out of the water themselves, leap in their thousands and come flopping, open-mouthed and goggle-eyed, to one's very door" (*CT* 12: 20). In Maud's likening Marshal to the zero-shaped emptiness of a "large clean china plate" (*CT* 12: 78), James further indicates that this economy of fame is structured upon its lack. The pair, Beadel-Muffet and Mortimer Marshal, thus play out mass publicity's symmetrical and dialectical oppositions, with the terms of success and failure defining each other.

In this theater of dialectical desire the players rehearse the new but already stale drama of fame. On the one hand, fame possesses a capacity to advance itself, which amounts to a sort of newness; but these advances occur only along a predetermined and predictable trajectory, hence it is already stale. Though it requires "genius," as Maud Blandy remarks, "to get yourself so celebrated for nothing" (*CT* 12: 23), such genius can reproduce only more fame, as we witness, for instance, in Beadel-Muffet's ever expanding press coverage. The steady increase in his self-accumulation serves as constant reinforcement of his genius merely for mastering and perpetuating "the 'terrific forces of publicity,'" as Howard has heard Beadel-Muffet say

(*CT* 12: 58). At the same time and perhaps more important, James reveals that the social significance of his actions is also inscribed within the same venerable set of Judeo-Christian values: "the accumulation was a triumph – one of the greatest the age could show – of *industry and vigilance*" (*CT* 12: 19, emphasis added). For all his brilliant manipulation and accumulation – to the extent of making his disappearance as publicly tantalizing as his presence, to the extent, moreover, of duping the Papers (thinking, as he lures them to do, that he wants to fake a disappearance from public view so as gradually to effect a real one) – James suggests in this passage that Beadel-Muffet's unheard of "triumph" is in fact more of the same work ethic. It is similar to the triumph portrayed in Dreiser's *Sister Carrie*, whose titular character continually exceeds herself by desiring and obtaining yet more wealth and fame as an actress. James creates a celebrity who can only reproduce more of himself. Beadel-Muffet, as the truism goes, is increasingly successful because he is successful – such is the tautological circularity that governs fame.

Much, then, in James's narrative serves to support the Habermasian claim that with the emergence of the mass circulation press, the newspaper as an institution traded its critical edge for manipulative and more lucrative sensationalism. Such an account renders the readers of newspapers "willing victims," as Salmon puts it, of corporate capitalist publicity.[30] Thus not unlike the turn of the century's reactionary social psychologists such as Gustave Le Bon and Boris Sidis, contemporary Marxist critics view modern readerships as essentially passive, manipulable and uncritical crowds.

I want to suggest, by contrast, that in "The Papers" James introduces a very different conception of readership, one that resonates with the contemporaneous ideas both of the sociologist Gabriel Tarde and certain progressive evolutionists. In his 1901 essay, "The Public and the Crowd," Tarde comments that he "cannot agree with that vigorous writer, Dr. Le Bon, that our age is the 'era of crowds.' It is the era of the public or publics, and that is a very different thing."[31] Tarde does not really reject here Le Bon's claims about the psychological primitivism of crowds; rather, he rejects his claims about their pervasiveness in society. In arguing that modern society is dominated not by crowds but by publics, Tarde stresses first of all the latter's absence of physicality:

We speak of the public at a theater, the public at some assembly, and here public means crowd. But this is neither the sole nor even the primary meaning, and while the importance of this type of public has declined or remained static, the invention of printing has caused a very different type of public to appear, one which never ceases to grow and whose indefinite extension is one of the most clearly marked traits of our own period . . . [T]he public, understood in this other sense [is] a purely spiritual collectivity, a dispersion of individuals who are physically separated and whose cohesion is entirely mental.

Arguing that the public is essentially a modern phenomenon, then, one that "could begin to arise only after the first great development in the invention of printing, in the sixteenth century," Tarde emphasizes the literate, reflective capacity of the public. The subsequent effect of this public's presence, according to Tarde, is a perpetual counterbalancing of a society's most volatile and potentially violent tendencies, thus contributing to a more peaceful, tolerant, and skeptical society.[32]

The mental "cohesion" of the public to which Tarde alludes derives from an awareness on participants' part of their simultaneous similarity. That is, the public's "currents of opinion" differ from the crowd's psychic current in that they constitute a mental state that does not differ from each of its participant's. This distinction is what leads Tarde with confidence to claim that "[f]rom the crowd to the public is an enormous leap," while at the same time asserting the public's homogeneity and essential bonding structure:

What then is the bond between them [members of a journal-reading public]? This bond lies in their simultaneous conviction or passion and *in their awareness* of sharing at the same time an idea or a wish with a great number of other men. It suffices for a man *to know* this, even without seeing these others, to be influenced by them *en masse* and not just by the journalist, who is the common inspiration of them all.[33]

Awareness and knowledge, then, are key features of Tarde's public. Granted, the last sentence in this quotation, with its references to influence, mass response and a journalist-*cum*-leader, makes Tarde's public look precariously like a crowd. While I have been at pains to show how the turn-of-the-century conceptions of the crowd and the public operated according to two distinct modes of human being, thus rendering the "leap" as one between kinds, not merely degrees, the deployment by Tarde (and other theorists) of the same images and metaphors to describe the two modes of collectivity is but one indication of how closely related they were seen to be. As historian Terry Clark comments, Tarde's public is "at once its [the crowd's] extension and antithesis."[34]

Indeed, the relation according to Tarde was historical and genetic: "Of course, in order for this *remote suggestion* [*suggestion à distance*] of individuals composing a public to become possible, it is necessary that they have practiced intimate suggestion [*suggestion à proximité*] for a long time, through the habit of intense social and urban life."[35] If a logic of accumulative evolution can thus be seen to underwrite Tarde's social-psychological theory of collectivity, nevertheless he maintains a clear distinction between one mode of evolved collectivity and another. On the other hand, Tarde's self-aware, knowing public remains conditioned by that mysterious bonding mechanism, imitation-suggestion. It draws its vitality from "opinion" which, Tarde writes, "is to the modern public what the soul is to the body." Thus a public, though markedly more rational, tolerant, peaceful, and understanding than a crowd, is at bottom unhinged from ethical reason. A public can become "overexcited" – and itself engender "fanatical crowds" – just as it can become "unstable," even "capricious."[36] Though Tarde conceives of public opinion as "in perpetual border disputes with" tradition and reason, which implies the possibility of its overlapping with ethical practices and ideas, these overlaps would be contingent merely:

[I]nstead of serving as a link between its neighbors [i.e., tradition and reason], Opinion likes to take part in their squabbles and sometimes, becoming intoxicated with new and fashionable doctrines, it pillages established ideas or institutions[.] ... [S]ometimes, under the authority of Custom, it expulses or oppresses rational innovators.

Public opinion, according to Tarde, is but one of these "three forces."[37] Mass publicity, through advances in print technology and distribution, has unified and stabilized public opinion, generally fostering its reflective more than its affective elements. But with imitation-suggestion as its first principle, mass publicity possesses no ethical essence.[38]

If Tarde's notion of evolution by social-psychological accumulation (as opposed to Darwinian inheritance or Lamarckian acquisition) thus renders both the hypnotic crowd and the conscious public ethically adrift, by contrast, some of the progressive evolutionists of the era echoed Thomas Huxley in arguing, as he did in 1896, for the bifurcation of evolution and ethics, the latter being anchored to a voluntaristic moral faculty and "common understanding." "Cosmic evolution," according to Huxley, "may teach us how the good and evil tendencies of man may have come about; but, in itself, it is incompetent to furnish any better reason why what we call good is preferable to what we call evil than we had before... Social progress means a checking of the cosmic process at every step and the substitution for it of another, which may be called the ethical process."[39] Similarly Lester Ward endeavors in the 1890s to articulate a dualistic analytic of the human being so as to identify certain faculties such as the intellect as undetermined (apart from their genesis) by natural or biological laws. As historian William Fine comments, "Intellect itself was not seen [by Ward and other early sociologists] as a social force, but instead as a separate faculty which guides the operation of social forces in the most beneficial directions." Most social theorists of the era were unable to abandon entirely the idea of a "social force," which, even if no longer biologically determined (as Spencerians claimed), still required the assertion of one or another quasi-mystical glue – what Charles Horton Cooley designated as a society's "genius" or "soul."[40] Still, the conception of a "working dualism" enabled the possibility of imagining a newspaper reading public as ethically and politically unmanipulated by such forces or by sensationalism.

Such is the vision of readership James offers in his narrative's most avid and conspicuous readers, namely Howard and Maud, the journalists themselves. Besides being actual or potential contributors to the Papers, they read and discuss both their contents and the conditions of their existence. In "The Papers" James works out Tarde's distinction between the conscious, newspaper-reading public and the hypnotic, newspaper-devouring crowd as well as the progressive evolutionist's distinction between ethics and evolution. In the following discussion I hope to show how James uses these two characters to dramatize these distinctions; that is, he shows them to be constituted through both public and crowd states of mind, through both ethical and evolutionary modes of being and transformation.

James's treatment of Howard and Maud as evolutionary phenomena, as discussed above, does not preclude each character's possession of a critical-ethical faculty. As though anticipating Habermas's identification of the coffee house as a choice site for critical debate, James repeatedly places his protagonists in "pothouses" where they share their latest discoveries and exchange viewpoints over cheap food and tea. During one of these rendez-vous, for instance, the conversation moves from noticing an article announcing the state of marital affairs of Beadel-Muffet's daughter to remarking critically on this celebrity's willingness to exploit his family for publicity's sake. Like James himself, Howard and Maud find such public traffic in private lives reprehensible, akin to being "hurtl[ed] through the air, clubbed by the paternal hand, like golf-balls in a suburb!" (*CT* 12: 20). Moreover, these remarks provoke self-reflection: "he and his companion were alike prompted to one of those slightly violent returns on themselves and the work they were doing which none but the vulgar-minded altogether avoid" (*CT* 12: 20). As the conversation ensues, it becomes clear that the primary moral problem animating their interactions revolves around reconciling their occupational involvement in the mass press with their disapproval of some of its practices. At this point in the plot they espouse different positions. Howard distances himself from the "vulgar" by being self-aware, but he also verges on cynicism:

"I haven't a scrap of faith left in a single human creature. Except, of course," the young man added, "the grand creature that *you* are, and the cold, calm, comprehensive one whom you thus admit to your familiarity. *We* face the music. We see, we understand; we know we've got to live, and how we do it. But at least, like this, alone together, we take our intellectual revenge, we escape the indignity of being fools dealing with fools. I don't say we shouldn't enjoy it more if we *were*. But it can't be helped; we haven't the gift – the gift, I mean, of not seeing. We do the worst we can for the money." (*CT* 12: 21)

Maud, by contrast, wants to imagine herself as one of the "fools," so as to preserve her professional integrity: "I require a working faith, you know. If one isn't a fool, in our world, where *is* one?" With each critical of the other's position – Maud declaring to Howard that he "certainly do[es] the worst [he] can," Howard worrying that Maud with her fool's faith will "fail" him—the two engage in moral debate, testing the implications of each position (*CT* 12: 21).

Maud will at one point call Howard "more than cynical," accusing him in his pursuit of Beadel-Muffet of becoming "sardonic," "[w]icked," "devilish"; and Howard will impatiently complain that Maud really does "*see* nothing" (34). Such scenes serve not to mark them as beyond the pale of moral or public consciousness, which would be the case if they in fact were wicked or oblivious. To the contrary, they demonstrate Howard's and Maud's adherence to rational-critical principles. Indeed, much of their interpersonal drama turns on Howard's possible role in what initially appears to be Beadel-Muffet's suicide. "I'll not have you if you've killed him," Maud tells Howard, when she suspects he has delightedly assisted in Beadel-Muffet's disappearance by "hound[ing] him on" (*CT* 12: 60–61). Howard himself is "scared" when he thinks he may well bear some "responsibility" (*CT* 12: 92). Neither morally nor socially vacuous, Howard and Maud are models of public consciousness. Their exchanges disclose the ground rules to which each implicitly consents: recognition of each other as reasonable, ethical beings, and a modicum of "working faith" in modern human society and its print media.

Aligned with this recognition is their mutual acknowledgement of being capable of communication not by way of imitation-suggestion but by way of intelligible agreement. In contrast, say, to Tarde whose theory has language originating in the speaker's ability to transmit through suggestion the meaning of a word along with its sound, James pointedly stresses that the public sphere's mode of communication implies reason's consent.[41] He does this by throwing into relief the idiosyncrasies of Howard's and Maud's language game, which reveals each character's commitment to what Wittgenstein calls a "form of life."[42] Early in the narrative James describes Maud as having an "accent not absolutely pure" (*CT* 12: 16). Nevertheless, in his reproductions of her and Howard's dialogues, her direct speech is unmarked by accent or dialect. This is important because at the same time, Maud and Howard have developed a mild habit of adopting a mock accent when pronouncing certain words. Equally significant, when James phonetically spells these words spoken in mock accent, they resemble other English words. Thus "play" converts into "ply," "lane" into "line," "tale" into "tile," and "literary" into "littery" (*CT* 12: 24, 37, 75, 95, 115). When Maud or Howard speaks one or another of these words in mock accent, James uses quotation marks to signal the fact. Occasionally, when the interlocutor repeats the word, the quotation marks are absent, such as in the following exchange, in which they discuss the potential literary merit of Beadel-Muffet's self-constructed situation. The first line of speech is Maud's:

"Something perhaps *could* be done with it – only it would take imagination."
      He wondered, and she seemed to wonder that he didn't see. "Is it a situation for a 'ply'?"
      "No, it's too good for a ply – yet it isn't quite good enough for a short story."
(*CT* 12:24)

In this manner James indicates the way in which a new rule is introduced into their language game, or an infrequently invoked rule is recalled. The quotation marks setting off "ply" signal Howard's ironic or mock tone. Just as Howard considers himself and Maud to be occupationally "in the know" (*CT* 12: 21), here he assumes Maud's attunement to his irony – "their general irony," James remarks in the narrative's opening paragraph, is something "which they tried at the same time to keep gay and to make amusing at least to each other" (*CT* 12: 13). That Maud gets it, his applied irony, is indicated in her subsequent use of "ply" without the stressed intonation, as indicated by the absence of quotation marks. In having his characters' mock-accented words appear as other English words, James implies his own assumption that his readers too will easily get the language game's rule of irony, rather than mistake "ply" for an intrusion of semantic mumble-jumble. In other words, James lays out a speech community's mode of existence and transformation: rather than being subject to the force of evolution or the miracle of imitation-suggestion, it depends on a prior capacity to apprehend the principle of rule and to gather contextual evidence of a specific rule's application. Such, in James's narrative, is the communicative basis for a rational-critical public sphere.

Within a few years of the publication of "The Papers," James published the lecture he delivered to the graduation class at Bryn Mawr College, "The Question of Our Speech" (1905). The greater portion of this lecture is devoted to promoting the importance of "the definite preliminary of a *care* for tone;" thence to care for and work to uphold a "tone-standard." Among other effects, such care would keep at bay the vulgarities of the modern newspaper that "affect us positively as the roar of some myriad-faced monster – as the grimaces, the shouts, shrieks and yells, ranging over the whole gamut of ugliness, irrelevance, dissonance, of a mighty maniac who has broken loose and who is running amuck through the spheres alike of sight and sound."[43] James's obvious disparagement of the daily papers' quality of speech *content*, however much it may reveal about his high-brow preferences for more eloquent, discriminating speech acts, nevertheless keeps to the same formal strictures found in "The Papers." For, as he states earlier in the essay, in order for speech to function as such for "any gathered group" there must first be agreement:

A virtual consensus of the educated, of any gathered group, in regard to the speech that, among the idioms and articulations of the globe, they profess to make use of, may well strike us in a given case, as a natural, an inevitable assumption. Without that consensus, to every appearance, the educative process cannot be thought of as at all even beginning[.][44]

The hyperboles James employs to describe the daily papers – a monstrous maniac in this essay, a rabid dog in "The Papers" – suggest that in his view the vulgarization of speech threatens to reduce "the colloquial *vox Americana*" to "no language at all," to "a mere helpless slobber of disconnected vowel noises." Again, whatever elitism such comments exhibit (which itself is arguably neutralized by James's claim that "within us all" reside "the tonic possibilities" he hopes to hear manifest), they also reveal the formal distinction between what "beasts" do, which is spontaneously to express – that is, "to snort or neigh, to growl or to 'meaow'" – and what humans do, which is to consent to communicate.[45]

In "The Papers" ethical transformation takes a tack similar to James's conception of a speech community's. Though Howard appears most susceptible to moral vacuity, given his negligible faith in humanity and his inclination toward cynicism, Maud is the one who undergoes the more notable adjustment. Having warned Howard that she will neither pity nor marry him if he turns out to be mixed up in Beadel-Muffet's demise, later, when he quite seems to be, she is compelled to face "the impassable," "the wrong," that she thinks he has "placed... between them." Her reflection on the matter initially leads to a dim view: "It was a wrong, it was a wrong – she couldn't somehow get out of that; which was a proof, no doubt, that she confusedly tried" (*CT* 12: 74). The most she achieves at this point is a recognition of "the obscurity and ambiguity in which some impulses lived and moved – the rich gloom of their combinations, contradictions, inconsistencies, surprises." Such recognition "rested her verily a little from her straightness... that she *could* be queerly inconsistent" (*CT* 12: 74).

Still later, when both are even more certain of Howard's involvement, Maud's moral sensibility veers. James writes, "the logic of her situation, she was sharply conscious, would have been an immediate rupture with Bight... Their hour had struck, the hour after which she was definitely not to have forgiven him" (*CT* 12: 92). But "in spite of logic" she moves "not in the sense away from him, but in the sense nearer." She now imagines Howard, in "the roused Strand, all equipped both with mob and with constables," to be endangered by "the very voice of justice" – a mode of justice, that is, that with the presence of constables and a mob threatens to be overly swift and punitive rather than deliberate and retributive. She is consequently taken by "an impulse of protection that had somehow to do with pity without having to do with tenderness. It settled, at all events, the question of leaving him; she couldn't leave there and so" (*CT* 12: 93). While on the surface Maud might seem in this scene to disavow moral "logic" and "justice," I would argue that it discloses not her abandonment of, but rather her shifting priorities within, a moral-public sphere. Not only does the justice at hand threaten to be anything but reasonable, but also the logic propping up her threat to leave Howard seems anything but watertight. Her previous reflections prepare her to acknowledge the obscurity and ambiguity not of moral principle but of moral application and responsiveness. Unlike Dr. Sloper and his daughter, Maud is willing to abandon her logical axiom when it has clearly ossified, when it proves to be merely personal, programmatic conviction. If her new decision to protect Howard emerges as an "impulse," it appears nonetheless to be grounded in moral awareness. Indeed James's significant qualification, that she is acting out of pity *without tenderness*, suggests that she has adopted the attitudinal orientation most suitable to political-moral liberalism: disinterested interest. This mode of "protection" underlies one of liberalism's most cherished maxims, the assumption of innocence until proven guilty. By the end of the story, of course, Howard proves not to be guilty nor Beadel-Muffet to be dead.

Having thus far examined how James shows the claims of the public sphere in the era of sensationalist journalism to depend on the state of the reader's consciousness, rather than, as Habermas and others imply, on the commercial structure and the content of the publication, I want now to reverse in a sense the flow of analysis. For what "The Papers" also explores is the limit of the rational-critical consciousness, hence of the public sphere. Much happens in the narrative that reflects the presence of what I have been calling a crowd or aesthetic state of mind. For if Howard and Maud exercise their public consciousness with respect to their engagement as journalists and newspaper readers, when it comes to other – even if related – realms of experience and action, they exhibit an alternate orientation. Just as the Press, which according to Howard generally serves as "the watchdog of civilisation," can press itself into a "chronic state of *rabies*" (*CT* 12: 63–64), thereby becoming effectively unreadable and unconscionable, the protagonists themselves at times appear pressed beyond readability and reasonability.

In other words, James, like his American-born, cosmopolitan friend Henry Brewster, is unwilling to rule out entirely the attraction and even the attractiveness (which is not to say the legitimacy) of a-moral action. In his 1887 *Theories of Anarchy and of Law* – which by 1890 James had read, recommending it as well to William James as "rather exquisite and remarkable" – Brewster lays out in a "midnight debate" among friends the distinctions among a variety of moral and political positions, most centrally, the formalist, the utilitarian-rationalist, the religious, and the anarchic. In the debate, the formalist and the anarchic advocates find resonance with each other. Wilfrid the formalist "protest[s] against" the utilitarian-rationalist and religious requirements of "some autocratic principle, some one great law – as, for instance, evolution; some one great force... [or] some supreme being in whom all things are summed up." He urges instead the idea of a "confederacy of equal states... without a ruler."[46] Harold the anarchist similarly refutes the claim of a unifying first principle, while also asserting the existence in humans of a "feeling of formal origin [which] can have no positive expression; it is by nature an antithesis to our perceptions." On this view, "mutual intelligence," rather than an external source (God or natural law) provides the moral basis for "our relations with others."[47] The formalist and the anarchist thus both value a liberal socio-political structure.

But also on the anarchic view, social maintenance and progress – the "gregarious ideal" of the utilitarian-rationalist – are not the only attractions in life. Revolt is too, and not merely out of egotistic self-interest. Harold insists on this point, arguing that the anarchic impulse "will lift...a man [of] high intelligence...above the level of personal interests as surely as the most genuine public spiritedness." Later in the debate Ralph the utilitarian-rationalist identifies this capacity as "the gift of affect and of self-forgetfulness" such as "our children" sustain. Thus emerges from their discussion a conception of a pluralistic mode of being, one that admits both law based on mutual intelligence and anarchy based on self-forgetting, one whose faculties thus operate "like distinct and complementary functions of an organism." Even though such functions are formally mutually exclusive, Wilfrid contends that "We are all of us, in some wise, in some spot, here anarchists, and there partisans of the law."[48] While no one in the debate clarifies how the particular functions are triggered to respond to particular "spots," the discussion makes clear that the anarchic propensity may have its existential attractions but is in no wise to be accepted as at all applicable to social or political relations. Affection and self-forgetfulness – the marks of crowd collectivity and aesthetic absorption – combine to render the anarchist beyond the ethical pale.[49]

In "The Papers," most prominently affected by this aesthetic or crowd orientation are actions and passions that provoke, indeed instantiate, Maud's abandonment of the journalistic profession. Her transformation from worker to non-worker is portrayed by James as distinctly unmotivated by ethical reason, neither deliberate nor impulsive. She enacts a mode of transformation that is more akin to spontaneous mutation, though of a psychical rather than biological sort. Where Darwin's theory of spontaneous mutation applied to an organism's reproductive potential, wherein offspring possess characteristics not manifest in the parents, thereby incarnating new variations within a species or, if functionally distinct, entirely new species, James applies it to his protagonists' psychical dynamics.[50]

His characterization particularly of Maud, the "product of the day," indicates a pluralistic mentality constituted in such a manner that certain states of mind are keyed to respond to certain kinds of circumstance. Thus Maud exhibits reasoning and remembering capacities when it comes to judging Howard's moral disposition and the journalistic profession; yet simultaneously she is "[b]orn afresh each morning" (*CT* 12: 14) when it comes to carrying out journalistic tasks. To be sure, "she had recognized, she believed, in keen moments, a vocation" (*CT* 12: 17). And she is not overly afflicted with what one Mrs. Margaret H. Welch in her 1894 paper,

"Is Newspaper Work Healthful for Women?" (presented before the American Social Science Association), argued were the usual "handicaps" of female journalists, "improper dressing and unhygienic eating."[51] In any case, Maud suffers no more than Howard from pothouse food. But not only is she unable to place a story on her own or obtain interviews apart from the hapless Mortimer Marshal's; she also has no memory for the details of news surrounding even the most celebrated figures. Howard has to remind her of the months-long fanfare regarding Beadel-Muffet's remarrying plans (*CT* 12: 34–35). Mortimer Marshal experiences what she herself admits, namely that she is a "fatal influence," a "non-conductor"; in terms of journalistic success, "she was herself nowhere, herself nothing" (*CT* 12: 39, 42).

Maud is ultimately undone as a journalist by her affective propensity. When James likens Maud to "certain agitated ephemeral insects," and tropes her as "really herself...an edition, an 'extra-special,'" and then later describes how "the extra-specials swarmed" on the occasion of Beadel-Muffet's alleged disappearance (*CT* 12: 14–15, 69), he associates her with the crowd's potential to attain affective heights that are beyond the pale of dutiful consciousness. More specifically, Maud possesses an extra-special capacity to *pity*. She pities, for instance, the pathetic Mortimer Marshal – despite her awareness that he is motivated by "rank greed" (*CT* 12: 73) – for latching onto so ineffectual a journalist as herself. Eventually, though, James reveals the indiscriminate nature of her pity: "she pitied [Marshal] too much, pitied herself, and was more and more, as she found, now pitying everyone." "Everyone" includes the master of publicity himself, Beadel-Muffet, whom she wants "to pity...in sufficient quantity." As Howard remarks, this means pitying "with extravagance and to the point of immorality" (*CT* 12: 41, 36). Indeed it is Maud's pitying extravaganza – that is, pity without the formal constraint of tenderlessness that structures, as we have seen, her orientation toward Howard himself – that morally and professionally derails her. However satisfied Maud ultimately is with this outcome, James shows that the means through which she meets this outcome lack a moral basis.

The height of Maud's drama of affection is reached when Mrs. Chorner, Beadel-Muffet's on-again, off-again fiancée, becomes the center of her attention. As a mode of "working faith" pity is what prompts her, upon visiting Mrs. Chorner under the auspices of a professional interview, to have "made friends" with her, so that now she "want[s] nothing...but to help her" (*CT* 12: 62). Yet when she later withholds from the Papers the story based on her final, exclusive, sensational interview, in which Mrs. Chorner tells Maud "everything about everything" (*CT* 12: 108), and which

Mrs. Chorner expects and hopes to see published, it is precisely this "working faith" that Maud abandons. She knows she will have "disappointed and cheated" (*CT* 12: 110) her "friend"; but as she later explains to Howard, "I would rather choose *that* shame, that of not doing for her what I had offered, than the hideous honesty of bringing it out. Because you see... it was – well, it was too much... Quite beautiful! Awful!... Charming, interesting, horrible. It was *true* – and it was the whole thing... Not a bit made up, just the poor woman melted and overflowing, yet at the same time raging – like the hot-water tap when it boils" (*CT* 12: 109).

In this episode (as retold to Howard) Maud's aesthetic involvement in Mrs. Chorner's story – taken in as she is by its beauty, charm, horror, interest, truth – seems to conflict with and to override her initial ambition to "help" the woman by getting the interview published. In other words, her aesthetic affection warrants her claim that the story is "too much" for her to follow through with the intention and agreement to help Mrs. Chorner as she wants to be helped. Aesthetics, then, not a journalistic "working faith," intensifies her affection "to the point of immorality." Maud admits to Howard that she "do[es]n't quite [her]self" understand why she will keep the story in her pocket; she offers only the description of sentiment: "well, I felt that I didn't *have* to, after all, if I didn't want to" place it (*CT* 12: 109). Such a description obviously eliminates reason as a guiding factor, but it may be understood as also eliminating self-interest. Her decision marks the end to her potential income as a journalist, thus negating rational-utilitarian interest. Moreover, the post-facto normative grammar – "I didn't want to" – seems poorly fitted to the initial overwhelming occasion of being party to Mrs. Chorner's confessional "rag[e]," to which Maud responds by discovering that she "*couldn't*" bring the story to the Papers (*CT* 12: 109). The story, then, incapacitates her will before it informs her normative subjective desire; it is from this external limit of capacity that her future course of a-social inaction originates.

Taking, in effect, the friendship with Mrs. Chorner so far as to oppose the latter's wishes, so far in fact as to terminate it, Maud embodies the extra-special, which is now to say the dysfunctional, journalist. As Howard tells her, "You've played, you see, a most unusual game. The code allows for everything *but* that" (*CT* 12: 110).[52] Spelling as Maud's personal code does the end of her barely begun career in journalism, Maud's insectile ephemerality adds another dimension to what she has earlier identified as the "combinations, contradictions, inconsistencies, surprises" of "some impulses" (*CT* 12: 74). The impulses shown to operate in this later scene might well be circumstantially related to Maud's public (that is, moral, occupational, reasoning) consciousness; but they are ultimately at odds with it. Tethered instead to affective extravagance, these impulses figure for James the human being's alternate affiliation with the inhuman swarm.

In his insightful monograph *Henry James and Modern Moral Life*, Robert Pippin has recently observed that in James the broad moral question – of trust, of interdependency, of the role of historical contingency – is more often than not "concentrated on the concrete issue: 'What *makes* a marriage.'" James's characters "are simply trying to get or stay married, or to endure a marriage, or to avoid marriage."[53] Normative and formative interpersonal experience provides the situational structure through which James gets at what it means, morally, to live a modern life. Both *Washington Square* and "The Papers" fit this skeletal description. But a slightly different way to frame James's mode of moral inquiry is to see him as investigating the conditions of the modern family, of private life, within a culture of crowds. In *Washington Square* James discloses the implications of enclosing a private sphere within an affective logic, be it passionate or patient; though he also gestures, through the figure of Mrs. Almond, toward a different order – one in which the twin syndromes of father knowing best and daughter persisting longest give way to a reasonable respect for a young adult's capacity to make her own choices, even poor ones.

On view in "The Papers" is a young man and a young woman, inching towards marriage, who also exhibit aesthetic and passional inclinations, but whose interactions with each other appear to be anchored in mutual, at times even tenderless, respect. The story ends with their leaving the Papers; and the reader is left with some confidence that the family they look forward to starting will be less authoritarian than the Slopers and less Darwinian than Maud's own. They may well succeed in neutralizing the crowd effect at home.

Such home-bound narratives of crowd culture will find their street-bound counterparts in the work taken up in the following chapter on Stephen Crane.

CHAPTER 3

A "gorgeous neutrality": social justice and Stephen Crane's documentary anaesthetics

In contrast to the Jamesian attention to urban domesticity, Stephen Crane's narratives and sketches make homelessness practically a condition of urban being. If the characters populating his cityscapes are not literally homeless, as are those seeking shelter in flophouses in "The Men in the Storm" and "An Experiment in Misery," then they are usually depicted as psychically or physically a very long way from home, as are the urchins in "An Ominous Baby" and "A Great Mistake," as well as the adults in "The Broken-Down Van." Others, such as the titular character in *Maggie*, are driven away from home or have veritable war zones as homes, as in "A Dark Brown Dog" and *George's Mother*. In short, Crane's urban homes, if depicted at all, are rather ferocious than sweet.

This anti-sentimental depiction of domesticity conforms of course to the late nineteenth-century realist imperative: to expose the sordid, hellish underbelly of modern city life. Thus Crane's city streets are equally troubled. But they do, at least, seem to offer his homeless population certain attractions and pleasures. One main attraction, literally in the psycho-physiological sense, is the crowd. Crane's street people are chronically forming crowds: to battle an opposing gang of urchins, to demand charity, to eat lunch in a restaurant; to look at a burning building, a fallen man, a traffic accident, or simply at the crowd itself.

Many of Crane's crowd configurations, I want to suggest, contribute to the imagination of a kind of home away from home. In putting it this way, I do not mean to imply that the crowd offers itself as a refuge of inconspicuousness for someone like Maggie who "departed from home" after being all too conspicuously shunned by her exhibitionist mother.[1] When she, now a streetwalker, enters the crowd, it is to find a client, even though she pretends otherwise: "She hurried forward through the crowd as if intent upon reaching a distant home" (*PP* 70). (An arguably more sentimental Dreiser will indeed create such a crowd refuge for Carrie Meeber to slip into, upon being defeated by her initial and unsuccessful search for work in Chicago.)² Rather, the street crowd becomes a home away from home in the sense that its intensive crowdedness instantiates, ironically enough, the site of radical privacy or separation.

In this chapter I examine how for Crane the crowd could represent something like the last holdout against a progressive-reformist threat – the contemporaneous political-economic movement of which Crane himself was obliquely a part. In an extreme form, Progressivism could threaten the political-liberal foundation of separate spheres by becoming what John Rawls calls *fully comprehensive*. That is, with Progressivism's ends-oriented ambition of socio-economic equality, it could embrace a political-moral conception which "covers all recognized values and virtues within one rather precisely articulated system."³ (Such a totalizing system contrasts with a partially comprehensive doctrine, which comprises a society's loosely knit religious, philosophical, and other non-political values, and forms the background culture of a given political system.) As a collective entity embodying the very idea of internal differentiation (as discussed in the Introduction), the crowd emblematized for Crane the antithesis of totalized socio-economic equality.

Progressive reformers at the turn of the century saw their mission as manifold. Among other things it entailed bringing public attention (as Jacob Riis's photojournalism did) to the wretched living conditions of the underclasses; providing the means and the places (as Jane Addams's Hull House did) for self-improvement; and proposing and enacting (as advocates of public utilities did) legal measures to counteract the laissez-faire policies that widened American society's disparities in wealth and well-being. This third task was predicated on accepting as within the purview of government the material welfare of the polity's populace – in other words, accepting political agencies' significant participation in defining and bringing about the public good.

There were milder and stronger versions of Progressive reformers' vision of such an ends-oriented mode of governance. Frederic Howe, best known for his municipal reformism, represents the milder version. In *The City: The Hope of Democracy* (1905) he contends that "*a priori* philosophers have reduced the functions of the state to those of the constable, to the protection of life, liberty, and property from external and internal violence"; whereas he, along with what he calls "public sentiment," favors the "formula of Locke that 'the end of government was the welfare of mankind.'" What makes Howe's argument mild is that, however critical of a priori philosophers, he harbors no desire to relinquish their commitment to democratic-liberal principles. Indeed he advances the "city-republic" as the ideal political entity, which in the form of "home rule" will enable citizens collectively to improve their quality of life by adopting "socialistic" measures such as improved public education and medicine, as well as municipal ownership of public utilities and some institutions of employment.[4]

Howe regards the municipal public as better able to effect change in social welfare than national or state publics, which are "less alert, much less able to act collectively or to concentrate attention upon a given issue." But besides being more effective, the city under home rule will be more affecting: it will become "a thing to be loved and cared for"; the home-ruled city will be "sense[d] ... *as a home.*" Howe's proposed municipality thus begins to take on attributes of a cozy, pre-modern social order; his "citizen will be attached to his community just as were the burghers of the medieval towns."[5] While Howe does not press hard on these analogies, his alignment of polity and home points to the extended reach into the private or intimate sphere that Progressive reformers envisioned. Without a priori political-liberal checks in place, which not only protect rights and liberties but also serve to separate out political and non-political domains, an ends-based political system might well reach all the way down. "Home" might no longer occupy a place in the background culture – sometimes overlapping with political conceptions, sometimes not – but instead find itself in lockstep with a fully comprehensive Progressivist system.

Edward Bellamy was a Progressive reformer who moved toward this stronger version. Following the publication of *Looking Backward* in 1888, the 1890s witnessed the meteoric rise of Bellamy's Nationalist movement, which garnered interest from all manner of political thinkers and activists – socialists, progressivists, populists, anarchists, as well as cultural conservatives. Described as being one of the most influential books of the turn of the century, *Looking Backward* responded to the era's economic instabilities and brutal labor conditions by seeking "to reason out a method of economic organization by which the republic might guarantee the livelihood and material welfare of its citizens on a basis of equality corresponding to and supplementing their political equality."[6] Having in view a fully comprehensive social justice system, the book's envisioned solution involved a "rearrangement of the industrial and social system on a higher ethical basis" whose "aim was to nationalize the functions of production and distribution" of material goods and services.[7]

Bellamy's Nationalist clubs are known historically to have spurred public movements early in the 1890s that effected social welfare legislation, such as bringing utilities (gas and electric) under municipal control. They also later influenced the Populist Party platform, which favored "government ownership of the railroads, telegraph, and telephone; civil service for all government employees; government postal savings banks; and the popular election of United States senators."[8] Despite such inspiring activism, critics frequently find fault with the authoritarian, militaristic aspect of Bellamy's political vision. They see him as less concerned with social justice than with disciplinary and managerial control. His notorious description of an industrial army of workers, in which "young men are taught habits of obedience, subordination, and devotion to duty," has contributed greatly to the negative reception of his work.[9] Such criticisms, however, overlook Bellamy's explicit commitment to democracy and fraternal co-operation, that is, to his premise that the nation's citizens enter into the social contract of the industrial army not only willingly but gratefully, because they understand the result to be social security and material well-being for one and all.

If not exactly authoritarian, then, Bellamy's vision of the nation in the year 2000 remains nonetheless political-theoretically problematic. This has to do with what one critic, Catherine Tumber, recently analyzes as his "gnostic vision of industrial reform – of rational, secular, managerial control and liberated, unmediated spiritual democracy." In her highly illuminating account, Tumber goes on to argue that Bellamy participates in the nineteenth century's demise of civic culture by constructing a political vision that effectively collapses the distinction between the public and the private. The "gnostic" element takes Bellamy beyond Christianity's morally overlapping agreement with liberal democracy (via its golden-rule justice and equality) by moving toward transcendental, mystic knowledge: "gnostic spiritual democracy – conceived as equal access to psychic power for use in gaining freedom from earthly conditions – serves to evade inherent limitations of human life." She finds evidence for this tendency primarily in Bellamy's short stories and notebooks. In these texts fantasies of mind-reading, thought transference, and other means of direct communication get played out, thereby obliterating "formerly meaningful intellectual distinctions that made sense of human limits."[10]

But even if, as Tumber says, his religious views are "muted" in *Looking Backward*, this text's utopian vision rests on the assumption that the political economy can and should amount to a fully comprehensive and scientific doctrine.[11] The public sphere is thus rendered superfluous. Not only do economic administration and distribution function solely according to scientific procedures worked out by experts, but also the public good itself is a fully rational, utilitarian affair. It is particularly this latter point that poses problems for a liberal democracy, because it implies that highly

subjective phenomena such as evaluations of the good life are objectifiable
and purely rational, thus in no need of prioritization through public nego-
tiation and debate. Bellamy avoids of course the totalitarian extreme: when
Edith goes shopping she enjoys the freedom to make selections according
to her "personal taste."[12]

But Bellamy appears not to appreciate the relevance of public-political
deliberation over, say, the social benefits of particular values and needs,
a procedure which enables a general calibration of social goods and services when conflicts arise and choices become necessary. He makes the
utilitarian assumption that, as Norman Barry puts it, "everybody's taste for
money income is the same," and furthermore depends "on the interpersonal
comparability of individual utilities and their cardinal measurability."[13] In
short, Bellamy's comprehensive doctrine relies on a self-evident gnostic
epistemology in which each citizen's consciousness is empirically knowable
and comparable. "Missing," consequently, "is any conception of the public
and the goods specific to it."[14]

Stephen Crane's urban stories and sketches recall the terms of the public
sphere that Bellamy leaves out; and, in more confrontational or dramatic
ways, they expose this public sphere's epistemological limits. They sub-
stantiate Rawls's observation that a "crucial assumption of liberalism is
that equal citizens have different and indeed incommensurable and irrec-
oncilable conceptions of the good."[15] Himself a part-time member of the
realist branch of Progressivism's reform movement, Crane seems nonetheless attuned to the epistemic fallacy underwriting a fully comprehensive,
Bellamyite version. Succinctly exemplifying this two-part and essentially
liberal claim (of the necessity of, yet epistemic limitation on, the public
sphere) is his brief sketch of a police court scene, entitled "An Eloquence
of Grief" (1896). It juxtaposes two court cases, one in which a servant girl
stands accused by her employer of theft, the other in which an old man faces
charges of public drunkenness. After the judge hears the evidence related
to the first case and decides in favor of a trial, "a great cry rang through the
court-room" with the girl claiming, "I am innocent!" (*PP* 836). However
"graphic a grief" as her cry expresses, Crane the journalist-narrator resists
the omniscient-sentimentalist device of using this kind of emotional display as an unequivocal sign of a character's innocence. While remarking
in high melodrama that the scream "slit with a dagger's sweep the curtain
of the common-place," prompting the courtroom spectators to undergo
"a spasmodic movement," Crane underscores his own epistemic limits by
leaving unanswered the question of the girl's status – "innocent or guilty"
(*PP* 863). Crane the realist-journalist is no Bellamyite mind-reader, nor is

he a spasmodically affected member of the courtroom crowd. He is situated somewhere in between those two limits of being.

Accepting the deep and moving pathos of the girl's eloquent grief, but not admitting it as uncontrovertible evidence of innocence, Crane conforms to liberal democracy's institutional conception of jurisprudential procedure. For if her anguished self-proclamation were accepted as epistemically certifying her innocence, then the judge in the second case, involving an "aged, almost toothless wanderer, tottering and grinning," would also be compelled to accept as proof of innocence the man's claim, "I've niver been dhrunk befoor" (*PP* 864). When a court officer responds to this statement by "lift[ing] his hand to hide a smile," he registers how inconclusive his own personal skepticism is (*PP* 864). Just as Crane has no insider knowledge as to the truth behind the servant girl's cry, this officer has none as to the falsity behind the aged wanderer's (who might simply have a speech impediment and be dizzy with hunger). The liberal polity builds its legal procedures and institutions on the absence, on the very impossibility, of fully comprehensive insider knowledge. With no hook-up to Bellamy's telepathic lines of communication, the courts rely on confessions of the guilty or evidence of guilt beyond a reasonable doubt. This is why in "An Eloquence of Grief," Crane has "the judge sa[y] that, considering the evidence, he would have to commit the girl for trial" (*PP* 863).

ANAESTHETIC REVELATIONS

More often than by representing public-political institutions such as criminal courts, Crane articulates his concern about the potential overreach of Progressivism through representations of crowds. For the crowd makes visible a simultaneously psycho-physiological and social condition of *anaesthesia*, thus becoming a figure of impenetrable privacy, of a home far away from home. At the turn of the century the anaesthetic state received much scientific attention as an accompanying feature of the hypnotic state, which as we know informed crowd psychology. As, for instance, William James writes in *Principles of Psychology*, under hypnosis "*sensations may be abolished*[.] ... Legs and breasts may be amputated, children born, teeth extracted, in short, the most painful experiences undergone."[16]

The anaesthetic condition inscribes itself in James's work not simply as a phenomenal fact but as a non-phenomenal figure. It contributes to James's articulation of physiology and philosophy, more specifically, to his ontological conception of a "pure" experiential condition that constitutes neither subjective nor objective experience but manifests itself instead as "neutrals, indifferents, undecideds, posits, data, facts."[17] As early as 1874 (in a book review for the *Atlantic Monthly*) and as late as 1910 (in "A Pluralistic Mystic," the last piece published in his lifetime) James registers his admiration for his eventual acquaintance Benjamin Paul Blood's small book, *The Anaesthetic Revelation and the Gist of Philosophy* (1874). Between these dates he refers to the book regularly: in the 1879 version of "The Sentiment of Rationality"; in "On Some Hegelisms" (1882); in *The Principles of Psychology* (1890); and in his chapter on mysticism in *Varieties of Religious Experience* (1902). As the title suggests, Blood attempts to align the "forgotten" "condition (or uncondition) ensuing about the instant of recall from anaesthetic stupor to sensible observation" with the philosophical limit, that is, with the conception of "life without personality, or consciousness that is not of some particular in logical form."[18]

James makes a similar venture, though with less mystical aspirations. Where Blood hails the anaesthetic revelation as an "initiation into the Secret of Life," James muses more pragmatically over the way anaesthesia enters into the physiological experience of *interest*. He first describes interest according to conventional physiology: "Our *interest in things* means the attention and emotion which the thought of them will excite, and the actions which their presence will evoke." Later, however, he remarks that interest is capable of reaching a limit of intensity, where the "absorption may be so deep as not only to banish ordinary sensations, but even the severest of pain." As an illustration he then quotes from an account of the mathematician Vieta who " 'was sometimes so buried in meditation that for hours he bore more resemblance to a dead person than to a living, and was then wholly unconscious of everything going on around him.' "[19] Vieta, in other words, presses his conscious interest so far as physiologically to reach a radically altered state of "unconscious" interest.

Vieta is but one of several figures of anaesthetic deadness deployed by James to articulate his conception of an inarticulate, anonymous limit pressing upon lived experience. But perhaps most remarkable of all is the "subject" who is "absolutely anaesthetic inside and out, but not paralytic, so that emotion-inspiring objects might evoke the usual bodily expressions from him, but who, on being consulted, should say that no subjective emotional affection was felt." As he notes, "Cases like this are extremely hard to find. Medical literature contains reports, so far as I know, of but three."[20] Despite or perhaps because of this empirical infrequency, the anaesthetic limit serves well to exhibit James's conception of pure experience, embodying as it does this ontological principle of "experience in its 'pure' state, plain unqualified actuality, a simple *that*, as yet undifferentiated into thing and thought." James registers dissatisfaction with the way conceptual thought and grammar are "too discriminative" and force him to call pure experience something, even something as nondescript as "a mere *this*," maintaining that it "would be better expressed by the bare interjection 'lo!' "[21] Figures such as the absolutely anaesthetic subject and the deadly interested mathematician dramatize this pure experiential condition: they are something like prolonged interjections.

The condition of anaesthesia informs Crane's similar conception of what he calls in one sketch (discussed below) a "gorgeous neutrality," which predicates his mode of realism and marks his representations of crowds. At once a realist and journalist in New York, Crane is engaged in the hunting and gathering of social documents; that is, he participates in late nineteenth-century realism's dominant project of making urban topoi, especially the situations of the "other half," sensibly and cognitively available to the newspaper and journal reading public. This realism, Alan Trachtenberg explains, could assure itself of "distance" from the underclasses of the slums by an aesthetics of moral and sentimental paternalism. But as he goes on to argue, Crane's realism does not adhere entirely to the conventions. Crane refuses to cultivate this comfortable distance by "aim[ing] at accuracy, not compassion." "Crane's concern is with the phenomenon before him[.] ... He writes to achieve an accurate statement of the feeling of the scene and his details are physical correlatives[.] ... He writes as a phenomenologist of the scene, intent on characterizing the consciousness of the place" and on "converting sheer data into *experience*."[22]

I want to suggest, however, that Crane refuses this distance in essentially the opposite manner: by converting lived experience back into *sheer data*, back into pure, anaesthetic experience. In effect he sabotages the realist and Progressivist project of making sense of phenomena. He dramatizes the propensity of the underclasses to render themselves conspicuous to the point of invisibility, material to the point of impalpability, verbal to the point of incommunicability: in sum, being human to the point of becoming inhuman.[23] By this means Crane documents the underclasses' modes of functionally confounding the dominant culture's efforts to locate, understand, and thereby contain them.

It is difficult to ascertain whether or not Crane ever read James's work, but he would have come across quotations and citations of James in the pages of journals in which he published. In the muckraking, reformist *Arena*, for instance, in which articles on psychical research regularly appeared, the editor B.O. Flower (to whom Hamlin Garland, himself a member of the American Psychical Society, had recommended Crane)[24] authored a couple of articles in 1892 on hypnotism (citing James as a source), both of which discuss the phenomenon of anaesthesia. "[T]he entire body," he says in one, "is as insensible to pain as if perfectly etherized, at [the hypnotist's] command the body instantly becomes as rigid as if all life had departed." And in an 1893 issue of *McClure's Magazine*, R. H. Sherard reports that there are "numerous cases of persons to whom hypnotism has been administered, just as chloroform is in other cases, as an anaesthetic."[25] Such was the state of psycho-physiological intrigue at the turn of the century.

The following section examines more fully how the discourse of anaesthesia informs Crane's literary practice, producing what might be called a documentary anaesthetics.

GORGEOUS NEUTRALITIES

Where James is more or less restricted to natural science's fund of evidence in his reach for figurations of the anaesthetic interjection, Crane's occupation as journalist makes available a representational mode that is arguably more elastic, blending as it does (especially in the sensation-mongering 1890s) documentation and imagination. Initial indications of this orientation can be found in a comment made by Elbert Hubbard, editor of *The Philistine*, who published some of his poems. "I do not confess to an unqualified liking for your work," he writes to Crane. "When you hand me the book [*The Red Badge of Courage*] I am grown suddenly blind. It rather appeals to my nerves than to my reason – it gives me a thrill. Your work is of a kind so charged with electricity that it cannot be handled. It is all live wire."[26]

To be "grown suddenly blind": in a culture in which vision is the dominant register of sense-perception and means of determining geographic, social, and psychic distance, optical relations play a central role in Crane's documentary anaesthetics.[27] Though he worked without a camera, his special interest in representing visual experience (often noted by commentators) means that he participated as much as documentary photographers in the production of visibility in which the late nineteenth century, with its improvement and proliferation of such technologies as the camera and the mass circulation press, was immersed. We may begin to see more clearly the nexus of relations between documentation, anaesthetics and Crane's literary practice by turning to what might count as the primal scene of anaesthesia: the first public demonstration of a surgical operation performed on an etherized patient. It happens that this scene, which predates Crane's decade of literary production by forty or fifty years, was photographed

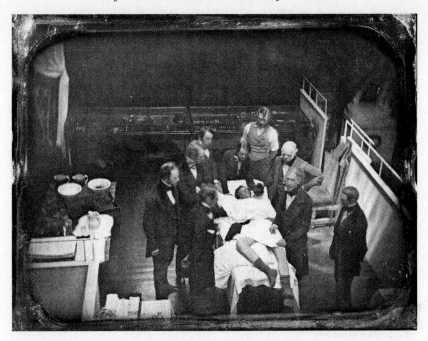

1 *Dr. W. T. G. Morgan recreating the first use of ether for anaesthesia in a surgical operation,* 16 October 1846, A. S. Southworth and J. J. Hawes. Courtesy of the J. Paul Getty Museum, Malibu, California.

(see illustration 1). William Welling, an historian of photography, considers the daguerreotype of this event to be "possibly the earliest documentary photograph taken in the United States."[28]

One can assume with full confidence that Crane knew nothing of this photograph (whose composition will be discussed in more detail below). But he did know rather well the work of the nineteenth century's famous documentarists, Mathew Brady and Jacob Riis, the latter of whose work is associated often enough with Crane's.[29] Moreover, the documentary genre was firmly established in mainstream culture by the 1890s. We find, for example, Sarah Orne Jewett, in 1893, inaugurating a series called "Human Documents" in the first issue of *McClure's Magazine*. In her comments the intent of the photographic series is shown clearly to be one of making human beings visible and legible: "when childhood has passed, one of the things we are to have learned, is to read the sign-language of faces[.] . . . There is no such thing as turning our faces into unbetraying masks. A series of portraits is a veritable Human Document, and the merest glance may discover the progress of man, the dwindled or developed personality, the history of a character."[30]

In contrast to this practice of making the "Human Document" cognitively transparent, Crane tends to draw out the human subject's pure experiential and consequently opaque ground, rendering the figure at hand epistemologically unavailable, hence indeed an "unbetraying mask." In a Sunday feature article for the New York *World* entitled "The Devil's Acre" (1896), one that has received little critical attention, Crane articulates the ontological predications of his documentary anaesthetics. In this article he records his impressions of the Sing-Sing prison, its electric chair, and graveyard. In his description of the electric chair he conveys a sense of the way animate mobility inheres in the inanimate, motionless object. As a "commonplace bit of furniture" that "waits and waits and waits" in all its "structural precision," this chair also marks "the terrible, the beautiful, the ghastly pass[ing] continually before our eyes."[31] Later, in his comments on the convicts' graveyard, Crane reverses his emphasis, to suggest as well the inanimacy inhering in the animate. Dispelling the reverential solemnity usually accorded cemeteries, Crane calls attention to the "[k]ind, motherly, old cows" grazing there, and remarks that a "certain Roman class taught magnificent indifference as the first rule of life. These cows are disciples of the Romans" (*W* 8: 667). This bovine indifference – not unlike Nietzsche's grazing, happily unhistorical animal, that, conditioned by forgetting, perpetually encounters its own death[32] – is an aspect borne most often in Crane by corpses, beasts, children, and crowds. As it affirms a certain deadness, it simultaneously demands, like James's pure experience, to be the first rule of *life*. It thus confirms this inanimacy *as* the first rule – and not the opposite – of life.

In the same non-dialectical vein yet with greater implications for the present discussion, Crane discovers a "gorgeous neutrality" in the state's graveyard community, in the way the convicts' burial sites, rather than being personalized and differentiated, are marked with like tombstones all bearing the same inscription: "At Sing Sing the author of the inscription preserves a gorgeous neutrality. When he formulated one he formulated them all. 'Here lies at rest —'" (*W* 8: 668). On the one hand this inscription serves to depersonalize the human subject buried underneath by disembodying the person's name (which would be filled in the blank), by severing it from everything that might recall the subject's personhood or history, thus, in effect, rendering the person anonymous. In other words, Crane discloses the State's efforts to secure not only criminal justice for the living but something like Bellamyite social justice for the dead. Alternately, it could be argued that the State, in being so reductive, assumes a respectable modesty and respectful distance by not presuming to know which particulars belonging to the convict's past, apart from the name, to highlight.

In any case the tombstones' gorgeous neutrality does not lie in the state's attempt to absorb the particular individual into a socialized and ordered general. Instead it derives from a different sort of anonymity, the anonymity inscribed in the very blank Crane evokes, the "—" that does not visibly exist, but non-visibly subsists and insists in each tombstone. This anonymous space-bar, marking the reciprocal interpenetrations of human beings and inhuman becomings, of the concrete and the abstract, is embodied in the tombstone itself: when the inscription is filled out with whichever name circumstances require, the entire enunciation of that naming points as much to human exchangeability, to the banal reproduction of the verbal coin, "Here lies at rest," as it does to the has-been human beneath it, the singularity that may be named but is no longer sufficiently composed to qualify as being "Here." Crane registers this inscriptive decomposition in a comment about the graveyard's visitors: "If people ... gaze at these tombstones they probably find that they can just make the inscriptions out at the distance and just can't make them out at the distance. They encounter the dividing line between coherence and a blur" (*W* 8: 669). A decisive word in this passage is the twice appearing "and," for by means of this most neutral of conjunctions he affirms two seemingly antithetical conditions, seeing and not seeing. Just as significantly, this visual assemblage produces – or is the product of, the sequence of cause and effect is indeterminate – a third quality, a "dividing line," in other words, another sort of anonymous "—" that renders the limit of both coherence and blur. Crane's verb choice here is also decisive. The line is not seen, but *encountered*, suggesting that its relation to visibility is a non-relation, that the line's linearity is distributed in a general economy of sight; that is to say, it is exterior to sight.[33] In other words, the "gorgeous neutrality" of the "—" obtains when sight is pushed to its limit of blindness – which Crane registers, not in the undifferentiated "blur," but the radically singular, non-phenomenal "dividing line."

As the basis for a documentary anaesthetics, Crane's "gorgeous neutrality" opens up the space of being-becoming invisible, of a becoming-anaesthetic that functionally (which is not to say politically) resists realism's and extreme Progressivism's imperative of being sensible. Crane's mode of documentation can be seen to resemble the radically neutral intensity of such later documentary photographers as Paul Strand. His well-known photograph, "Blind Woman" (1916), serves as an allegory for how little the realist camera

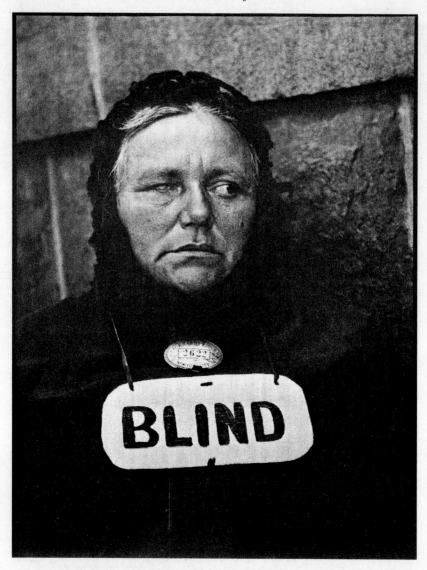

2 *Blind woman*, 1916, Paul Strand. Courtesy of the Metropolitan Museum of Art, The Alfred Stieglitz Collection, 1933 (33.43.334).

sees (see illustration 2). It is a frontal close-up of an aged, and obviously impoverished, blind woman's face whose unseeing eyes – one wandering, the other half-closed and opaque – render her indifferent to the camera. The camera is incapable of coercing her to participate in a dialectic of recognition; she remains, in other words, outside the intentionally structured economy of intersubjectivity. The metal badge under her chin reflects New York's numerical hold on her occupational status as a peddler; but the sign "BLIND," while identifying the woman's physical handicap, also reflects back onto the viewer his or her severely limited insight into her radically private world. Strand's photograph formally conceals nothing (there is, for instance, no obscuring or softening touch of a shadow or angular perspective), but to the contrary carries exposure to the point of opacity. It is as though the scrutinized object's "gorgeous neutrality" interjects itself into the relation between the viewer's sense-perceptual sight and cognitive insight.

In his urban sketches Crane often figures this anaesthetic limit-experience as a quotidian, violent, and literal descent – the breakdown of a van, the collapse of a man, the stumbling actions and passions of a drunk. These scenarios often involve crowds. A prime example is his 1894 sketch, "When Man Falls, a Crowd Gathers," which documents the psycho-physiological transactions between a crowd and its object of attention: a fallen man who seems only nominally or anaesthetically alive. But before turning to this sketch it is worth noting the ways in which it formally duplicates the photograph of the first anaesthetic operation. For while this photograph historically registers the primal scenes of documentary photography and anaesthetic surgery, its pictorial composition resembles nothing so much as this other primal scene, the hypnotized crowd surrounding and enthralled by its leader. In the photo, however, as in Crane's sketch, the leader, the figure attracting everyone's attention, lies prostrate and inert, vulnerably exposed (in the photo, indeed, overexposed, stripped as the patient's slightly parted legs are to their socks) rather than masterfully poised. The composition thus partly derails the document's intended social function, namely, to testify to the regular and orderly dissemination of science and technology. With its circle of gentlemanly spectators within the operating pit – the eye-witness bearers of new knowledge and expertise who come, see, and conquer the event of anaesthesia – the photograph's semiotics tell of the bright day and equally bright future for medicine. But the object of these men's collective gaze seems to be the corpse-like patient rather than the doctor administering the ether (who scarcely distinguishes himself from the others), suggesting that the spectacle of human inanimacy may be mimetically anaesthetizing them as much as the ether is the patient.[34]

In "When Man Falls" this mimetic transaction between the inanimate and the animate receives dramatic attention, making apparent how little sight sees. The sketch stages, in other words, how magnetically confounding those who have fallen into anaesthetic space can be to the realist viewers who attempt to follow them. Little more happens in this sketch than the title suggests: an unnamed Italian immigrant walking along during evening rush hour "suddenly" collapses in what appears to be an epileptic seizure; his boy companion screams and "[i]nstantly from all directions people turned their gaze upon the prone figure." A policeman and doctor arrive, and alternately scold the crowd and demand more space; finally, after an ambulance arrives to cart the "limp body" away, members of the crowd "resume... their ways" (*PP* 600–604). The sketch's diachronic scheme thus reproduces the "rhythmical roar" of the elevated railroad nearby, "suddenly begun and suddenly ended" (*PP* 602). It models what the sociologist Robert Park would analyse a decade later in his dissertation *The Crowd and the Public*. Focusing less on the psychological disposition of the crowd or its historical emergence, Park foregrounds the crowd's active role as a pre- or inter-institutional entity, a force that transforms existing institutions and groups into new ones. "Since the crowd is short-lived," Park writes, "it often seems preferable to speak of it as a phenomenon undergoing formation and dissolution rather than as a static entity."[35]

Crane's sketch combines Park's diachronic phenomenology of the crowd's metabolic transitoriness with what could be called the crowd's synchronic transitoriness, its metabolic ontology. That is, Crane depicts the crowd's condition as neither simply static being nor simply mobile becoming, but as being-becoming qualitatively other. This gets played out in his dramatization – or rather, parody – of the fallen man as leader, and the crowd's subsequent imitation of him. Dropping to the literal ground, as well as to the figurative ground of his body, this figure inaugurates yet doubly removes himself from the role of the leader. Neither leading nor being led, he performs instead the role of non-leader. Crane blocks the leaderliness of the leader by rendering him effectively dead on arrival. As such the fallen man remains external to the restricted economy of power: neither superordinate nor subordinate, he embodies the inordinate, the radically neutral condition that remains "the first rule of life" – the "lo!" of pure experience. As though to emphasize further the limited significance of crowd psychology's leader-crowd theory, Crane depicts the crowd as momentarily obedient when a "tall German suddenly appeared and resolutely began to push the crowd back... He had psychological authority over this throng; they obeyed him" (*PP* 602). This obedience is clearly secondary to the drama of the sketch, since the tall German, from whom nothing more is heard, is neither affiliated with the fallen man nor ultimately distracting much attention from him.[36]

Pure, anaesthetic experience thus embodied, the fallen man's optical relation to the crowd resembles Strand's blind woman's to the camera:

"Through his pallid half-closed lids could be seen the steel-colored gleam of his eyes that were turned toward all the bending, swaying faces and in the inanimate thing upon the pave yet burned threateningly, dangerously, shining with a mystic light, as a corpse might glare at those live ones who seemed about to trample it under foot" (*PP* 601). His eyes' "steel-colored gleam," much like her sign "BLIND," reflects back onto the spectators what cannot be seen more than what "could be seen." Hypnotically, "those live ones" – and Crane's pronominal use, as Michael Fried observes, invites the reader to substitute "corpses" for the pronoun "ones" – are able to stare but not see, or at least not cognize, "held" as they are "in a spell of fascination."[37] In his troping the crowd later in the sketch as a "sea of men" (*PP* 603), Crane likewise evokes the crowd's disjunctive conflation of being animate ("men") and becoming inanimate ("sea").

The hypnotic relation becomes more pronounced through Crane's attention to the scene's spatial relations. Situating himself at a distance through much of the "drama," he describes how in the "centre of the crowd," "[d]own under their feet," lies the fallen man, "about" whom is circled a "dodging, pushing, peering group." Realistically enough, "[o]ver the heads of the crowd" hangs an "immovable canvas sign"; but verging on the surreal, the crowd's verbal expressions are also airborne: "A volley of questions, replies, speculations flew to and fro above all the bobbing heads;" and "Always the same question could be heard flying in the air. 'What's the matter?'" (*PP* 600–602). The relation between "air" and "matter" turns out to play a crucial role. Crane describes how the spectators "pressed and crushed again" and how those near enough to see the man become as stiff as he: they "hung back," they are held "chained" and "seemed scarcely to breathe." With the crowd hypnotically or mimetically immobilized by way of absorbing the corpse-like qualities of the "inanimate thing" below as well as the "immovable sign" above, Crane stages the human being's sublime materiality: the crowd becomes so crowded that it reaches the qualitatively other point of crow*dead*ness. It performs a radically inhuman pressing beyond itself. Within its volatile unity of "bending, swaying faces," of persons who "crowded savagely... like starving men fighting for bread" (*PP* 600–601), obtains the zero-space of uttermost solidity and solidarity. (In "The Men in the Storm" [1894] this condition is equally pronounced: "One expected that from the tremendous pressure, the narrow passage to the basement door would be so choked and clogged with human limbs and bodies that movement would be impossible" [*PP* 583].) If the fallen man inspires the gathering of the crowd he also embodies its utter expiration.[38]

As though to drive home the point, Crane represents the "space" between the man and the crowd – the "air" in which words "could be heard flying" – as offering no communication. The man's boy companion is engaged in an interaction with the crowd that amounts to anaesthetized action or inaction: "The men near him questioned him, but he did not seem to understand. He answered them 'Yes' or 'No,' blindly, with no apparent comprehension of their language" (*PP* 601). Communication in this sketch is derailed by the Jamesian "bare interjection." Crane further reinforces the condition of incommunicability by imaging a "curtain" that is "rung down," an "impenetrable fabric suddenly intervening" between the crowd and the fallen man, when finally the ambulance carts him away (*PP* 604). The members of the crowd, like Strand's camera, "still continued to stare at the ambulance" but the fallen man, like the blind woman, does not look back. Insofar as this fall of a curtain in the sketch's final passage reproduces its initial and central event – the "fall" of a man – the visibility of that event is always already closed off from the crowd whose identity it at once inaugurates and forecloses. The anaesthetic remains of the fallen man are thus from beginning to end external to the economy of power and signification inscribed in crowd psychology. Conspicuous as he is, his actions resist legibility; but illegible as he is, the crowd cannot resist him. It follows its non-leader into its own crowdedness. He enacts the gorgeous neutrality of simultaneously having "suddenly begun and suddenly ended."

If Crane's anaesthetic realism in this sketch serves effectively to burlesque crowd psychology's ostensible insight into the leader-crowd relation, it further undermines the discipline's tenets by exposing the weakness of the hypnosis model's unilateral structure. Tarde (as noted in the Introduction) maintains that "the magnetised subject imitates the magnetiser, but that the latter does not imitate the former," and goes on to conclude that "the unilateral must have preceded the reciprocal."[39] In contrast to this conceptual hierarchy, Crane suggests that hypnotic forces are reciprocally at work. For before the man falls – before, that is, he becomes a non-leader – Crane recounts how he and his boy lumber down the street "*crowded* with laborers, shop men and shop women," "blinking their black eyes at the passing show." Evidently the man's own specular participation precipitates his "fit," for the next thing the reader learns is that "[s]uddenly the man wavered on his limbs and glared bewildered and helpless *as if some blinding light had flashed before his vision*; then he swayed like a drunken man and fell" (*PP* 600, emphasis added). In a sense, then, before forming a crowd, the crowd already was a crowd, but as such it was also a leader, hypnotizing its soon-to-be non-leader. Tarde, as it happens, envisions a similar scenario when he discusses the more general pattern of imitation taking place in the urban environment. He claims that the "animate environment" of the city serves to "stultif[y]" city dwellers and render them "somnambulistic": "The noise and movement of the streets, the display of shop-windows, and the wild and unbridled rush of existence affect them like magnetic passes." According to Tarde, this occurs because "their attention is so bent upon everything they have previously seen and heard," that their memory is "absolutely paralysed" and "spontaneity is lost."[40] But what he fails to imagine is Crane's moment of spontaneity when the subject literally and figuratively drops out of the imitative structure.

Elsewhere in his oeuvre Crane enlists that vision-dependent phenomenon, *color*, to render yet also, as it were, to anaesthetize social phenomena. Profoundly impressed, apparently, by Goethe's analysis of "the effect which the several colors have upon the mind," Crane's metaphorics of color is more often affectively blinding than cognitively illuminating.[41] As Jonathan Crary explains in his engaging study of modern optics, *Techniques of the Observer*, Goethe's theory of colors was among the first to break with Newtonian optics and to locate color not in the object but in the observer: "As Goethe explains at length, they [that is, undulating colors of an afterimage observed in a dark room] are 'physiological' colors belonging entirely to the body of the observer and are 'the necessary conditions of vision'. . . The human body, in all its contingency and specificity, generates 'the spectrum of another colour,' and thus becomes the active producer of optical experience." As Crary tells it, Goethe's physiological account creates the conditions of possibility for the English painter Turner's direct, visionary "confrontation with the sun," his "solar preoccupations" that call into question "the very possibility of representation." A characteristic late Turner work thus "[o]n the one hand stands as an impossible image of a luminescence that can only be blinding and that has never been seen, but . . . also resembles an afterimage of that engulfing illumination."[42] As it happens, Crane himself trafficked a bit in "solar preoccupations," in afterimages of the sublime, as is registered, for instance, in lines near the end of the poem *War Is Kind*: "For that love is now to me / A supernal dream, / White, white, white with many suns" (*PP* 1344). More important to the present discussion, however, are the ways in which Crane images scenes of everyday urban life as colorfully blinding.

One technique used to this end is to riddle these scenes with color, to the point, as it were, of producing chromatic blockages. We see this in his story, "The Broken-Down Van" (1892). Briefly, the story recounts the event of a traffic jam that ensues when a horse-drawn furniture van breaks down, consequently blocking the horse-drawn street-cars' passage – not surprisingly, a crowd gathers here too. What is particularly striking in this sketch, compared to others, is that, on the surface, Crane's interjection of colors is almost exclusively realistic – that is, plausible, even accurate, as Trachtenberg would say. But this color co-ordination by no means renders the scene cognitively visible. Indeed, in Crane's hands the scene becomes comically *obscene*, in that "most literal sense" of the word that Crary lends to it: "the shatter[ing of] the *scenic* relationship between viewer and object."[43] In "The Broken-Down Van" Crane achieves this shattering by interjecting color with a joyful vengeance. The scene decomposes under the pressure of his outlandish, positively distracting repetition: "red" occurs in the second paragraph (about one and a half pages long in the Library of America edition) more than fifteen times, ten times within the first six sentences. Lights are red, cars are red, the driver's hair, the van's "landscape" (that is, its sides), and the dashboards are all "red" (*PP* 521–522). The repetition does more than contribute to the atmosphere of a "wild, maniacal dance," as Crane calls it (*PP* 521). By the end of the paragraph Crane's narrative belligerence has beaten red redless (other colors are also involved in the scene, but they receive by comparison only bruising treatment). No longer seeing the color red, but only the word "red" in all its corpse-like materiality, the reader witnesses the exhaustion of red's redness. When red falls, anaesthetic affectivity gathers.[44]

What is more, a sort of sonic or verbal blockage joins this chromatic one, thereby exhibiting a collectivity's will to mimetic nonsense:

Well, the van was wrecked and something had got to be done. It was on the busiest car track on Manhattan Island. The cliff-dwellers got down in some mysterious way – probably on a rope ladder. Their brethren drove their van down a side street and came back to see what was the matter.
"The nut is off," said the captain of the wrecked van.
"Yes," said the first mate, "the nut is off."
"Hah," said the captain of the other van, "the nut is off."
"Yer right," said his first mate, "the nut is off."
The driver of the red car came up, hot and irritated. But he regained his reason.
"The nut is off," he said.
The drivers of the green and of the blue car came along. "The nut," they said in chorus, "is off." (*PP* 522)

By the time the "chorus" – another sort of crowd – sings out, "The nut is off," the information transmitted in the speech act is absurdly uninformative. Crane's sketch is a joyful confirmation of collective non-communication, of social anti-scenes in which realist, would-be reformers face nonsensical, banal repetition.

Thus far we have seen how Crane hunts and gathers various forms of disruptive insensibility in scenes either of inanimate single figures or of collectively behaving entities, be these latter drivers, spectators or tombstones. I want now to turn to two sketches, "An Ominous Baby" (1894) and "A Lovely Jag in a Crowded Car" (1895), in which Crane deals with the insensibility of individuals animated to the extreme. It is as though the central figures in these two sketches enact, not unlike the "dodging, pushing, peering" crowd of "When Man Falls," that symptom oddly concomitant with both surgical and hypnotic anaesthesia, namely, *hyperaesthesia*. As Tarde observes of hypnotized subjects, "a singular mixture of anaesthesia and hyperaesthesia of the senses is the dominant characteristic," going on to clarify how "under the gaze of another person" a hypnotized subject experiences not only a "kind of momentary paralysis of mind, tongue and arm, [but also] the profound agitation of the whole being and the lack of self-possession."[45] With his dramatization of the "baby rage" of a "small barbarian" in the first sketch and the jag of a "wild red demon of drink and destruction" in the second, Crane unleashes the hyperaesthetic potential of one of the nineteenth century's abiding aesthetic motifs, the urban *flâneur*. Charles Baudelaire, the *flâneur's* great champion, draws on this figure's affinity with the child and the drunk, yet he tends to idealize the *flâneur* as one who encounters harmonious beauty by adopting a childlike or intoxicated "Sensibility" and by wending his way (rarely *her* way in the nineteenth century) through the crowd on a Poe-inspired quest for concealment.[46] By contrast, Crane decomposes this harmless, turtle-toting ego-ideal into its highly visible and downright obnoxious constituents – a temperamental baby and an all too happy drunk.[47]

"An Ominous Baby," with its fabulous opening, "A baby was wandering in a strange country," recounts the *flânerie* of a "soiled" and "tattered" boy as he toddles away from the "poor district," sallying forth "to investigate the new scenes" of a wealthier neighborhood (*PP* 527).[48] "Dragging behind him a bit of rope," this pedestrian clearly needs no turtle at the end of it to disturb the tempo of urban industriousness: "Passengers had to avoid the small, absorbed figure in the middle of the sidewalk"; his attentive, awe-filled gaze alone disturbs two nursery maids in conversation. More disruptive yet is the "scuffle" that ensues when his "infant tranquility" transmutes into the "baby rage" of a "small barbarian": having communicated to a "pretty child in fine clothes" his desire to "play wif" the latter's toy fire engine, and having been denied the request, the boy finally gets what he "want[s]" by dint of a "supreme tug." Whereupon he "prepare[s] the toy for travelling": the geographically uncontained and socially intrusive *flânerie*, evidently, will continue (*PP* 527–529). A final point about this sketch: in having the triumphant tattered boy leave the scene "weeping with the air of a wronged one who has at last succeeded in achieving his rights" (*PP* 529), who thereby enacts a might-equals-right political logic, Crane sends up a warning flare of sorts. It is directed not at the Bellamyites or other Progressives, but at the laissez-faire capitalists who, in neglecting public welfare and in leaving unchecked socially corrosive disparities in wealth, education, and well-being, have created the social conditions for random if not planned acts of violence.

The hyperaesthetic interjection of this baby's fellow wanderer in "A Lovely Jag in a Crowded Car" is at once more volatile and less violent. The story's headline, as it originally appeared in the New York *Press*, serves well as a summary: "A LOVELY JAG / IN A CROWDED CAR // A Blithe Episode of the Busy/ Shopping Days. // JOY UNCORKED AND EXUBER- ANT / This Man Had a Great Time All by/ Himself" (*W* 8: 872). In this "episode" of everyday life we find another *flâneur*, "a wild red demon of drink and destruction," whose wandering through crowds is limited to the interior of a crosstown car, but who experiences traumas and shifting pleasures with as much relish and sensitivity as any ambler-aesthete on a Parisian boulevard. Now "totter[ing] greatly in his excitement" or "feel[ing] a keen humor" when the car's "sudden jerk" causes him "to be precipitated violently into a seat," now suffering "astonishment" and "grief," now "spend[ing] some anxious moments in reflection" or "overcome by [a] wild thought," Crane records how the man "rejoiced that the world was to him one vast landscape of pure rose color," seen as it is "through a pair of strange, oblique, temporary spectacles." But the drunken man, like the ominous baby, disrupts others as much as himself. The "atmosphere" of the car, before he enters, is "as decorous as that of the most frigid of drawing rooms," filled as it is with middle-class women shoppers sitting "in austere silence regarding each other in occasional furtive glances and preserving their respectability with fierce vigilance." But once having embarked, the drunk in his "benign amiability" effectively deterritorializes this space by conducting a "great celebration," by singing and beating time "as if he was leading a grand chorus," by pounding the floor with his umbrella and calling to all aboard, in barely intelligible speech, to have a drink with him, whereupon with "infinite pains and thoroughness he canvasse[s] the passengers, putting to each one the formidable question: 'What'll yeh drink?'" (*W* 8: 361–364).

Transgressing property or propriety, Crane's hyperaesthetic *flâneurs* leave visible impressions on the social and material surfaces of everyday life. Yet in "A Lovely Jag" Crane seems as intent as in "The Ominous Baby" on creating the impression – an afterimage, perhaps – that another impeachably quotidian but highly visible figure remains – both in spite and because of this visibility – uncannily invisible. His concluding sentence thus reads: "They both [that is, the conductor and the one sympathetic passenger, who could well serve as Crane the reporter's surrogate] turned to watch him [that is, the drunk who has disembarked] and they remained there deep in reflection, absorbed in contemplation of this wavering figure in the distance, *until observation was no longer possible*" (*W* 8: 364, emphasis added).[49] Furthermore, in "A Lovely Jag" we witness the man falls-crowd gathers metabolics – for here too, immediately preceding this conclusion, Crane records how the man, upon disembarking, "sprawled out upon the cobbles." Then the drunk "arose instantly and began a hurried and unsteady journey back up the street, retracing the way over which the car had just brought him. He seemed overwhelmed with anxiety" (*W* 8: 364). Like the crowd, he dissolves and reforms, forms and moves on.

In both stories the protagonists' hyperaesthetic modes of subjectivity mime, as though having internalized, Le Bon's characterization of the crowd. They enact the spontaneity, the anarchic indifference to consequences, to a certain extent the irritability and violence, and certainly the mobility, impulsiveness and transience that Le Bon ascribes to the crowd, but that Crane redescribes as a constitutive feature of modern urban ontology. Such hyperaesthetic spontaneity is obviously incompatible with the Bellamyite vision of a fully comprehensive socio-economic regime of equality and justice. Nor does it comply with liberal democratic principles. But liberal democracies with a self-limiting reach, Crane's work implies, allow such features of human being to flourish in non-political domains. What we find operating in these sketches, then, are conceptions of optics and visibility that counter the epistemological assumptions (or fantasies) of Progressive utopianists and literary realists, but that ultimately confirm the attractions of privacy inhering in a political-liberal order.

CHAPTER 4

Vicious gregariousness: White City, the nation form, and the souls of lynched folk

In June 1893 *The Atlantic Monthly* ran an article entitled "A National Vice" in which the essayist (and later biographer of Bret Harte) Henry Childs Merwin reprehends Americans for their "undue gregariousness." Citing various trends of "modern life" – railroad travel, apartment dwelling, urban migration, the predominance of clubs, and so forth – Merwin then settles on a few of the very worst signs of this vice: "To dine in a crowd; to be charitable in a crowd; to go out in a crowd to view the face of nature; and, perhaps greatest absurdity of all, to read poetry in a crowd, – such are the ambitions of a typical American." Merwin worries that gregariousness, though necessary at an earlier stage in human history for the protection of the species, now promotes imitativeness; it "dulls the higher intellectual powers," and "prevents men from attaining their proper individuality of mind and of character." While conceding that the "social instinct" beneficially "fosters sympathy and pity and charity," the bane of modern life is urbanization, according to Merwin; it threatens to render extinct the "man of genius," the man who "becomes a law unto himself." Such men, he rues, "seldom arise in large cities."[1]

While disparagement of urban crowdedness appears regularly in nineteenth-century social commentary, Merwin amplifies the sense of peril by rendering gregariousness a "national" problem. By this he means not simply that gregariousness is a problem especially afflicting Americans as private individuals; rather, it is a problem for Americans as political subjects and for the United States as a nation. To bolster his views he turns to the renowned British physiologist and eugenicist Francis Galton: "the blind instincts" "have been ingrained into our breed, and . . . are a bar to our enjoying the freedom which the forms of modern civilization are otherwise capable of giving us. A really intelligent nation might be held together by far stronger forces than are derived from the purely gregarious instincts." Like genius, like nation: each requires its own "law," its own "force." A modern nation committed to freedom will realize its intelligence only insofar as its citizens abandon the gregariousness "still [applicable] to a large part of the black population of Africa." While anthropological racism informs Merwin's case against gregariousness, it also betrays – despite his anti-urban barking – a deep-seated commitment to modernity. That is, where other opponents of the city extol the virtues of rural life and call for a return to the small community, to the *Gemeinschaft*, Merwin's preferred form of collectivity is the modern nation. He invokes the countryside (New England and Scotland) not for its communal coziness, but for its provision of solitude; he looks to the modern nation to replace the "clannish[ness]," such as one finds in "various African tribes," with civilized intelligence.[2]

What Merwin wants, like countless armchair and professional social philosophers before and after him, are indeed private persons who think and act for themselves; he wants "intellectual workers" who leave behind "gossiping, tea-drinking society," carry out "abstract thinking...in solitude," and create "great," "strong and original works" of art. The Brontë sisters, Millet, Turner, Emerson, and Carlyle count among his examples of this commitment to solitude and to aesthetic and intellectual production. Similarly, he wants citizens and nations to think for themselves, to overcome the ways of "the earlier ancestors of our European stock."[3] What is remarkable about Merwin's boilerplate view is that he seems to have in mind one and the same method for realizing them, namely, the recovery of a solitude (both individual and collective) derived from "becom[ing] a law unto [one]self." Were we all in touch with our inner law, Merwin implies, we might all become great artists, thinkers, and citizens; we might all participate in the making and maintenance of a "really intelligent" nation. Thus would he restore the personal self, the political self, and the nation-state to their respective individualities.

By invoking this idea of becoming a law unto oneself as the solution to the problem of imitative gregariousness, Merwin shows himself to be strikingly inattentive to the discursive ambiguities, indeed antinomies, inhering this idea. More often than not, as I discuss more fully below, the phrase connoted highly intense, anarchic gregariousness – as in a lynch mob. This oversight on Merwin's part might seem hardly worth noting – his article appeared in a popular monthly, after all, not a scholarly journal; and Merwin himself is far from being a household or even schoolroom name. It does, in my view, nevertheless warrant attention. For the oversight bespeaks a broader cultural logic operative at the turn of the century, one that shaped simultaneously the era's politics of race and politics of national collectivity.

Over the course of this chapter I examine a chain of discursive links that enabled the US's imagination of itself as an urban, white nation whose people constituted a body of primarily nation-affirming and only secondarily (if at all) public-minded citizens. This imagination, I argue, depended on eliding the distinction between – or facilitating the adequate exchangeability of – the crowd and the public. It was also bound up with the discourse of genius, insofar as from this figure emanated the idea of becoming a law unto oneself. In other words, the project of imagining the nation as a racially homogeneous collectivity hinged on an understanding of becoming a law unto oneself as alternately (if not simultaneously) entering the public square or (and) entering the crowd mind. In Merwin's solution to the problem of the national vice of gregariousness one begins to see how such elisions and interchanges took shape.

Before returning to Merwin's concerns, it may help to touch on the specific way representations of crowds factor into this project of imagining a white national collectivity at the turn of the century. This chapter focuses on two types of crowd that I see as particularly germane to this collectivity's imagined coherence. First, there are the ones that gathered at expositions such as the 1893 Chicago World's Fair, one of the era's most prominent crowds-producing and nations-imaging events (which opened just one month before the appearance of Merwin's article). An event of national cathexis, the Fair would be charged with the task of representing the nation's "people." Arguably more than Philadelphia's Centennial Exposition in 1876, when the United States had not yet established itself as an industrialized geopolitical power (and was still preoccupied with Reconstruction), and more than the St. Louis World's Fair in 1904, when the United States was enmeshed in controversial imperialist enterprises, Chicago's Columbian Exposition was particularly well poised to accept this task, to represent the nation both to its constituents and to other nations as a homogeneous people pledged to Americanism. Such, certainly, is how the President of the Columbian Exposition, T. W. Palmer, envisioned it, as is evident in his proclamation three years before the Fair opened that one of its central purposes was "the commingling of our people from East, West, North, and South, from farm and factory. Such great convocations as that of our projected Fair are the schools wherein our people shall touch elbows, and the men and women from Maine and Texas, from Washington and South Carolina, learn to realize that all are *of one blood*, speak the same language, worship one God, and salute one flag."[4] This fair was also particularly well-suited to promote, as historian Peter Hales explains, "the concepts underlying the American urban renaissance movement," namely, "planning, order, monumentality, and symbolic historicism." "The 'White City,'" he argues, "was not merely the most concerted and unified exposition of the principle of that movement; it was also a consciously conceived public relations effort aimed at disseminating the movement's message about urban civilization to both the nation and the world."[5]

Second, there are the crowds that gathered largely in the South to commit what civil rights activist Ida B. Wells (later Barnett) in 1894 called the "national crime" of lynching, a practice whose frequency, according to public record, reached its first peak in 1892.[6] Turn-of-the-century lynch mobs and fair crowds turn out to be kissing cousins. It has been remarked often enough that the Fair's appellation, White City, not only referred to the fairground's white classical architecture and general pristine aura, but also bespoke its racial politics – its devastatingly effective ad hoc manner of excluding the nation's black population from self-representation at the Fair as well as from employment by the Fair (apart from the most menial labor). As Wells put it in *The Reason Why the Colored American Is Not in the World's Columbian Exposition*, an 1893 anti-lynching pamphlet distributed at the Fair, "Theoretically open to all Americans, the Exposition practically is, literally and figuratively, a 'White City,' in the building of which the Colored American was allowed no helping hand, and in its glorious success he has no share."[7]

Thus, at the same time as Chicago emblematized the nation's full entry into urban modernity, it also registered the post-Reconstruction accommodation of the South's vision of the nation's racial constitution: albeit not the extremist South's preferred Anglo-Saxon white, but certainly melting-pot white.[8] In 1894 Frederick Douglass may have been the first explicitly to correlate the effects of the Columbian Exposition with those of the lynch mob. Protesting against the fact that "not one of them [the "eight millions of colored people in the United States"] was deemed worthy to be appointed a Commissioner, or a member of an important committee, or a guide, or a guard on the Exposition grounds," he goes on to gloss this maltreatment:

It says to the world that the colored people of America are deemed by Americans not within the compass of American law and civilization. It says to the lynchers and mobocrats of the South, go on in your hellish work of negro persecution. What you do to their bodies, we do to their souls.[9]

In short, the national vice of physically peaceful but in other ways distressingly gregarious gatherings and the national crime of horrifyingly violent mob gatherings amounted to a nationalist virtue: these crowds shouldered as it were the stage upon which the US publicized its birth as a white nation fit for urban modernity.

The Columbian Exposition fairly revelled in its staginess, its theatricality. Historian Wim de Wit describes in "Building an Illusion" how the Fair's illusory quality was indeed acknowledged by its movers and shakers, "[t]he architects themselves." Chief of Construction "[Daniel] Burnham called the exposition halls 'architectural sketches' ... [and Henry] Van Brunt compared the facades to scenery 'executed on a colossal stage.'" Architecture critic "Montgomery Schuyler called the fair 'a success of illusion.'" Here "illusion" is used loosely as a synonym for spectacle and grandeur – not, then, to indicate deception. While the enjoying of spectacle may well accompany Americans' loving to be deceived – the latter being P. T. Barnum's famous insight – the two pleasures are by no means identical. As de Wit goes on to remark, "In essence an illusion, the fair was never intended to be presented as a real alternative to the American city or, especially, to the city of Chicago."[10] Nor could its buildings of staff and plaster, and its evanescent, transient status, possibly have been mistaken as such. Indeed, as White City (or Dream City or Magic City, as the fairgrounds were variously called) exuded an openly – not deceptively – illusory aura, the six-month long event in a sense prepared the nation for what, three years later, the dissenting Supreme Court Justice Harlan in the *Plessy* case condemned as the "thin disguise" of Jim Crow.[11] The social-psychological oppressiveness of this disguise similarly turned less on its deceptiveness than on its thinness. Wells too spoke of white Southerners' "infamously false excuse" of defending women's virtue and honor – a falseness that was recognized as such but nevertheless circulated in the press as justification or at least explanation for white mobs' lynching of blacks.[12] The re-emergence a few years later of the Ku Klux Klan's popularity (in literature and then later in film) would signal the success of deploying disguise not to conceal at all but to reveal. As Walter Michaels explains, the "purpose of the [Klan's] sheets, then, is not to conceal the identities of individual clansmen for, far from making their visible identities invisible, the sheets make their invisible identities [their racial whiteness] visible." The nation's general accession to illusion and phantasmagoria arguably culminated, as Michael Rogin has suggested, in D. W. Griffith's transformation of American history as such into film per se. "Presented as a transparent representation of history, ... the film [*The Birth of a Nation*] actually aimed to emancipate the representation from its referent and draw the viewer out of history into film."[13]

This appreciation of the illusory helps to explain why, as I argue in the final section of this chapter, W. E. B. Du Bois, in his 1903 short story of a lynching, "Of the Coming of John," alludes to Wagnerian opera – a paradigmatic site of grand, indeed grandiose, illusion. Further, he countervails the

American penchant for varieties of personal, public, and national farce by representing a black person's shift into something like a supra-operatic mode of consciousness. Du Bois noted elsewhere not only that the lynch mob operated behind "a veil of vengeance," but also that Southern "[w]hite men *became a law unto themselves.*"[14] In this story he indicts both the affective falseness of lynch mobs and their disingenuous appropriation of law. In *The Souls of Black Folk*'s single fictional narrative he redirects the lynch scenario away from its conventional signification of blacks' abused, terrorized place within Southern (or, more generally, American) socio-economic matrices and toward his own project of deracialization and the neutralization of power. Moreover, insofar as the protagonist's actions and passions in the South are intimately bound up with his experience of urban crowds in the North, Du Bois rewrites Douglass's terminal logic in which the black urban soul goes the way of the black rural body. At the end of the story what remains is a profoundly unlocatable and anonymous shrillness – the bareness of the world whistling in the lynch victim's ears, as though he has entered the domain of pure law, pure force.

When Du Bois uses the phrase, becoming a law unto oneself, he obviously means something quite different from Merwin's idea of self- and nation-strengthening solitude. Du Bois's anarchic lynch mob, carrying out what was known as lynch *law*, embodies violent force, not intelligent "serenity" or imaginative "inward[ness]."[15] And yet the differences between Du Bois's version and Merwin's version of the phrase are less stable than they appear. Merwin's exhortation to become, as an artistic genius does, a law unto oneself seems at first to echo the Kantian account of the artist who does not conform to established rules and instead creates his or her own. In many respects this is also, for instance, what Merwin's contemporary George Du Maurier means in his bestselling novel *Trilby* (1894) when he, paraphrasing Kant, describes the "genius" of the two (fictional) reigning English painters: "absolutely original, receiving their impressions straight from nature itself; they founded schools instead of following any, and each man was a law unto himself, and a law-giver unto many others."[16] The focus here is on the artist's *production*, rather than the artist's *being*.

Yet *Trilby*, like so many accounts of genius, is also deeply concerned with the artist's mental state. From Diderot's proto-romantic self-forgetting actor to Nietzsche's post-romantic self-surpassing Dionysus, modernity's paradigmatic artistic genius is one whose inwardness resembles a crowd-like loss of personality. In *Trilby* the two acclaimed, law-giving painters are marked by a tendency to fall into such self-forgetfulness. In one scene Du Maurier depicts the two playing cup and ball together at an elite soirée: "both so rapt in the game that they were unconscious of anything else, and both playing so well (with either hand) that they might have been professional champions!" Of course, it is the tone-deaf Trilby herself who exemplifies this state *in extremis*. Hypnotized by the evil genius-musician Svengali, she becomes the most sensational vocalist ever to appear on the Continent and in England. She possesses the "mathematically pure" voice, embodying the "apotheosis of voice and virtuosity." And it is in this mode of borrowed genius that she, in turn, magnetizes the audience, which "bursts once more into madness" at the conclusion of her performance. Additionally, "journalistic acclamation" has itself "gone mad."[17] In other words, Trilby and her crowds of admirers mirror each other's transported states of being. Like genius, like (lynch or spectator) crowd: each becomes a law unto itself.

In such flights of genius Merwin ostensibly has no interest. He envisions artistic genius as a means of producing solitary individuals fit for a modern civilized nation, not one diva with her primal horde. But in his bid to key genius to this purpose he scants constitutive features of aesthetic and political discourses that would advance his cause. And without them Merwin, like the social psychologists discussed in the Introduction, has no conceptual mechanism to separate categorically the innovative artist from the imitative artist, the "civilized" nation from the "primitive" clan. The mechanism with the potential to sever genius from a crowd mentality and to bind it to a civil collectivity is Kantian common sense. It is not merely originality that makes a genius, according to Kant. As he remarks, "there may also be original nonsense."[18] Rather, a genius is one whose mental aptitude, in giving the rule to art, enables him or her to create communicable, intelligible works of art. As discussed in previous chapters, this communicability undergirds the beholder's ability to make aesthetic judgments about it and implies this autonomous beholder's a priori reflective and critical capacities, who then occupies a place within a public, not a crowd.

The absence of a public common sense is more pronounced where Merwin brings his arguments to bear on the state of the nation. While he does envision an artistic genius whose works are intelligible, he stops short of providing this "proper individual" with the mental aptitude required of a liberal democratic nation. He overlooks the ethical component that, for instance, John Dewey foregrounds in his 1888 account of what it means to be politically a law unto oneself. Inflected, to be sure, with Hegelian more than strictly Kantian concepts, in his essay, "The Ethics of Democracy," Dewey defends democracy against Plato's and Henry Maine's charge of its anarchic dangers, insisting that its ideals of liberty, equality, and fraternity comprise "the highest ethical idea that humanity has yet reached." Dewey goes on to claim that democracy is engendered by "the spirit of personality indwell[ing] in every individual." This mode of individualism is not lawless but lawful:

[F]rom the democratic standpoint, it must be remembered that the individual is something more than the individual, namely, a personality. His freedom is not mere self-assertion, nor unregulated desire. You cannot say that he knows no law; you must say that *he knows no law but his own*, the law of personality ... Liberty is not a numerical notion of isolation; it is the ethical idea that personality is the supreme and only law, that *every man is an absolute end in himself.*

Dewey's democrat not only is his own law but knows it; this self-knowledge is what distinguishes him from the force-fed artistic genius. He realizes the "universal" ideal of "freedom, of responsibility, of initiative"; he manifests his "devotion to the interests of the social organism." He is thus capable of being united with others also so inclined – capable, that is, of forming a more numerous public.[19]

In effect Dewey updates the biblical version of being a law unto oneself. In the New Testament the apostle Paul speaks of Gentiles in this manner: "For when the Gentiles, which have not the law, do by nature the things contained in the law, these, having not the law, are a law unto themselves." The remaining verses in the chapter clarify that a law is not so much something to possess in letter as to embody in spirit: "which shew the work of the law written in their hearts, their conscience also bearing witness."[20] In this case the gentiles who conform to the law seemingly need no external or divine threat to motivate their conformity because individual conscience already guides them. Dewey's Kantian redescription of Christian conscience as secular, democratic ethics, in which each man is an end in himself, brings with it a number of implicit stipulations. In presupposing self-consciousness and reasonable respect for others, it eliminates from the field of being a law unto oneself both the artist's self-forgetting and the lynch mob's anarchic vengeance. It fortifies the common sense of Merwin's proper individual by making a *socius*-directed self-knowledge rather than inward solitude the standard measure. Further, it excludes the appeal that lynch-law proponents sometimes made to a supra-human "higher law," by understanding human personality as the seat of law.[21]

With Merwin's general anthropological slant, backed by pointed references to Galton's work, it is easy to see why the political-liberal version of becoming a law unto oneself held little appeal. For while it might open the way for a meditation on the political structure of the United States, it offered little for someone interested in national identity. And it is the nation's character – its vices and virtues – that exercises Merwin. In this discursive market Galton's scientistic authority offered much. Galton's understanding of genius as an inherited, psycho-biological reality dovetailed with evolutionary anthropology's understanding of genius as a racial, hence *national*, characteristic. Gustave Le Bon, for instance, uses "genius" and "soul" interchangeably in his account of the relation between race and nation. In his *Psychology of Peoples* (published in 1894 as *Les lois psychologiques de l'evolution des peuples*, translated into English in 1898), Le Bon claims that a nation's homogeneity derives from racial stability. While conceding that only among savages "is [it] possible to find peoples of absolute purity," the "civilized" "historical races are sufficiently ancient," and to be understood as anatomical, psychological, and physiological realities, hence as "unaltering." The "invisible" racial soul thus constituted, it "proceeds from the most general, the most primordial of these permanent laws... [which] govern the general course of each civilisation." Le Bon can thus claim that the "national soul" *precedes* the "notion" of a "native country." When Le Bon sums up his argument of *The Psychology of Peoples* in his subsequent book *The Crowd*, he refers to the way an historical race "possesses, as the result of the laws of heredity such power that its beliefs, institutions, and arts... are merely the outward expression of its genius." Here he also contends that a nation, whose "race carries in its mental constitution the laws of its destiny," thus abides by the "secret forces" of nature.[22]

In short, the soul (the genius) is the law (the force) that animates the race (the nation). This constellation enables Le Bon to imagine a racially homogeneous nation becoming a law unto itself. Soul and genius make race inhere in national identity. The "really intelligent" nation that Merwin and Galton hold dear will emerge, according to this logic, when its people leave off the primitive gregarious instincts and tap into the race's yet more primitive genius. Merwin's seamless slide from the aesthetic to the political, from solitary artistic genius to solitary national genius, exemplifies one manner in which an intelligent modern nation could be imagined without a nod to the political-liberal public. That is, Merwin looks not to the crowd's categorical antithesis, the public, but rather to the crowd's racial relative: the more restrained, more intelligent, more innovative genius in the family.[23]

As an indirect but well-timed message to his readers, the likes of whom would be on their way to exercise their gregariousness at the Columbian Exposition, Merwin preaches to a sympathetic but not entirely indoctrinated choir. Other, more direct responses to the Fair as a site of collectivity prove less averse to either enthused crowds or reasoning publics. Indeed, they discursively require both conceptions of collectivity. Nevertheless, as we shall see, they too contribute to the diminishment of the public as a constituent feature of the national polity. They too thereby enable the imagination of the United States as a homogeneously white, highly civilized, urban nation.

WHITE CITY: THE CROWD, THE PUBLIC, THE NATION

Frederick Douglass's post-Exposition comments on the Chicago World's Fair's treatment of black Americans reiterate his views published earlier in March, 1893 (that is, before the Fair opened but after the October, 1892 inauguration ceremonies, which he attended as United States ambassador to Haiti). In both publications, even as he condemns the Fair for forsaking, in its methodical exclusion of blacks, the nation's principles of justice and equality, he praises the Fair's general purpose and function. For, as he puts it in the earlier article, it "spoke of human brotherhood, human welfare, and human progress." He goes on to describe how the Fair stages its celebration of these ideals not so much by speaking as by making sounds "more eloquent than speech": The "occasion [being] too great for oratory, too great for music or poetry," the "thronged" and "crowded" spectators let their approval be expressed through "shouts of applause."[24] Semantically grounded as the word "eloquent" is in speech, it is technically suitable to qualify manners *of* speech, rather than manners of expression *other than* speech. Yet Douglass's linguistic jolt fits the occasion; for he goes on figuratively to disjoin this festive crowd from itself, much as turn-of-the-century social psychologists do when they diagnose crowd collectivity as entailing, to quote Robert Park from 1904, a "suggestive reciprocity reach[ing] a certain degree of intensity" so as to produce a "psychic current," a "unity" whose "collective being [is] different from its component members."[25] In other words, the reciprocity between participants is so intense as to eliminate reciprocity itself: rather magically a single unself-conscious unity appears where there once was a multiplicity of self-conscious units.

Similarly Douglass: "I heard that strange and weird hum and buzz of the one hundred thousand voices blended into one sound, like the roar of many waters. I observed the profound and miraculous hush which fell upon that vast human ocean at the first call to order."[26] As the crowd weirdly buzzes and hums like a swarm of insects and roars like water, its constituent members simultaneously ratify their membership within the human community and are themselves disengaged from that realm. Using metaphors of the inhuman and inanimate, along with onomatopoeia, to represent a more eloquent – and a more than eloquent – unity, Douglass's rhetorical strategies resemble, as we shall see, Fair boosters' representations of municipal, public, and national unity.

Records show that the Columbian Exposition attracted over twenty-seven million visitors, more than any previous World's Fair. This pleased the Chicago Fair's boosters, whose general outlook was bigger meant better and biggest meant best. Their Fair could also boast the largest indoor structure in the world, the Liberal Arts and Manufactures Building, which, at 31.5 acres, held some 100,000 persons for the Fair's dedication ceremony.[27] The largest crowd of all turned out on Chicago Day, 9 October, the anniversary of the city's great fire in 1871, prompting James Buel, author of the 1894 book of photographs of the Fair, *The Magic City*, to make the following remarks in the caption to a photograph of this day's crowd:

Never before in the history of the world was there such a crowd as was drawn to the World's Fair on October 9th[.] . . . Immense preparations had been made in anticipation of an unprecedented number of visitors[.] . . . People gathered there from every point of the compass to take part in the rejoicing, and the citizens opened their treasures of wealth to make the triumphant jubilation an occasion of unexampled splendor . . . A tremendous procession, martial, commercial, and civilian, paraded the streets with what appeared an endless line of allegoric floats, and banners waved everywhere, the insignia of patriotic pride. The joyful multitudes poured into the Exposition grounds until the six hundred and thirty three acres could scarcely accommodate any more. The record of the day showed 751,000 admissions, more than double the number of persons that attended the great Paris Exposition on any one day.[28]

The "patriotic pride" that these remarks both record and exhibit, I want to suggest, is not simply pride in the immensity of the Exposition's crowds per se but in these crowds' capacity to represent a nationalized public of whose purpose the crowd itself is proudly aware. In other words, insofar as the Exposition literally and figuratively moves the nation's masses to gather anonymously, to be educated, and to reinforce a national identity, it seems to dramatize, by in effect incarnating, what political theorist Ernest Gellner in *Nations and Nationalism* describes as the basic requirements of the modern nation: that it be a "mobile, anonymous, literate, identity-conferring culture."[29]

Another Fair publicist, George Miles, makes explicit the endeavor to co-ordinate municipal, public, and national collectivity when he describes Chicago in his *World's Fair from London 1851 to Chicago 1893* (1892) as having "a right to claim the enthusiastic co-operation of the whole country," and as a "municipality, equal to every demand, and [possessing] a public-spirited citizenship whose Americanism is pledged, as is the Nation, to [the Fair's] splendid success."[30] If the Fair's success hinges on the practical co-operation of a municipality's Americanism and a nation's Americanism, Buel's and Miles's rhetorical success hinges on the conceptual co-operation – in effect, the interchangeability – of two modes of aggregation: the state of *being united* through reasoned consent, as in the case of public-spirited urban dwellers, and the state of *being unified* through affective fusion, as in the case of the nation's patriotic crowds.

Certain official nationalists, for their part, exalted affective fusion, under the sign of patriotism. Theodore Roosevelt, for instance, urges "love of country [as] one of the elemental virtues" of being American. Unequivocal, single-minded patriotism is essential to meet "the dangers that confront us," specifically, the dangers of immigrants' hyphenated allegiance, of natives' "unwholesome parochial spirit," and of anarchists' "provincial patriotism." In Roosevelt's Manichean universe of "either fail[ing] or succeed[ing] greatly" in the face of these "many threatening evils," the "one quality which we must bring to the solution of every problem... [is] *an intense and fervid* Americanism."[31] Such affective unity derives its conceptual plausibility from a crowd collectivity.

On the other hand, the nation also requires discerning and discriminating aptitudes. As Gellner clarifies, it requires an internally functioning mode of recognition:

[T]wo men are of the same nation if and only if they *recognize* each other as belonging to the same nation... [Persons become] a nation if and when the members of the category firmly recognize certain mutual rights and duties to each other in virtue of their shared membership of it. It is this recognition of each other as fellows of this kind which turns them into a nation, and not the shared attributes, what ever they may be.

Such recognition comes about, according to Herbert Croly in *The Promise of American Life* (1909), only when citizens assume a "disinterested patriotism." It takes a patriotism "reinforced by intellectual insight" to maintain not only "loyalty" but also political "responsibility."[32] In other words, it takes a public.

However categorically distinct as the crowd and the public were, World's Fair boosters tended to splice the two together, as though hoping to overcome their constitutive incompatibilities through rapid oscillation. Illustrative of this rhetorical method is Palmer's speech cited earlier. In it he goes on to remark that civic instruction is necessary both to sharpen the nation's future geopolitical edge and to overcome its recent violent past of civil war:

If we are to remain a free people, if the States are to retain their autonomy, if we are to take a common pride in the name of America, if we are to avoid the catastrophe of former years, Americans must *commingle*, be brought in contact and acquire *that mutual sympathy* that is essential in a harmonious family. Isolated, independent travel may do this, but not to any such extent as will be accomplished by gatherings like this, where *millions will concentrate to consult and compare* the achievements of each other and of those from across the sea . . . Many will come from selfish motives, possibly, but the social atmosphere they will here breathe, *that indefinable influence that pervades and affects people who come together in masses* with a common purpose, will broaden them and teach them that discussion and not violence is the proper way to adjust differences or promote objects – and thus prepare humanity for that good time so long coming.[33]

This hopeful imagination of the Fair as a sort of site-specific performance piece dedicated to transforming spectator crowds into public- and nation-minded citizens mixes and matches the laws of the crowd and the public. Palmer's collected population is at once deeply sympathetic and readily educable, exhibiting an ambidexterity that runs counter to the claims of contemporaneous psychology. According to the era's crowd psychologists, if the visiting "millions" "concentrate" so as to imbibe that "indefinable influence" of the masses, education will be the least of their capacities. Far from engaging in the cognitive activities of consulting and comparing achievements, of discussion and education, as Palmer envisions the millions touching elbows to do, Le Bon claims that crowds "do not reason, that they accept or reject ideas as a whole, that they tolerate neither discussion nor contradiction, and that the suggestions brought to bear on them invade the entire field of their understanding." Where Palmer imagines that the "indefinable influence" pervading gathered crowds will instruct them in citizenship, Le Bon argues that this very condition – this "indefinable influence," which he often calls "contagion" – induces precisely the "hypnotic order" that renders crowds uneducable, indeed, entirely unreasonable and unreasoning. A "crowd," he contends, "is no more capable than an inorganic mass of following [logical] associations, nor even of understanding them."[34]

Where Palmer's splicing conjoins the unconjoinable (by putting the crowd's sympathy and influence in the service of public consciousness-raising), other Fair representations show the gathering effect to resolve into something like individual persons' own private crowd minds – minds that are fully alert but nonetheless fully detached from the civic activity of consulting and comparing. For instance, one report on Chicago Day describes the visitors' thwarted efforts to be civic-minded:

Nobody could study the exhibits on this occasion. When the visitors entered the mighty current they were carried along like so many pieces of wood on the surface of a river. Once and a while they would drift by some interesting thing and stop for a moment to gaze at it only to be started on in the stream of humanity by an irresistible force behind.

Such visitors exhibit not so much the empirical *loss* of consciousness (others, in fact, do faint in the crush)[35] as the material *limit* of consciousness. Like Douglass's applauding crowd, but in a more random, less synchronized manner, the water-borne woodenness of these visitors marks them as intermittently alive neither to the instructional nor entertainment value of the displays. "Still," the same (unnamed) writer continues, "they enjoyed it. They were part of the mightiest gathering the world had ever witnessed, and it was something to be proud of."[36] This adverb of contrast ("still") points to a disjunction – rather than an alignment as in Palmer's depiction – between the crowd's absent-mindedness and the public's presence of mind, the latter being capable of "pride" and cognizant of "being part of" the crowd drift.

   Given the propensity, as these verbal representations suggest, of Fair visitors to enter into their own private, hence unco-ordinated, crowd-like domains, visual images of gathered participants visibly in sync and resembling a public more than a crowd offered perhaps a more promising way of figuring the American people's self-awareness of their national unity: one blood, one language, one God, one flag (to recall Palmer's terms). Surely something along these lines is what Fair organizers had in mind when they elected to have public school children, during various ceremonies, not simply salute one flag but visually *incarnate* one flag (see illustration 3). Donning, in their sartorial collectivity, the symbols of the nation – the stars and stripes – these children make visible the unified identity of a national-ized public sphere. It is worth considering this photograph in the context of contemporary debates that couple embodiment with a politics of inclusion and, conversely, abstraction with a politics of exclusion. Michael Warner, for instance, remarks that "it would be better . . . to make reference to one's marked particularities without being specified thereby as less than pub-lic," suggesting that embodiment does not but should have a fundamental, legitimate presence in the public sphere.[37]

   At first glance the image of the live flag seems to verify the historical claim that public inclusion involves an erasure of particularity, of personal

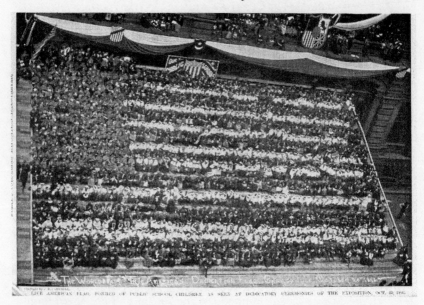

3   *Live American flag, formed of public school children as seen at the dedicatory ceremonies of the Exposition,* 20 October 1892. *World's Columbian Exposition Illustrated,* 1893.

embodiment. For the purposes of this panoramic photograph, at least, the organizers of the "live American flag" might as well have dressed man- nequins in the appropriately co-ordinated uniforms. However, further con- sideration suggests (assuming that the sign at the top of the human flag and the caption beneath the image are meant as truth claims) that the only way to be actually or associatively included in this public perfor- mance is through the *particular* qualification of childhood. But this does not mean that particularity has *replaced* the abstract individual as the only necessary condition of the public's possibility. Quite the contrary: it means that any materialized public will necessarily possess particularities, whether these publics be socio-politically negligible (such as children) or acceptable (such as white adult males). As an artifact of turn-of-the-century official culture, this photograph obviously subscribes to the conventional view that properly educated children (in contrast, of course, to the era's greatly feared hordes of uneducated immigrant adults) will someday become proper citizens, or at least voting citizens' wives; which is to say that their partic- ularities promise eventually to be masked by historically contingent tech- nologies of personhood so as to make these embodied persons look like abstract individuals. In short, the principle of abstraction might be visually obscured by the school children's bodies but it is by no means conceptually eliminated.

As important for securing the conceptual validity of the abstract individual as showing the inclusion of embodied persons is the photograph's allegorization of the exclusion of the abstract individual, which it accomplishes by including the person on the extreme left, in the middle of the flight of stairs, outside the frame of the flag. There are two figures: the one on the right, in top hat and trousers is obviously an adult male; the other, however, the one halved by the photograph's edge, is far less easily identifiable. It might be a boy or a girl, a child or an adult doubled over. The distance needed by the camera to capture the live American flag renders this "excluded," isolated individual far more abstract than the color-co-ordinated public children.[38] The terms boy, girl, child, and adult, are of course categories of identity, of embodiment, hence incompatible with the principle of abstraction, or related to it only as epiphenomena. While historical contingencies may have rendered some of these identities sociopolitically more negligible than others, the sliced, shadowy figure recalls the logical necessity of the ontologically abstract.

The image's success at conveying school children's (proleptic) public value, at foregrounding their abstract uniformity, and at bestowing particularity on group identity rather than personal identity, goes far to confirm abstract being (singular or plural) as a fundamental principle of the public sphere. It also goes far to confirm official culture's pedagogical ideal, as articulated by President Cleveland during the Fair's opening ceremonies. It is an ideal that pertains both to the public school system and the Columbian Exposition:

We who believe that popular education and the stimulation of the best impulses of our citizens lead the way to [the] realization of the proud national destiny which our faith promises, gladly welcome the opportunity here afforded us . . . We have made and have gathered together objects of use and beauty, the products of American skill and invention; but *we have also made men who rule themselves.*[39]

This vision of American education producing self rule maps onto the photograph of uniform public school children only if self rule is understood in a manner akin to Dewey's democratic public individuation, so that uniformity is seen not to be externally enforced by clothes, but simply the outcome of each child's accession to his or her inner law of reason.

But as the flag incarnate effaces practically all personal particularity, and as the persons incarnating the flag have not yet attained majority (and thus remain biologically marked, according to crowd psychologists,

4 *The surging sea of humanity*, 1893, Benjamin Kilburn. Courtesy of the Charles Rand Penney 1893 World's Columbian Exposition Collection.

as particularly susceptible to the forces of imitation-suggestion), the image also goes far to make the individuating principle of the public look like the homogenizing principle of the crowd. Recalling that the Columbian Exposition occasioned Francis Bellamy's drafting of the "Pledge of Allegiance," these children of the "live American flag" might well be understood as saluting themselves – as having fallen prey to a crowd-like psychic reciprocity, in which case they redundantly pledge themselves to themselves. The circular attentiveness of this auto-attracted crowd would thus render public school children essentially uneducable (in the Le Bonian sense). Either their conduct happens to accord with pedagogical directives, and they take their places within the flag frame, or it does not, and they are relegated to the steps.[40]

An image of collectivity that reinstates personal particularity as diversity is Benjamin Kilburn's stereograph of the Exposition's opening day. Kilburn, who with his partner was the only party granted official permission to make stereographs of the Exposition, offers in his popular and widely distributed image entitled *The Surging Sea of Humanity* (illustration 4), a nearly eye-level yet also panoramic view of a vast outdoor space completely filled with homogeneously well-dressed, only mildly rambunctious, Fair visitors. Unlike conventional panoramas (such as the frequently reprinted photograph of the crowds on Chicago Day), where the camera's elevation is so great that persons are registered as more or less discrete, evenly nondescript entities, Kilburn's stereograph ranges from the specific, animated features of persons in the foreground to the synecdochically functioning derbies in the middle-ground, and finally to the background of abstract marks of black and grey. This representation of collectivity, perhaps more than any other discussed in this chapter, renders virtually indistinguishable the crowd and the public. Just as the blank space separating the nearly but not quite identical left and right images amounts to a spatial analogue of the viewer's physiological blind spot (which enables the stereoscopic apparatus to function – that is, to make two two-dimensional images look like one three-dimensional, crowd-filled space), the combined pictorial and verbal components of the stereograph concoct the illusion of a gathered "humanity" that resolves itself simultaneously into a crowd and a public.

As Kilburn's stereograph indexically registers both the highly resolved details of the persons up front, thereby imbuing them with specificity and recognizability, and the essentially exchangeable figures in back, the image serves as proof positive of the public's twin constitutive features, embodiment and abstraction. The male figure slightly left of and below the center of the crowd, who points back at the camera or viewer, as though to establish eye contact and identification, marks this group's capacity to create a bond based on intelligent, self-aware conviction.

Yet superimposed on these graphic indicators of a public sphere are the image's kinetic and metaphorical conceits, supplied verbally by the caption's reference to the "surging sea." Kilburn's ekphrasis turns away from photochemical literalness and toward figurative literariness, counting heavily on the viewer's attraction to the phantasmagoric illusion of crowdedness. From this standpoint the slightly admonitory arm gesture of the male figure mentioned above has the effect of a miniature ego before a monstrous id. The viewer's (literary) eye sweeps over and beyond him, induced by the cropped frame to imagine an endless horizontal expanse of multitudes not shown. The affective intensity of, say, the gleefully open-mouthed woman near the bottom right (or the grimacing man clutching his throat three heads behind her) points to that "surge" of psychic reciprocity that liquifies united persons into a unified crowd. Her emotional surge toward inanimate homogeneity is echoed by what might be called the formal or technological surging brought about by the ever so slight difference between the stereograph's two images. It keeps the roving eye – *sans* stereoscopic apparatus – ever so slightly off balance.

It was suggested earlier that, at the turn of the century in Europe and the United States the *deus ex machina* that co-ordinated the crowd and the public, keying both to the nation, took the form of race. Bearing the trappings of a biologically and anthropologically natural perpetuity, race could serve to prop up the very idea of unified homogeneity. In the United States, however, the topography of race and heredity, nation and tradition, was markedly shiftier than in Europe. Facing the nation's past, present, and likely future of immigration, nationalists who invoked race often echoed Crèvecoeur in their appeal to the people's on-going capacity to mix blood and melt difference. Since the late 1880s Roosevelt had espoused the making of a new American race, a "new and distinct ethnic type."[41] Similarly Croly: though he envisions a "living nation" as one populated by an "invisible multitude of spirits" (quoting Bismarck from 1847), he does not go so far as to confer on this "true people" a collective racial past. Indeed, he distances Americanism from a "merely instinctive national tradition" whose source is a military or "racial political principle." Race has – as his endorsement of Crèvecoeur's designation of America's "new race of men" suggests – proleptic, not historical, relevance.[42] More precisely, as an historical phenomenon, race registers the proleptic *becoming* of an American, not the a priori *being* of one, as biological nationalism demands. Transformation itself thus becomes the American tradition. The stipulation of being racially "new" replaces Le Bon's of being "sufficiently ancient."

While Roosevelt's and Croly's validation of a new American race makes, as Michaels explains, "the very idea of American citizenship...a racial and even racist idea," insofar as "it confers on national identity something like the ontology of race," it is not until this idea of race is anchored specifically in whiteness that racial identity and national identity coincide, and that Northern and Southern sectional divisions are reconcilable.[43] The following discussion takes up how postbellum lynching, as a specific mode of collectivity, contributes to this whitening of the American race, thence to the homogeneous unity of the nation. Predictably it does so by appropriating the demonic energy of the mob; but also, less predictably, by appropriating the decency, the civilized serenity, of a collected public.[44] When Harriet Beecher Stowe's mulatto paragon of virtue and intelligence George Harris reappears as a minor character in Thomas Dixon Jr.'s *The Leopard's Spots* (1902), he embarks on a "strange journey" across the country, placing "wreath[s] of costly flowers" on the ash-heap[s] of lynch victims: "strangest of all, he found one of these ash-heaps in the public square."[45] As the national crime of lynching goes public, it thereby falls in step with the nation's preferred self-representation as modern and urban.

THE LAWFULNESS OF LYNCHING

Lynch law opponents and apologists alike drew attention to the frenzied, mobbish behavior of the lynchers. In *Southern Horrors*, for instance, Wells contrasts the lynchers' violent beastliness to the codes of conduct governing modern civility, through whose institutions the lynchers pass:

They go into the town where everybody knows them, sometimes under the gaze of the governor, in the presence of the courts, in the presence of the sheriff and his deputies, in the presence of the entire police force, take out the prisoner, take his life, often with fiendish glee, and often with acts of cruelty and barbarism which impress the reader with a degeneracy rapidly approaching savage life.[46]

Even Roosevelt – garden variety white supremacist, gradualist, and North-South conciliator – decried in 1906 lynchers' actions as "avenging in bestial fashion a bestial deed, and reducing themselves to a level with the criminal."[47]

With equal vehemence the lynching proponent Senator Ben Tillman in 1907 appealed to mob violence as the necessary and inevitable response to blacks' transgressions:

And shall such a creature [the black rapist]...appeal to the law? Shall men cold-bloodedly stand up and demand for him the right to have a fair trial and be punished in the regular course of justice? So far as I am concerned he has put himself outside the pale of the law, human and divine... Civilization peels off us, any and all of us who are men, and we revert to the original savage type whose impulses under any and all circumstances has always been to "kill! kill! kill!"[48]

Tillman's notoriously brazen advocacy of mob violence was only slightly more extreme than Dixon's version in *The Leopard's Spots*. Even though the hero Charles Gaston balks at the violent lynching of his childhood playmate Dick for the assault on Flora, the crowd gains magnitude and legitimacy by taking on a mythical, cosmic, hence inevitable, life of its own. It has "melt[ed] into a great crawling swaying creature, half reptile half beast, half dragon half man, with a thousand legs, and a thousand eyes, and ten thousand gleaming teeth." Such mobbing beastliness makes possible, as Sandra Gunning in *Race, Rape, and Lynching* observes, the imagination of a "classless racial solidarity." Dixon writes: "the white race had fused into a homogeneous mass of love, sympathy, hate and revenge. The rich and the poor, the learned and the ignorant, the banker and the blacksmith, the great and the small, they were all one now." As both Dixon's fiction and Tillman's propaganda graft the crowd's primitive energies onto a socio-political fantasy of racial and class homogeneity, they imbue the lynch mob with the auratic appeal of what Rogin calls a crusading "sacred brotherly horde."[49]

Tillman's comments, moreover, make explicit the ever-present tension between mob action and statutory law, what Dixon melodramatizes as the Clan's choice "to violate for the moment a statutory law" for the sake of "a higher law."[50] "Lynch law," of course, predates its racialized connotation and application, earlier associated as it was with colonial and frontier society's ostensible need to resort to "popular justice" when civic institutions regulating and punishing offenders proved insufficiently effectual. "Lynch-law," James Cutler writes in his 1905 social scientific study of the phenomenon, "has always been considered as operating wholly without, or in opposition to, established laws of government." Maintaining that lynch-law in "its origin...was no more blameable than were the laws established by the Pilgrim fathers," Cutler explains how the practice could be refashioned at the turn of the century to meet the sensibilities of a modern public, one committed to at least a semblance of democratic governance and due process. Indeed, Cutler's treatise itself participates in this refashioning.[51] It serves to close the gap – or to effect the exchange – between lawlessness and lawfulness, between the crowd mind and the public square.

Cutler achieves this rapprochement by in effect rehabilitating antebellum lynching episodes; he does this both by empathizing with frontier society's ostensible needs for swift punishment, and by minimizing lynchers' retributive impulses while stressing their commitment to natural rights and freedoms. He quotes from the ever-trustworthy Northern Unitarian W. E. Channing's 1839 comments on lynching: "In such a case, the public without law do the work of law, and enforce those natural, eternal principles of right, on which all legislation should rest." By this logic, when "congregated thousands" – and here Cutler quotes the "rightly named" Judge Lawless from an 1836 account of a Saint Louis lynching – have worked themselves into a "mysterious, metaphysical, and almost electric phrenzy" so as to be "beyond the reach of human law," they do so in the name of that which governs human law: eternal right.[52]

Yet more consequential for Cutler's refashioning of lawlessness as lawfulness is Judge Lawless's opinion that the lynching action is legitimate if accomplished by "the multitude," and not by "a *small* number of individuals, separate from the mass." For later in the book Cutler suggests how mob action might accord with the principles of democracy. Contending that the "democratic spirit" makes it "inevitable that the legal machinery will prove powerless to control popular excitements," he goes on to clarify how "spirit" in effect converts lawlessness into lawfulness:

In a democracy... [t]he *people consider themselves a law unto themselves*. They make the laws; therefore they can unmake them. Since they say what a judge can do, they entertain the idea that they may do this thing themselves. To execute a criminal deserving of death is to act merely in their sovereign capacity, temporarily dispensing with their agents, the legal administrators of the law.

Not unlike contemporary postmodern theorists' privileging of particularity, Cutler's claim about the "inevitab[ility]" of lynching rests on the equation of the "democratic spirit" with state and local *difference*, what he calls the "republican form of government." The "moral sentiment of the community" determines the law.[53]

Such privileging of the local, Herbert Croly argued, cannot avoid the "error" of confusing a bona fide "authoritative popular Sovereignty" – based on a nation's "collective purpose" and its intractable assertion of "fundamental law" – with "the majority vote" whose "arbitrary and dangerous tendencies" must not be ignored. In other words, only the peremptory, authoritative assertion of liberal principles, rights, and protections, only the maintenance of what Croly sees as the national "tradition" of "absolute Sovereign authority," can parry the attacks of Cutler's all too democratic spirit.[54]

Wells's anti-lynching campaign strategies reflect this turn-of-the-century tension between Cutler's populist democracy and Croly's liberal nationalist democracy. That is, she pragmatically acknowledges yet conceptually rejects the era's conflation of the crowd mind and the public square. Her acknowledgement is implicit in the dramatic, at times sentimental form of her activism, bent as she was on swaying public sentiment via the press and publicity (as opposed, say, to working through legislative channels). Her concomitant rejection is visible in the content of her anti-lynching appeal. Facing a climate of opinion that held lynch law to be what Cutler called a "species of common law," Wells harped on American society's "hypocrisy and duplicity," its "false and shallow pretense" of racially equitable conditions (whether in the realm of hiring practices, judicial due process, or self-representation). This is a line of argument that in principle excludes the personal or particular element from the democratic public sphere. "Virtue knows no color line," Wells maintains, going on to demand "Equality before the law."[55]

While Wells herself was committed rather to Croly's than to Cutler's description of the national democratic form, the evidence she collects of the era's lynching practices – an era in which there appears to have been more lynchings than due-process executions – indicates the widespread acceptance of Cutler's common law. She indicts Americans for not even attempting to conceal their moral and civic degeneracy, their abandonment of liberal principles:

Masks have long since been thrown aside and the lynchings of the present day take place in broad daylight. The sheriffs, police and state officials stand by and see the work well done. The coroner's jury is often formed among those who took part in the lynching and a verdict, "Death at the hands of parties unknown to the jury" is rendered... Under these conditions, white men have only to blacken their faces, commit crimes against the peace of the community, accuse some Negro, nor rest till he is killed by a mob.[56]

Charles Chesnutt's 1899 story, "The Sheriff's Children," dramatizes this sort of unconcealed duplicity. Upon the murder of a white man and the sheriff's arrest of a black stranger, the white men of the town decide, after drinking enough "moonlight whiskey" to obliterate lingering "vague notions of the majesty of the law and the rights of citizen," to lynch the suspect. The sheriff, who "had sworn to do his duty faithfully and knew what his duty was, as sheriff," successfully fends off the mob from inside the jailhouse. But, as he negotiates with the men from behind "a little wicket in the door" enabling him to see them, he also makes a point of not seeing them, of calling them "strangers": "The sheriff did not think it necessary to recognize anybody in particular on such an occasion; the question of identity sometimes comes up in the investigation of extra-judicial executions."[57]

Not only would the lynch mob pass with impunity by the governor, the courts, and the police, as Wells describes, but the lynching event could occasion a relatively grand and formal public gathering. Wells's reproduction in *A Red Record* of excerpts from the New York *Sun's* account of an 1893 lynching in Paris, Texas reveals striking parallels between people gathering to witness a lynching and people gathering to look, say, at school children saluting the flag at the Columbian Exposition. Not only is much made of the "special trains" hired to bring in spectators, but also, recalling Exposition President Palmer's vision of the "commingling of our people from East, West, North, and South," the report describes how "[p]eople were here from every part of this section. They came from Dallas, Fort Worth, Sherman, Denison, Bonham, Texarkana, [and] Fort Smith." Kilburn's stereograph caption re-appears almost verbatim: the "surging mass of humanity" in attendance is described as alternately "worked up to a great... frenzy," in which "[n]o one was himself," and "look[ing] calmly on" the acts of torture inflicted on the still living victim. Yet more illustrative of a deliberative public-spiritedness propping up the national crowd crime is Wells's documented account of the Memphis daily paper, the *Public Ledger's* complicity. In anticipation of a lynching, it sent a telegram to Chicago's *Inter-Ocean* requesting them to "send Miss Ida Wells to write it up."[58]

Most revealing of all are two visual representations (one being an 1891 photograph, the other an 1893 engraving most likely made from a photograph) included in Wells's *The Reason Why* as well as *A Red Record*. They show proud, dignified, serene white men and boys squarely facing the camera, standing by their still hanging victim. Here we are confronted not so much with a nation's duplicity or false pretense as with its appallingly unpretentious, unprepossessed public sentiment. As representations of collectivity, these images establish retrospectively the lynchers' crowd-like homogeneity through the presence of the hanging man. His ritualized capture and execution would have necessarily involved brutal – but to the participants by no means unjust or criminal – action. And his blackness, expelled as it is from the living *socius*, registers this crowd's racial homogeneity. Meanwhile, the lynchers establish their public unity, fit for the nation form, through the men's and boys' direct, deliberate, reasoning gaze, signifying their reciprocal recognition of each other and their awareness of the camera that documents their group consensus. National crime shades into national virtue: these images represent a distinctively white collectivity's becoming a law unto itself in both senses of the phrase. Virtue indeed knows no color line because the only color to which virtue now applies is white. The photographs document Dixon's grand illusion, namely, "that the Negro was an impossibility in the newborn unity of national life."[59]

UNLYNCHING THE SOUL: THE MARRIAGE OF ONE AND ZERO

In Du Bois's *Black Reconstruction in America* the tone in which he describes the postbellum lynching epidemic is understandably defeatist:

A spirit of lawlessness became widespread. White people paid no attention to their own laws. White men became a law unto themselves . . . and the South reached the extraordinary distinction of being the only modern civilized country where human beings were publicly burned alive.[60]

The South's raising of the specter of black criminality succeeded, as Frederick Douglass put it at the time, in "lull[ing] the conscience of the north into indifference and reconcil[ing] its people to such murder."[61] If the effort to expose Southern crowds' lawlessness failed in part because of the South's success in subsuming it under democratic lawfulness, and the North's accession to this thin disguise, Du Bois's short story, "Of the Coming of John," can be understood as challenging this national picture of North-South reconciliation and public-crowd exchangeability. This chapter's final section examines how he does so, on the one hand, by exposing through melodramatic realism the sham conditions that enable such reconciliation and exchangeability; and on the other hand, by articulating through what might best be described as operatic impressionism a mode of de-racialized consciousness, one that entails appropriating the lynch mob as a site of affectively sublime aesthetics. He thus resignifies American racism's primal and paramount scene of the lynched black body. The effect of this resignification is to neutralize the lynch scene's conventional social and political signification of populist triumph, of racial distinction, and enforced African-American abjection.[62] Thus "Of the Coming of John" operates on two narratological fronts: the one enacts, not unlike Wells's campaign, an oppositional public protest against United States racial politics; the other affirms a sublime aesthetics of racial erasure. As this aesthetics entails the erasure of human identity per se, its telling formally necessitates a third-person point of view, such as Du Bois's fiction offers.

To begin with Du Bois's melodramatic realism, it can be seen as a response to modernity's racial and representational dialectic. No matter how grand the illusion of the Columbian Exposition's whiteness, no matter how thin the disguise of *Plessy's* equal accommodations or of the KKK's white sheets, the era's racial and representational topography was dialectically mapped out. There obtained the distinction between and reciprocal presupposition of illusion and reality, concealment and revelation, the essential whiteness of the American and the ineradicable blackness of the black. Affective correlates thickened this binary structuration: aesthetes enjoyed the non-deceiving illusion; white supremacists took pride in their whiteness; race activists deplored hypocritical politics and practices. For African-Americans, this social dialectic primed the melodramatic pump, reinforcing as it did their socio-economic deprivation and oppression – conditions which, as Du Bois explains in earlier chapters of *Souls*, foster a "tendency to excess, – radical complaint, radical remedies, bitter denunciation or angry silence."[63] His well-known autobiographical account of being "peremptorily" rejected by a schoolmate as a social equal, of having "with a certain suddenness" to see himself as "different from others" (*SBF* 44), further suggests the appropriateness of deploying melodrama, with its abrupt shifts in plot and its moral, affective, and situational extremes, to represent the dire realities of African-American life.

As Du Bois's fictional narrative unfolds, detailing the scientific, social, and aesthetic education of John Jones (both in the South at Johnstown's Institute and in New York City), it shows the protagonist's growing awareness of what it means to be black in the United States: educational and economic handicaps and Jim Crow ordinances comprise the external modes of oppression; susceptibility to "sarcasm," "bitterness," and "dread," the internal modes (*SBF* 250–251). The episode in which John Jones's white Southern counterpart John Henderson and the latter's white Northern date consort to have John Jones removed from the theater suggests how reconciliation of the South and North entails nationalizing Jim Crow policies and attitudes. The urban North's high culture, in the form of Wagner's *Lohengrin*, may offer John Jones aesthetic solace, a "world more beautiful than anything he had known" (*SBF* 252). But when he attempts to assimilate this beauty to his own life-world, so that the "infinite beauty of the [swan's] wail lingered and swept through every muscle of his frame, and put it all a-tune" (*SBF* 252), it becomes clear that the aesthetic mode best corresponding to his situation is not Wagnerian opera but some banal version of melodrama, with its all too glaring emotional colors, its all too obvious social divisions and moral dilemmas. For in the next scene John is thrust out of high aestheticism's contemplative mode and into the faux pas of having "touch[ed] unwittingly" the arm of a white woman, causing her to "dr[a]w away" (*SBF* 252). Social impropriety's real-life melodrama is compounded by narratological melodrama in the prefiguration of John's expulsion – both imminently from the theater's "dreamland" (*SBF* 252) and ultimately from life – when, just prior to this scene, Henderson's date "roguishly" comments, "you must not lynch the colored gentleman simply because he's in your way" (*SBF* 251). Besides adopting Jim Crow, North–South reconciliation invites adapting the subject of lynching to heterosexual flirtation.

Du Bois also puts melodrama's moral schematism to use. John Jones, having returned to his hometown Altamaha, faces both the uncomprehending black folk whom he has decided his mission is to educate and the obnoxious white folk who suspect him of stirring up trouble and subsequently shut down his school. This conflict culminates in John's fighting racist vice with moral virtue and heroic violence when he kills his sister's assaulter John Henderson. The story's villain, however, is not so much this white John as his father, Judge Henderson, who repeatedly puts John Jones down and blocks his efforts to uplift the black population. In making the foremost antagonist a civic leader, and then having this "haggard white-haired man, whose eyes flashed red with fury" lead the lynch mob that murders John (*SBF* 263), Du Bois draws attention to the means and effects of conflating the crowd and the public. He discloses the erosion of liberal justice when arbitrary crowd action poses as, or is confused with, publicly sanctioned law; and when public agents fail to exclude from their public actions personal or particular sentiments. Melodrama thus serves to display the thinness of Jim Crow's disguise as well as to indicate the peril of exchanging as though equivalent the crowd's and the public's modes of becoming laws unto themselves.

That "Of the Coming of John" makes law a central theme becomes clear at the turning point in the action. When John decides to return to Altamaha to educate the black population and "help settle the Negro problems," he bolsters his resolve by quoting from the Book of Esther: "'I will go in to the King, which is not according to the law; and if I perish, I perish'" (*SBF* 254). The law John obviously has in mind is the written and unwritten code of segregation and conduct designed to pre-serve racial distinctions and socio-economic hierarchies. Violating that law, John knows, will be personally detrimental, both physically harmful and, as Priscilla Wald glosses this passage, involving a "more figurative 'perishing' as a recognizable (and self-recognized) subject." Wald understands the story primarily in terms of a protagonist who "challenges the dominant narrative that constitutes social existence," while concluding that John "is unable, in the end, to turn the double-consciousness of his self-estrangement into an aesthetic principle through which to shape a counternarrative."[64] To the extent that John's aesthetics and social existence are dictated by double-consciousness's dialectic of recognition and self-recognition, Wald's argu-ment is persuasive. (Such an aesthetics and such a sociality would accord with the general structure of the public sphere, as discussed above.) Still, what remains to be examined more fully is the way "Of the Coming of John" articulates through John an alternative mode of aesthetics and social existence – a "counternarrative" that, however, does not counter socio-politically oppressive forces in an oppositional, resisting, or reactive sense; for ultimately John is no martyr. Rather, engaged in an aesthetic apprehen-sion of his circumstances, he registers a mode of impersonal consciousness and action that counters oppression by in effect not acknowledging its ex-istence, by not recognizing it as a coloring or even a killing agent. This engagement is most visible in his appropriation of the biblical narrative of Esther and of Wagner's opera *Lohengrin*. In contrast to Wald's claim that Esther and Lohengrin represent "heroic," "prewritten scripts" to which John "too willingly submits," with the consequence that he is "unable to rewrite the tragic ending," I would argue that precisely these narratives, as he rewrites them nearly beyond recognition, enable him to bypass the entirely too predictable and melodramatic script of martyrdom, of glorified victimization.[65]

Engaging this alternative aesthetic principle necessitates John's dissociation of the impending violence to his person from the signs of blacks' oppression and powerlessness – signs which the lynching event, as a national and regional phenomenon, conventionally serves to keep in circulation. (The circulation of these signs could benefit civil rights activists and militant white supremacists alike. It serves the first group obviously by exposing ongoing social inequities and abuses; only slightly less obviously, it serves the second group by intimidating blacks, by reminding them of their precarious, imperilled position in white America.) It is an aesthetics John derives from his experiences of the urban North, especially from his exposure to Wagner's opera. It amounts to what I called at the beginning of this chapter his supra-operatic mode of consciousness, which itself banks on the cultural prominence of Wagner's opera at the turn of the century.

As is well known, Du Bois was an ardent fan of Wagner's music-drama. Eric Sundquist explains in his compelling study, *To Wake the Nations*, that Du Bois "responded not as a racist but as a race nationalist to the power of Wagnerism – to its conjunction of aesthetics, prehistorical myth, and national identity." With the promotion of a cultural and racial nationalism as one of Du Bois's central tasks, he accomplishes it, Sundquist argues, primarily through a revaluation of the tradition of African-American sorrow songs.[66] But where Sundquist understands "Of the Coming of John" as squaring with this mythic-nationalist project, I see the story as squarely at odds with it. What Du Bois significantly resists in this story, unlike Wagner, is the grandiose mythifying of his protagonist, as well as the equally grandiose glorifying of a national people.

According to historian Joseph Horowitz's fascinating and well-documented *Wagner Nights*, by the 1880s, once Anton Seidl had arrived from Germany (and from Wagner's household, which he inhabited for several years as devoted famulus) to conduct New York's Metropolitan Opera, the United States Wagner cult was in full swing. Adopting Wagner's methods of empathetic identification, Seidl's conducting charisma not only spellbound the musicians on the boards and in the pit, but also magnetized the audiences, which reportedly applauded and screamed for hours.[67] When Du Bois describes John Jones as "sitting...silent and rapt," listening to the "last ethereal wail of the swan that quivered and faded away into the sky" (*SBF* 253), he registers his protagonist's susceptibility to the infamous "Wagnerian narcosis," the hypnotic surrender that was considered by Wagner fans to generate a wholesome elevation of the moral faculties.[68]

As one among Wagner's many critics, Nietzsche was less persuaded of the salutary effects of such enthrallment. Identifying *Lohengrin* as "the first example, only too insidious, only too successful, of hypnotism by means of music," Nietzsche derides Wagner's charlatanry, his false inflation of essentially modern "bourgeois" concerns – "[a]lways five steps from the hospital" – into mythological hugeness, into eternal verities.[69] Worse, Wagner's mythic pretensions end by confirming the Christian capitalist modernity he presumed to overcome. Nietzsche sees *Lohengrin*, for instance, whose plot revolves around Elsa's vow never to demand to know her rescuer-betrothed's name or provenance, as "contain[ing] a solemn excommunication of inquiry and questioning. Wagner thus represents the Christian concept 'you ought to and must *believe*.' It is a crime against what is highest and holiest to be scientific." Ultimately Wagner disappoints Nietzsche because he propagates an "opera of redemption." "The need for *redemption*," he explains, "the quintessence of all Christian needs," is reprehensible because it is nihilistic: "The Christian wants to be *rid* of himself. *Le moi est toujours haïssable.*" By contrast, what Nietzsche calls a "master morality" is "rooted in a triumphant Yes said to oneself – it is self-affirmation, self-glorification of life."[70]

In his *In Search of Wagner* Adorno explains how Wagner's mythologizing works in part to appropriate violence for myth's own legitimation and redemption. His *Gesamtkunstwerk* – that is, his "dogma of the identity of music and poetry" and of "universal immanence" – enabled Wagner, first of all, to reclaim myth as the proper aesthetic sphere: "[he] acknowledges neither history nor the supernatural nor even the natural, but [rather that] which lies beyond all such categories... This stratum, where all is undifferentiated, is that of myth." It thus serves "to merge irreconcilables – the positivistic with the metaphysical." Once myth is established as the origin of culture, the pre-contractual condition of humanity becomes aesthetically available to modernity. It is the realm in which law "itself becomes lawlessness," in which "mythic violence and legal contract are confounded." In this manner the "opacity and omnipotence of the social process is [*sic*] then celebrated as a metaphysical mystery." History itself in this aesthetic mode becomes myth: "Wagner fraudulently presents the historical German past as its essence. In this way he has invested such concepts as 'ancestors' and 'the people' with... absoluteness."[71]

In "Of the Coming of John" Du Bois in a sense rewrites Wagner to suit Nietzsche, if not Adorno. *Lohengrin* becomes the means by which Du Bois articulates a non-redemptive "self-affirmation" in the face of race-based slaughter, by which he disarticulates this violence from the lynch mob's "veil of vengeance," of primitive, mythic, and mythologically legitimating (which is to say redemptive) fury. Much pivots on Du Bois's representation of John succumbing to the hypnotic state. In Dixon's *The Clansman* (1905), the Southern stalwart Dr. Cameron hypnotizes Gus, the black man who has raped the white, virginal (and perversely surnamed) Marion Lenoir, in order to have him re-enact the scene of the crime. Gus, who "is peculiarly sensitive to hypnotic influence," does so with "fearful realism," prompting the clansmen present to assault him, at which point Dr. Cameron "beat[s] them off" while enjoining, "Men! Men! You must not kill him in this condition!"[72] The problem of killing Gus in "this condition" is that he would be unaware of his death as a capital punishment; he would die in a psycho-physiologically and morally absent manner.

This is the condition John Jones's prior exposure to Wagner enables him to re-enter after killing John Henderson in his sister's defense. He looks "dreamily" at the slain body, recalling the "half-daze," the "dreamland" in which "he sat" while attending the opera (*SBF* 262, 252). Indeed, as though back in the opera house, he then "seat[s] himself on [a] great black stump" and thinks "of the gilded ceiling of that vast concert hall, [and hears] stealing toward him the faint sweet music of the swan" (*SBF* 262–263). When he begins to think back on his schoolmates at Johnstown, wondering how "they" "turned out" and including John Jones as one of "the[m]," the hypnotic spell is evidently profound enough to cause him momentarily to forget his identity, to dissociate his current experience from personal pastness. Awaiting the lynch mob in this self-absent manner, and as it were re-scoring "the tramp of horses and murmur of angry men" as a "[c]lear and high...faint sweet melody [that] rose and fluttered like a living thing," John shifts into operatic high gear. On the one hand he converts the mob, as Tillman and Dixon might, into a heroic, mythic creature, "thundering toward him...[and] sweeping like a storm" (*SBF* 263). On the other hand, he upstages the mob's operatic mode of being by converting himself supra-operatically into both hypnotized spectator and hypnotic deliverer of a death-aria. While John does not literally sing an aria, he does "hum" *Lohengrin's* famous "Bridal Song." This humming, combined as it is with John's intensely impressionistic if not hallucinatory visions during this final interval of life, can be likened to what Herbert Lindenberger describes as "the lengthy interval in many operas between the infliction of a fatal wound and the victim's actual death." This interval serves "less [as] an occasion for agony than for a pleasurable display of musical eloquence." While such an interval can verge on the ludicrous, such as when Wagner's Siegfried "has to *sing* a long passage with a spear sticking between his shoulder-blades – and presumably into his lungs," in Du Bois's story it heightens and draws out his protagonist's strange joy.[73]

John receives his fatal wound in effect when he assaults John Henderson. From that moment on, he is back in opera's "dreamland."

"Joy" is a crucial term in Du Bois's narrative; it comes to replace John's earlier affects, cited above: sarcasm, bitterness, and above all dread. It enters by way of the hummed German, and constitutes John's (and Du Bois's) literal rewriting of *Lohengrin*. Instead of Wagner's *treulich* (faithfully), John hums the word *freudig* (joyously). Russell Berman suggests that, however unintentional the misquotation, "Du Bois would want to insist that John assumes his role or mission joyously" – that mission being, in his view, his service to the cause of black activism.[74] Yet Du Bois's rewriting of Wagner has profounder significance. It does well to recall, first, that when John assumes his race-work mission, he does it not so much with joy as with grim, biblical resolve: if I perish, I perish. Second, the humming of the rewritten line happens at the end of the road, after his school has been shut down and his white counterpart killed – implying that, John's mission of service accomplished (or at least ended), he now embarks on a mission impossible, namely of rendering his death by lynching as a marriage of one.

For what is crucial about the introduction of *freudig* is not only its marking of an affective reversal; rather, it eliminates *treulich*, the opera's semantic and conceptual keystone, appearing as it (or its etymological relation, *trauen* [trust]) does on nearly every page of the libretto, and referencing as it does the marital object-oriented structure, not to mention Christianity. Du Bois's elimination of *treulich* takes on yet more significance in light of the fact that faith is also the moral and political axis around which Dixon's racial fantasy rotates in *The Leopard's Spots*. "[F]aith's the word," replies Tom Camp, the poor, hard-working, and loyal farmer-soldier to his former General's eulogy: "A man's just as big as his faith. I've got faith in the South. I've got faith in the good will of the people of the North." As Dixon depicts the postbellum Southern socio-political sphere as one in which the "complete alienation of the white and black races" takes the place of "the old familiar trust" between master and slave, his same-race romance hinges on the lovers' unconditional mutual trust. "You will trust me, will you not, dear?" pleads the Anglo-Saxon girl, Sallie Worth. "I have trusted you with my immortal soul," assures the Anglo-Saxon boy, Charles Gaston. Near the end of the novel, after Gaston declares in his winning political speech that the "Anglo-Saxon race is united and has entered upon its world-mission," Dixon makes explicit, ventriloquized by Gaston, that the fate of racial homogeneity – which is also to say political reconstruction, Southern style – hangs on faith and trust: "I love mine own people. Their past is mine, their present is mine, their future is a divine trust." Charles Gaston and Sallie Worth succeed where Wagner's Elsa fails. It makes sense that in his short story Du Bois would erase altogether these constitutive elements of race and folk phantasmagoria.[75]

Berman makes the persuasive case that Wagner's drama of a woman's breach of domestic (spousal) faith bears a certain resemblance to Du Bois's story of the United States's public betrayal of its black citizens. Elsa's insistence on knowing Lohengrin's name and provenance places secondary attributes of personal identity before what a rational, egalitarian political order would designate as Lohengrin's primary attribute: his "civil integrity," his status, no more nor less, as a human.[76] (This account has to exclude from Lohengrin's current identity as husband and state protector the magic powers enabling his arrival in and departure from the kingdom, powers which make him something other than human.) Similarly, African-Americans' civil integrity is disallowed in John Jones's world, where the abstract principles of justice and equality are under Jim Crow's siege.

Du Bois's story, however, does not end with this "tragedy of egalitarianism."[77] It ends rather with a redescription of marriage as a severely private, indeed solitary affair. The supplantation of *treulich* by *freudig* signals Du Bois's shift in the narrative from a public sociality, based on intersubjective recognition and exchange, to a crowd sociality – more precisely, asociality – based on inexchangeable self-absence. As it happens, Elsa herself supplies models for both ontological propositions. For the most part, as Berman implies, her spousal function circulates in a world which wants both public and private realms to adhere to a Habermasian "audience-oriented" sociality. The domestic sphere would thus mirror the political sphere. Yet it does well also to recall that Habermas himself argues that the strength of a democratic-rational polity lies in the way its abstract universalism secures, rather than eliminates, concrete, subjective individuation. Elsa notably demands to know Lohengrin's name only *after* they have performed the public marriage ceremony. Only within the depths of *"Liebestille"* (tranquil, silent love), only when they are "alone, when nobody is awake," does she lodge her plea.[78]

This is because Elsa understands the civil ceremony of marriage to allow in private a dissolution of "civil integrity." She explicitly indicates as much when, directly preceding the ceremony, she declares her love to Lohengrin: "My hero, *in whom I must perish!* / High above the power of all doubt / My love will survive" (*Mein Held, in dem ich muss vergeh'n! / Hoch über alles Zweifels Macht / . . . soll meine Liebe steh'n*).[79] The interplay between passing and standing (*vergehen* and *stehen* – in both English and German the words are semantically grounded in spatial relations), along with their respective meanings of dying and living, captures precisely the experiential situation of John Jones facing the lynch mob, which he revealingly "pitie[s]," that is, joins in passion (*SBF* 263). In meeting the mob not with self-preservationist dread nor even self-reflective bitterness, but rather self-dissolving joy, John in an involuntaristic sense beats the crowd to the punch.

The lynch scene notably takes place near the sea. Next to its "great brown" and "silent" massiveness, the lynch mob is but a mere "storm"; John, watching it, is its eye. Silent as the sea may be, it is also the source of music, the site "whence rose the strange melody" of Lohengrin's swan (*SBF* 262–263). Indeed, in John's consciousness the sea is both aesthetic source and central aesthetic figure, for when he arrives in New York and seats himself to observe the crowded streets, "brilliant with moving men," they "remind... [him] of the sea... so changelessly changing" (*SBF* 251). This crowd he also calls "the World"; and being "suddenly seized" by "the notion... to see where the world was going," John follows his Northern sea of men as it flows into the North's aesthetic site, the opera house (*SBF* 251). Now, in this later scene, possessed of certain knowledge of his imminent lynching, John tells his mother, "I'm going – North," and returns to the assault site where he "smile[s] toward the sea" (*SBF* 250–251). With this impressionistic chain of associations John in effect reclaims the New York street crowd as a site of de-racialization, of pure, neutral, self-dissolved being.[80]

When, very near the end, John "turn[s] his closed eyes toward the Sea," Du Bois's narrative distinctly resembles the final scene of Kate Chopin's *The Awakening* (1899), in which the protagonist Edna Pontellier "there beside the sea, absolutely alone," "felt like some new-born creature, opening its eyes in a familiar world that it had never known."[81] As Chopin's novel revolves around the contingencies of gender, Edna's self-impressions of gender neutrality, of feeling like an "it," take on dramatic significance. The biological impossibility toward which she reaches parallels the post-*Plessy* legal and cultural impossibility John Jones faces. Du Bois describes in a previous chapter his own new-born, but tragically already dead creature, his son, as having "kn[own] no color-line," in whose "little world walked souls alone, uncolored and unclothed" (*SBF* 230). Like Chopin, he reaches toward images of identity-neutral being – uncolored souls who will not go the way of the nation's blackened and blacked out bodies.

Toward the end of "Of the Passing of the First-Born," Du Bois's lyrical evocation of the uncolored soul modulates into rather bitter grief. This surfaces in an imagined dialogue with his dead son: "Well sped, my boy, before the world had dubbed your ambition insolence, had held your ideals unattainable, and taught you to cringe and bow. Better far this nameless void that stops my life than a sea of sorrow for you" (*SBF* 231). But recognizing in the next breath how he has projected onto his son's generation his own generation's experience, Du Bois rhetorically cancels his speech with more speech. "Idle words," he now claims, and goes on more hopefully to envision a better future (*SBF* 231–232). I have been arguing that in "Of the Coming of John" Du Bois in an important, more severe sense returns to idling. In the above quotation "idle" refers to Du Bois's misplaced emotion of bitter grief and his misreading of the future, that is, to judgmental errors with respect, to put it crudely, to the emotional and historical use-value of his son's death. Whereas, applied to the later chapter, "idle words" means something like: words giving expression to the condition of being literally idle – empty, useless, valueless. The "nameless void that stops life" returns as an agent of life, of life stopped but life nonetheless.

In the final line of "Of the Coming of John" Du Bois offers perhaps his severest image of stopped life, of identity-neutral being: "And the world whistled in his ears." As the lynch mob's "storm burst[s] around him," John's consciousness is elsewhere; the eye of this storm, he has entered the anonymous, neutral space of "the world." Such whistling is opera at its purest. Friedrich Kittler argues that Wagner, over the course of his composing career, developed an ever-deeper commitment to what Kittler calls the "acoustic field as such, with its senseless noises and disembodied voices." Further, by *Lohengrin*, he suggests, Wagner has "acoustic hallucinations take the place of optical ones," referring specifically to the way Elsa's initially visual dream of being rescued by a knight yields to an acoustic hallucination, whereby the sheer medium of "pleas, laments, and moans" (rather than the contents of a message) "have successfully commanded Lohengrin to appear from a distance of some four hundred miles."[82] This supra-operatic modality – the acoustic field as such, the sheer medium – governs John Jones's parting experience. The joyous "hum" of self-absent marriage returns as the world-crowd's sheer "whistle." The paragraph indentation and the grammatically superfluous conjunction "and" at the beginning of the line draw attention to the line's appended relation to the rest of the text.

Thus reminding readers of the textual field as such, Du Bois also subtly hints at the significance of his rewriting Wagner's opera. For he has done nothing less than expose the fatuity of redeeming (and prescribing) the viciously gregarious crowd mind as equivalent to the political-liberal public square. Simultaneously he reclaims the deeply attractive crowd-world as a site of a sublime limit of experience. Relishing its strangest fruits, he thus reserves for the aesthetic realm what the stridently illiberal Wagner evidently embraced as a political maxim: "Life is law unto itself."[83]

CHAPTER 5

A "moving mosaic": Harlem, primitivism, and Nella Larsen's Quicksand

If, as the preceding chapter suggests, African Americans were discursively excluded from the nation form, they might well form a city. At the time and place of the Harlem Renaissance, multitudes – arriving during the Great Migration northwards – were crucial to Harlem's physical establishment as a black domain. Crowds as *residents* were essential to Harlem's very definition, to quote James Weldon Johnson's well-known description, as "a city within a city, [as] the greatest Negro city in the world," as the place that "contains more Negroes to the square mile than any other spot on earth."[1] To make Harlem "the recognized Negro capital," Johnson further suggests, African Americans had to become an aggressive crowd of capitalists. He describes the means by which savvy black real estate investors finagled the purchases of property and the rental to other blacks in heretofore white neighborhoods, resulting in a "whole movement [which], in the eyes of whites, took on the aspect of an 'invasion'; they became panic-stricken and began fleeing as from a plague." If Johnson expresses some amusement over whites' mob-like exodus, he equally delights in the behavior of Harlem's new masses – the "colored washerwoman or cook" – who, like the moneyed elite, did their capitalist part. When the "Rev. W. W. Brown, pastor of the Metropolitan Baptist Church, repeatedly made 'Buy Property' the text of his sermons," a "large part of his congregation carried out the injunction . . . Buying property became *a fever*."[2] Crowds thus contributed to the possession of black individuality, that is, to the emergence of a middle class and its individually recognized writers, artists, performers, academics, businesspersons, and so forth.

However "fever[ish]," then, Johnson's black consumer crowds stood as emblems of utilitarian-rational conduct. With the memory still fresh of the race riots of the late 1910s (most prominently in East St. Louis in 1917 and Chicago in 1919), in which blacks were associated, both as victims and perpetrators, with brutal savagery, images of respectable collective behavior such as buying property advertised African Americans' capacity to participate in and enjoy normative American pursuits of happiness. Concomitantly, such images brought attention to the African-American population as an autonomous political-economic power. However opposed in principle to segregation, race activists generally advocated autonomy as a practical economic measure. Even as high-minded an activist as W. E. B. Du Bois did. As Adolph Reed explains, "[c]ooperativist racial economics long had held an attraction for Du Bois. Both as an economic practicality and as a model for economic democracy, the cooperative recommended itself to him." Particularly after World War I, "he felt that the slogans of political democracy developed a hollow ring; the pressing problems were then economic rather than political 'in an oligarchic world.'"[3] To be sure, as Johnson recounts, when in 1919 the Department of Justice, suspecting seditious radicalism, inquired into the purpose of the NAACP, Du Bois responded, "We are fighting for the enforcement of the Constitution of the United States," which is to say, in Johnson's own words, the organization was "insist[ing] upon the impartial application of the fundamental principles of the Republic without regard to race, creed, or colour."[4]

While commitment to these universalist civil liberties and obligations was obviously not abandoned, the shift in focus toward the race's autonomous economic and cultural advancement contributed to the emergence of a racialized "comprehensive doctrine," to borrow Rawls's phrase once again. In other words, race became – even when biologically repudiated – an essential structuring element of value and belief. As long as the political work arising from this race consciousness did not overtly contravene the fundamental principles of the liberal democratic polity, a racialized comprehensive doctrine met the requirement of reasonability – as reasonable as, say, an Episcopalian or Protestant comprehensive doctrine.[5]

But unlike those adhering to religious comprehensive doctrines, who might undergo all manner of lapses, conversions, and changes of denominational affiliation, a racially marked American could not relinquish with impunity a race-based doctrine. Even a black-identified person capable of passing could not become ex-colored without, as James Weldon Johnson shows in his novel *The Autobiography of an Ex-Colored Man*, the sense of betraying his race and deceiving others. In the early decades of the twentieth century, as Walter Michaels has persuasively argued, racial and cultural consciousness converged. Cultural identity thus became a matter of inheritance rather than practice, a matter of ideology rather than mere anthropological fact. The consequence is the emergence of what Michaels calls "nativist modernism":

Promoting a conception of identity as both description and responsibility, it [nativist modernism] made Americanness into a racial inheritance and culture into a set of beliefs and practices dependent on race – without race, culture could be nothing more than one's actual practices and therefore could never be lost or recovered, defended or betrayed – but not reducible to race – if it were nothing but race, it could also not be lost or recovered, it could only be a fact, never a project.

Michaels further explains that this project of Americanness succeeded in disarticulating American identity from American citizenship, so that ethnically or racially marked persons might, say, participate in elections but still not be American.[6] Thus on one level it appeared that political and cultural consciousness were fully separable. But on another level the knitting of political and economic consciousness complicated this neat division. When Du Bois called for economic change, it was not the case that he simply turned from issues related to public-political civil rights and obligations to those related to private commerce and consumption; it was, rather, that he inclined more toward championing economic causes *as* political causes. In *Darkwater* (1920) he supplemented his advocacy of political democracy with a socialist-progressivist demand, in the name of justice and fairness, for "industrial democracy": "we must face the fact that the final distribution of goods – the question of wages and income is an ethical and not a mere mechanical problem and calls for grave public human judgment and not secrecy."[7] Calling for moderate collectivist measures such as public ownership of utilities and inheritance taxation, Du Bois registers a political-liberal concern to meet the era's tenacious challenge of devising acceptable procedures for material redistribution.

While Du Bois himself would steer clear of conflating this kind of political-economic advocacy and his advocacy of African-American economic autonomy – the latter motivated by his sense of historical contingency rather than by ethical principle – the double articulation of political and economic justice on the one hand, and economic and cultural power on the other, invited confusion and indistinction. Not only would racial-cultural identity become an object of affection rather than a set of practices, as Michaels adduces, but also a black individual's personal affections and practices would be taken as signs of political orientation – of betraying or embracing race solidarity. Thus Helga Crane in Nella Larsen's *Quicksand* (1928) feels exiled from the Tuskegee-like school Naxos when she becomes aware that her devotion to "spontaneity" and "enthusiasm" clashes with "the Naxos policy of uplift," which demands conformity to puritanical orderliness and which is invested in carving out a humble political-economic place for agriculturally and industrially trained blacks.[8] Thus also her later friend in Harlem, Anne Grey, who is "obsessed by the race problem," deems that the mulatta Audrey Denny "ought to be ostracized" for her "outrageous, treacherous" behavior of keeping company with whites (*Q* 48, 61).

This chapter examines more closely Larsen's representation in *Quicksand* of the psychical distresses brought on by racialized worlds in which the formal distinction between a background comprehensive doctrine and its political conception has been lost, so that the political domain is no longer free-standing and the background culture is in effect saturated by a racialized political consciousness. In this novel Larsen depicts two black worlds (akin to Booker T. Washington's vocationally trained Tuskegee Institute and Du Bois's professionally and aesthetically cultivated Talented Tenth) where the prevailing assumption is that race solidarity should reach to the bottom depths of conscious being, where violations of these worlds' codes of personal conduct and affect reverberate with political significance. Larsen's novel, I argue, provides one of the more incisive if also oblique critiques of Harlem's capitalizing renaissance and the race consciousness it purposes to mold. This critique crystallizes around crowd scenes in which the protagonist Helga Crane trades in her race consciousness for the ecstatic state of having no consciousness at all, of reaching the limit of consciousness – suggesting that during the Harlem Renaissance, the only alternative to being racialized is self-evacuation.

As indicated at the start of this chapter, the establishment of Harlem as African-America's "culture capital" entailed an increasing awareness of it as an autonomous site of group solidarity. Lewis Alexander's poem, "Streets," published in the first volume of *Fire!!* in 1926, illustrates how this awareness maps onto the discourse of urban crowds: "Avenues of dreams / Boulevards of pain / Moving black streams / Shimmering like rain."[9] As the speaker attributes a feeling, dreaming consciousness to the streets, he also defines this stream of consciousness as black. Further illustrating this collective consciousness, as Johnson points out, is Harlem's relish for publicly gathering and displaying itself. "One of its outstanding features is brass band parades. Hardly a Sunday passes but that there are several of these parades of which many are gorgeous with regalia and insignia. Almost any excuse will do – the death of an humble member of the Elks, the laying of a cornerstone, the 'turning out' of the order of this or that."[10] If such public rituals were numerous, they were not all equally significant. Johnson depicts with special pride the crowd that gathered for the funeral of Florence Mills, the fabulously (and transracially) popular Broadway star. In this passage it becomes clear that the crowd's massiveness, "such as Harlem, perhaps all New York, had never seen before," functions as symbolic or indexical capital, and thereby serves to reinforce Harlem's status as "culture capital":

Her funeral was one such as Harlem, perhaps all New York, had never seen before. Five thousand people were packed to suffocation in Mother Zion Church. The air quivered with emotion. Hall Johnson's choir sang Spirituals, and the whole throng wept and sobbed . . . Women fainted and men were unnerved . . . Outside the church more than a hundred thousand people jammed the streets. A detail of one hundred and fifty police was necessary to handle the crowd. The procession moved slowly through this dense mass . . . [A]n airplane circled low and released a flock of blackbirds. They fluttered overhead a few seconds and then flew away.[11]

This passage compresses many of the historical, ideological and icono-graphic significations of the crowd in African-American urban conscious-ness. It underwrites what might be called the capitalization of and on Harlem. The collective, if also cathectic, regard for Florence Mills reiter-ates the centrality, indeed the superiority, of Harlem vis-à-vis the African-American diaspora; in the context of the general project of racial uplift it reiterates the very need for such a geographical and cultural focal point if such uplift is to succeed. The crowd gathering at Mills's funeral thus memo-rializes more than a Broadway star; it memorializes itself as a whole.[12]

On one hand, such uplifting representations were surely necessary for the consolidation of cultural and economic power. On the other, their constant reiteration by those holding the reins to African-Americans' po-litical, social and aesthetic capital also would have the detrimental effect of steadily amplifying Harlem's self-consciousness, and then of depending on this self-consciousness as the dominant means of strategically opposing Anglo-America's political and economic discrimination. Harlem would thereby risk becoming too insulated, hence too dependent on a politics of power and racial identity. A closer examination of Johnson's depiction of Mills's funeral gathering discloses the way a power politics of capital and identity bears in it a self-undermining potential, one that ushers in what can be understood as Harlem's collective headlessness. First, the very fact that Mills's funeral is the occasion for the exceptional display of Harlem's massive solidarity indicates a certain irredeemable deadness inhering in its collective vitality; she embodies, in other words, the limit at which an organic crowd transforms into its inorganic other. In a twist on crowd psy-chology's leader-crowd relation – one that recalls Stephen Crane's sketch, "When Man Falls, a Crowd Gathers" – the five thousand comprising the crowd within the church follow Mills by miming her deadness, "packed to suffocation," "unnerved" and fainting. Yet similar to Le Bon's crowd, their emotional pitch is extreme, seized as they are by weeping and sobbing. The air itself "quiver[s] with emotion." They thereby enact what Gabriel Tarde remarks is "the singular mixture of anaesthesia and hyperaesthesia of the senses [that] is the dominant characteristic of [urban] somnambulists."[13] This doubled condition, furthermore, is reproduced in the funereal rites, that is, in the inanimate flying machine which gives birth to an entire crowd of animate signifiers, a flock of blackbirds. Besides signifying both Mills's latest success as the star of the musical revue *Blackbirds* and the increasingly significant role of blacks in transracial commercial entertainment, these blackbirds also serve an iconographic function: in their movement first downward, after the release from the airplane, then upward, they enact the divine recovery and heavenly transport of the spirit inhabiting Mills's corpse. Moreover, the transition that the flock makes, "flutter[ing] overhead a few seconds," between its gravitational descent and airborne ascent dramatizes the third, externally related condition of suspension between a corpse's inert materiality and a spirit's evanescent immateriality. The live icon enacts thereby not so much Florence Mills's condition of being dead but her pure, anonymous experience of becoming dead, the being-becoming of death. In this scene, Johnson configures a collective will to mindless anonymity subtending Harlem's dominant will to identity as capital, as "Harlem."

Larsen's novel draws a similar configuration of African-American capitalization and anonymity as countervailing pressures. In a letter to Carl Van Vechten, Larsen once listed the "things there are to write, if only one can write them": "Boiler menders, society ladies, children, acrobats, governesses, businessmen, countesses, flappers, Nile green bath rooms, beautifully filled, gray moods and shivering hesitations, all presented in an intensely restrained and civilized manner and underneath the ironic survival of a much more primitive mood."[14] As facetious as her list of "things" is, her commentary regarding the presentation of them warrants closer consideration. Much like Henry James, Larsen is engaged in a writing practice of restraint, of social decorum, which renders the "shivering hesitations," that is, the subterranean eruptions of "a much more primitive mood," all the more intense.[15] We will see that in her dramatization of what Helga Crane at one point thinks of as her pattern of "explosive contact" (Q 51), Larsen explores the anonymous decapitalization conditioning subjective and collective experience. She carries this out in her representation of Helga Crane's overdetermined relation both to crowds (within and without Harlem) and to her self – to her self as capital and to the physiological capital constituting her self.

We will see further how Larsen, as narrator, embodies this primitive mood when towards the end of the novel her irony turns savage. In contrast to other modernists who engage primitivism as a therapeutic means of revitalizing an overly civilized bourgeois world (as Jackson Lears and Robert Nye have shown), or who deploy the crowd psychological idiom to "embod[y] the communal alternative to individualism," Larsen's primitivism pulls her narrative into the theater of the absurd.[16] By her double means of characterization and narrative filtration, Larsen reveals the difference between an idealization of *aesthetic* experience, as wrought by the Harlem Renaissance's capitalization of both art objects and artistic subjects (manifested, for instance, in its profusion of literary contests), and the enactment of pure *anaesthetic* experience which presses on both the racial-politicized aesthetic object and subject. That is, anaesthetic pressure bears both on Larsen's novel and Helga Crane's selfhood – to the point of narratological absurdity in the first case and psycho-physiological rupture in the second.

As a troubled, fickle mulatta who flees from her past, moving from and to various urban milieus – Chicago, Harlem, Copenhagen – Helga's psychology has understandably intrigued the novel's critics. Many have analyzed the novel from a Freudian perspective, diagnosing Helga as neurotic, sexually repressed, and/or narcissistically self-centered. Yet, in my view, in Larsen's representation of Helga's psychically restrictive economy of desire and repression, attraction and repulsion, such drives animate a larger, more complex and unpredictable psycho-physiology which repeatedly disrupts the dialectical determinations of her consciousness, thus redistributing its directives within a general economy of thinking and non-thinking, of feeling and non-feeling, of desiring and – *laughing*.[17]

Affective jolts and interjections are central to Larsen's characterization of Helga Crane, often expressed as the recurring event of a "sudden attack of nerves" (*Q* 17). This condition is first revealed when Helga experiences an attack while walking to the administration building of the detested Naxos and preparing to submit her resignation to its principal Dr. Robert Anderson. "This was a disease from which [she] had suffered at intervals all her life, and it was a point of honor, almost, with her never to give way to it" (*Q* 17). Yet the next scene shows her distinctly giving way to it, if only momentarily. As Robert Anderson greets her, "her lips formed speech, but no sound came. She was aware of inward confusion. For her the situation seemed charged, unaccountably, with strangeness and something very like hysteria. An almost overpowering desire to laugh seized her" (*Q* 19). If such paralyzing occasions cause Helga to "suffer" – and indeed they prove in the narrative to jar the smooth surface of her aestheticized life – they also constitute what might be called Helga's will to adventure. Critics have noted the picaresque structure of the novel, yet scant attention has been paid to her psycho-physiological adventuresomeness. This *will* to adventure, one must hasten to add, is not exactly the same as a *sense* of adventure, for of this latter, more deliberate trait she possesses but little. To be sure, at times she longs consciously for spontaneity, but more often for security, for "lavish contentment and well-being" (*Q* 67). In contrast, her will to adventure describes what her self spontaneously enacts, willy-nilly.

In the 1920s the Chicago School sociologist Robert Park, influenced by the social philosopher of modernity Georg Simmel, identifies the urban milieu as particularly conducive to adventure. He suggests that this has to do with the urban population's mobility, as well as the city's physical structure, which he likened to "a mosaic of little worlds":

This makes it possible for individuals to pass quickly and easily from one moral milieu to another, and encourages the fascinating but dangerous experiment of living at the same time in several different contiguous, but otherwise widely separated, worlds. All this tends to give to city life a superficial and adventitious character; it tends to complicate social relationships and to produce new and divergent individual types. It introduces, at the same time, an element of chance and adventure which adds to the stimulus of city life and gives it, for young and fresh nerves, a peculiar attractiveness.[18]

No wonder that Helga, who stems from Chicago, is about to return there. With her nerves, her race-based social complications, and her divergence from the uplift-activist norms, she is practically destined to carry out Park's "fascinating but dangerous experiment of living" in a self-dividing manner.

Moreover, she will do so in ways that formally resemble Georg Simmel's conception of the adventure, as outlined in his 1911 essay, "The Adventure." Simmel describes the adventurer as one who "treats the incalculable element in life in the way we ordinarily treat only what we think is by definition calculable." Thus, "in the adventure we abandon ourselves to the world with fewer defenses and reserves than in any other relation, for other relations are connected with the general run of our worldly life by more bridges, and thus defend us better against shocks and dangers through previously prepared avoidances and adjustments." Paradoxically, it is by abandoning oneself to the world's relations that one becomes "torn off" from those relations, forming a "non-organic relation to the world" and "dropping out of the continuity of life." Simultaneously engaged to and disengaged from the world's and the self's past and future, this "ahistorical" figure conflates chance and necessity. Simmel's paradigmatic adventurer is the gambler, who "lets the accident somehow be encompassed by the meaning which controls the consistent continuity of life, even though the accident lies outside that continuity."[19] In this sense the self does not simply embark upon an adventure; the adventure likewise embarks upon the self.

Helga Crane similarly conflates chance and necessity. This is evident, for instance, in the scene with Dr. Anderson. During their interview he at first persuades Helga not to leave Naxos: "she resolved not only to remain until June, but to return next year... He had won her. She knew that she would stay" (*Q* 20–21). Yet in the next moment, at hearing him proffer a compliment – "'You're a lady.' You have dignity and breeding" – Helga suddenly recoils. "At these words turmoil rose again" (*Q* 21). The reader already knows that she is overly sensitive to her "lack of family" (*Q* 8), but in the present circumstances this sensitivity works in her favor (that is, to induce her to leave what the narrator has implied is the oppressive world of Naxos). She defies his compliment by abruptly leaving, but only after retorting with the truth about her family: "I was born in a Chicago slum... *My father was a gambler* who deserted my mother, a white immigrant. It is even uncertain that they were married" (*Q* 21 emphasis added). Later that day, on the train out of Naxos, she reflects back on the morning interview:

Just what had happened to her there in that cool dim room under the quizzical gaze of those piercing gray eyes? Whatever it was had been so powerful, so compelling, that *but for a few chance words* she would still be in Naxos. And why had she permitted herself *to be jolted into a rage so fierce, so illogical, so disastrous,* that now after it was spent she sat despondent, sunk in shameful contrition? (*Q* 22, emphasis added)

As Simmel and Park suggest, the will to adventure carries its dangers. Nevertheless, in becoming so overwhelmed with the present as to take decisive – which is not to say decided, or premeditated – action based on "a few chance words," Helga exhibits the adventurer-gambler's ahistorical propensity, one forceful enough to supplant her libidinal attraction to her superior. At the same time, however, in her very act of gambling she demonstrates an undeniable relatedness to her past, that is, to her father, the gambler who deserts home and family. We see here as well as elsewhere in the narrative that Helga's adventures – producing in her as they do a sort of self-fissure, a nervous incapacitation that impinges on her capacity to deliberate – turn out to constitute many of Helga's most original, spontaneous, uninhibited, and indeed *ridiculous* moments. Though she gathers her wits soon enough to suppress her laugh here at the start of the interview with Robert Anderson, in another nervous attack she does not, but gives "a little unpremeditated laugh and slip[s] out" (*Q* 29). This is Helga's response to having the door virtually closed in her face by the new white wife of her one remaining family member, the white Uncle Peter, whom she seeks in Chicago after leaving Naxos. Here is the residual, meaningless laughter undermining her restricted economy of self-conscious thought and signification; it is a manifestation of Helga's "primitive mood."

In the opening scene of the novel, its first primitive, "shivering hesitation" presents itself. As Ann Hostetler observes, the first action attributed to Helga becomes significant as it recurs throughout the text: "Helga Crane tried not to think" (*Q* 2).[20] Of course, trying not to think amounts to more thinking – thinking about not thinking, about forgetting: "She wanted forgetfulness, complete mental relaxation, rest from thought of any kind" (*Q* 2). Helga is still using her head. But this self-possession does not persist. Sitting alone in her beautifully cultivated and ordered room, "a comfortable room, furnished with rare and intensely personal taste," she soon feels "a surge of hot anger and seething resentment" towards Naxos, the Southern school for blacks where "[e]nthusiasm, spontaneity, if not actually suppressed, were at least openly regretted" (*Q* 1–2, 4). It is worth noting the subtle ways in which Larsen heightens the sense of this scene's "primitive mood" – specifically, the mood suppressed by Naxos and resurfacing in Helga as anger and resentment. For she achieves this partly by hinting at a pervasive presence or, more precisely, *pressure* of crowdedness. Larsen describes, among the many lovely things surrounding Helga, a "shining brass bowl" as being "crowded with many-colored nasturtiums" (*Q* 1). The book Helga finally selects to read, Marmaduke Pickthall's 1903 *Said the Fisherman*, which is set primarily during the 1860 Damascus massacre, is dotted with literally dozens of allusions to mobs, crowds, and multitudes. It ends with the depiction of a "yelling, furious mob, all rushing in one direction."[21] This novel she chooses for "relaxation," given that her "day had been more than usually crowded with distasteful encounters and stupid perversities" (*Q* 2). Even her desk, "the old bow-legged secretary," seems under pressure, holding "*with almost articulate protest* her school-teacher paraphernalia" (*Q* 4, emphasis added).

While Helga sits there "motionless," the room itself starts to move about her: "a newly-risen breeze...suddenly parted the thin silk curtains at the opened windows," causing a "slender frail glass vase [to fall] from the sill with a tingling crash." Though Helga initially remains motionless ("Helga Crane did not shift her position"), she "at last" stirs "uncertainly, but with an overpowering desire for action of some sort. A second she hesitated, then rose abruptly and pressed the electric switch with determined firm-ness, flooding suddenly the shadowy room with a glare of light." Though determination usually suggests foresight, hers clearly emanates from an unpremeditated, "overpowering desire," a desire that provokes a sort of physiological mimesis of her physical surroundings. For her next move, af-ter a "quick nervous tour" about the room, is to grab her school papers and "fl[i]ng them violently" to the floor (Q 3–4). She is compelled to re-enact the fall of the vase. Having "hesitated," having thought about not thinking to the point of not thinking, and instead, heedlessly (or headlessly) act-ing, Helga breaks the bounds of the "self-restraint" she normally possesses (Q 5).

Moreover, in doing violence to the loveliness of her room, which, apart from her physical attire, represents her capital investment in, and expression of, the aesthetic ideals of harmony, order, and "personal taste," she shatters the narcissistic sphere of her identity.[22] In Hazel Carby's important discus-sion of the novel, she calls attention to the fact that *Quicksand* may be the "first text by a black woman to be a conscious narrative of a woman embed-ded in capitalist relations." In Carby's view Helga Crane is represented as a "consumer" and "defined through the objects that surround her." Naxos too is "represented as being symbolic of the acceptance of [an] oppressed social condition. Within this order," Carby thus concludes, Helga is "an expression of powerlessness, the alienated individual who [cannot] change her social condition and [feels] only a sense of individual failure."[23] What Carby overlooks in drawing this conclusion, however, are these scenes of mimetic action in which Helga Crane shuts down her capitalizing ten-dencies, and consequently indeed alters her social condition. After all, she does not remain in Naxos, where the option of settling into a respectable bourgeois marriage is in the offing. My point, however, is not that in these episodes of mimetic action Helga Crane exchanges her "powerlessness" for powerfulness; rather, she enters what Mikkel Borch-Jacobsen explains (as discussed in my Introduction) is the crowd's condition of *unpower*.

As the narrative unfolds, it becomes increasingly clear that the valua-tive content of Helga's normative thought processes is not entirely reliable. Larsen's genius as narrator lies in her rendering Helga as a central conscious-ness equipped with an ample amount of capitalizing self-awareness but only a modest amount of self-understanding. She is capable, for instance, of as-sessing her "commercial value" (Q 35) and of selecting for herself the outfit to suit every occasion (from her Chicago job-hunting "suit of fine blue twill faultlessly tailored" to the "cobwebby black net [dress] touched with orange" that she dons when wishing to signify her intention "to fly" from

Harlem [*Q* 31, 56]). Yet she is largely incapable of discerning what it is she "wants":

There was something else, some other more ruthless force, a quality within herself, which was frustrating her . . . [and] kept her from getting the things she had wanted . . . But just what did she want? . . . Helga Crane didn't know, couldn't tell. (*Q* 10–11)

Moreover, even when she is capable of understanding herself, this by no means guarantees self-control. While in Copenhagen, for instance, troubled by unwanted homesickness, she witnesses how "[h]er old unhappy questioning mood" effects a sort of self-sabotage: "for she knew that into her plan for her life had thrust itself a *suspensive conflict* in which were fused doubts, rebellion, expediency, and urgent longings" (*Q* 83, emphasis added). Here, as in Naxos, self-reflection devolves into suspense and conflict rather than deliberative resolution. Again, if this incapacity to think clearly or to understand herself properly causes her to suffer, indeed to experience a sort of paralysis, it also inflames her to remove herself from what Larsen indicates is a highly exploitative, sexist, and racist situation, namely, Copenhagen's high society and the potential marriage to its famous painter and chauvinist Axel Olsen.

The condition of "suspensive conflict" shadows Larsen's representations of crowds, beginning indeed with her titular image. Quicksand was once thought to be a special kind of sand in which, if one were caught, one inevitably sunk. It has since come to be understood to consist of ordinary sand "quickened" or animated to a certain viscosity by upward flows of water equal to or exceeding the buoyant weight of sand, in which the human being in fact is easily suspended. In Larsen's novel quicksand turns out to be emblematic not simply of the social and personal forces that pull Helga down but of Helga herself: Helga *as* quicksand.[24] For all of her flightiness, indeed on account of her flightiness, Helga embodies the principal qualities of quicksand, inert materiality and immaterial animation. Her actions or plans are repeatedly suspended and redirected by what she calls in herself an "imp of contumacy" (*Q* 51). At the time of formulating this thought, Helga, living in Harlem, is reflecting on her most recent "explosive contact," having suddenly fled from the visiting Robert Anderson, to whom she is still attracted (though unwilling to admit it to herself). "Until the very moment of his entrance, she had no intention of running away, but something, some imp of contumacy, drove her from his presence, though she longed to stay" (51). Despite this later self-chastisement, Helga's overdetermined "imp" is what prevents her from entering into the predictable, all too purposeful life of disciplinary and routinized race work that the drab, aptly grey-eyed Robert Anderson would likely offer her. Derailing her original intention to follow through with the visit, Helga resembles Poe's "imp of the perverse," which he describes as "a *mobile* without motive, a motive, not *motivirt*" (*sic*).[25] Similarly, Helga's imp affectively quickens her to the point of spontaneous disruption.

Helga, moreover, before arriving in Harlem, exhibits the impishness of Poe's well-known urban imp, the man of the crowd. Critics have shown how "the man" of Poe's short story applies equally to the nameless "decrepid old man" (*sic*) who meanders "backward and forward, without apparent object, among the throng" and the nameless narrator who observes him first from behind the bow window of a coffee house and later "resolve[s] to follow the stranger whithersoever he should go."[26] Similarly, Helga, upon reaching Chicago from Naxos, becomes both observer of and participant in the city crowd. She first observes it from the distance of her room at the YWCA, registering, as Robert Park would a couple of decades earlier, its metabolic movements: "She stood intently looking down into the glimmering street, far below, swarming with people, merging into little eddies and disengaging themselves to pursue their own individual ways" (*Q* 30). She reaches the limit of self-restraint, however, and is unable to maintain this distanced perspective:

A few minutes later she stood in the doorway, drawn by an uncontrollable desire to mingle with the crowd. The purple sky showed tremulous clouds piled up, drifting here and there *with a sort of endless lack of purpose. Very like the myriad human beings pressing hurriedly on.* Looking at these, Helga caught herself wondering who they were, what they did, and of what they thought. What was passing behind those dark molds of flesh. *Did they really think at all?* Yet, as she stepped out into the moving multi-colored crowd, there came to her *a queer feeling of enthusiasm*, as if she were tasting some agreeable, exotic food – sweetbreads, smothered with truffles and mushrooms – perhaps. And, oddly enough, she felt, too, that she had come home. She, Helga Crane, who had no home. (*Q* 30, emphasis added)

In rhetorically positing the question, "Did they really think at all?" Larsen suggests the opposite, that crowds do not think. Miming instead the inorganic state of clouds, the crowd radically materializes itself; it embodies the "endless lack of purpose" of inorganic matter, of consciousness pressed to its limit of non-thinking. Helga is compelled to join this mass. What she affirms as "home," then, is unsheltered rootlessness. Momentarily at least, she shares with Baudelaire's *flâneur* "the hate of home, and the passion for roaming."[27] Over the next days and weeks, while looking for work, Helga circulates within a pecuniary economy of excess that mirrors her physiology. She "spent hours in aimless strolling about the hustling streets of the Loop district" and, in true Baudelairean fashion, squandering her money on "things which she wanted, but did not need and certainly could not afford" (*Q* 32).

Perhaps more significant, however, is that immediately preceding this crowd scene Helga undergoes one of her most emotionally – and physiologically – battering experiences, in which she demonstrates not so much a love of traumatic adventure, as Baudelaire's male *flâneur* would, as a propensity to deploy the traumatic state of being as a weapon, as perhaps a vulnerable female must. Having been refused entrance into her uncle's home in Chicago, Helga "flee[s]." Larsen describes her as being so "torn with mad fright" that she is "unconscious of any change [in the weather], so shaken she was and burning. The wind cut her like a knife, but she did not feel it." It is at this limit of consciousness and feeling, at this self-fissure ("torn" and "cut" as she is), that Helga perversely yet successfully fends off a man who "accost[s] her":

> On such occasions she was wont to reply scathingly, but, tonight, his pale Caucasian face struck *her breaking faculties* as too droll. Laughing harshly, she threw at him the words: "You're not my uncle."
> He retired in haste, probably thinking her drunk, or possibly a little mad. (*Q* 29, emphasis added)

"Laughing" and "a little mad," this is Helga at her most spontaneous and adventuresome. She is temperamentally quickened to the "breaking" point of linguistic nonsense. The series of events leaves her feeling "vulnerable" and "wound[ed]" but also not feeling: "Night fell, while Helga Crane in the rushing swiftness of a roaring elevated train sat numb" (*Q* 29). In "rushing" motion but also anaesthetically inert, Helga's quicksand-like capacity for self-suspension primes her for visions of and immersion in the quicksand-like crowd. If she looks "intently" at the crowd, it is not with the insight of aestheticizing intentionality, but the blindness of anaesthetizing intensity, the "queer feeling of enthusiasm."

Later in the novel, in her depiction of a Harlem cabaret scene Larsen heightens the crowd's – and along with it, Helga's – resemblance to quicksand:

> They danced, ambling lazily to a crooning melody, or violently twisting their bodies, like whirling leaves, to a sudden streaming rhythm, or shaking themselves ecstatically to a thumping of unseen tomtoms... *The essence of life seemed bodily motion*... the crowd became a swirling mass. For the hundredth time [Helga] marvelled at the gradations within this oppressed race of hers. A dozen shades

slid by. There was sooty black, shiny black, taupe, mahogany, bronze, copper, gold, orange, yellow, peach, ivory, pinky white, pastry white. There was yellow hair, brown hair, black hair; straight hair, straightened hair, curly hair, crinkly hair, wooly hair. She saw black eyes in white faces, brown eyes in yellow faces, gray eyes in brown faces, blue eyes in tan faces. Africa, Europe, perhaps with a pinch of Asia, in a fantastic motley of ugliness and beauty, semi-barbaric, sophisticated, exotic, were here. But she was blind to its charm, purposely aloof and a little contemptuous, and soon her interest in *the moving mosaic* waned. (*Q* 59–60, emphasis added)

In this proliferation of human fragments – color, skin, hair, eyes and faces, all in a "swirling mass" – Larsen decomposes the human being into its inorganic components: matter and motion. Helga withdraws from this crowd to a "purposely aloof" distance, marking her return to self-consciousness, partly the consequence of her general prudishness but also of the specific situation in which she finds herself, namely, having "discovered Dr. Anderson sitting at a table on the far side of the room" (*Q* 59–60). Initially, however, and "for a while" she is not "blind to" but distinctly blinded by the "charm" of this crowd: "Helga was . . . oblivious of the oblivion of the other gyrating pairs, oblivious of the color, the noise, and the grand distorted childishness of it all. She was drugged, lifted, sustained by the extraordinary music, blown out, ripped out, beaten out by the joyous, wild murky orchestra" (*Q* 59).

Helga may come to censure this behavior but Larsen clearly does not. Helga's participation in the crowd dramatizes her being "lifted" or "sustained" in "bodily motion" as though a "moving mosaic" herself. Moreover, the syntax – the double passive construction in the last full sentence quoted above, coupled with its ellipsis of the second series of participles' pronoun and verb (that is, of "which was," which would connect the second series to "extraordinary music") – presses Helga to the limit of plausible human experience: besides being drugged, lifted and sustained, Helga is "blown out, ripped out, [and] beaten out" by the "joyous music." In contact with this moving mosaic, Helga simultaneously explodes out of it. In this manner Larsen revaluates and stands apart from what Helga, following convention and stereotype, disparages as being "in the jungle" (*Q* 59). Larsen's "primitive mood" neither disparages nor mystifies African-American culture. Rather, it imagines a new discursive possibility: the condition historically made available by urban modernity of becoming anonymous, of being-becoming matter in motion.[28]

This suspension of human identity animates Larsen's representation of what is perhaps the novel's most intense crowd scene, Helga Crane's "conversion" among the "frenzied women" in a storefront church. It animates, however, not the conversion experience per se, that is, the replacement of skepticism with Christian faith, but the affective arrest that Helga enters during the conversion, "in [which] moment she was lost – or saved" (*Q* 113). This is the arrest inhering in the *versio* of conversion, in pure turning; it is registered in Larsen's punctuating dash.[29]

Up to this point in the novel Larsen has attended little to Helga Crane's religious or, more precisely, non-religious inclination. The reader learns only of her contempt for the white preachers to whom she was required to listen in Naxos and of her willingness to put the Christian church in the service of her job hunt while in Chicago:

Helga Crane was not religious. She took nothing on trust. Nevertheless on Sundays she attended the very fashionable, very high services in the Negro Episcopal church on Michigan Avenue. She hoped that some good Christian would speak to her, invite her to return, or inquire kindly if she was a stranger in the city. None did, and she became bitter, distrusting religion more than ever. (*Q* 34)

Given religion's minimal thematic presence in the novel, along with Helga's general hostility towards the Christian faith and its practices, her sudden conversion and subsequent move to Alabama at the end of the novel have annoyed critics who, invested in a realist aesthetics, regard these events as implausible. Deborah McDowell observes that critics "have consistently criticized the endings of her novels... which reveal her difficulty with rounding off stories convincingly." She goes on both to agree with these criticisms and to offer an explanation that smooths over the abruptness of Larsen's endings:

Critics of Larsen have been rightly perplexed by these abrupt and contradictory endings. But if examined through the prism of black female sexuality, not only *do they make more sense*, they also illuminate the peculiar pressures on Larsen as a woman writer during the male-dominated Harlem Renaissance. They show her grappling with the conflicting demands of her racial and sexual identities and the contradictions of a black and feminine aesthetic... [These endings become] radical and original efforts to acknowledge a female sexual experience, most often repressed in both literary and social realms.[30]

As valuable as this interpretation is for an advanced understanding of Larsen's realist sexual politics, it overlooks how Larsen, much like her protagonist, ventures toward the limits of her writerly experience. She explodes, as it were, her contact to realist prose and its epistemological imperative to make conventional sense.

In a letter to Van Vechten, Larsen expresses as much frustration with her ending as her later critics: "Yes, I do think the thing is perhaps not so much *too short*, as *too thin*."[31] The next line suggests that this shortcoming has less to do with skill than will, that is, her will to writerly abjection. With Helga-like impetuosity she writes, "The truth is that I got awfully tired of it about the middle of the Copenhagen episode. That and the last chapter ought to be longer. I should hate terribly to have to write even one more word for the damned thing." Turning from a realist to what she might call a primitivist mode, Larsen suggests that the latter's "ironic survival" is contingent upon something like an authorial "attack of nerves." Though later she in fact does revise the manuscript, this attack left its narratologically violent mark. If up to now Larsen has been venturing primarily – though by no means exclusively – in a realist project, a project which demands credible relations of cause and effect, in the final episodes all bets are off. Reader and writer have been abandoned to the cause of narratological causelessness. Dragging her protagonist through the burlesqued world of lower-class faith-healing, Larsen renders the final episodes ludicrously absurd. Much like the Chicago street crowds that Helga compares to clouds, the novel enacts "a sort of endless lack of purpose" – a primitivist aesthetics, one could say, of crowdedness.

At the start of the conversion scene Helga Crane takes up where she left off in Chicago: wandering aimlessly and dejectedly through Harlem's streets because she has tried and failed to lure the now-married Dr. Anderson into bed. "In the streets, unusually deserted, the electric lights cast dull glows. Helga Crane, walking rapidly, aimlessly, could decide on no definite destination. She had not thought to take umbrella or even rubbers. Rain and wind whipped cruelly about her, drenching her garments and chilling her body... Unheeding these physical discomforts, she went on" (*Q* 110). When Helga comes across a storefront church, one might say that she meets her nomadic match.

Historically, the storefront church was an urban phenomenon. Not only were they geographically shifty, but so were their members. "Nobody knows," the sociologists Benjamin Mays and Joseph Nicholson quote one minister as saying, "how many folk are in a Baptist church." Another minister comments, "It is difficult to keep up with the people who join the church. Quite a few of them are renters and roomers. They move frequently, leaving no addresses. Many of them leave the city without notice."[32] Members of Harlem's talented and capitalizing tenth were less than enthusiastic over the African-American Christian cults and their storefront churches. James Weldon Johnson registers his distaste with particular clarity: "There are something like one hundred and sixty coloured churches in Harlem. A hundred of these could be closed and there would be left a sufficient number to supply the religious needs of the community... The superfluous one hundred or more are ephemeral and nomadic, belonging to no established denomination and within no classification. They are here today and gone somewhere else or gone entirely tomorrow." Johnson's annoyance with such "excess churches" of no classification derives from his ambition to see and make Harlem attain classified centrality. He writes, "In a community like Harlem . . . the church is [i.e., should be] a stabilizing force," going on to praise capital "churches like Mother Zion, St. Philip's, and Abyssinian, each of which is an organization with over a hundred years of continuous historical background."[33] Mays and Nicholson exhibit more sympathy for the nomadic churches, explaining that they may not be as short-lived as they appear, since "the church proper may exist for a long time, but move from one store-front to another," and that, in any case, they help rural people new to a metropolis adjust. Yet they too complain of the "promiscuous crowding together of churches," claiming that "the Negro has more churches than he can maintain in healthy condition"; thus they wish for "[i]ntelligent church planning" for the future.[34]

This prescription of institutional health entails a rationalist economy of proportion which would eliminate what Johnson calls "the waste brought about by the needless churches."[35] What annoys the Harlem capitalists is a promiscuity fermenting in and among these churches, the "crowding together" both of their physical structures and their physical members, whose effect is to deterritorialize the position and identity of any one discrete church, as well as any one discrete member. It disables the capitalizing will to hierarchical organization.

Larsen's novel dramatizes just how decapitalizing these nomadic churches can be. Their open- or revolving-door policy enables Helga, "drenched and disheveled," to take refuge in the "improvised meeting house" that she literally almost stumbles across: "She had opened the door and had entered before she was aware that, inside, people were singing a song" (*Q* 110–11). Although she recognizes the song from "years ago," the effect, with its constant refrain, "Showers of blessings," is "too much":

The appropriateness of the song, with its constant reference to showers, the ridiculousness of herself in such surroundings, was too much for Helga Crane's frayed nerves. She sat down on the floor, a dripping heap, and laughed and laughed and laughed. (*Q* 111)

When a crowd gathers, woman falls. Helga's abject laughter is at first met with the congregation's "shocked silence," yet it seems to function as an initiation rite, a password: "in a moment there were solicitous voices; she was assisted to her feet and led haltingly to a chair" (*Q* 111). This pattern of falling and rising will be repeated in the episode, grotesquely and in high burlesque. First there is the woman next to Helga who, as the crowd warms up, "in wild, ecstatic fury jumped up and down...clutching at the girl's coat, and screamed: 'Come to Jesus, you pore los' sinner!'" The drama builds as Helga shrinks away from the woman but loses her coat in the process. This reveals her "bare arms and neck growing out of the clinging red dress," causing the woman to "shriek," "'A scarlet 'oman. Come to Jesus, you pore los' Jezebel'" (*Q* 112). If this is not the first time that Helga has been identified as a prostitute (besides the stranger in Chicago, Axel Olsen also identifies her as such), it may well be the most perversely ironic. It is precisely Helga's virginity, her crowning failure to lure a man into adultery, that galls her into abject action.

Larsen's absurd, primitivist burlesque reaches full bloom when she shows the crowd, along with Helga, coming into – and, as it were, out of – its own. To gain an adequate view of this devolution the passage must be quoted at length:

Little by little the performance took on an almost Bacchic vehemence. Behind her, before her, beside her, frenzied women gesticulated, screamed, wept, and tottered to the praying of the preacher, which had gradually become a cadenced chant... Fascinated, Helga Crane watched until there crept upon her an indistinct horror of an unknown world. She felt herself in the presence of a nameless people...[T]he horror held her. She remained motionless...And as Helga watched and listened, gradually a curious influence penetrated her...she felt herself possessed by the same madness; she too felt a brutal desire to shout and sling herself about...she gathered herself for one last effort to escape, but vainly...She fell forward...For a single moment she remained there in silent stillness...And in that moment she was lost – or saved. The yelling figures about her pressed forward, closing her in on all sides...[W]ith no previous intention [she] began to yell like one insane... She was unconscious of the words she uttered, or their meaning...Some of the more exuberant worshippers had fainted into inert masses, the voices of others were almost spent. (*Q* 114–115)

This is primitive decapitalization at its uttermost, both Helga's and Larsen's. Unleashing implausibility with a vengeance, the author pitches the character to the crowd's hyperaesthetic heights of Bacchic frenzy and anaesthetic lows of "silent stillness," rendering her in effect one of the "nameless people." The crowd, in its "exuberan[ce]" (etymologically defined as *beyond abundance*), passes out of its human definitions and into the inhuman anonymity of "inert mass," linguistic nonsense, and "spent" voices.

If failing at luring a man into adultery triggers Helga's fall into abjection, her success at finding pure unadulterated sex with the Reverend

Mr. Pleasant Green seems to convert her back into a conscious being. As such she possesses two kinds of thought: the deluded variety, as when she aims, now in rural Alabama with her husband, "to subdue the cleanly scrubbed ugliness of her own surroundings to soft inoffensive beauty, and to help the other women [of the town] to do the same" (Q 119); and the awakened variety, as when she feels "an astonished anger at the quagmire in which she had engulfed herself. She had ruined her life" (Q 133). But in fact, there is no basis for assessing Helga's seemingly awakened thoughts as any less deluded. Her rapid oscillation between the two varieties indicates that her entire thinking process has become so insecure and polymorphously infantile as to immerse her in reflexive, indeed spasmodic, rather than reflective thinking. In effect, Helga has exhausted her human capital. Any thought goes; Larsen allows the reader to invest as little in her final recognition of having "been a fool" as in her conviction that, now full of hatred for her husband and the South, she "couldn't desert" her children (Q 133, 135).

In short, there is no telling that Helga will remain submerged in the quagmire of Southern rural life and child-bearing. Her fate, as I have tried to suggest, is both *of* quicksand and *as* quicksand; and, as bodily motion is the "essence of life," she may indeed resurface. Larsen's narrative strategies and dominant metaphors render her protagonist's fate irredeemably suspended rather than inevitably fatal.[36] As such, the novel confirms Larsen's own personal philosophy: "I don't have any way of approaching life," she once explained to an interviewer, "it does things to me instead."[37]

In her novel Larsen suggests that this assertion of the agency of "life" over and above race consciousness, as it occasions self-dissolution, may be the only alternative to a politicized comprehensive doctrine of being black. As Larsen herself, in her status as author, exhibits a certain attraction to this self-abjecting propensity, she all but suspends contact with the political-liberal perspective that underwrites her satirical critique of Harlem's politics of identity. But where Larsen's character becomes quicksand, Larsen herself ultimately does not. She signs off on the novel's publication, however irritated she is by its quality. Implied therein is the recovery of a reliably intentional consciousness – one that functions, in fact, apart from racial or cultural identity. And it is from this perch of contractual consent and satirical critique that Larsen contributes to what I have been suggesting throughout this book is a particular literary history: one confirming, however understated, the abiding virtues of political-liberal ideas and practices.

CHAPTER 6

Breaking the waves: mass immigration, trauma, and ethno-political consciousness in Cahan, Yezierska, and Roth

"The street paused." Only metaphorically would a street pause because only metaphorically could a street move. Yet where this sentence appears in the penultimate chapter of Henry Roth's *Call It Sleep* (1934), a chapter famous for its Joycean lyricism, the effect is more realistic than lyrical. In invoking the street Roth quite clearly refers to the people in the street who do indeed pause – and moments later form a crowd – when David the boy-protagonist short circuits the trolley line's third rail. However, most of the people who pause are not in the street per se, but rather indoors where they are distracted by the incident from "their tasks, their play, from faces, newspapers, dishes, cards, seidels, valves, [and] sewing machines."[1] Still, as a literary conceit the pausing street draws little attention; it pales in comparison to the synaesthetic phantasm appearing a few lines later in which Roth depicts the short circuit incident itself: "a quaking splendor dissolved the cobbles, the grimy structures, bleary stables, the dump-heap, river and sky into a single cymbal-clash of light. Between the livid jaws of the rail, the dipper twisted and bounced, consumed in roaring radiance, candescent –" (*CS* 419). Next to such verbal turbulence, the pausing street looks veritably like *terra firma*.

I belabor this point about the street's inconspicuousness as a figure of speech because this very feature reinscribes the ordinary neglect of an important truth about most streets: they result from a publicly recognized need for transportation systems and are integral to a municipality's political-economic infrastructure. On the most basic level public street maintenance facilitates, in the civil-libertarian vein, citizens' equal access to available goods and services, and, in the economic vein, a municipality's commercial and industrial transactions. Overlooking this prosaic truth, figurative invocations of "the street" tend to associate it with more dynamic, more scenic socio-cultural phenomena – with, say, strangers commingling, whether leisurely or for business; with like-minded individuals congregating for spontaneous or scheduled political demonstration; or, as in Roth's case, with neighbors residing. Hence Peter Jukes in *A Shout in the Street* can make the affirming assertion that "the street, by definition, is a place of debate between ambivalent clashing perspectives."[2] Be that as it may, the street is also a place of public consent.

In *Call It Sleep* the semantic elision of the street's prosaic public-municipal identity makes thematic sense. Roth depicts a vibrant crowded world of immigrants, the Lower East Side in the early twentieth century, that, occupied with the troubles and pleasures of everyday life, takes only the faintest notice of the public infrastructure and organization. Yet the elision makes thematic sense for essentially the opposite reason as well. Roth shows how the ethnic-immigrant adults populating this world conduct themselves largely in accordance with prevailing liberal public principles and with the municipality's infrastructural designs. The publicness of the public street, in other words, may be lost to fingertip consciousness but it is by no means forgotten. That the child protagonist David's intensely personal, quasi-delusional odyssey involves the engagement (as near-executioner) of a quite prominent public utility, the trolley system's electric line, suggests the lengths to which Roth goes to delineate the dual significance of this elision. It is integral to his larger portrait of what might be called liberal-democratic society's dualistic imagination. There is David's idiosyncratic, phantasmatic imagination, which sees the third rail as unadulterated "titanic power" (*CS* 419); and there is the public functional imagination, as represented by Dan MacIntyre who, in his capacity as motorman, engages the third rail to move the trolley car and who frets when a vendor dawdles on the tracks, putting him behind schedule. While this motorman of the trolley franchise is himself personally so "enraged" at "this lousy dago blocking traffic" that "[h]e'd like to smack the piss out of him," he conducts himself according to a liberal-municipal ethos: "He pounded the bell instead" (*CS* 412). Both David and Dan rely on the steady presence and the predictability of the public utility's electric current to carry out their diverse projects.[3]

Later in this chapter I develop the argument that Roth represents the "eclipse" of the public and of liberalism – to borrow John Dewey's phrase from the late 1920s and early 1930s – in order to disclose the liberal public's abiding if also ignored functional and principled relevance. His articulation of a dualistic imagination draws together his specific focus on David's childhood experiences and his broader view of the East Side immigrant population. They converge dramatically at the end of the novel in one of the most prolonged crowd scenes in literary history. Ultimately, then, Roth's dualism informs his orientation toward the nation's history of mass

immigration and the concomitant emergence of an ethnic-immigrant subjectivity. As we shall see, Roth importantly rewrites what Randolph Bourne
called in 1916 the nation's "great social drama" which presented itself "as
the waves of immigration broke over it."[4]

Narratives from within the immigrant population of what has come to be
known as the second great wave of immigration occurring in the late nineteenth and early twentieth centuries often mirrored American commentators from without in their sense of arriving among teeming multitudes, of
belonging to the tides, waves, and streams of newcomers, estranged and
estranging.[5] In support of their cause for immigration restriction, nativists
needed to look no farther than an immigrant's own depiction of his or her
world, such as Abraham Cahan's in *Yekl* (1896):

Suffolk Street... [on] the East Side... is one of the most densely populated spots
on the face of the earth – a seething human sea fed by streams, streamlets, and rills
of immigration flowing from all the Yiddish-speaking centers of Europe... [I]n
fine, people with all sorts of antecedents, tastes, habits, inclinations, and speaking
all sorts of subdialects of the same jargon, thrown pellmell into one social caldron –
a human hodgepodge with its component parts changed but not yet fused into
one homogeneous whole.[6]

Not only do immigrants depict themselves living in such nearly inhuman
conditions, but some of them yearn for it. Anzia Yezierska's protagonist
in *Bread Givers* (1925), for example, hates the New Jersey town to which
she has had to move with her parents. She misses the ghetto pulse: "The
crowds sweeping you on, like waves of a beating sea. The shop. The roar of
the rushing machines. The drive and the thrill of doing things faster and
faster."[7]

Such self-representations could confirm nativist sentiment that the immigration population was not made of the right stuff. "At the deepest
level," the historian John Higham explains, "what impelled the restriction
movement in the early decades of the twentieth century was the discovery that immigration was undermining the unity of American culture and
threatening the accustomed dominance of a white Protestant people of
northern European descent."[8] The protection of white culture, of course,
required more than a culture war waged on paper; it required *policy*. The
immigration restriction policies of the era, as they set the terms regarding
which ethnic groups and how many from each would be permitted entry, reflected the degree to which race or ethnicity per se had become a
public-political matter. In other words, a newcomer's political status as an
immigrant and his or her personal status as belonging to an ethnic group

were rendered inseparable. However "hyphenated" such a person's ethnic identity might become through assimilation, there would be no operative dualism along the personal-political axis. According to nativist logic, what one was personally matched what one was politically.

It is the contention of this chapter that Roth's retention of an operative dualism in *Call It Sleep* enables him to break with the ethno-political ideology in which the personal and the political converge. This is what distinguishes his novel from such predecessors in immigrant fiction as Cahan's *The Rise of David Levinsky* (1917) and Yezierska's *Bread Givers*. Moreover, as we shall see, Roth disarticulates the personal and the political by appropriating a psycho-discursive phenomenon so often connected to the immigrant narrative of assimilation, namely, *trauma*. Historically coinciding with a resurgent psychoanalytic interest in the nature of neurotic and normative trauma, these three writers adapt various elements of its logic to their accounts of ethnic-immigrant psychic life.[9] In secondary literature on immigrant narrative, casual references to the traumatic dimensions of assimilation abound, such as Alice Kessler Harris's comment that Yezierska's "work is suffused with the unending trauma of adjustment, with the psychic stress of adaptation"; and Jules Chametzky's more general description of Americanization as "cultural trauma familiar to all new immigrants." William Boelhower describes the "perspectival system inherent in the immigrant experience" as one involving "a catastrophic act of topological dislocation."[10] As a means of organizing the storm and stress of Old World and New World conflicts, particularly in relation to the nuclear family, the discourse of trauma appears to fill the psychic bill.

While it is probably going too far to say that a nativist politics was conceptually dependent on a logic of trauma in its effort to define ethnic immigrants as constitutively un-American, what should become clear over the course of this chapter is how neatly an immigrant narrative detailing the traumas of assimilation dovetailed with nativist claims.[11] Implying as conventional trauma theory did that the traumatized subject's history was always with her or him, that this subject was always possessed by her or his history, such a psychic economy matched the nativist claim that an immigrant was constitutively unfit to assume an American identity. As a function of personal history, one's psychic economy mapped onto one's ethno-political identity.

Of the three novels discussed in this chapter, only Roth's puts trauma theory – and notably an unconventional version of it – to work *against* this convergence of personal, ethnic experience and public-political identity. Resonating instead with some of the arguments advanced by John Dewey in the 1920s and 30s about the need to preserve a dualism in the formation of a democratic public, Roth's novel may be understood as breaking from the literary waves treating immigrant ethnicity in the early twentieth century, as washing against the ideological and essentially nativist tendency to conflate the personal and the political.

SUCCESSIVE SUCCESSES

The Rise of David Levinsky (1917) is a fictional memoir of a Russian Jew who, now around sixty years old and very wealthy due to his success in the cloak-making industry, had arrived destitute in New York in the 1880s. Cahan himself was an immigrant, and through his work as political activist, literary writer, public intellectual and journalist in both Yiddish and English, he became fully versed in the era's ethno-political discourse propagated by such personages as Theodore Roosevelt, Woodrow Wilson, and Calvin Coolidge, Edward Ross and Horace Kallen, Herbert Croly and Randolph Bourne. His novel is shaped by this discourse; it treats the impact of the ethno-political ideology on the Jewish immigrant consciousness, laying out the impossibility of ever becoming a true American.

In his appeal to "true Americanism," Theodore Roosevelt offers within the space of half a dozen lines two ways for immigrants to reconstruct their history of becoming Americans. The first involves naturalization: "After passing through the crucible of naturalization... we are Americans." The second involves physical relocation: "We are Americans from the moment we touch the American shore."[12] Given Roosevelt's notoriously demanding patriotism, which fueled his exhortations that immigrants shed their past allegiances and identities, it must be assumed that the second way of becoming an American, touching the shore, is good only retroactively, that is, after the conditions of the first way, naturalization, have been met. Only if one has assimilated to the American way can one describe oneself as having become American in the moment of touching its shore. This retroactive reconstruction, one could say, is the poetic license granted by the offices of Roosevelt's true Americanism to the immigrant who tells the true tale of true Americanization.

For Cahan's protagonist David Levinsky, however, neither reconstruction – neither touching the shore nor embracing the crucible – delivers him properly to the state of being an American. This is because the self-reflexive narrative logic to which he adheres operates under the sign of nativism rather than assimilationism. No personal narrative can produce for him an American identity because none can eliminate the brute fact of his foreign birth: "That I was not born in America was something like a physical defect." Roosevelt's stringent assimilationism included the directive that "[w]e must Americanize [newcomers] in every way" including "speech."[13] But Levinksy perceives himself as essentially, not simply circumstantially, inadequate in this regard. He "lack[s]" the "special slang sense" with which Americans are "born," and consequently finds himself always lagging behind the natives who "were so quick to discern and adopt these phrases" (*RDL* 291). Of course, only someone who learns slang at quite a clip, and thus possesses a fair command of idiomatic English, can perceive a discrepancy as subtle as the rate of learning slang. Nevertheless a nativist self-perception works to cast Levinsky's adaptability as defected. Earlier too he remarks that "[p]eople who were born to speak English were superior beings... [They] were real Americans" (*RDL* 176).

With the narrator-protagonist's nativist determination of identity as a matter of being rather than doing – to apply the distinction Walter Michaels lays out in *Our America* – the question arises as to what his autobiographical account of Americanization, of doing things as Americans do them, signifies. *The Rise of David Levinsky* is most often read as a rags-to-riches tale of Americanization and the loss of ethnic identity. Chametzky, for instance, describes the novel's "lacerating theme" as "the price an individual or group pays when, for the sake of success in material terms, it temporizes with its best self," the best self being a non-Americanized Russian Jew.[14] The novel ends as it begins, with the backward-looking narrator registering his regret, finding himself a captain of industry with only empty, nostalgic attachment to Antomir, Russia, his birthplace. In my view, however, Levinsky's nativism essentially reverses the flow of psychic affliction: his constitutive resistance to being American, not his process of Americanization, is what precipitates much of his grief and his yearning for the land of his birth.

Levinsky's nativist sentiment, which is refracted throughout the novel in expressions of self-disappointment and embarrassment about his Old World ways, seems to override both his general description of "the immigrant's arrival in his new home [as being] like a second birth to him" (*RDL* 86) and his personal account of celebrating the 25th anniversary of his own "Landing Day," which is more important to him than his "real birthday" (*RDL* 513). Indeed the date of his touching the shore is more important because it retroactively marks the day that he does *not* become a "real American." He is at once born and aborted; he launches an on-shore odyssey of Americanization, just as he launches what retroactively emerges as an overgrown obituary reiterating the fact of not being an American.

Phillip Barrish has instructively elucidated how, from a sociological point of view, David Levinsky's distanced expertise in the marginal, hence exotic, life of Jews in New York authorizes his position as narrator.[15] By contrast, I would emphasize that, from a psycho-subjective point of view, Levinsky's trenchant nativism traumatizes his relation to Americanization. Supplying him as it does with a birth defect, nativism is what spurs him to narrate at all. Further, the nativist narrative resulting from Levinsky's traumatized psyche dictates the subsumption of a purely neutral or abstract public identity, namely his official status as an immigrant, into a personal-political consciousness in which the contingency of birthplace defines him ethno-politically as non-American.

Cahan's novel itself supplies an account of the implications of trauma's effect on memory and narrative representation. Levinsky recounts an episode from his severely impoverished childhood in which his mother is devastated upon learning of the damage done to the family drinking cup when David slips and falls on his way home from the tinsmith's where the cup has just been repaired: "When my mother discovered the damage she made me tell the story of the accident over and over again, wringing her hands and sighing as she listened" (*RDL* 7). The mother's need to relive, through narrative reproduction, the crisis as a crisis is symptomatic of the traumatized mind. Freud encountered patients who were "obliged to *repeat* the repressed material as a contemporary experience instead of, as the physician would prefer to see, *remembering* it as something belonging to the past."[16] In the novel, the remembered contents of the young son's narrative constituting its pastness are of secondary importance relative to the narrative's formal function of enabling the mother's absorptive reliving of the past as immediately and distressingly present.

The older, Americanized Levinsky exhibits symptoms similar to his mother. In his self-introduction as narrator he comments on his relation to his past, describing how he "love[s] to brood over [his] youth" (*RDL* 3). What is significant about this statement is not so much the specific disposition of mourning associated with brooding as the fact that he desires to brood, and that there is nothing in his psychic economy to block this grief-inducing desire. The autobiography itself is evidence of Levinsky's veritable compulsion to recollect. Additionally, Levinsky goes on to describe long past events as "com[ing] back to [him] with the distinctness of yesterday"; he defines "the dearest days in one's life" as "those that seem very far and very near at once" (*RDL* 3). While the capacity to render "very near" events or representations that are distant is not exclusive to the traumatic subject – as this study has shown, those capable of an absorptive aesthetic relation are similarly disposed – it does conform to the traumatic subject's compulsive presentism.

Furthermore, there is much evidence of multiple traumatizing events in David Levinsky's life history. First, there is his mother's brutal death at the hands of Russian anti-Semites:

It was not until I found myself lying on this improvised bed [in the synagogue] that I realized the full extent of my calamity... I had been in an excited, hazy state of mind, more conscious of being the central figure of a great sensation than of my loss. As I went to bed on the synagogue bench, however, instead of in my old bunk at what had been my home, the fact that my mother was dead and would never be alive again smote me with crushing violence. It was as though I had just discovered it. I shall never forget that terrible night. (*RDL* 53–54)

Here the young Levinsky's "excited, hazy state of mind" and, some time later, the "crushing" sense of having "just discovered" his mother's death, indicate the self-dissociation brought on by shock, as well as the cycle of forgetting and remembering that trauma was thought often to entail. Less crushingly traumatic but seemingly more in need of psychic repetition is the prior death of David's father, which leaves "a great blank in [his] family nest" (*RDL* 5). Not unlike Freud's account of the child who develops a *fort/da* game as a means simultaneously of coping with and reproducing the pain of his mother's departure, young David attempts to erase the "blank" by using his father's "rusty old coat...as a quilt" but only ambivalently succeeds:

I would pull it over my head, shut my eyes tight, and evoke a flow of fantastic shapes, bright, beautifully tinted, and incessantly changing form and color. While the play of these figures and hues was going on before me I would see all sorts of bizarre visions, which at times seemed to have something to do with my father's spirit. (*RDL* 5)

Where a "blank" once was is now an equally vacuous, if more colorful, "spirit." Finally, there is David Levinsky's demographic history. He counts himself among the "[o]ver five million people [who] were suddenly made to realize that their birthplace was not their home" (*RDL* 61).

Moreover, these trauma-related incidents of childhood past have a way of reappearing later in life. The homelessness of persecuted Jews resurfaces as his own chronic homelessness in New York (like Dreiser's Carrie, his final station is a "high-class hotel" [*RDL* 526]). The relic of his father, the coat, resurfaces as Levinsky's prized object of manufacture. The fantasy of incessant changefulness resurfaces as his consummate talent for role-playing. In other words, as an autobiographical, self-loathing narrator who loves to brood over his painful youth, Levinsky dwells on traumatic incidents from his Antomir years that are bound to repeat themselves in New York. He thereby creates for himself a host of opportunities to imitate his trauma-tized mother, "wringing her hands and sighing as she listened" to what she already has heard.

It is important to understand that the claim that traumatic events early in Levinsky's childhood shape his life history is not inconsistent with the claim that his traumatic consciousness is tightly bound up with his recogni-tion of his birth defect, which occurs only after he is deeply Americanized. Given, first, the often retroactive (that is, latent) manifestation of trauma; second, the retrospective structure of autobiography; and, third, the se-lectivity of memory, it is impossible to ascertain whether the childhood crises trigger his life of repetition compulsion, or conversely, whether the later traumatic discovery of his birth defect triggers his selection of par-ticular events that typologically reiterate his condition. The actual source of his trauma is less important than the fact of his current enactment of a traumatic consciousness.

Whatever its source, the traumatic consciousness offers the means for an Americanized, nativist ethnic-immigrant to tell his life story not so much as one of self-betraying material success, but as a series of self-confirming successes. This series underscores Levinsky's plight: his condition of perpet-ual succession, his condition of doing rather than being. "Success! Success! Success! It was the almighty goddess of the hour" (*RDL* 445). Levinsky's account of a particularly winning business hour also bespeaks his currently winning story hour, which in turn evinces his traumatic self-constitution. Success succeeds success: the defect that prevents him from being a real American locks him into a mode of self-loathing confession wherein he endlessly bests himself in doing things as Americans do them.

But even as Levinsky's traumatic consciousness persistently confirms his sense of not being a real American, its conditions and compulsions ulti-mately conspire to render indistinguishable his Old World and New World modes of doing. Isaac Rosenfeld observed decades ago that Levinsky does things so well in the American way because he does them so well in the Jewish way. Rosenfeld goes on to argue that Levinsky's career "draws our attention to the considerable structural congruity that must underlie the character and culture of the two peoples." His self-reliance, ingenuity, in-dustriousness, and tradesman duplicity have roots in both cultures. But Rosenfeld singles out as the most significant parallel Levinsky's yearning and dissatisfaction, which, "turning on itself and becoming its own object," amounts to a "reflexive" "desire for desire."[17] Though operating in a dif-ferent psychoanalytic register, Rosenfeld's diagnosis of Levinsky's reflexive desire dovetails with what I see as his traumatic nativism. Both identify him as in a state of perpetual succession. But through the lens of traumatic nativism we also discern the significance of Levinsky's self-identification according not to his deeds but to his birth. Actions, passions, and character are thus subordinated to a nativist-oriented ethno-political discourse that renders the autobiographical "confession" a mode of talking therapy that has no cure in sight. The more he achieves in the American way the more firmly his immigrant status settles into his consciousness as an ethnic status that cannot be overcome. Bearing witness to his past proves to be the most successful means of reiterating this invention taken for truth.

BLOOD AND IRON

Where David Levinsky suffers the psychic injury of not having been born in America, Sara Smolinsky, the autobiographical protagonist of Anzia Yezierska's *Bread Givers* (1925) is chronically struck by the thought of having never been born at all. The initial occurrence of this thought happens in her childhood during a family argument in which her tyrannical Old World father deems it "nonsense" that his daughters should choose their own spouses. The mother's contribution to the argument reflects her usual divided state of sharing her daughters' point of view while ultimately acquiescing to the father's: "Maybe if I had the sense of my daughters in America, I would have given you a good look over before the wedding" (*BG* 76). Her accompanying "funny smile" and head shake make clear her intention to tease her husband with this remark, but its effect on young Sara is much more drastic: "In the stillness that followed Mother's words, I was thinking: Suppose Mother had not felt like marrying Father, then where would all of us children be now?" (*BG* 76). The invoked "stillness" – absence of motion, of sound – indicates the obvious answer, that these particular children simply would not "be" anywhere. Sara demonstrates her grasp of this personally appalling reality when she chastises herself for "foolish[ly]" wishing that just as "girls [should] pick out for themselves the men they want for husbands...children also could pick out their fathers and mothers" (*BG* 76). However much social "sense" it might make for women to choose their spouses, she recognizes the logical "nonsense" of children choosing their parents.

When in 1915 Horace Kallen famously invoked the fact that persons can't change their grandfathers, he did so to promote what he came eventually to call "cultural pluralism," wherein persons define themselves according to their ethnic past.[18] When Yezierska has her protagonist run up against essentially the same fact, she does so to dramatize the shock of recognizing one's existential precariousness. Thus where Kallen mobilizes biological reproduction to underwrite an ethnic psycho-subjectivity that redeems the past, that repudiates assimilationism by calling for a re-attachment of the ethnic-immigrant's past to his or her present affective consciousness, Yezierska mobilizes biological reproduction to imbue her protagonist with an awareness that her possession of a past and present, whatever their relation, but for the grace of contingency, would not have been possible at all.

In an ethnic-immigrant novel about a historically and geopolitically specific "struggle" – as the subtitle puts it – "between a father of the Old World and a daughter of the New," this episode of existential crisis stands out for its secularly universal applicability. Possessing nothing more than self-consciousness and an understanding of causality, human beings anywhere and anytime might contemplate the contingencies of their secular birth. Yet for all its universality, in *Bread Givers* the traumatizing thought of being nothing or nobody instead of something or somebody is intimately bound up with Sara Smolinsky's self-identification as an Americanized ethnic American. This has not to do with, say, her taking literally Roosevelt's hyperbolic threat directed at immigrants that "the man who does not become Americanized ... becomes nothing at all."[19] Rather, it has to do with how she understands her relation to her Old World Jewish parents, specifically her father. What inspires her fantasy about being able to choose parents is her hatred for her misogynist, self-centered, unemployed, indigent, impractical, imperiously patriarchal, Torah-studying father. He is the one who perpetually abuses her with threats of being nothing, by for instance reminding her that "a woman without a man" (such as the rebellious Sara seems then destined to become) amounts to "[l]ess than nothing – a blotted out existence" (*BG* 205). More extreme and devastating is a later incident, when their hostilities reach the boiling point and she reveals to him that she ran away because she "hated" him, provoking him to expel her from the family: "How came you ever to be my child? I disown you. I curse you. May your name and your memory be blotted out of this earth" (*BG* 207–208). His curse reproduces her hate-inspired traumatic thought of having never been born.

Since her father is one of the parents who brought her into being, Smolinsky cannot accept the fact that she hates him enough to wish him not to be her father – as that wish implies in turn a wish to be herself nothing instead of something. In other words, Smolinsky cannot distinguish between a hatred of her father's doing, his conduct, and a hatred of his being, the biological fact of his being alive. By the end of the narrative Smolinsky resolves the traumatizing fact of hating her birth-parent not by separating out his hateful doing from his biological being, but by ceasing to hate him:

How could I have hated him and tried to blot him out of my life? Can I hate my own arm, my hand that is part of me? Can a tree hate the roots from which it sprang? Deeper than love, deeper than pity, is that oneness of the flesh that's in him and in me. (*BG* 286)

Having by this point obtained a college degree, a teaching post, nice clothes, and other accoutrements of Americanization, Smolinsky is no longer motivated to hate her father because she no longer has to view him as the massive barrier to her successful Americanization. Indeed she can now say that he contributes to her success: "Who gave me the fire, the passion, to push myself up from the dirt? If I grow, if I rise, if I ever amount to something, is it not his spirit burning in me?" (*BG* 286). Not unlike David Levinsky, then, Sara Smolinsky becomes a New World girl by exercising her Old World "spirit." In this roundabout way she effectively confirms Kallen's cultural pluralism in which ethnic birth remains the primary source of identity.

Over the course of the novel Sara Smolinsky's trauma of discovering herself wishing away her life by wishing to pick out a different father plays itself out in the form – as opposed to the manifest content – her Americanization takes. The point I wish to emphasize is not so much that Smolinsky, in ceasing to hate her father and in accepting her Polish-Jewish roots as that which helped her to Americanize, has resolved the polar tension between ethnic identity and assimilation. Rather, what needs to be understood is that she succeeds in smuggling in her father's "spirit" of tyranny to organize her project of Americanization.[20] The New World Smolinsky, of course, is no visible tyrant. From the glimpses provided of her teaching persona, she is not even bossy – she laughs good-naturedly while encouraging her pupils to pronounce words correctly (*BG* 271–272). Nevertheless, her motivating imagination of Americanization retains the logic of dominance and power. She envisions even the best of human relations accordingly: her spousal ideal is an "American-born man who was his own boss... [a]nd would let me be my own boss" (*BG* 66). In other words, her ideal American is a laissez-faire libertarian. Over the course of the narrative it becomes clear that what she calls "the bottom starting-point of becoming a person" (*BG* 159) conforms to this ideal of negative freedom and self-interest. For instance, the specific situation giving rise to this phrase is Smolinsky's first-ever rental of a room of her own. She describes the event marking her independence with libertarian flourish and glee: "Like a drowning person clinging to a rope, my tired body edged up to that door and clung to it... This was the door of life" (*BG* 159). Having now a "separate door to [her]self – a door to shut out all the noises of the world" (*BG* 159), Smolinsky reinscribes the libertarian vision of negative freedom as an assertion of her sovereign individuality over the restrictive claims of society. As will be discussed more fully in the following section, it is this adversarial version of the American political system that her teacher and one-time intimate friend, John Dewey, stands up against in his 1927 *The Public and Its Problems* and elsewhere.

Throughout *Bread Givers* the notion of becoming a "person," of being a "person among people," functions as a touchstone against which Smolinsky measures the success of her Americanization and her rejection of her father's Old World ways. As a child, for instance, she likes to peddle herring because she earns money, which "made [her] feel independent, like a real person" (*BG* 28). Yet being "a person among people" is precisely the claim her father makes for himself (*BG* 75). And when he is among "people," not just his family, he exhibits a consummate incapacity to accommodate or respect public law, due not least to his "fear" of God's law (*BG* 64). Foremost among the examples of this non-assimilative streak is his violent assault on the obnoxious landlady who, demanding back rent, disrespects his devotion to the Holy Torah. When she has him arrested the father retains for the ensuing court trial a lawyer who in effect argues that public law should accommodate his client:

In high American language the lawyer made a speech to the judge and showed with his hands all those people who looked up to Father as the light of their lives. And then he told the Court to look on Father's face, how it shined from him, like from a child, the goodness from the holy life of prayer... And he called on the neighbors to give witness how Father loved only stillness and peace and his learning from his books. And if he hit the landlady, it was only because she burst into the house in the midst of his prayers, and knocked his Bible out of his hands and stepped on it with her feet. (*BG* 24–25)

The family's neighbors who "have crowded themselves into the court to hear the trial," reinforce this flouting of the public laws against assault. After the judge dismisses the charge, "[a]ll the people stamped their feet and clapped their hands, with the pleasure of getting even" (*BG* 24, 26). Among people, then, Smolinsky's father manages to shape a collective sentiment according to his own religious lights; he manages to sway even the public institution of justice into accommodating his logic of "getting even," whose manifestations include assault with impunity.

While Sara Smolinsky's own actions against public-political principles are not so egregious, in her orientation toward the public institution to which she commits herself, education, she exhibits a similar disregard for its political-liberal underpinnings. For one thing, she imagines school as a "battle-field" and herself as a "soldier in battle" who has to "fight for every bit of [her] education" (*BG* 233, 178, 218). Such combativeness inspires her to rail against "those bosses of education who made us study so much dead stuff," such as geometry, which "stupef[ies her]" (*BG* 181, 187). Embattlement turns out to describe not merely her relation to institutions of learning but also to knowledge itself. Education, for her, is a drama of conquest: "Nothing was so beautiful as to learn, to know, to master by the sheer force of my will even the dead squares and triangles of geometry" (*BG* 201).

That geometry is her least favorite and worst subject (failing it as she does both in night school and college), reveals her scant appreciation for abstract thinking. Indeed, the only knowledge she cares to obtain is the kind she already knows: "I only want to know what interests me. Why should I have to choke myself with geometry? ... I want the knowledge that is the living life" (*BG* 181). She rejects geometry not only because it is "dead" in her view, but because it is "the *same* deadness that we all got to know *alike*"; it does not take into account the fact that students comprise "all kinds of *different* people" (*BG* 181, emphasis added). Despite the semantic neutrality imbuing her mantra, to become a person among people, knowledge counts for Smolinsky primarily to the extent that it accommodates difference; public education is valuable insofar as it is personalized. No wonder that in college psychology becomes her favorite subject and that her greatest achievement there is winning first prize for her submission to the essay contest on "What the College Has Done for Me." Accepting the award at Commencement, Smolinsky recalls "standing before that sea of faces," before the students who were "cheering and waving and calling [her] name, like a triumph" (*BG* 233–234). Being honored by a crowd of what she, like David Levinsky, calls "real Americans" (*BG* 210), whose earlier exclusions made her feel like "nothing and nobody" (*BG* 219), this event marks her success at becoming a highly personalized person among people.

This is not to say that Sara Smolinsky has no regard for any sort of reason. Indeed, her account of attending college is in large part about her ultimate grasp of reason. But for her, reason means either self-restraint or scientific objectivity. It does not seem to encompass the political-liberal principles of justice or consensus. She considers herself "now a person of reason" when, having "learned self-control," she does not erupt in anger after students in class laugh at her naive comment (*BG* 233). She expresses deep gratitude for her professor Mr. Edman's lessons in the "new world of reason and 'objectivity'": "through him, I had learned to think logically for the first time in my life... Through him I have gained this impersonal, scientific state of mind" (*BG* 226). By the evidence supplied, however, the mode of logic and reasoning she has learned stops at causal relations and extrapolation. For instance, in order to grasp the concepts of apperception, the reflex arc, and inhibition, Mr. Edman asks his students to search through their "own experience" to find examples of psychological conflict, of interference between emotion and intellect, a task which Smolinsky carries out with zeal (*BG* 222). Such processes of objective extrapolation are indeed necessary to a liberal-democratic polity – the viability of whose judgments of procedure and policy depends on their relevance to human experience. But they are not sufficient. As Dewey maintained, in Robert Westbrook's well-formulated paraphrase, "Scientific reasoning was of inestimable value in determining what one should do to live the life one wished to live,... but it could render no definitive judgment about what sort of life one should want to live. This was the work not of scientific intelligence but of moral imagination."[21]

In her bid for a laissez-faire, libertarian mode of Americanization Sara Smolinsky accordingly associates herself with three particular icons of Americanism: Columbus, the pilgrim fathers, and the pioneers (*BG* 209, 232).[22] With the first two operating historically under the auspices of a monarchy seeking geopolitical power (to which the pilgrims added their own ambition of manifest theocracy), and the third emblematizing the will to "survive" in the "wilderness" against all odds (*BG* 232), these icons evoke willpower and unflinching commitment. Smolinsky's nickname from her father, *Blut und Eisen*, blood and iron, bespeaks her destiny as an ethnic-immigrant-pilgrim-pioneer. In sum, Smolinsky's entire American identity is conditioned by one element: force. "A triumphant sense of power fill[s]" her, not only because she finds herself "a teacher in the public schools" (*BG* 241), but because where there is no power in her being, there is, as the reader learns time and again, "nothing." Interestingly enough, at one point when she is feeling particularly triumphant in her solitary achievements, she associates this power with a crowd power: "The strength of a million people was surging in me... I was alone with myself, was enjoying myself for the first time as with the grandest company" (*BG* 157). Where one so easily becomes two, and two multiplies into a million, Smolinsky, once she hits her libertarian stride, need never face becoming nothing.

Yet as it also happens, the only time she thinks of nothingness favorably is when, on a date, she encounters the dancing crowds in a New York nightclub: "To lose myself in the mad joy of the crowd... This was the life" (*BG* 193). Her association here of the crowd with "life" allows her to convert nothingness itself into a force. Thus does it become life itself. And thus does it accord with comments appearing elsewhere in the narrative, such as when she imagines herself, pursuing knowledge, as "touch[ing] the fiery center of life," or when she likens herself to "the sun so active with life" (*BG* 230, 282). Though she abandons the theological dogma fueling her father's imperiousness, Sara Smolinsky's converts his blood and iron into her empowered, indeed burning, sense of being a person among people. This translation may well ward off the traumatizing thought of not being born, but it will also conform to the personal-political (and nativist) ideology that Dewey, for one, found in need of eradication.

BORN IN THE CRACK

Where in *Bread Givers* the crowd functions as a sort of objective correlative of the force Sara Smolinsky endeavors to harness so as to become an ethno-political person among ethno-political people, in *Call It Sleep* (1934) the crowd contributes to Roth's annulment of this conflationary picture. That is, the crowd levers his reconfiguration of the dualistic immigrant. On the one hand, Roth constructs a big picture of those immigrants who constitute a wave breaking over the Lower East Side. The novel opens in 1907, "the year that was destined to bring the greatest number of immigrants to the shores of the United States. All that day [when David's father comes to meet the newly arrived wife and child at the boat] her decks had been thronged by hundreds upon hundreds of foreigners, natives from almost every land in the world" (*CS* 9). Such throngs resolve into adults who might occasionally "swirl... about in a dense, tight eddy" when a boy electrocutes himself nearly to death, but who ordinarily function as adequately socialized, autonomous beings. What is striking about the novel's resplendent final crowd scene, where this eddying formation occurs, is not, as Leslie Fiedler has it, that it stages how polyglot verbiage "dissolves into a cacophony of disembodied voices, clearly symbolizing the 'futility and anarchy' of modern life."[23] To the contrary, it stages how the Lower East Side's polyglot verbiage preserves within itself the operative conditions of communication, namely speakers and listeners who presume to – and evidently do – understand each other, notwithstanding their heavily accented and grammatically poor English.

On the other hand, Roth dwells on one boy who constitutes only a tiny droplet in this immigrant wave and who seems not to resolve into anything but a molecular form of a breaking wave. "*Resounded, surged and resounded, like / ever swelling breakers*": with these lines Roth inaugurates the penultimate chapter's psycho-narration of David's third rail pursuit (*CS* 410). They describe the obsessive-compulsive state into which he has fallen, absorbed by the recent memory of having been "*[d]ouble dared*" by some boys to make contact with "*the light in the crack*" (*CS* 410). What is again striking about this episode is that when David soon replaces the surge of ocean breakers with a surge of electricity, Roth does not have the ensuing aggregation of spectators follow suit. They do not resemble Stephen Crane's hypnotically entranced "sea of men" surrounding the collapsed Italian immigrant in "When Man Falls, a Crowd Gathers." David's spectators may have "confused, paralyzed, babbling" moments (*CS* 421), but by and large they retain their wits, their field sense, and their intelligibility. This is evidenced by their collective effort to locate a wooden broom and their subsequent orchestration of David's removal from the tracks before the medical intern arrives (*CS* 421). As they wait for the ambulance they also debate intelligently enough whether or not the unknown boy could have fallen onto the rail by accident, thus, whether he should "sue" the trolley company for being "de fault" (*CS* 424–425). That Roth throughout this chapter italicizes his psycho-narration of David's inner experience of these events reinforces the constitutive discrepancy between the boy and his crowd.

The significance of Roth's reconfiguration, then, is in effect to reverse both socio-cultural and novelistic expectations. Where the era's preferred metaphors would associate aggregated immigrants with a wave or herd mentality, Roth's immigrants manage to come across, despite his representation of their voices as disembodied, as competent individuals making decisions on the spot. In effect, they are not a wave, but a public. Roth similarly reverses the protagonist's usual function. Where protagonists of ethnic-immigrant novels conventionally differ from background characters by occupying a privileged position of self-awareness and achievement, Roth's David has scarcely more self-possession than "an ever swelling breaker." Indeed, viewing the course of his trials and travails from the hindsight of the novel's final episodes, it becomes clear that throughout the narrative Roth depicts David as something like a crowd waiting to happen, a wave waiting to break. Roth's characterological reversal is one among many novelistic strategies by means of which he reveals his ambition both to resonate with and to sound against the ethnic-immigrant novel.

However, what I aim to demonstrate in the following discussion is that Roth's reversals do not signify a simple reversal of ideological values, whereby, say, his representation of immigrants' group competence indicate his favorable view of them or his privileging collectivism over individualism.

Rather, his reversals conduce a much more significant reconfiguration, whereby, as stated earlier, the ethnic and the political are rendered categorically distinct. One might call Roth's *Call It Sleep* a postethnic novel, to adopt Werner Sollor's and David Hollinger's felicitous phrase. Hollinger stresses postethnicity's alignment with a Bourne-inspired cosmopolitanism so as to underscore the prime value of voluntary – in contrast to heritable – association. "A postethnic perspective challenges the right of one's grandfather or grandmother to determine primary identity. Individuals should be allowed to affiliate or disaffiliate with their own communities of descent to an extent that they choose."[24] Brought to bear on Roth's novel, postethnicity implies the attraction both of inherited and non-inherited ethnic circumstance and particularity as sources of experiential engagement; but it also implies the marginality of either form of ethnic engagement with respect to public-political consciousness.

Viewed in this light, Roth's novel can be seen to dovetail with John Dewey's contemporaneous efforts to shift the political-theoretical debate away from one about competing claims of the individual and society, and toward the more difficult task of determining what ought and ought not to count as politically relevant, that is, as matters of public policy. The dogged methodicalness on display in *The Public and Its Problems* (1927), as Dewey lays out his case in support of the latter schema, suggests the degree to which proponents of laissez-faire capitalism and democratic defeatists dictated the terms of political debate.[25] In the early 1930s Dewey's criticisms of the New Deal are born out of a similar frustration with Roosevelt's willingness to accept the prerogatives of corporate capitalism.[26] As long as the core liberal conflict could be conceived as revolving around the protections of individual or corporate freedoms against the encroachments of society, laissez-faire capitalism could count on the nation's ideological commitment to libertarian autonomy to favor its claims. Dewey, on the other hand, as a progressivist proponent of "a more equitable distribution of rights among individuals," such as would foster a modestly socialist form of public welfare, maintains that liberalism entails more than negative liberties.[27] He joins political liberalism to the ontological claim that human beings are at once wholly socialized – given their prolonged dependency as children (*PP* 62) – and wholly individualized – given their "mental and moral" singularity (*PP* 75). Thus dispensing with the false opposition between individual and society, Dewey reveals liberalism's task to be one of properly identifying issues of public concern.

His criterion for identifying such issues is the nature of an action's or transaction's "consequences"; if these consequences extend problematically "beyond those directly [and consensually] engaged in producing them," an "organized public," as distinct "from other [non-political] modes of community life" such as religious, artistic, or scientific groupings, must deliberate with the impartial intelligence of a scientist or expert how best to regulate such consequences (*PP* 26–27). In his effort to reclaim impartial intelligence and communication as the baseline of the public sphere, Dewey plays up the primacy of scientific method and *a posteriori* reasoning, while underplaying a priori principles as the propagator of ethical decision-making. Troubled by laissez-faire capitalism's co-optation of eighteenth-century liberalism's universalist claims, Dewey promotes a pragmatic consequentialism as a means of keeping the focus on average society's economic malaise and other current socio-political problems. He attacks formal reason for producing legal sophistry and rigidity (*PP* 57). But at the same time he practically recapitulates Kant's categorical imperative when he rejects the view that laws are coercive commands, arguing instead for "their plausible identification with reason": law "operates as a condensed available check on the naturally overweening influence of immediate desire and interest over decision. It is a means of doing for a person what otherwise only his own foresight, if thoroughly reasonable, could do" (*PP* 56).[28]

Dewey's ambitions in *The Public and Its Problems* are both theoretical and practical. He argues that "the outstanding problem of the Public is discovery and identification of itself" (*PP* 185). His account counters Walter Lippmann's mystification of a "phantom public" by insisting on the absurdity of setting Society as a thing apart from its constituents (*PP* 188). In his later *Liberalism and Social Action* (1935) Dewey recapitulates many of the claims made in the earlier work, but also adds his oft-made argument that the "freed intelligence" of the scientific method stands over and against a politics of force. As a mode of "cooperatively organized intelligence," it promises to promote "the liberation of the capacities of individuals for free, self-initiated expression [which] is an essential part of the creed of liberalism." While Dewey exhibits a polemical commitment, especially in this later text, to the historicity and relativity of liberalism, his entire project of arguing for and preferring the virtues of the scientific method and mentality (against the alternatives of violent force or improvisational "drift") implies a formal commitment to liberalism's universalist ethical propensities.[29]

While undoing "the celebrated modern antithesis of the Individual and the Social" (*PP* 87), as well as dispelling the myth that economic "laws" are "natural" and therefore not to be tampered with by public policy (*PP* 90), Dewey does recognize the real practical problems liberalism faces. These problems revolve essentially around political-liberalism's requirement that persons accept and exercise their "dual capacity" as both public officers and persons with private interests. A public, he acknowledges, "arrives at decisions, makes terms and executes resolves only through the medium of individuals...As a citizen-voter each one of these persons is, however, an officer of the public," much like "a senator or sheriff." Yet these individuals "still have private interests to serve, and interest of special groups, those of the family, clique or class to which they belong" (*PP* 75–76). Bearing witness to such interests, especially as they give rise to powerful if not plutocratic economic conglomerates, "the democratic public," Dewey complains, "is still largely inchoate and unorganized" (*PP* 109).

Despite this political-economic criticism, Dewey remains adamant about avoiding "'the great bad,' the mixing of things that need to be kept distinct" (*PP* 83). He has specifically in mind those arguments that blur the distinction between the "claims of democracy as a social and ethical ideal" and the history of how political democracy arose (*PP* 83–84). But this injunction also has important implications for his assessment of the era's perceived immigration problem. Dewey seems to go out of his way not to lay political democracy's failures at the feet of immigrants, as nativists at the time were wont to do. Offering glimpses of his technocratic optimism, Dewey attributes to "[r]ailways,...the mails, telegraphs and telephone, newspapers, [et cetera]" the nation's ability to maintain a unified state despite its "large and racially diversified population" (*PP* 114). The nation's history of immigration is especially remarkable for its negligible political impact:

The wonder of the performance is the greater because of the odds against which it has been achieved. The stream of immigrants which has poured in is so large and heterogeneous that under conditions which formerly obtained it would have disrupted any semblance of unity as surely as the migratory invasion of alien hordes once upset the social equilibrium of the European continent. (*PP* 115)

While such praise of political stability is in turn undercut by Dewey's dismay over the current state of the public's apathy, its lack of communication, and its general incompetence, his recognition that as a current public issue "the regulation and distribution of immigrants" requires "technical" attention (rather than an ethno-political culture war) goes far to disinvest immigration of nationalist-identitarian rhetoric (*PP* 124–125).[30] His treatment of immigration as one among other current concerns such as health and sanitation, housing and transportation, urban planning and education (*PP* 124–125), also goes far to separate out immigrants' public-political status as such from what may be their personal ethnic consciousness and contingencies.

Returning to Roth's novel, we see that it too articulates this formal separation of the political and the personal, albeit with rather different emphases. Indeed, with the novel's scant attention to public-political affairs, Dewey could justifiably argue that *Call It Sleep* confirms his point about the current apathetic, inactive, eclipsed state of the public. When David's mother Genya asks her sister Bertha whether Nathan her fiancé is a citizen, to which Bertha replies in the affirmative, that marks the beginning and end of their political conversation (*CS* 194). Elsewhere Bertha suspects that David's father Albert attends a campaign speech before Election Day only to avoid her and Nathan (*CS* 190–191). Yet as indicative as such signs may be of a minimally operative political consciousness, in my view they join the signs cited earlier in confirming Dewey's other point about the ease with which "the stream of immigrants" poured into liberal democracy's normative channels.

Moreover, such signs of public-political awareness as do emerge mark the distinction between the consciousness of the immigrant adults in David's family and David's own. The most he seems to grasp about Election Day, in keeping with his general attraction to dazzling light and power, is that it occasions a "big, big fire" (*CS* 193). As suggested above, Roth's adoption of the third-person point of view is crucial for the purposes of underscoring this distinction between the sensibility of adult and child. He departs from his literary predecessors (not only Cahan and Yezierska but also Michael Gold, whose *Jews without Money* appeared some months before Roth began writing *Call It Sleep*),[31] whose backward looking, self-describing and self-interpreting adult protagonists formally register their assumption of a developed ethno-political consciousness. Instead, Roth deploys a narrative technique that formally dissociates narrator and protagonist. No matter how deeply aligned the two may be through focalization, this dissociation enables the narrator to play at will against the protagonist's self-knowledge. (An autobiographical narrator may claim in the narrative present to know more than or differently from what she or he knew in the past, but as a present protagonist narrating, she or he cannot make such a claim.) Equally significant is the fact that throughout the novel's time span Roth's protagonist remains under the age of ten, which is to say a legal minor. This renders dubious such claims as Brian McHale's about David's "civic marginality," about his status as a "marginalized citizen," by means of which designation McHale establishes a resemblance between David and Joyce's politically alienated Mr. Bloom. At best one might view the novel as Kenneth Burke did in 1935, namely, as capturing "the 'pre-political' thinking of childhood."[32]

With a narrative perspective that is sympathetic towards but not identical to the protagonist's, and with a protagonist whose consciousness is central and dominant but not definitive, Roth undertakes his project of squaring the ethnic-immigrant family circle. He brings to the typical ethno-political immigrant narrative a postethnic, post-identitarian relevance, whereby the terms and contingencies of Jewishness and Americanness may well be central and dominant but likewise are not definitive. As suggested earlier, much turns on Roth's representation of ethnic-immigrant trauma. Werner Sollors understates the case when he remarks that David is "easily traumatized."[33] David is a veritable traumatophiliac who submits himself to as many permutations as he can discover of a bedazzling crowd-wave consciousness.

Every opportunity a psycho-physiological crisis: very early in the narrative, for instance, David enters the traumatic state on his way down the tenement stairs as he goes out to play:

A few steps from the bottom landing, he paused and stared rigidly at the cellar door. It bulged with darkness. Would it hold?... It held! He jumped from the last steps and raced through the narrow hallway to the light of the street. Flying through the doorway was like butting a wave. A dazzling breaker of sunlight burst over his head, swamped him in [a] reeling blur of brilliance, and then receded... (*CS* 20 ellipses in original)

This rush leaves him "[b]linking and almost shaken... until his whirling vision steadied" (*CS* 20). David's precocious susceptibility to the traumatic state is one reason why he cannot be contained by or put in the service of an ethno-political drama that turns on the conflict between remaining Jewish or becoming American. He contrasts, in other words, to Sara Smolinsky whose traumatic disposition, as elaborated earlier, emanates from the universally available crisis of imagining never having been born. But then it later modulates into an ethnic-specific disposition circulating within a psychic structure that stakes itself on her father's Old World Jewishness and her modern Americanized identity. Instead, David's mode of trauma, no matter how deeply it involves elements from his family history as triggering devices, erases his ethnic identification. Overheard Old World family stories function just like a newly acquired Christian rosary, or a trip to the wharf where the "brilliance" of light on water is "hypnotic" (*CS* 217), or the chanted lines of Hebrew that "dissolve" his "senses" and leave him "[u]nmoored in space" (*CS* 255): they serve as the media but not the structuring source of David's compulsive self-erasures. Where Hana Wirth-Nesher reads the novel as "about an immigrant child's quest for a personal and cultural identity apart from his parents," and as "trac[ing] the arduous and bewildering path of assimilation," I suggest that the novel traces David's promiscuous practice of erasing such identitarian associations altogether.[34] Trauma becomes one of the means through which Roth articulates a postethnicity residing in the heart of the Lower East Side's polyglot population. Laying out trauma's extreme claims on personal consciousness, Roth discloses the pressing value of separating out the personal and the political.

Call It Sleep can be read as playing out the two sides, broadly construed, of the historical-theoretical account of trauma as it stood in the early decades of the twentieth century.[35] Ruth Leys has most thoroughly illuminated the analytical crossroads at which theorists such as Freud and Sandor Ferenczi found themselves as they attempted to reckon with the conflicting implications of their own claims. Briefly, on the one (and more widely received) side, a pregiven ego develops anxiety for "the purpose of protecting the psyche's coherence by allowing the ego to represent and master a danger situation that it recognizes as the reproduction of an earlier situation involving the threatened loss of an identifiable libidinal object."[36] In this scheme, trauma is thus subsumed by the libidinal economy which, with its mechanisms of repression, give rise to such neuroses as the Oedipal complex. The traumatizing object, such as the aggressor-father, is conceived as wholly external to the traumatized ego-subject, such as the son who wants exclusive possession of the mother. Further, the ego-subject, it is presumed, is able to represent to itself, if only in the unconscious, the initial traumatic event that it now wards off through anxiety. Psychoanalytic therapy, then, hopes first to identify the trauma through dream analysis or hypnosis, and then to bring it to the patient's conscious attention.

On the other side, psychic mechanisms are at work that precede ego-formation and do not readily assimilate themselves to psychoanalytic self-representation. Leys refers to this mode as the "archetrauma of identification," and it entails the stimulation of a primary affective bond that launches the traumatic subject into a state of full mimetic identification – an identification that, like hypnosis, "can never be remembered because it precedes the very distinction between self and other on which the possibility of self-representation and hence recollection depends." Trauma on this view consists of the subject's originary condition of "vacancy"; it is "the condition of the [subject's] birth" and thus "occurs prior to any conscious perception or any repression."[37]

In *Call It Sleep* Roth stages something like a traumatic duet, with father Albert and son David the two performers. Many critics have interpreted this relationship as a textbook case of the Oedipal complex, with their rivalry and phobias reproducing Albert's relationship to his own father. Perhaps one attraction of this account is that it squares so nicely with the ethno-political narrative of Americanization, wherein allegiances to the Old World father can be seen as necessarily sacrificed in order for the next generation to triumph in the New. In my view, however, the duet takes a different spin, with Albert indeed enacting the Oedipal neurosis, but with David enacting the second version of trauma outlined above. I hasten to add that by this distinction I do not aim (and do not think Roth aims) to reproduce in another register a narrative of supplantation – where New World trauma triumphs over Old. In terms of the novel's larger context, neither trauma wins, as neither is compatible with political liberalism. (The first is distinctly illiberal, in its adherence to a blood-and-iron, power-grabbing logic; the second is distinctly a-political, in its will to non-representational vacancy.)

Albert Schearl exhibits many pathological symptoms: repeated acts of unprovoked or undue violence; a persecution complex that makes him suspicious even of passersby on the street (*CS* 42); his purchase "for memory's sake" of bull horns attached to a plaque (*CS* 299); his wish-fulfillment that David not be his son; and not least his disdainful abuse of David. All these traits warrant the speculation that Albert never quite recovers from the shock and guilt of having impassively witnessed, back in Austria, an ox gore his father to death; and that he takes out his repressed self-loathing on his son. In the novel's final sequence Bertha reveals Albert's projective psychic repetition when, just as Albert is about to assault David with the broken whip, she holds him off, shrieking, "He'll trample on him as he let his father be trampled on" (*CS* 402). A sign that by the very end Albert may be breaking out of the Oedipal headlock appears in the form of a neighbor's report of what she overheard Albert holler after the attempted assault: "Ah'm khrezzy! I dun know vod I do!" (436). According to the Freudian therapy plan, recognition is a first step towards cure. If Roth's novel had centered on the father instead of the son, it might have been hopefully titled "Call It Quits."

In the title Roth did select, however, "sleep" bears no suggestion of person-to-person relationality, of, say, the love, desire, jealousy, aggression, protection, abandonment, or other affective elements that ordinarily comprise a Freudian family romance. Sleep is what a person in his or her full somatic solitariness enters at the limit of consciousness. The novel's title, then, is in keeping with what in my view is its central mission: to play out an archetraumatic drama as a way of indeed calling it quits with the traumatic family romance that so readily maps onto the ethno-political imagination. To be sure, in the novel's final paragraph in which David, verging on sleep, meditates dreamily on what exactly is being called sleep, one association he proffers is the feeling of "strangest triumph, strangest acquiescence" (*CS* 441). Such terms do indicate relationality – one triumphs over and acquiesces to someone or something. But with the qualifier "strangest" David signals that his version of triumph and acquiescence, more precisely, of triumph *as* acquiescence, is beyond the reach of ordinary apprehensible experience.

In near parody of the weighty significance the ethnic-immigrant narra- tive typically bestows on chronological time, so as to deliver up subjective experience to a structure of lost ethnic past and found American present, Roth's boy protagonist collects in a shoe-box the daily leaves of a calendar. He who "remember[s] nothing," according to his mother (*CS* 18) hoards these leaves as a "treasure," though also according to her he has little re- spect for time: "You peel off the year as one might a cabbage" (*CS* 19). Later, when he boasts of the calendar to an unimpressed playmate, "the one unique point" he can make about it is that his "fodder made it" (*CS* 21), printer that his father is. While here helping David save face, evocations of his father more often arouse dread. The calendar itself is a site of such anxiety; it ominously marks Sundays in red, "days his father was home," and "[i]t always gave David a little qualm of dread to watch them draw near" (*CS* 19). But if the novel starts out looking as though it were going to oedipalize David's psyche – replete with overdetermined admiration and castration fears – whose external traumatic incident, it could be claimed, is the father's sudden, violent ejection of the child's Old World hat upon his arrival in the United States (*CS* 10), it soon enough takes a different turn. As often as David's father-induced affective turbulence takes the form of dread, indicating his ego's self-preservation, it also inspires the kind of utter self-erasure associated with archetrauma. One highly charged instance is when Albert poises to assault him for the first time:

Like a cornered thing, he shrank within himself, deadened his mind because the body would not deaden and waited. Nothing existed any longer except his father's right hand... Transfixed, timeless, he studied the curling fingers that twitched spasmodically, studied the printer's ink ingrained upon the finger tips, pondered, as if all there were in the world, the nail of the smallest finger, nipped by a press, that climbed in a jagged little stair to the hangnail. Terrific absorption. (*CS* 83)

Shortly after this incident David himself adopts his father's "volcanic and incalculable force" (*CS* 85) when, taunted and threatened by a "pack" of schoolboys, David erupts: "Suddenly a blind, shattering fury convulsed in him," and he lunges at one of his antagonists (*CS* 91). What we begin to see, then, is David's oscillation between self-erasure through utter hypnotic withdrawal – David's "absorption" – and self-erasure through total mimetic identification – David's embodiment of his father's "fury." Coming full circle as this psychic logic does, from pure a-sociality to pure sociality, from anonymity to crowd-like unity, David enacts what Leys also calls the "archetrauma of birth." As such, its occurrence is prior to subjective identity or a pregiven ego, just as it is prior to "any perceptual object," which is to say any traumatizing agent such as a father.[38]

As we saw in Cahan's and Yezierska's novels, the circumstances of birth, the very thought of these circumstances, serve as traumatic fodder for the ethno-political psychic economy. Roth also makes use of this theme, but to different ends. Where Cahan's and Yezierska's protagonists are afflicted by thoughts of their own births – one taking place in the wrong country, the other hypothetically not taking place anywhere – David seems rather more taken with the thought of the world's own creation, albeit in relation to himself. The first chapter's opening scene has him feeling physically slighted by the kitchen. Too small to reach the water faucet, "David again became aware that this world had been created without thought of him" (*CS* 17). While not wishing to claim this moment as then and there traumatic, I do want to stress the congruence between this scene in which David, evidently not for the first time, contemplates his absence from the creation of "the world" he inhabits and the novel's final episode in which David pursues the one thing he seems able to "remember," the third rail's birth-power: "*Now! Now I gotta. In the crack, / remember. In the crack be born*" (*CS* 411).[39] Through the means of a metal milk dipper, an instrument associated with his father's most recent occupation as a milkman, David's tapping of the crack's current does not so much amount to the birth of his own ego-subjectivity as it stages his absolute identification with the birth-force itself. The limit-experience of self-absence during this birth event is driven home by Roth's high-modernist image, recounted in third-person psycho-narration and isolated even further by means of parentheses, of two mirrors facing each other:

> (*As if on hinges, blank, enormous*
> *mirrors arose, swung slowly upward*
> *face to face. Within the facing*
> *glass, vast panels deployed, lifted a*
> *steady wink of opaque pages until*
> *an endless corridor dwindled into*
> *night.*) (*CS* 427)

While Albert may himself unconsciously regard David as an Oedipal rival, David's omission of self from his all too literal power seizure effectively annuls his father's projection. In the paternal generation preceding David, the transference of power took the form of possession: Albert gains what his father loses, hence his satisfaction in owning and displaying a set of bull horns. David, on the other hand, never comes into the possession of power, but himself becomes its instrument. Such self-evacuation is the condition of birth archetrauma. The only trophy commensurate with David's "triumph" is indeed "strangest acquiescence" otherwise known as sleep.

Roth's third-person point of view enables him to represent through psycho-narration the dissociated consciousness that David himself would formally be precluded from representing; hence the narrator's comment, as David starts his final quest, that "the small sputter of words in his brain seemed no longer his own...but detached from him" (*CS* 409). This narrative perspective also enables Roth to situate David in a broader socio-political context: the impoverished, insecure world of the Lower East Side in the decades leading up to the Depression. With the hindsight of a Communist Party member writing during the Depression, Roth registers his skepticism toward the American way in the novel's Prologue, which he added after completing the novel in 1934 (he became a CP member in 1933). There he intertwines an ominous description of the national icon, the Statue of Liberty whose features are distorted by shadows, "her depths exhausted" (*CS* 14), with the novel's particular icon of unrestrained brutality, horns. They enter the scene by way of a rather conspicuous conceit – a description of the Statue as surrounded by "the horns of the harbor" (*CS* 14). Roth names New Jersey and Brooklyn as the literal landmasses constituting these horns, but the literary symbolism at work here, in addition to the sarcastic, lewd allusions to the Statue appearing later in the novel, suggest what Mark Schoening calls Roth's political "disaffection." Schoening maintains that Roth harbored none of the class interests that so often motivated Party members and that his "turn to the party was animated...by his commitment to rejecting – in the most fundamental way possible – the nation he inhabited." This biographical account buttresses Schoening's interpretation of the novel as offering, through the figure of David and his "redirecting of power," a vision of "genuine revolutionary possibility." David's culminating "paralysis" on this view "is embraced as a precipatory form of extreme alienation that can trigger the coming into being of a nation genuinely receptive to its citizen's concerns" (*sic*). Thus David's power seizure augurs politically "meaningful change."[40] Whereas for many critics David emerges as a figure of spiritual or aesthetic redemption, in this reading he figures political redemption.

By contrast, what I have attempted to shed light on is David's non-redemptive, non-political, bedazzled presence. In the novel's penultimate chapter Roth utilizes the formal distinction between italicized psycho-narration and direct dialogue to underline the distinctions of consciousness between David's mode of being entranced and the spectators' mode of being alert, engaged, communicative, and above all helpful. Unlike David, they function perfectly well as public citizens. This makes clear that David's revolt has no substantial bearing on their constitution as political-liberal subjects. The short circuit may momentarily disrupt the public infrastructure, and David's injury may disrupt the everyday life of "the street," but the event itself occasions his purely personal – which is also to say, given its entailment of self-erasure, impersonal – odyssey into the electrocutional sublime. Furthermore, however extremely disenchanted Roth himself may have been with the nation he inhabited, he depicts an immigrant populace – indeed a liberal public – that clearly depends on, enjoys, and expects the perpetuation of civil rights and responsibilities. They obviously appreciate not only free speech (which underwrites the lewd jokes about the Statue of Liberty), but also the rights and duties of contract and accountability (which make available the possibility of suing the trolley company) as well as the municipality's infrastructural cohesiveness (which renders a short-circuited third rail an unusual event). In my view, Roth's envisioned antidote to the political-economic discontent circulating through the novel's background takes the shape of a Deweyan recharge of political liberalism rather than a Davidian revolt. At one point in the novel Bertha reminds Genya of what "you don't see ... in this land," namely anti-Semitic "pogrom[s]" and "peasant[s]" who practice justice by going after their opponents with "an ax" (*CS* 154). In Roth's postethnic novel, "this land" remains politically devoted to more reasonable forms of administering rights and justice, even as it offers the space, however crowded on the Lower East Side, for radically vacuous forms of impersonal entrancement.

If Roth's novel can thus be seen to separate out what Hannah Arendt in *The Human Condition* envisioned conjoined – natality, action, and politics – it serves as a fitting conclusion to this study. Equally fitting is its image of the ethnically marked urban crowd: while it may appear at first glance to blandish the United States's currently favored self-image of diversity, it stands more insistently as an emblem of public sameness, a consensual public ably bearing the rights and obligations of the political-liberal condition.

Notes

INTRODUCTION

1 George Oppen, *Collected Poems* (New York: New Directions, 1975), p. 151.

2 William James, *The Principles of Psychology*, 2 vols. (New York: Henry Holt, 1890), vol. 1, p. v; Gustave Le Bon, *The Crowd*, trans. anon. (London: T. Fisher, 1896), p. 15; Friedrich Nietzsche, *Beyond Good and Evil*, trans. Walter Kaufmann (New York: Vintage, 1967), p. 197. The scholarly literature on the crowd in modern history is immense. For a brief but highly detailed overview of the crowd in American history from the antebellum period to the Gilded Age, see the first chapter of Gregory Bush, *Lord of Attention: Gerald Stanley Lee and the Crowd Metaphor in Industrializing America* (Amherst: University of Massachusetts Press, 1991). For a more sustained analysis of middle-class attitudes towards urban masses, see Paul Boyer, *Urban Masses and Moral Order in America, 1820–1920* (Cambridge, MA and London: Harvard University Press, 1978). For a valuable analysis of depictions of protest mobs and riots in American literature, see Nicolaus Mills, *The Crowd in American Literature* (Baton Rouge and London: Louisiana State University Press, 1986). Germinal studies of the rise of crowd psychology include Susanna Barrows, *Distorting Mirrors: Visions of the Crowd in Late Nineteenth-Century France* (New Haven and London: Yale University Press, 1981); Robert Nye, *The Origins of Crowd Psychology: Gustave Le Bon and the Crisis of Mass Democracy in the Third Republic* (London: Sage Publ., 1975); J. S. McClelland, *The Crowd and the Mob: From Plato to Canetti* (London: Unwin, 1989); Serge, Moscovici, *The Age of the Crowd: A Historical Treatise on Mass Psychology*, trans. J. C. Whitehouse (Cambridge, England: Cambridge University Press, 1985); and Jaap Van Ginneken, *Crowds, Psychology, Politics, 1871–1899* (Cambridge, England: Cambridge University Press, 1992). For a history of earlier popular protest in England and France, see George Rudé, *The Crowd in History, 1730–1848* (New York and London: John Wiley and Sons, 1964). For an account of the confluence of literature and political demonstrations in Victorian England, see John Plotz, *The Crowd: British Literature and Public Politics* (Berkeley and Los Angeles: University of California Press, 2000). For a broad study of the convergence of crowd psychology and theories of mass consumer culture, see Patrick Brantlinger, *Bread and Circuses: Theories of Mass Culture as Social Decay* (Ithaca and London: Cornell University Press, 1983). For an

analysis of high modernism's appropriation of crowd psychology for its articulation of collectivist politics, see Michael Tratner, *Modernism and Mass Politics: Joyce, Woolf, Eliot, Yeats* (Stanford: Stanford University Press, 1995).

3 McClelland, *The Crowd and the Mob*, pp. 1, 3–4.

4 Michael Schudson, *The Good Citizen: A History of American Civic Life* (Cambridge, MA and London: Harvard University Press, 1998), pp. 5, 7.

5 Gabriel Tarde, *The Laws of Imitation*, trans. Elsie Clews Parsons (New York: Henry Holt, 1903), pp. 83–84.

6 Ruth Leys, "Mead's Voices: Imitation as Foundation, or, The Struggle against Mimesis," *Critical Inquiry* 19 (1993), p. 279. As Leys also notes, the "origins" of the social self "go back to Adam Smith's theory of sympathy, which in the 1890s underwent a considerable revival in the United States," p. 278.

7 See Howard Horwitz's essay on Stephen Crane and American sociology, "*Maggie* and the Sociological Paradigm," *American Literary History* 10 (1998), pp. 606–638, for a more detailed account of this contradiction and how it prefigures contemporary social constructionist theory.

8 Edward Ross, "The Mob Mind," *Popular Science Monthly* 51 (1897), p. 398. Three years later in the same forum, a professor from Iowa, G. T. W. Patrick, would repeat the argument yet again:

> The inference which we seem compelled to draw from studies in social psychology is that social man is, in his ethical and intellectual development, many stages behind the individual man. The progress of civilization is a slow, painful, upward climbing, in which individuals are the thinkers, the planners, the promoters and the leaders. The mind of society, on the other hand, . . . is an imitative, unreflective, half-hypnotic, half-barbaric mind, always acting as a drag upon the upward and forward movement, and, in times of crazes, epidemics and social cataclysms, gaining temporary dominance and causing disastrous relapses to a lower plane of civilization.

See G. T. W. Patrick, "The Psychology of Crazes," *Popular Science Monthly* 57 (1900), p. 294.

9 Mikkel Borch-Jacobsen, *The Freudian Subject*, trans. Catherine Porter (Stanford: Stanford University Press, 1988), pp. 138–139, emphasis added.

10 Boris Sidis, *The Psychology of Suggestion* (New York: Appleton, 1898), p. 252; Boris Sidis, "A Study of the Mob," *Atlantic Monthly* (February 1895), p. 190.

11 Borch-Jacobsen, *The Freudian Subject*, pp. 143, 236; Le Bon, *The Crowd*, p. 133; Tarde, *Laws*, p. 79. It is worth mentioning that not all theorists or researchers agreed with this model of hypnosis. William James and Georg Simmel, for instance, suggest that the hypnotic scenario has a bilateral structure. In *Principles of Psychology* James comments that "Any sort of personal peculiarity, any trick accidentally fallen into in the first instance by some one [hypnotized] subject, may, by attracting attention, become stereotyped, serve as a pattern for imitation, and figure as the type of a school. The first subject trains the operator, the operator trains the succeeding subjects, all of them in perfect good faith conspiring together to evolve a perfectly arbitrary result." See James, *Principles*, vol. 2, p. 601. Similarly, Simmel, in his more general account of the sociological relation between super- and subordination, makes the following remark:

The most characteristic case of this type is shown, perhaps, by hypnotic suggestion. An outstanding hypnotist pointed out that in every hypnosis the hypnotized has an effect upon the hypnotist; and that, although this effect cannot be easily determined, the result of the hypnosis could not be reached without it. Thus here, too, appearance shows an absolute influence, on the one side, and an absolute being-influenced on the other; but it conceals an interaction, an exchange of influences [*eine Wechselwirkung, einen Austausch der Einflüsse*], which transforms the pure one-sidedness of superordination and subordination into a *sociological* form.

See Georg Simmel, *The Sociology of Georg Simmel*, trans. Kurt Wolff (London: Free Press of Glencoe, 1950), p. 186.

12 William James, *Writings 1902–1910*, ed. Bruce Kucklick (New York: Library of America, 1987), p. 1036.

13 William James, *Essays in Radical Empiricism* (Cambridge, MA and London: Harvard University Press, 1976), p. 42, emphasis added.

14 James, *Writings*, p. 754, second emphasis added.

15 Quoted in Ralph Barton Perry, *The Thought and Character of William James*, 2 vols. (Boston: Little, Brown and Co., 1935), vol. 2, pp. 764, 757.

16 For a fuller account of James's conception of pure experience, see my article, "William James's Onto-Physiology of Limits," *Genre* 29 (1996), pp. 341–358.

17 While the phrase "liberal republicanism" may be anachronistic, it conveniently combines the idea of individual autonomy and public conscience. Richard Dagger's recent book, *Civic Virtues: Rights, Citizenship, and Republican Liberalism* (New York and Oxford: Oxford University Press, 1997) explores more fully the significance of theorizing the compatibility of liberalism and republicanism. Other studies that have proved helpful in this and other matters related to the history of liberalism include James Kloppenberg's *The Virtues of Liberalism* (New York and Oxford: Oxford University Press, 1998) and Joyce Appleby's *Liberalism and Republicanism in the Historical Imagination* (Cambridge, MA and London: Harvard University Press, 1992). More frequently in this book I refer to "political liberalism," a Rawlsian phrase that is also anachronistic but that usefully separates out political-ethical ideas from political-economic ones (if only eventually to rejoin them).

18 Perry Miller, *The Transcendentalists: An Anthology* (Cambridge, MA: Harvard University Press, 1950), p. 71.

19 *Ibid.*, p. 423.

20 *Ibid.*, p. 234.

21 Quoted in William Pease and Jane Pease, eds. *The Antislavery Argument* (Indianapolis and New York: Bobbs-Merrill, 1965), p. 116.

22 John Rawls, *Lectures on the History of Moral Philosophy*, ed. Barbara Herman (Cambridge, MA and London: Harvard University Press, 2000), pp. 148–150.

23 Miller, *The Transcendentalists*, pp. 425–428.

24 Immanuel Kant, *The Critique of Judgement*, trans. James Creed Meredith (Oxford: Oxford University Press, 1957), sec. 40, p. 151.

25 Ralph Waldo Emerson, *The Complete Works of Ralph Waldo Emerson*, 12 vols. (New York: AMS, 1968), vol. 7, pp. 26–27.

26 Francis Bowen, *The Principles of Metaphysical and Ethical Science Applied to the Evidences of Religion* (Boston: Brewer and Teleston, revised edition, 1855), p. 282.

27 *Ibid.*, pp. 224, 297–299, 306, 269, 276, 288, 305, 299.

28 Rawls, *Lectures*, pp. 280–281; Bowen, *Principles*, p. 283.

29 Gregg Crane, *Race, Citizenship, and Law in American Literature* (Cambridge, England: Cambridge University Press, 2002).

30 John Rawls, "Themes in Kant's Moral Philosophy," in *Kant and Political Philosophy: The Contemporary Legacy*, eds. Ronald Beiner and William James Booth (New Haven and London: Yale University Press, 1993), pp. 305–306.

31 Jürgen Habermas, *The Structural Transformation of the Public Sphere: An Inquiry into a Category of Bourgeois Society*, trans. Thomas Burger (Cambridge, MA: MIT Press, 1991), p. 54.

32 For Habermas's concessions on these points, see "Further Reflections on the Public Sphere" and "Concluding Remarks" in the volume of essays entitled *Habermas and the Public Sphere*, ed. Craig Calhoun (Cambridge, MA and London: MIT Press, 1992), pp. 421–461, 462–479. Another valuable volume of essays devoted to the public sphere is *The Phantom Public Sphere*, ed. Bruce Robbins (Minneapolis and London: University of Minnesota Press, 1993).

33 Nancy Fraser, "Rethinking the Public Sphere: A Contribution to the Critique of Actually Existing Democracy," in *Habermas and the Public Sphere*, ed. Craig Calhoun (Cambridge, MA and London: MIT Press, 1992), p. 116.

34 Michael Warner, "The Mass Public and the Mass Subject," in *Habermas and the Public Sphere*, ed. Craig Calhoun (Cambridge, MA and London: MIT Press, 1992), pp. 383–384, 382.

35 Habermas makes this point quite clearly:

The bourgeois public's critical public debate took place in principle without regard to all preexisting social and political rank and in accord with universal rules. These rules, because universally valid, secured a space for the individuated person; because they were objective, they secured a space for what was most subjective; because they were abstract, for what was most concrete.

The domain of law was particularly crucial, Habermas suggests, for the institution of this model, for in principle it could replace the arbitrary power plays of a monarchy or state:

[T]he concept of law as an expression of reason preserved other, older elements of its origin in public opinion, still traceable in the connection between parliament and public. This is why Carl Schmitt gave first place not to the political definition of law but to the other: "Law is not the will of one or of many people, but something rational-universal; not *voluntas* but *ratio*." In its intention, the rule of the law aimed at dissolving domination altogether; this was a typically bourgeois idea insofar as not even the political safeguarding of the private sphere emancipating itself from political domination was to assume the form of domination. The bourgeois idea of the law-based state, namely the binding of all state activity to a system of norms legitimated by public opinion (a system that had no gaps, if possible), already aimed at abolishing the state as an instrument of domination altogether. Acts of sovereignty were considered apocryphal per se.

See Habermas, *Structural Transformation*, pp. 54, 81–82.

36 Warner, "Mass Public," p. 384.

37 Nancy Ruttenburg, *Democratic Personality: Popular Voice and the Trial of American Authorship* (Stanford: Stanford University Press, 1998), p. 12. This book offers a richly textured and learned history of what Ruttenburg calls the "*preliberal democratic tradition* for which the separation of the thinker from the mass, the theoretical articulation from the act, has not yet transpired," p. 6. While presenting a provocative account of the interpenetrations of the theological or supernatural and the political in early American history, Ruttenburg also seeks (with a nod to the guidance of Chantal Mouffe's political theory) more problematically to rehabilitate this mode of politics as a positive alternative to democratic liberalism: "How are we to convert these negative traits into positive ones; how are we to elicit the shape of preliberal democracy from the historical invisibility to which it has been consigned? The answer, I suggest, lies in reconceptualizing democracy as a theater of verbal (symbolic) action . . . The experiential dimension of this ground is thoroughly performative, for within it the coming-into-being of a radical democratic subjectivity is simultaneously modeled before and appropriated by others," pp. 15–16.

38 Philip Gould, *Covenant and Republic: Historical Romance and the Politics of Puritanism* (Cambridge, England and New York: Cambridge University Press, 1996), pp. 50, 184–185, 189.

39 Jonathan Elmer, *Reading at the Social Limit: Affect, Mass Culture, and Edgar Allan Poe* (Stanford: Stanford University Press, 1995), p. 153.

40 Steven Knapp, *Literary Interest: The Limits of Anti-Formalism* (Cambridge, MA and London: Harvard University Press, 1993), pp. 83–84.

41 Kant, *Judgement*, sec. 8, p. 54, sec. 22, pp. 84–85.

42 Anthony J. Cascardi, *Consequences of Enlightenment* (Cambridge, England: Cambridge University Press, 1999), pp. 149–150; Kant, *Judgement* sec. 22, p. 84). See also Lyotard, "*Sensus Communis:* The Subject in *statu nascendi*," in *Who Comes After the Subject?*, eds. Eduardo Cadava, Peter Connor, and Jean-Luc Nancy (New York and London: Routledge, 1991), pp. 217–235; and Deleuze, *Kant's Critical Philosophy: The Doctrine of the Faculties*, trans. Hugh Tomlinson and Barbara Habberjam (Minneapolis: University of Minnesota Press, 1984), pp. 21–24, 48–50.

43 It is beyond the scope of this study to elaborate fully the history and philosophy of the sublime. Particularly helpful analyses for my purposes include Frances Ferguson, *Solitude and the Sublime: Romanticism and the Aesthetics of Individuation* (New York and London; Routledge, 1992); Barbara Claire Freeman, *The Feminine Sublime: Gender and Excess in Women's Fiction* (Berkeley and Los Angeles: University of California Press, 1995); Luc Ferry, *Homo Aestheticus: The Invention of Taste in the Democratic Age*, trans. Robert de Loaiza (Chicago and

London: University of Chicago Press, 1993); Anthony Cascardi, *Consequences of Enlightenment;* and Andrew Bowie, *Aesthetics and Subjectivity: From Kant to Nietzsche* (Manchester and New York: Manchester University Press, 1990). For a different (ideological) analysis of the crowd as an urban sublime object, see Christophe Den Tandt, *The Urban Sublime in American Literary Naturalism* (Urbana and Chicago: University of Illinois Press, 1998).

44 Kant, *Judgement*, sec. 25, p. 94.
45 Nathaniel Hawthorne, *The House of Seven Gables* (New York: Penguin, 1985), pp. 165–166.
46 Kant, *Judgement*, sec. 28, p. 112.
47 Hawthorne, *House*, p. 158.
48 John Rawls, *Political Liberalism* (New York: Columbia University Press, 1993), pp. 12, 144, 39.
49 Hawthorne, *House*, p. 165.
50 *Ibid.*, pp. 166, 174.
51 Martin Jay, "Reflective Judgments by a Spectator on a Conference that Is Now History," in *Hannah Arendt and the Meaning of Politics*, eds. Craig Calhoun and John McGowan (Minneapolis: University of Minnesota Press, 1997), pp. 339–340.
52 Kimberly Curtis, "Aesthetic Foundations of Democratic Politics in the Work of Hannah Arendt," in *Hannah Arendt and the Meaning of Politics*, eds. Craig Calhoun and John McGowan (Minneapolis: University of Minnesota Press, 1997), pp. 28, 35; Jay, "Reflective Judgments," p. 344.
53 Anthony J. Cascardi, "Communication and Transformation: Aesthetics and Politics in Kant and Arendt," in *Hannah Arendt and the Meaning of Politics*, eds. Craig Calhoun and John McGowan (Minneapolis: University of Minnesota Press, 1997), p. 104.
54 Kant, *Judgement*, sec. 47, p. 172; Jay, "Reflective Judgment," pp. 342–343.
55 Wai Chee Dimock, *Residues of Justice: Literature, Law, Philosophy* (Berkeley and Los Angeles: University of California Press, 1996), pp. 124, 139.
56 Rawls, *Political Liberalism*, p. 136.

I ANTEBELLUM AESTHETICS AND THE CONTOURS OF THE POLITICAL

1 Nathaniel Hawthorne, "The Old Apple-Dealer," in *Tales and Sketches* (New York: Library of America, 1982), p. 719. Hereafter this volume is cited as *TS*, with page references appearing in the text.
2 Alexis de Tocqueville, *Democracy in America*, trans. George Lawrence (New York: HarperPerennial, 1988), p. 182.
3 Nicolaus Mills, *The Crowd in American Literature* (Baton Rouge and London: Louisiana State University Press, 1986), p. 50.
4 Mills, *Crowd*, pp. 12, 76.
5 Mills's account of democracy's conflict between man and men is not theorized in the post-structuralist manner of Claude Lefort. Where the latter discovers in democratic hegemony a constitutive self-erasing instability – due to its "empty

place" at the hierarchical top – Mills relies on a sociological or psychological model of internal conflict. See Lefort, *Democracy and Political Theory*, trans. David Macey (Minneapolis: University of Minnesota Press, 1988), p. 17.

6 Mills, *Crowd*, 12.

7 Tocqueville, *Democracy*, pp. 250, 260, 253.

8 *Ibid.*, p. 278.

9 Paul Boyer, *Urban Masses and Moral Order in America, 1820–1920* (Cambridge, MA and London: Harvard University Press, 1978), pp. 13, 72.

10 Perry Miller, *The Transcendentalists: An Anthology* (Cambridge, MA and London: Harvard University Press, 1950), p. 185.

11 Arthur M. Schlesinger, Jr., *The Age of Jackson* (Boston and Toronto: Little, Brown, 1945), p. 406.

12 Lydia Maria Child, *Letters from New York* (New York: Charles S. Francis and Co., 1843), pp. 104, 182. Hereafter this volume is cited as *LNY*, with page references appearing in the text.

13 Dana Brand, *The Spectator and the City in Nineteenth-Century American Literature* (Cambridge, England: Cambridge University Press, 1991), p. 8.

14 Quoted in Frank Otto Gatell and John M. McFaul, eds., *Jacksonian America 1815–1850: New Society, Changing Politics* (Englewood Cliffs, New Jersey: Prentice-Hall, 1970), pp. 102–103.

15 Walt Whitman, *Leaves of Grass* (New York: Library of America, 1992), p. 165. Hereafter this volume is cited as *LG*, with page references appearing in the text.

16 Kerry C. Larson, *Whitman's Drama of Consensus* (Chicago and London: University of Chicago Press, 1988), pp. 73, 10.

17 Allen Grossman, "The Poetics of Union in Whitman and Lincoln: An Inquiry toward the Relationship of Art and Policy," in *The American Renaissance Reconsidered*, eds. Walter Benn Michaels and Donald Pease (Baltimore and London: Johns Hopkins University Press, 1985), p. 192.

18 Quoted in Larson, *Drama*, p. xviii.

19 Regarding policy, Allen Grossman offers the insight that, with respect to Whitman's work, "A poetry that authorizes a personhood reflexively validated by its own discourse can have no category of fictionality...A poetry that has no category of fictionality is a policy." See "The Poetics of Union," p. 186. Other analyses that inform my reading of Whitman include Larzer Ziff, "Whitman and the Crowd," *Critical Inquiry* 10 (1984), pp. 579–591, which focuses on the dialectic between the individual one and the undistinguished many; Donald Pease, *Visionary Compacts: American Renaissance Writings in Cultural Context* (Madison: University of Wisconsin Press, 1987), which examines Whitman's "'body electric,' the incipient crowd formation at work in everybody, constitut[ing] a physical basis for the spontaneous and momentary associations of urban [and, as Pease goes on to argue, national] life," p. 110; and Philip Fisher, "Democratic Social Space: Whitman, Melville, and the Promise of American Transparency," *Representations* 24 (1988), pp. 60–101, which sees in Whitman's work an aesthetic politics of uniformity, one that "imposes

the requirement that the common be expanded until it fills out the real,"
p. 67.

20 Chantal Mouffe, "Democracy, Power, and the 'Political,'" in *Democracy and Difference*, ed. Seyla Benhabib (Princeton: Princeton University Press, 1996), pp. 246, 248; Judith Butler, *Bodies that Matter: On the Discursive Limits of "Sex"* (New York: Routledge, 1993), pp. 15–16.

21 Butler, *Bodies*, p. 15.

22 Mouffe, "Democracy," pp. 247, 246.

23 Calvin Colton, "Democracy," *Junius Tracts* no. 6 (New York: Greeley and McElrath, 1844), pp. 95, 87.

24 *Ibid.*, pp. 85, 90, 96.

25 Schlesinger, *Age of Jackson*, p. 414.

26 Russell L. Hanson, *The Democratic Imagination in America* (Princeton: Princeton University Press, 1985), p. 131.

27 John Calhoun, *Disquisition on Government and Selections from the Discourse*, ed. C. Gordon Post (New York and London: Macmillan, 1953), p. 28.

28 *Ibid.*, pp. 5–6.

29 Hanson, *Democratic*, p. 152.

30 Tocqueville, *Democracy*, pp. 251, 272.

31 George Fitzhugh, *Cannibals All!* in *Antebellum: Writings of George Fitzhugh and Hinton Rowan Helper on Slavery*, ed. Harvey Wish (New York: G. P. Putnam's Sons, 1960), pp. 151, 148. As though an unwitting prophet of contemporary radical democratic theory, Fitzhugh goes on to proclaim that "[r]iots, mobs, strikes and revolutions are daily occurring. The mass of mankind cannot be governed by Law. More of despotic discretion and less of Law is what the world wants. We take our leave by saying, 'THERE IS TOO MUCH OF LAW AND TOO LITTLE OF GOVERNMENT IN THIS WORLD,'" p. 156. In contrast to contemporary theorists, of course, Fitzhugh condemns such violent struggles and hopes despots will quash them. It is nevertheless important to see how a politics of power produces world pictures that are congenial to opposite ends of the political spectrum.

32 George Fitzhugh, *Sociology for the South*, in *Antebellum: Writings of George Fitzhugh and Hinton Rowan Helper on Slavery*, ed. Harvey Wish (New York: G. P. Putnam's Sons, 1960), pp. 49, 57.

33 Fitzhugh, *Sociology*, p. 44; *Cannibals* pp. 104, 151.

34 Fitzhugh, *Sociology*, pp. 49, 60.

35 Fitzhugh, *Cannibals*, p. 149.

36 Michel Foucault, *The History of Sexuality: An Introduction*, trans. Robert Hurley (New York: Vintage, 1978), pp. 93, 92.

37 Walt Whitman, *Complete Poetry and Collected Prose* (New York: Library of America, 1982), p. 929.

38 For an extended analysis of the rhetoric of weather and nature in antebellum political culture, especially in Emerson, see Eduardo Cadava's *Emerson and the Climates of History* (Stanford: Stanford University Press, 1997): "Referring to whatever is incalculable and uncontrollable, [climate] is at times another word

for chance and time," p. 4. In his detailed and nuanced account of Emerson's politics of transformation and historical contingency, Cadava acknowledges but in my view severely scants Emerson's articulation of "a categorical imperative, of a morality and justice incommensurate with the strategies of self-interest at work within this or that civil law," p. 66.

39 In emphasizing Child's public persona, my analysis contrasts with Carolyn Karcher's. In her formidable critical biography of Child, *The First Woman of the Republic* (Durham: Duke University Press, 1994), she stresses the "personal" aspects of *Letters from New York*, pp. 295–319.

40 In his *Lectures on the History of Moral Philosophy*, John Rawls clarifies the role of sentiment in Kant's moral philosophy, which, I am arguing, finds exemplification, at least in its broad contours, in Child's work. While feeling does not enter into the deliberation over this or that political-moral choice, it is absolutely essential to the very existence of moral life:

Th[e] capacity for moral feeling does not by itself determine our power of choice; rather, without it there is no possibility of this power's ranking the moral law as supremely regulative and in itself a sufficient motive. In its absence, the moral law would be for us just an intellectual object, like a mathematical equation[.] . . . [M]oral feeling itself is incorruptible and present in everyone so long as humanity (in Kant's usual sense) is not dead in us . . . We have a susceptibility to be moved by pure practical reason, and this susceptibility is moral feeling, but as such it is sui generis.

See Rawls, *Lectures on the History of Moral Philosophy*, ed. Barbara Herman (Cambridge, MA and London: Harvard University Press, 2000), p. 293.

41 Foucault, *History*, p. 93.

42 F. O. Matthiessen, *The James Family: A Group Biography* (New York, Vintage, 1980), pp. 400, 401–402.

43 Joel Headley, *The Great Riots of New York, 1712–1873* (Miami, FL: Mnemosyne Pub., 1969), pp. 66–67.

44 Charles Baudelaire, *The Painter of Modern Life and Other Essays*, trans. Jonathan Mayne (London: Phaidon Press, 1964), pp. 1, 13; Walter Benjamin, *Illuminations*, ed. Hannah Arendt (New York: Schocken, 1969).

45 Benjamin, *Illuminations*, p. 188.

46 *Ibid.*, pp. 188, 164–165, 189–190. This account of Benjamin's essay is informed in part by Alexander Gelley's essay, "City Texts: Representation, Semiology, Urbanism," in *Politics, Theory, and Contemporary Culture*, ed. Mark Poster (New York: Columbia University Press, 1993), pp. 237–260.

47 Poe, "The Man of the Crowd," *Poetry and Tales* (New York: Library of America, 1984), p. 396. Hereafter this edition is cited as *PT*, with page references appearing in the text.

48 Benjamin, *Illuminations*, p. 179.

49 Dana Brand, *Spectator*, pp. 92–93.

50 *Intention*, of course, is a key word of formalist literary criticism, one garnering much attention in the 1980s with the publication of Steven Knapp and Walter Benn Michaels's essay, "Against Theory." For this essay and responses to it, see

W. J. T. Mitchell, ed., *Against Theory: Literary Studies and the New Pragmatism* (Chicago and London: University of Chicago Press, 1985). My discussion of Poe's story adheres closely to the account of authorial intention advanced by Knapp and Michaels; indeed, the narrative in my view might profitably be read as an allegory of the logic on which is grounded the distinction between an intentionless, nonsensical state of being and an intentional, intelligible state.

51 David Henkin, *City Reading: Written Words and Public Spaces in Antebellum New York* (New York: Columbia University Press, 1998), p. 168.

52 For yet another analysis of the socio-political conditions of reading in "The Man of the Crowd," see Terence Whalen's *Edgar Allan Poe and the Masses* (Princeton: Princeton University Press, 1999). He understands the story as a "parable of the predicament Poe faced as a commercial writer," that is, of being "impelled to seek out and appropriate all salable secrets, even the secrets of 'deep crime' perpetrated in the city of mass consumption," p. 105. This impulsion derives from the writer's need to respond to what Whalen describes earlier as the "Capital Reader," the reader for whom "knowledge does not culminate in virtue, wisdom, or happiness; instead knowledge reenters an endlessly expanding process of intellectual production that closely parallels the 'ceaseless augmentation' of capitalism itself," p. 14. Provocative as Whalen's general thesis is, its application to "The Man of the Crowd" is unpersuasive, given the narrator's designation of the man not only as unreadable but also as unable to read his face-to-face beholder.

53 Henkin, *City Reading*, pp. 12–13, 7, 11.

54 Jonathan Elmer, *Reading at the Social Limit: Affect, Mass Culture, and Edgar Allan Poe* (Stanford: Stanford University Press, 1995), pp. 12–13.

55 Mary Ryan, "Gender and Public Access: Women's Politics in Nineteenth-Century America," in *Habermas and the Public Sphere*, ed. Craig Calhoun (Cambridge, MA and London: MIT Press, 1992), p. 268.

56 Elmer, *Reading*, p. 153.

57 Although the story takes place in London, hence the plausible presence of "noblemen" (*PT* 389), I am guided by other critics such as Elmer and Robert Byer who read this story as reflecting Poe's concerns about American politics and culture. Poe's general gothic or fantastic literary style invites such critical license. See Elmer, *Reading*; Robert Byer, "Mysteries of the City: A Reading of Poe's 'The Man of the Crowd,'" in *Ideology and Classic American Literature*, eds. Sacvan Bercovitch and Myra Jehlen (Cambridge, England: Cambridge University Press, 1986), pp. 221–246.

58 See Larzer Ziff, *Literary Democracy: The Declaration of Cultural Independence in America* (Middlesex and New York: Penguin, 1982), pp. 67–86.

59 Darrel Abel, *The Moral Picturesque: Studies in Hawthorne's Fiction* (West Lafayette, IN: Purdue University Press, 1988), p. 1.

60 *Centenary Edition of the Works of Nathaniel Hawthorne* 23 vols. (Columbus, Ohio: Ohio State University Press, 1962–), vol. 23, pp. 273, 278. Hereafter this edition is abbreviated as *CE*, with volume and page references appearing in the text.

For a highly valuable and incisive analysis of Hawthorne's representation in *The Scarlet Letter* of specifically *good* citizenship, see Brook Thomas, "Citizen Hester: *The Scarlet Letter* as Civic Myth," *American Literary History* 13 (2001), pp. 181–211. On his view, the novel "illustrates how important it is for liberal democracies to maintain the space of an independent civil society in which alternative obediences and loyalties are allowed a chance to flourish," p. 185.

61 "The Old Apple-Dealer" conforms to the literary genre of the sketch. Its brevity and fragmentary quality foster this double-play of offering and withdrawing. In *The Spectator and the City* Dana Brand provides ample evidence of the emergence in the antebellum United States of a literary *flânerie*, which drew on more established European discursive practices, and which advanced the sketch as a modern belletristic form.

62 Henry James, *Hawthorne*, in *The Shock of Recognition*, ed. Edmund Wilson (Garden City and New York: Doubleday, 1943), p. 458, emphasis added.

63 *Ibid.*, p. 456.

64 Harriet Beecher Stowe, *Uncle Tom's Cabin: Or Life Among the Lowly*, ed. Elizabeth Ammons (New York: Norton: 1994), p. 294.

65 For an informative and insightful account of Hawthorne's abiding interest in the natural sciences, see Taylor Stoehr's *Hawthorne's Mad Scientists. Pseudo-science and Social Science in Nineteenth-Century Life and Letters* (Hamden, CT: Archon Books, 1978).

66 Many other American notebook entries from the 1830s and 1840s reflect Hawthorne's curiosity about psycho-physiological anomalies and near-death experiences. In one he considers writing an essay "on various kinds of death, together with the just-before and just-after" (*CE* 8: 239). In others he records the idea of a man who exists for ten years in "suspended animation" (*CE* 8: 16); the idea of a "[w]oman to sympathize with all emotions, but to have none of her own" (*CE* 8: 169); the conversation he had with an amputee who affirmed that "he still seemed to feel the hand that had been amputated" (*CE* 8: 91–92); the case cited in Andrew Combe's *Principles of Physiology* of a man who was "seized with a fit of frenzy, which terminated in mania" after he shut himself up for days with various sources of excitement (that is, alcoholic spirits, colognes, a singing girl) as an experiment (*CE* 8: 235–236).

67 Wolfgang Schivelbusch, *The Railway Journey: Trains and Travel in the Nineteenth Century*, trans. Anselm Hollo (New York: Urizen Books, 1979), p. 119, emphasis added.

68 Ruth Leys, *From Sympathy to Reflex: Marshall Hall and His Opponents* (New York: Garland, 1991). As Leys explains, this line of modern scientific inquiry had its predecessors:

[T]he reflex concept had its remote origins in the ancient doctrine of *sympathy*, according to which one organ or part of the body had extensive inter-relations with other, often distant parts, by virtue of the sympathy between them. In ancient thought, the cause of sympathy was supposed to be an immaterial psychic principle or soul, which pervaded the body and mediated between the parts without necessitating a direct connection between the tissues involved.

See Leys, *From Sympathy to Reflex*, p. 3. This physiological model provided eighteenth-century philosophers such as Shaftesbury, Smith, and Hume with a way of understanding relations between persons as well.

69 Stoehr, *Mad Scientists*, p. 81.

70 Andrew Combe, *Observations on Mental Derangement*, ed. Anthony Walsh (Delmar, NY: Scholar's Facsimiles and Reprints, 1972), p. 297, emphasis in original.

71 See Stoehr, *Mad Scientists*, pp. 68, 80–81, 239.

72 Combe, *Observations*, pp. 94, 112–113.

73 *Ibid.*, pp. 295–296, emphasis in original.

74 Mary Gove (Nichols), *Lectures to Ladies on Anatomy and Physiology* (Boston: Saxton and Pierce, 1842), pp. 211, 214.

75 Combe, *Observations*, pp. 40, 34, 87–88.

76 Abel, *Moral Picturesque*, pp. 11, 2.

77 Brand, *Spectator*, pp. 113, 7.

78 Headley, *The Great Riots*, p. 66.

79 James, *Hawthorne*, p. 463.

80 Gillian Brown, *Domestic Individualism: Imagining Self in Nineteenth-Century American Literature* (Berkeley and Los Angeles: University of California Press, 1990).

2 JAMES AND THE PUBLIC SPHERE

1 Henry James, *The Complete Tales of Henry James*, 12 vols., ed. Leon Edel (Philadelphia and New York: J. B. Lippincott, 1962–1965), vol. 12, p. 86. Hereafter this edition is cited as *CT*, with volume number and page references appearing in the text.

2 Immanuel Kant, *Political Writings*, ed. Hans Reiss (Cambridge, England: Cambridge University Press, 1970), p. 55, emphasis omitted.

3 Jürgen Habermas, *The Structural Transformation of the Public Sphere: An Inquiry into a Category of Bourgeois Society*, trans. Thomas Burger (Cambridge, MA: MIT Press), p. 105.

4 *Ibid*, pp. 28–29.

5 *Ibid.*, pp. 46–47, 160, 178.

6 See, for instance, Ross Posnock, *The Trial of Curiosity: Henry James, William James, and the Challenge of Modernity* (Oxford: Oxford University Press, 1991); Ian Bell, *Washington Square: Styles of Money* (New York, Twayne, 1993); Andrew Scheiber, "The Doctor's Order: Eugenic Anxiety in Henry James's *Washington Square*," *Literature and Medicine* 15 (1996), pp. 244–62; Richard Salmon, *Henry James and the Culture of Publicity* (Cambridge, England: Cambridge University Press, 1997); Sara Blair, *Henry James and the Writing of Race and Nation* (Cambridge, England: Cambridge University Press, 1996); Jean-Christophe Agnew, "The Consuming Vision of Henry James," in *The Culture of Consumption: Critical Essays in American History, 1880–1980*, eds. Richard Wightman Fox and T. J. Jackson Lears (New York: Pantheon, 1983), pp. 67–100.

7 Henry James, *A Small Boy and Others* (New York: Charles Scribner's Sons, 1913), pp. 309–310; Henry James, *The American Scene* (Bloomington: Indiana University Press, 1968), p. 131.

8 James, *Small Boy*, pp. 103, 20; James, *American Scene*, p. 68.

9 Henry James, *Washington Square* (London: Penguin Classics, 1984), p. 46. Hereafter this edition is cited as *WS*, with page references appearing in the text.

10 Marshall Berman calls such face-to-face encounters the "primal modern scene." See Berman, *All That Is Solid Melts into Air* (New York: Simon and Schuster, 1982), p. 229. See chapter 1 of this study for discussions of Poe's, Hawthorne's, and Whitman's renditions.

11 By the 1840s mesmerism had become a veritable cult in the United States, coinciding, as the historian Robert Fuller explains, with the Second Great Awakening as well as with the "surging tide of American rationalism." See Fuller, *Mesmerism and the American Cure of Souls* (Philadelphia: University of Pennsylvania Press), pp. 21, 75. By the time James was writing *Washington Square* in 1879, this spiritualist cult had lost much of its fervor and the scientistic cult of hypnosis had not yet reached full swing. Nevertheless there is evidence of his abiding interest in the theme. In 1874 he published the short story "Professor Fargo" which revolves around a charlatan mesmerist, his deaf and dumb subject, and her father, a mathematical genius bordering on madness. In his 1876 review of the Goncourt brothers' work, he remarks that their volumes "are a magazine of curious facts, and indicate a high relish for psychological research." See James, *Literary Reviews and Essays*, ed. Albert Mordell (New York: Twayne, 1957), p. 158. Moreover, he indicates a knowledge of Oliver Wendell Holmes's novel, *The Guardian Angel* (1867), as he mentions it in a letter to his sister Alice James when the novel was being serialized. See James, *Henry James: Letters*, 4 vols., ed. Leon Edel (Cambridge, MA and London: Harvard University Press, 1974–1984), vol. 1, p. 69. It is a "medicated novel" by Holmes's own account and treats the recovery of an hysteric beauty, who in one phase receives magnetic treatment. Holmes's medicated style reverberates well into the 1870s, as evidenced by Bayard Taylor's *Diversions of the Echo Club* (published first in the *Atlantic Monthly* in 1872 and republished in a volume in 1876) in which Holmes is fondly caricatured in a poem called "The Psycho-Physical Muse," the caricaturist having first "surrender[ed] ... like spiritual mediums, to the control of the first stray idea that enter[ed his] brain." See Taylor, *Diversions of the Echo Club* in *The Shock of Recognition*, ed. Edmund Wilson (Garden City and New York: 1943), pp. 350, 354.

12 William James would refer to the forehead, following current parlance, as a "hypnogenic zone." See James, *The Principles of Psychology* 2 vols. (New York: Henry Holt, 1890), vol. 2, p. 594. In *The Guardian Angel* Holmes describes how the young doctor, only recently acquainted with his magnetizing capability, treats the traumatized, hysterical and aptly named Myrtle Hazard: "All the strange spasmodic movements, the chokings, the odd sounds, the wild talk, the laughing and crying, were in full blast ... The Doctor could hardly refuse

trying his *quasi* magnetic influence, and placed the tips of his fingers on her fore-head . . . the storm was soon calmed, and after a little time she fell into a quiet sleep." See Holmes, *The Guardian Angel* (Boston and New York: Houghton, Mifflin, 1895), p. 134. One might also think of Poe's narrator of "The Man of the Crowd," the convalescent who, with his "brow to the glass" of the restaurant in which he sits, seems to be hypnotically seized by the old man's appearance whose "countenance . . . at once arrested and absorbed [his] whole attention." See Poe, *Poetry and Tales* (New York: Library of America, 1984), p. 392.

13 Ian Bell, *Washington Square: Styles of Money* (New York: Twayne, 1993), p. 23; Andrew Scheiber, "The Doctor's Order: Eugenic Anxiety in Henry James's *Washington Square*," *Literature and Medicine* 15 (1996), p. 245.

14 Bell, *Styles*, pp. 5, 63, 95–96. See also Millicent Bell, "Style as Subject: *Washington Square*," *Sewanee Review* 83 (1975), pp. 19–38.

15 Scheiber, "Doctor's Order," pp. 246–247, 248–249.

16 Bell, *Styles*, p. 5; Scheiber, "Doctor's Order," p. 252.

17 It is worth noting at this point that Catherine possesses, oddly enough, certain salient features that James attributes also to Nathaniel Hawthorne in his monograph, which appeared shortly before *Washington Square*. For all of the controversy this book has raised, owing to its ostensible deprecation of Hawthorne's work, it reveals James's undeniable admiration for the author himself. He is fascinated not so much with Hawthorne's imaginative genius or authoritative assertiveness – the *sine qua non* of the romantic and realist writer, respectively – but with Hawthorne's *silence*. James describes Hawthorne's relish for the "incommunicative periods" when his wife was absent, and his habit of "going into the village [and coming] home without having spoken a word to a human being." See James, *Hawthorne* in *The Shock of Recognition*, ed. Edmund Wilson (Garden City and New York: Doubleday, 1943), p. 515. Not unlike Catherine Sloper's "dumb eloquence," as James calls her reticence to speak, the "silence-loving and shade-seeking side of [Hawthorne's] character," his "natural shyness and reserve," the "extraordinary blankness" of his diaries, the "moon-lighted air of his intellect," all seem to attract and intrigue James, pp. 446, 459, 514. He quotes a "singularly beautiful and touching passage" from Hawthorne's notebooks, in which the latter describes himself as sitting "a long, long time, waiting patiently for the world to know me . . . And sometimes it seems to me as if I were already in the grave, with only life enough to be chilled and benumbed . . . Indeed, we are but shadows; we are not endowed with real life," pp. 466–467, ellipses added. For all of Hawthorne's ghostliness, James insists (as he does similarly with regard to Catherine) that "there was nothing unamiable or invidious in his shyness, and above all that there was nothing preponderantly gloomy," p. 447.

18 James Esdaile, *Mesmerism in India* (Chicago: The Psychic Research Co., 1902), pp. 116, 77, 116, emphasis in original.

19 Marcel Gauchet, *L'inconscient cérébral* (Paris: Édition Seuil, 1992), p. 60, my translation here and below. See also Ruth Leys, *From Sympathy to Reflex: Marshall Hall and His Opponents* (New York: Garland, 1991).

20 *Ibid*, pp. 92–93, emphasis in original, ellipses added.
21 Quoted in Allan Angoff and Eric Dingwall, eds., *Abnormal Hypnotic Phenomena: A Survey of Nineteenth-Century Cases* vol. 4 (London: J. and A. Churchill, 1968), pp. 31–32, emphasis added.
22 Bell notes the similarity between Catherine's and her father's modes of observation:

> Suspension registers the immobility into which Catherine is pressured. But here we recognize also the extent to which she herself is obliged to wield, unwittingly perhaps, the very forces that instigate her immobility. In part she is adopting a stance akin to Sloper's in watching the experiment herself. In part she is beginning to acknowledge the need for some element of performance in her personal relations, the performance that... is to be a hallmark of the new social reality within consumer culture. In part she is displaying the alienation of the self that is customarily associated with the effects of developing industrialism.

See Bell, *Styles*, pp. 95–96.
23 Andrew Bowie, *Aesthetics and Subjectivity: From Kant to Nietzsche* (Manchester and New York: Manchester University Press, 1990), p. 21.
24 Walter Benjamin, *Illuminations*, ed. Hannah Arendt (New York: Schocken, 1969), p. 124.
25 Habermas, *Structural Transformation*, p. 133.
26 Quoted in Patrick Brantlinger, *Bread and Circuses: Theories of Mass Culture as Social Decay* (Ithaca and London: Cornell University Press, 1983), pp. 6–7.
27 Salmon, *Culture of Publicity*, pp. 139–140, 141. Salmon thus importantly reverses the conventional view of Henry James as a conservative critic of newspaperism, such as one finds even recently in Michael Robertson's first chapter, "Journalism as Threat: William Dean Howells and Henry James," of *Stephen Crane, Journalism, and the Making of Modern American Literature* (New York: Columbia University Press, 1997).
28 *Ibid*., pp. 148, 139, 146.
29 Philip Fisher, "Appearing and Disappearing in Public: Social Space in Late-Nineteenth Century Literature and Culture," in *Reconstructing American Literary History*, ed. Sacvan Bercovitch (Cambridge, MA and London: Harvard University Press, 1986), p. 167.
30 *Ibid*., p. 139.
31 Gabriel Tarde, "The Public and the Crowd," in *Gabriel Tarde: On Communication and Social Influence: Selected Papers*, ed. Terry Clark (Chicago and London: University of Chicago Press, 1969), p. 281.
32 *Ibid*., pp. 277, 279, 281.
33 *Ibid*., pp. 278, 281, 283, 278, emphasis added.
34 Terry Clark, "Introduction," *Gabriel Tarde: On Communication and Social Influence: Selected Papers*, ed. Terry Clark (Chicago and London: University of Chicago Press, 1969), p. 52.
35 Gabriel Tarde, *L'opinion et la foule* (Paris: Presses Universitaires, 1989), p. 34, my translation. This passage appears in the same essay, "The Public and the Crowd," in its original French version, but was eliminated from Terry Clark's

substantially abbreviated translated version. The same holds for other passages referred to below.

36 Gabriel Tarde, "Opinion and Conversation," in *Gabriel Tarde: On Communication and Social Influence: Selected Papers*, ed. Terry Clark (Chicago and London: University of Chicago Press, 1969), pp. 297, 281, 283–284.

37 *Ibid.*, p. 299.

38 Robert Park was an American sociologist who in 1904 reiterated and elaborated Tarde's ideas. He exemplifies turn-of-the-century social psychology's internal difficulties with its own terms and classifications. Precision and consistency are at times wanting. For instance, at one point in *The Crowd and the Public* he defines the public as "at the same stage of awareness-development as the crowd," namely at the stage of "unreflective perception"; but at another point he defines the public as unlike the crowd in its capacity for "rational reflection," in that reason, not instinct, prevails when its members interact with each other. See Park, *The Crowd and the Public and Other Essays*, trans. Charlotte Elsner (Chicago: University of Chicago Press, 1972), pp. 57, 80–81.

39 Thomas Henry Huxley, *Evolution and Ethics*, eds. James Paradis and George C. Williams (Princeton: Princeton University Press, 1989), pp. 115, 138–139.

40 William F. Fine, *Progressive Evolutionism and American Sociology, 1890–1920* (Ann Arbor: UMI Research Press, 1976), pp. 120, 132.

41 In *The Laws of Imitation* Tarde offers the following argument:

> But let us go back still further, to that pre-historic dawn when the art of speech was unknown. At that time how was the secret content of the mind, its desires and ideas, transfused from one brain to another? . . . Hypnotic suggestion can give us some vague idea[.] . . . It is not difficult to understand how the first inventor of speech set to associating in his own mind a given thought and a given sound (perfected by gesture), but it is difficult to understand how he was able to *suggest* this relation to another by merely making him hear the given sound. If the listener merely repeated this sound like a parrot, without attaching to it the required meaning, it is impossible to see how this superficial and mechanical *re-echoing* could have led him to understand the meaning of the strange speaker or carried him over from the *sound* to the *word*. It must then be admitted that the sense was transmitted with the sound, that it reflected the sound. And whoever is acquainted with the feats of hypnotism, with the miracles of suggestion, that have been popularized to so great an extent of late, should certainly not be reluctant to admit this postulate.

See Tarde, *The Laws of Imitation*, trans. Elsie Clews Parsons (New York: Henry Holt, 1903), pp. 204–205.

42 In *Philosophical Investigations* Wittgenstein makes the distinction between agreement regarding truth claims and agreement regarding the framework of communication, the latter being the accepted "form of life":

> "So you are saying that human agreement decides what is true and what is false?" – It is what human beings *say* that is true and false; and they agree in the *language* they use. That is not agreement in opinions but in form of life.

Such agreement registers the end of explanation. Interlocutors either apprehend agreement as a human capacity or they don't. See Wittgenstein, *Philosophical*

Investigations, trans. G. E. M. Anscombe (New York: Macmillan, 1958), sec. 241, p. 88.

43 Henry James, *The Question of our Speech* and *The Lesson of Balzac* (New York: Haskell House Pub., 1972), pp. 13, 12, 43.

44 *Ibid.*, p. 6.

45 *Ibid.*, pp. 35, 46, 25, 36, 47.

46 Henry Brewster, *The Theories of Anarchy and Law* (London: Williams and Norgate, 1887), pp. 30–31; Henry and William James, *William and Henry James: Selected Letters*, eds. Ignas K. Skrupskelis and Elizabeth M. Berkeley (Charlottesville and London: University of Virginia Press, 1997), p. 234.

47 Brewster, *Theories*, pp. 104, 93.

48 *Ibid.*, pp. 52, 61, 130, 80, 148.

49 In a 1970 essay on *The Princess Casamassima*, Taylor Stoehr importantly argues that Henry Brewster's book anticipates Wittgenstein in its attack on linguistic referentiality as the source of meaning. He contends that the stripping away of referential authority is essentially anarchistic; but he stops short of allowing that the substitute linguistic order, "linguistic solidarity among men" based on a belief that "language [is] shared," is essentially Kantian and liberal. On my view, when Brewster's Harold invokes "mutual intelligence" as the basis for social relations, he trades in his anarchic card for a liberal one; where he invokes disinterested "revolt," he reverses the trade. See Stoehr, "Words and Deeds in *The Princess Casamassima*," *ELH* 37 (1970), pp. 130, 133.

50 Here too James resembles social psychologists such as Tarde; for Tarde the notion of spontaneous generation serves to explain the emergence of crowds, new political parties, and so forth. See Tarde, *L'opinion*, pp. 46, 53. Tarde's aim is to move away from evolutionary biological explanations and toward dynamic psychological ones. Thus transformations from broad "organized social groups" to more narrowly circumscribed publics he calls "inorganic." See Tarde, "Public," p. 289. It is also worth noting Morse Peckham's argument about Darwin's conception of species. In "Darwinism and Darwinisticism" (1959) he contends that Darwin "demonstrates that to the term there is no corresponding reality or entity in the biological world. It is essential to his argument that species should not be regarded as fixed . . . since the term is only of convenience in creating hypotheses[.] . . . To him a scientific law was a mental convenience." From this perspective, the spontaneity of spontaneous generation has no intrinsic value, moral or otherwise – nor for that matter does the continuation of a species – for it is merely descriptive. As Peckham goes on to argue about such a "mechanism," "[i]t reveals a world not of accident precisely but rather one in which 'accident' becomes a meaningless problem." Where in "The Papers" the main characters take evident personal pleasure in the consequences resulting from their spontaneous actions, James stakes no claims on the political or moral value of these consequences. See Peckham, "Darwinism and Darwinisticism," in *Darwin*, second edition, ed. Philio Appleman (New York: Norton, 1979), pp. 303, 304.

51 Margaret Welch, "Is Newspaper Work Healthful for Women?" *Journal of Social Science* 32 (1894), p. 113.

52 In the interests of brevity I have bypassed the elements in the narrative that I think point to Howard's own "unusual game." A case can be made for his similarly "immoral" abandonment of the public sphere and journalism. Although he repeatedly intimates his willingness to leave the profession on account of its vulgarity, when he finally does bail out, he is otherwise motivated. While genuinely distraught when he thinks he might be responsible for Beadel-Muffet's demise, Howard also considers journalism a 'sport,' a 'game,' which is formally not unlike Maud's conversion of it into an aesthetic practice. Thus he decides to drop out once he sees his defeat. "I lose," he says, upon hearing the announcement of Beadel-Muffet's alleged death, "I *have* lost. So I don't matter" (*CT* 12: 97). The defeat, however, consists not so much in discovering himself responsible, but in learning the news through the hawkers' cries, instead of himself being "in the know," which to him is what being a journalist means. Having lost, he no longer wants to play, for as he says to Maud, "What is sport but success? What is success but sport?" (*CT* 12: 49).

53 Robert B. Pippin, *Henry James and Modern Moral Life* (Cambridge: Cambridge University Press, 2000), pp. 38, 59.

3 SOCIAL JUSTICE AND CRANE'S DOCUMENTARY ANAESTHETICS

1 Stephen Crane, *Prose and Poetry* (New York: Library of America, 1984), pp. 67, 65–66. Hereafter this edition is cited as *PP*, with page references appearing in the text.

2 Theodore Dreiser, *Sister Carrie* (New York and London: Viking Penguin, 1990). Dreiser describes how Carrie "gladly sank into the obscuring crowd," p. 20.

3 John Rawls, *Political Liberalism* (New York: Columbia University Press, 1993), p. 13.

4 Frederic C. Howe, *The City: The Hope of Democracy*, introd. Otis A. Pease (Seattle and London: University of Washington Press, 1969), pp. 299, 283, 287.

5 *Ibid.*, pp. 281, 282, emphasis added, 292.

6 Quoted in Robert C. Elliott, "Introduction" in *Looking Backward*, Edward Bellamy (Boston: Houghton Mifflin, 1966), p. x.

7 Edward Bellamy, *Looking Backward* (Boston: Houghton Mifflin, 1966), p. 153.

8 Sylvia Bowman, *Edward Bellamy* (Boston: Twayne, 1986), p. 114.

9 Bellamy, *Looking Backward*, p. 75.

10 Catherine Tumber, "Edward Bellamy, the Erosion of Public Life, and the Gnostic Revival," *American Literary History* 11 (1999), pp. 613, 612, 629.

11 *Ibid.*, p. 612.

12 Bellamy, *Looking Backward*, p. 66.

13 Norman Barry, *An Introduction to Modern Political Theory*, second edition (Hampshire and London: Macmillan, 1989), p. 154.

14 Tumber, "Gnostic Revival," p. 634.

15 Rawls, *Political Liberalism*, p. 303.
16 William James, *The Principles of Psychology*, 2 vols. (New York: Henry Holt, 1890), vol. 2, p. 606, emphasis in original.
17 Quoted in Ralph Barton Perry, *The Thought and Character of William James*, 2 vols. (Boston: Little, Brown, 1935), vol. 2, p. 405.
18 Benjamin Paul Blood, *The Anaesthetic Revelation and the Gist of Philosophy* (Amsterdam and New York: n.p., 1874), pp. 12–13.
19 Blood, *Anaesthetic Revelation*, p. 35; James, *Principles*, vol. 1, pp. 320, 419.
20 James, *Principles*, vol. 2, p. 455.
21 William James, *Essays in Radical Empiricism* (Cambridge, MA and London: Harvard University Press, 1975), pp. 36–37; James, *Principles*, vol. 2, p. 8.
22 Alan Trachtenberg, "Experiments in Another Country: Stephen Crane's City Sketches," in *American Realism: New Essays*, ed. Eric Sundquist (Baltimore and London: Johns Hopkins University Press, 1982), pp. 144, 145, 148. For related, more recent accounts of the intersection of Crane's work and contemporaneous moral frameworks, see Keith Gandal, *The Virtues of the Vicious: Jacob Riis, Stephen Crane, and the Spectacle of the Slum* (New York and Oxford: Oxford University Press, 1997); and Bill Brown, *The Material Unconscious: American Amusement, Stephen Crane, and the Economies of Play* (Cambridge, MA and London: Harvard University Press, 1996). Gandal's book situates Crane within the context of his era's Christian charity writing, arguing insightfully that Crane advances a redescription of personal morality, one based on slum-dwellers' self-esteem engendered by peer approval. Brown's book emphasizes Crane's specifically anti-Methodist interest in amusement, revealing Crane's appropriation of popular cultural phenomena such as freak shows and war-game excitement.
23 If my account diverges from Trachtenberg's insightful reading, it can be seen in some ways to take up where Michael Fried in *Realism, Writing, Disfiguration: On Thomas Eakins and Stephen Crane* (Chicago: University of Chicago Press, 1987) leaves off: a reference appears in one of his concluding footnotes to the interest at the end of the nineteenth century in a "range of phenomena that included partial aphasias, anaesthesias, automatic writing, and split consciousness," p. 204. The major thrust of Fried's work has been to map out the ways in which Crane's work draws attention to the materiality of writing, a materiality that "threaten[s] to abort the realization of the 'impressionist' project," p. 120. His concern, then, is primarily with Crane's dramatization of the limits of representation and the act of writing. My concern is with Crane's dramatization of the limits of experience within a nexus of physiological, social, and political relations. Where Fried draws on Derrida's analysis of the ontological status of writing, I draw on Deleuze's brief but trenchant commentary on Crane in *The Logic of Sense*. There he sets forth a constellation of neutrality, indifference, and anonymity in his reading of the limit-experience of battle in *The Red Badge of Courage*. See Fried, *Realism*, pp. 163, 185; see Gilles Deleuze, *The Logic of Sense*, trans. Mark Lester (New York: Columbia University Press, 1990), pp. 100–101.

24 As is well known, Garland was convinced of Crane's automatic writing capacity. See, for instance, R. W. Stallman's account in *Stephen Crane. A Biography* (New York: George Braziller, 1968), p. 90, or Christopher Benfey's in *The Double Life of Stephen Crane. A Biography* (New York: Alfred E. Knopf, 1992), p. 130.

25 B. O. Flower, "Hypnotism and Mental Suggestion," *The Arena* 6 (July 1892), p. 210; R. H. Sherard, "The Hypnotic Experiments of Doctor Luys," *McClure's Magazine* 1 (November 1893), p. 551.

26 Stephen Crane, *The Correspondence of Stephen Crane*, 2 vols. (New York: Columbia University Press, 1988), vol. 1, p. 115.

27 For an account of Crane's optics that differs from the one I give below, see Mark Seltzer's essay "Statistical Persons," *diacritics* 17 (1987), pp. 82–98. He makes the provocative but unconvincing claim that Crane operates (in) a "realist" "seeing machine in which everyone is caught," an apparatus of the nineteenth century's "single technology of regulation," producing a "compulsory and compulsive visibility" and "making everything, including interior states, visible, legible, and governable," pp. 84–85. It is not only Seltzer's totalizing hyperboles ("everything," "everyone") that weaken his argument; it is also the fact that the better part of his analysis relies on the claim that Crane, like most realists and naturalists, "seems to require the figure of the prostitute," p. 86. But apart from *Maggie*, prostitutes hardly appear in Crane's work at all, a fact that is all the more remarkable in light of his intimate (as well as scandalous) association with them.

28 William Welling, *Photography in America: The Formative Years 1839–1900* (New York: Thomas Y. Crowell, 1978), p. 54. Needless to say, one expectation of the documentary genre (be it in the medium of photography, film, sound recording or print) is that it document, that it produce eye-witnessed images, synecdochal proof of the existence of particular events or conditions. Such is the function of documentary or news photography, a practice that became current in the 1870s. Yet what is striking about this photograph, as Welling goes on to report, is that it was shot not at the original, actual operation in 1846, but at its re-enactment, perhaps as long as ten years after the event. While the doctor, John C. Warren, who performed the operation appears in the photo, the dentist, W. T. G. Morton, who momentously administered the anaesthetic does not, nor does the original patient. Furthermore, the patient was to have a tumor removed from his jaw; thus he received the ether vapors sitting up (probably in the chair on the right), not prostrate. See Welling, *Photography in America*, p. 54. What we find, then, is a primal scene of documentation fully saturated with both newsmaking drama and theatrical fabrication. Another historian, Helmut Gernsheim, places the date of the daguerreotype at 1847, but provides no explanation. See Gernsheim, *The Origins of Photography*, revised edition (New York: Thames and Hudson), p. 104. The J. Paul Getty Museum's date, which appears in the caption, is that of the actual operation. For a colorful but reliable (yet at odd moments comically sexist) account of the history of surgical anaesthesia, see Howard Riley Raper, *Man against Pain: The Epic of Anesthesia* (New York: Prentice-Hall, 1945). Other valuable accounts include

Victor Robinson, *Victory over Pain: A History of Anesthesia* (New York: Henry Schuman, 1946) and Thomas E. Keys, *The History of Surgical Anesthesia* (New York: Schuman's, 1945).

29 R. W. Stallman reports that Crane used Brady's work as source material for *The Red Badge of Courage*. See Stallman, ed., *The Stephen Crane Reader* (Glenview, IL: Scott, Foresman and Co., 1972), p. 169. Regarding Jacob Riis, as a young reporter in Asbury Park Crane covered Riis's lecture there.

30 Sarah Orne Jewett, "Human Documents," *McClure's Magazine* 1 (June 1893), p. 17.

31 Stephen Crane, *The Works of Stephen Crane*, 10 vols. (Charlottesville: University Press of Virginia, 1969–1976), vol. 8, pp. 665–666. Hereafter this edition is cited as *W*, with volume and page references appearing in the text.

32 In "On the Uses and Disadvantages of History for Life" (in *Untimely Meditations*) Nietzsche writes: "Then the man says 'I remember' and envies the animal, who at once forgets and for whom every moment really dies... Thus the animal lives *unhistorically*[.] ... Forgetting is essential to action of any kind, just as not only light but darkness too is essential for the life of everything organic." See Friedrich Nietzsche, "On the Uses and Disadvantages of History for Life," in *Untimely Meditations*, trans. R. J. Hollingdale (Cambridge, England: Cambridge University Press, 1983), pp. 61–62.

33 Here I am drawing upon Derrida's distinction between a general and restricted economy. Whereas the latter is circumscribed by signification and representation, the former ruptures these containments with the excessive laughter of non-signification: "It opens the question of meaning. It does not describe un-knowledge, for this is impossible, but only the effect of unknowledge." See Jacques Derrida, "From Restricted to General Economy. A Hegelianism without Reserve," in *Writing and Difference*, trans. Alan Bass (Chicago: University of Chicago Press, 1978), p. 270.

34 The exception is the surgeon, who, hands on the patient's thigh, looks toward the camera. Not foregrounded, however, he figures much less prominently than the prostrate patient.

35 Robert Park, *The Crowd and the Public and Other Essays*, trans. Charlotte Elsner (Chicago: University of Chicago Press, 1972), p. 29. Originally written in German (*Masse und Publikum*, 1904) under the direction of the philosopher of history Wilhelm Windelband, Park's dissertation reflects the influence not only of his mentor and former teacher, Georg Simmel, but also of his American teachers, William James and John Dewey. For an excellent study of Park's role in establishing the Chicago school of sociology, see Fred H. Matthews, *Quest for an American Sociology: Robert E. Park and the Chicago School* (Montreal: McGill-Queen's University Press, 1977). Winifred Raushenbush's biography, *Robert E. Park: Biography of a Sociologist* (Durham: Duke University Press, 1979) is also informative. Like Crane, Park's tenure as a newspaper reporter in New York took place in the early 1890s; he also contributed stories to the *World*. There is no evidence that the two were acquainted, but it happens that Park also had an interest in tombstones. A grand-daughter reports that he once

"wrote a poem about the Ossified Man, something to the effect that when he dies he will become his own tombstone," quoted in Raushenbush, *Robet E. Park*, p. 16.

36 That Crane was aware of crowd psychology and wary of its influence on the city police's strategy for managing crowds is evident in what appears to have been an altercation with Theodore Roosevelt, then Police Commissioner of New York (who later, as former President of the United States, would insist on meeting Le Bon while on a visit to France). This occurred following an evening of clashes between the police and the crowd attending a William Jennings Bryan meeting at Madison Square Garden. The *New York Times* (13 August 1896) reported that "Twenty mounted police and 100 men on foot charged the crowd cautiously but inexorably, and pressed the people back," p. 3. Crane seems to have criticized the police or perhaps Roosevelt himself, for the latter dispatched the following note to Crane: "This evening [the occasion of a Bourke Cockran meeting] I shall be around at the Madison Square Garden to see exactly what the Police do. They have a very difficult task with a crowd like that, because they have to be exceedingly good-humored with the crowd, and they also have to please the Managers of the meeting who know nothing about crowds, and yet they have to control twenty thousand people." See Crane, *Correspondence*, p. 249. With his implicit distinction between those "who know nothing" and himself, Roosevelt reflects the attitude of superior knowingness so often cultivated by scientific objectivists, as crowd psychologists generally presumed themselves to be.

37 Fried, *Realism*, pp. 94, 102.

38 This sketch is also central to Fried's examination of Crane's thematization of writing, given its numerous images (for example, the sign, the letters on the ambulance, the curtain, not least the fallen man) that lend themselves to interpretation as allegorical props for the scenes and acts of writing. As he also points out, with regard to this and other stories, the optical relations between the "unseeing stares" of corpse-like entities and their "overinvolved" spectators serve to threaten the latter: "One way in which that threat is registered by Crane's protagonists is as a loss of all sense of distance and very nearly of distinction between themselves and the corpselike beings that obsess their attention." See Fried, *Realism*, pp. 108, 117. In their losing all sense of distance and distinction (a sort of motor anaesthesia), I would add further that the fallen man and the crowd are nonetheless never homogenized, given the man's external relation to the scene (he has both dropped into and out of it). This fundamental differentiation is registered in the impalpable "room" or "space" separating him from the crowd (*PP* 603).

39 Gabriel Tarde, *The Laws of Imitation*, trans. Elsie Clews Parsons (New York: Henry Holt, 1903), p. 79.

40 *Ibid.*, pp. 83–84.

41 John Berryman, *Stephen Crane: A Critical Biography*, revised edition (New York: Farrar, Straus, Giroux), p. 24. Robert Hough seems to be the first to analyse in depth Crane's deployment of Goethe's theory of colors. His essay, "Crane

and Goethe: A Forgotten Relationship," *Nineteenth Century Fiction* 17 (1962), pp. 135–148, is valuable for its exposition of Crane's dramatic – usually metaphoric or psychological – rather than descriptive use of color. I part ways with his analysis, however, in its normative understanding of metaphor and symbol. That is, where Hough views Crane's color use as an emotional extension of or correspondence to a given scene (for example, "In *The Red Badge of Courage*, the title itself is a metaphor of violence, and war is symbolized throughout by red, crimson, or flame color," p. 143), I see Crane's metaphorics of color as producing more disjunctive or antagonistic relations.

42 Jonathan Crary, *Techniques of the Observer: On Vision and Modernity in the Nineteenth Century* (Cambridge, MA: MIT Press, 1990), pp. 68–69, 139.

43 *Ibid.*, p. 127.

44 Fried points out how such repetition draws out the materiality of writing, citing William James's "parallel phenomenon, the way in which 'if we look at an isolated printed word and repeat it long enough, it ends by assuming an entirely unnatural aspect.'" See Fried, *Realism*, pp. 130–131.

45 Tarde, *Laws*, p. 85. In the case of surgical anaesthesia, two of its mid-nineteenth-century discoverers, Horace Wells and Crawford Long, came to it by witnessing or experiencing the phase of hyperaesthesia induced by inhaling nitrous oxide, a form of entertainment then called "ether frolics." Raper gives an account in *Man against Pain* of Horace Wells's encounter. On the advice of P. T. Barnum, a certain "Professor Colton" brought to Hartford Connecticut "A GRAND EXHIBITION of the effects produced by inhaling NITROUS OXIDE," as its 1844 newspaper advertisement announced. Wells attended and even participated in the evening entertainment, observing how indeed one effect of the gas was, as the advertisement went on to state, "to make those who inhale it either Laugh, Sing, Dance, Speak or Fight, &c., &c., according to the leading trait of their character." But he also observed that it had an anaesthetizing effect:

Then he sat and watched Citizen Samuel Cooley take it, become excitedly intoxicated, shout, stagger about, run into a bench, or settee, and batter his shins . . . Mr. Cooley had not seemed to experience pain when he ran into the bench . . . It did not make sense, skinning one's shins and not registering pain . . . so [Wells] made his way to Samuel Cooley's side and said, "Did you hurt yourself, Sam, when you ran into the bench?"

The question rather startled Mr. Cooley. "Hurt myself? Why no. What bench? What do you mean?"

See Raper, *Man against Pain*, pp. 70–72.

46 See Charles Baudelaire, *The Painter of Modern Life and Other Essays*, trans. Jonathan Mayne (London: Phaidon Press, 1964).

47 In a note to "On Some Motifs in Baudelaire," Walter Benjamin explains that around "1840 it was briefly fashionable to take turtles for a walk in the arcades. The *flâneurs* liked to have the turtles set the pace for them." See Benjamin, *Illuminations*, ed. Hannah Arendt (New York: Schocken, 1969), p. 197.

48 It is worth noting that this sketch appears in the same issue of *The Arena*
that contains an article by J. R. Cocke who discusses "hysterical paralysis" and
hypnotic anaesthesia. See Cocke, "The Power of the Mind as a Remedial Agent
in the Cure of Disease," *The Arena* 9 (May 1894), pp. 752, 755.

49 These two *flâneurs* thus prefigure Crane's description of his own writerly activity
as a realist-journalist. In 1896 he wrote to the editor Ripley Hitchcock: "After
all, I cannot help vanishing and disappearing and dissolving. It is my foremost
trait." See Crane, *Correspondence*, p. 213.

4 WHITE CITY, THE NATION FORM, AND THE SOULS
OF LYNCHED FOLK

1 H[enry] C[hilds] Merwin, "A National Vice," *The Atlantic Monthly* 71 (1893),
pp. 769, 770–772.

2 *Ibid.*, p. 770.

3 *Ibid.*, p. 771.

4 Quoted in George Miles, ed. *The World's Fair from London to Chicago 1893*
(Chicago: Midway Pub., 1892), p. 25, emphasis added.

5 Peter Hales, *Silver Cities: The Photography of American Urbanization, 1839–1915*
(Philadelphia: Temple University Press, 1984), pp. 133–134.

6 Ida B. Wells, *A Red Record: Tabulated Statistics and Alleged Causes of Lynchings
in the United States, 1892–1893–1894*, in *Selected Works of Ida B. Wells-Barnett*,
introd. Trudier Harris (New York and Oxford: Oxford University Press, 1991),
p. 149.

7 Ida B. Wells, *The Reason Why the Colored American Is Not in the World's
Columbian Exposition*, in *Selected Works of Ida B. Wells-Barnett*, introd. Trudier
Harris (New York and Oxford: Oxford University Press, 1991), pp. 134–135.

8 For a wide-ranging and intricate account of how immigrants to the US nego-
tiated whiteness and became white, see Matthew Frye Jacobson, *Whiteness of
a Different Color: European Immigrants and the Alchemy of Race* (Cambridge,
MA and London: Harvard University Press, 1998).

9 Frederick Douglass, "The Lessons of the Hour," in *The Oxford Frederick Douglass Reader*, ed. William Andrews (New York and Oxford: Oxford University
Press, 1996), p. 353.

10 Wim de Wit, "Building an Illusion: The Design of the World's Columbian
Exposition," in *Grand Illusions: Chicago World's Fair of 1893*, eds. Neil Harris
et al. (Chicago: Chicago Historical Society, 1993), pp. 69, 71. The iconoclast
architect Louis Sullivan's famous 1924 criticism of the Fair also notes its market-
driven propagation of the illusory. Likening the Fair's architectural productions
to a virus, Sullivan savages the entire enterprise:

There came a violent outbreak of the Classic and the Renaissance in the East, which
slowly spread westward, contaminating all that it touched, both at its source and outward. The selling campaign of the bogus antique was remarkably well managed through
skillful publicity and propaganda[.] . . . By the time the market had been saturated, all
sense of reality was gone. In its place had come deep-seated illusions, hallucinations,

absence of pupillary reaction to light, absence of knee-reaction – symptoms all of progressive cerebral meningitis: The blanketing of the brain.

See Sullivan, *The Autobiography of an Idea* (New York: Dover, 1956), pp. 324–325.

11 Brook Thomas, ed. *Plessy v. Ferguson: A Brief History with Documents* (Boston and New York: Bedford Books, 1997), p. 59.

12 Wells, *Red Record*, p. 147. See, for instance, the 1892 response by W. Cabell Bruce in the *North American Review* to Frederick Douglass's article, "Lynch Law in the South," published in the previous issue. Where Douglass takes to task one "Bishop Fitzgerald, of the Methodist Church South" for "complain[ing] of the North that it does not more fully sympathize with the South in its efforts to protect the purity of Southern women," Bruce practically defends the South's lynching practices:

If lynching is more prevalent in the South than elsewhere, it is because . . . in the last year or so, the negro there has violated the chastity of white women with such appalling frequency, and under circumstances so unutterably shocking to human nature, that the white race there has been goaded into a degree of excited feeling.

While claiming that "[n]othing can justify lynching, under any conditions not totally abnormal, no matter how heinous the crime," Bruce also ignores Douglass's evidence of lynching of black men for alleged crimes unrelated to white women. Further, he essentially apologizes for, and would have his reader understand why, "a widespread feeling on the part of the white race in the South, *however mistaken*, that the most flagitious of crimes has become almost epidemic in their midst, and that only a nemesis, following the offence as surely and speedily as does the thunder clap the lightning flash, is adequate to the protection of mothers, wives and daughters." See Frederick Douglass, "Lynch Law in the South," *North American Review* 155 (1892), p. 20; and W. Cabell Bruce, "Lynch Law in the South," *North American Review* 155 (1892), pp. 379–380, emphasis added).

13 Walter Benn Michaels, "The Souls of White Folk," in *Literature and the Body: Essays on Population and Persons*, ed. Elaine Scarry (Baltimore: Johns Hopkins University Press, 1988), p. 190; Michael Rogin, " 'The Sword Became a Flashing Vision': D. W. Griffith's *The Birth of a Nation*," *Representations* 9 (1985), p. 185.

14 W. E. B. Du Bois, *Darkwater: Voices from within the Veil* (New York: AMS Press, 1969), p. 26; W. E. B. Du Bois, *Black Reconstruction in America 1860–1880* (Cleveland and New York: Meridian, 1964), p. 700, emphasis added.

15 Merwin, "A National Vice," pp. 770, 771.

16 Du Maurier, *Trilby* (Oxford and New York: Oxford University Press, 1995), p. 146. For similar statements by Kant, see *The Critique of Judgement*, trans. James Creed Meredith (Oxford: Oxford University Press, 1957), sec. 46, pp. 168–169, where he stresses the artistic genius's originality, his "giv[ing] the rule as nature," and his production of exemplary models.

17 Du Maurier, *Trilby*, pp. 167, 203, 205, 209, 220.

18 Kant, *Judgement*, sec 46, p. 168.

19 John Dewey, "Ethics of Democracy," in *The Political Writings*, eds. Debra Morris and Ian Shapiro (Indianapolis and Cambridge: Hackett, 1993), pp. 62, emphasis added, 61. My alignment here of Dewey and Kant, specifically with Kant's concept of *sensus communis*, may seem blinkered, given Dewey's general hostility to Kant's transcendentalist system and his general adoption of Hegel's brand of idealism (particularly in Dewey's early work). However, I think there are good reasons for proposing this alignment, while also acknowledging its incompleteness. First, it has been shown that Dewey's view of Kant's formalist ethics as overly rigid, empty, and inapplicable to real-life circumstance, was largely the result of Hegel's own (mis)reading of Kant. See Robert B. Westbrook, *John Dewey and American Democracy* (Ithaca and London: Cornell University Press, 1991), pp. 44–47, 199–200; and Matthew Festenstein, *Pragmatism and Political Theory: From Dewey to Rorty* (Chicago: University of Chicago Press, 1997), p. 207. Second, Dewey's moral philosophy accords fully with Kant's anti-utilitarian claim that every man is an end in himself and is imbued with moral autonomy. See Festenstein, *Pragmatism*, p. 56. Dewey's rational-consequentialist tendency (discussed more fully in chapter 6) seems to follow from what Rawls points out is Hegel's rejection of "Kant's distinction between prudence and morality." Such a rejection, however, does not imply the supersession of rationality over reason: "The word Hegel uses for 'rational' here is *vernünftig* ... It must not be mistaken for instrumental, or means-ends, or economic rationality," as it is bound up with human history, hence with intelligible (as opposed to noumenal) reason itself. See Rawls, *Lectures on the History of Moral Philosophy*, ed. Barbara Herman (Cambridge, MA and London: Harvard University Press, 2000), pp. 335, 332. Third, in refuting evolutionary naturalists and neo-Platonists, Dewey joins Rousseau and Kant in their anti-elitist assertion of each sane adult person's autonomy. And fourth, even though Dewey's conception of a person's freedom is bound up with his or her self-aware relation to human history and its current manifestation (rather than with Kant's noumenal *sensus communis*), it is nonetheless directed toward, rather than away from, the *socius*.

20 *The Holy Bible: Authorized King James Version* (London and New York: Collins' Clean-Type Press, 1975), *Romans* 2.14–2.15.

21 For an illuminating account of the multiple meanings of higher law in the nineteenth century, see Gregg Crane, *Race, Citizenship, and Law in American Literature* (New York and Cambridge, England: Cambridge University Press, 2002).

22 Gustave Le Bon, *The Psychology of Peoples*, trans. anon. (New York: G. E. Stechere, 1924), pp. 16, 7, xviii, xix, 14; Gustave Le Bon, *The Crowd*, trans. anon. (London: T. Fisher Unwin, 1896), pp. 70, 110–111.

23 For an intriguing account of how, a couple decades later, the idea of national genius could become a function of culture rather than race, see Susan Hegeman, *Patterns for America: Modernism and the Concept of Culture* (Princeton: Princeton University Press, 1999).

24 Frederick Douglass, "Inauguration of the World's Columbian Exposition, in *World's Columbian Exposition Illustrated* 3, ed. James Campbell (Chicago: 1893), p. 300.
25 Robert Park, *The Crowd and the Public and Other Essays*, trans. Charlotte Elsner (Chicago: University of Chicago Press, 1972), pp. 15, 22.
26 Douglass, "Inauguration," p. 300.
27 See John E. Findling, *Chicago's Great World's Fairs* (Manchester and New York: Manchester University Press, 1994), p. 18.
28 James William Buel, *The Magic City* (New York: Arno Press, 1974).
29 Ernest Gellner, *Nations and Nationalism* (Ithaca and London: Cornell University Press, 1983), p. 86.
30 Miles, ed. *World's Fair*, pp. 2, 5.
31 Theodore Roosevelt, "True Americanism," in *American Ideals and Other Essays Social and Political*, second edition (New York: Putnam's Sons, 1898), pp. 15, 18–19, emphasis added.
32 Gellner, *Nations*, p. 7; Herbert Croly, *The Promise of American Life* (New York: Macmillan, 1919), p. 287.
33 Quoted in Miles, *World's Fair*, p. 25, emphasis added.
34 Le Bon, *The Crowd*, pp. 62, 10, 114.
35 For instance, James Wilson Pierce reports in his 1893 *Photographic History of the World's Fair* that during the Fair's opening ceremonies, over which President Cleveland presided, the danger of fainting was real:

The pushing and crowding at the northeast end of the Administration Building soon became so severe that many women fainted, while others became so sick that they had to be lifted bodily over the railing[.] ... City police mingled with the guards and endeavored to quiet the excited, swaying mass within the bounds of personal safety.

See Peirce, *Photographic History of the World's Fair* (Baltimore: R. H. Woodward, 1893), pp. 331, 333. Another attention-blocking factor, according to some, was the voluminous amount of instructional material. Henry Adams's account, for instance, confirms the difficulty of making sense, despite the best intentions, of the Fair's educational displays. In his third-person autobiography he describes the situation:

He set off to Chicago to study the Exposition again, and stayed there a fortnight absorbed in it. He found matter of study to fill a hundred years, and his education spread over chaos. Indeed, it seemed to him as though, this year, education went mad ... [A]t Chicago, educational game started like rabbits from every building[.] ... Education ran riot at Chicago.

See Adams, *The Education of Henry Adams*, ed. Ernest Samuels (Boston: Houghton Mifflin, 1973), pp. 339, 342.
36 Quoted in Campbell, *World's Columbian Exposition Illustrated*, vol. 3, p. 222.
37 Michael Warner, "The Mass Public and the Mass Subject," in *Habermas and the Public Sphere*, ed. Craig Calhoun (Cambridge, MA and London: MIT Press, 1992), p. 384.

38 The image's vagueness is not related to the quality of this book's visual reproductions; it is no more precise in Campbell's 1893 *World's Columbian Exposition Illustrated.*

39 Quoted in Campbell, *World's Columbian Exposition Illustrated*, vol. 3, p. 86, emphasis added.

40 For a fuller and astute analysis of this era's account of education as either coercive or an appeal to interest, and of its redescription of uneducability as positive individualism, see Walter Michaels's essay "An American Tragedy, or the Promise of American Life," *Representations* 25 (1989), pp. 71–98.

41 Quoted in Thomas G. Dyer, *Theodore Roosevelt and the Idea of Race* (Baton Rouge and London: Louisiana State University Press, 1980), 131. Although Roosevelt was by the middle 1890s deeply influenced by Le Bon (via Henry Cabot Lodge), his commitment to assimilation contrasts with Le Bon's view of the United States's future. See Dyer, *Theodore Roosevelt*, p. 11. Le Bon claims that the United States has succeeded not through the mixing of race but on account of the Anglo-Saxon's superlative homogeneity, which means that "the foreign immigrations are powerless to modify the general trend of the mind of the race." Equally certain is he that "the United States are now exposed to a gigantic invasion" of immigrants and that the disproportion of immigrants to Anglo-Saxons means that a "civil war ... is preparing." See Le Bon, *Peoples*, pp. 140, 146, 161–62.

42 Croly, *Promise*, pp. 265, 244, 215, 9.

43 Michaels, "Souls," p. 192. See also Rogin, "Sword," pp. 152–153. After the Civil War, lynching became more and more (though never exclusively) a racialized practice, and even more intensely a racialized discourse. My account of how lynching functions to whiten and unify the nation differs somewhat from Michaels's and Rogin's in that it stresses not the way the KKK embodies the nation's *ancient* white (yet invisible) soul, but rather in the way lynch collectivities ritualize the expulsion of the black, for whom, according to prevailing racial ideology, it would remain impossible to become white or, *a fortiori*, American. I discuss these issues more fully later in this chapter.

44 The lynch mob possessed the additional element of being seen as a primarily American mode of collectivity. Hence Le Bon's remark about the United States: "[t]he summary proceedings of Lynch-law are universally recognized to meet [the] case" of "dangerous" blacks. See Le Bon, *Peoples*, p. 147.

45 Thomas Dixon, Jr., *The Leopard's Spots: A Romance of the White Man's Burden 1865–1900* (New York: Doubleday, Page and Co., 1902), p. 403.

46 Ida B. Wells, *Southern Horrors: Lynch Law in All Its Phases*, in *Selected Works of Ida B. Wells-Barnett*, introd. Trudier Harris (New York and Oxford: Oxford University Press, 1991), p. 21.

47 Theodore Roosevelt, *The Writings of Theodore Roosevelt*, ed. William H. Harbaugh (Indianapolis and New York: Bobbs-Merrill, 1967), p. 205.

48 Quoted in Sandra Gunning, *Race, Rape, and Lynching: The Red Record of American Literature, 1890–1912* (Oxford and New York: Oxford University Press, 1996), p. 5. This redescription of the beastly savage as an agent of divine

and human lawfulness conforms to the fin-de-siècle conception of modernity as exhausted, overrefined, and thus in need of cultural revitalization such as crowd energies could supply. See Robert Nye, "Savage Crowds, Modernism, and Modern Politics," in *Prehistories of the Future: The Primitivist Project and the Culture of Modernism*, eds. Elazar Barkan and Ronald Bush (Stanford: Stanford University Press, 1995), p. 48.

49 Dixon, *Spots*, p. 380, 368; Gunning, *Race*, p. 40; Rogin, "Sword," p. 180.

50 Dixon, *Spots*, p. 161.

51 James Elbert Cutler, *Lynch-Law: An Investigation into the History of Lynching in the United States* (New York: Negro Universities Press, 1969), pp. 15, 195. It is somewhat misleading to claim, as Susan Mizruchi recently does, that Cutler has "obvious sympathies for lynching." See Mizruchi, *The Science of Sacrifice: American Literature and Modern Social Theory* (Princeton: Princeton University Press, 1998), p. 336. Like so many other of the era's social commentators, Cutler is patently equivocal. In the same paragraph, for instance, as he states that "[i]n the last analysis lynch-law is without any justification whatsoever," he also falls just short of justifying it:

> But if circumstances and conditions be taken into consideration and the history of the practice carefully noted, it is possible to see how justification has come about through the different points of view that have been taken. From the standpoint of the frontiersmen and pioneers summary procedure in certain cases was wholly justifiable. From the standpoint of the Southerners during the period of Reconstruction summary procedure was likewise wholly justifiable. To men living in a community where a particularly brutal and barbarous crime is committed upon a white person by a negro, the prompt lynching of the negro, even with some torture and cruelty, seems entirely defensible... [T]he fact remains that [lynching] has been repeatedly justified in one way or another.

See Cutler, *Lynch-Law*, p. 226. As Mizruchi more convincingly suggests, Cutler's "effort to explain lynching scientifically often amounted to explaining it away." See Mizruchi, *Science*, p. 336.

52 Cutler, *Lynch-Law*, pp. 194, 109–110. The specific case was the lynching (of a black man) that precipitated, first, the highly publicized destruction of the abolitionist Reverend Lovejoy's printing office and, later, Lovejoy's own lynching in Illinois.

53 Cutler, *Lynch-Law*, pp. 110, 268–269, emphasis added, It is worth noting that appeals to particularity and local difference, as well as indictments of abstract reason, similarly informed nineteenth-century European anti-Semitism. In his 1850 "Judaism in Music," anti-Semite Richard Wagner, ruing the current state of liberal "human justice," explains its evolution in the following way: "When we strove for emancipation of the Jews, however, we virtually were more the champions of an abstract principle, than of a concrete case: just as all our Liberalism was a not very lucid mental sport...so our eagerness to level up the rights of Jews was far rather stimulated by a general idea, than by any real sympathy." See Wagner, *Richard Wagner's Prose Works*, 8 vols., trans. William Ashton Ellis (New York: Broude Bros., 1966), vol. 3, p. 80. Later

in the century, anti-Dreyfusard Maurice Barrès would take up the cause in France:

This Kantism in our classrooms claims to classify the universal man, man in the abstract, taking no account of individual differences. Its tendency is to make our young Lorrainers, Provencaux, Bretons and Parisians of this year into an abstract ideal man, while our need is for men firmly rooted in our soil, in our history, in our national conscience, and adapted to the French necessities of this day and date.

Quoted in Peter G. J. Pulzer, *The Rise of Political Anti-Semitism in Germany and Austria* (New York: John Wiley and Sons, 1964), p. 57.

54 Croly, *Promise*, pp. 280–281. It does well to recall at this point Arendt's distinction in *On Violence* between authority, which is predicated on respect and consent (thus requiring neither coercion nor persuasion), and political power such as totalitarian regimes require for self-preservation. Croly's conception of "absolute Sovereign authority" corresponds to the former. See Hannah Arendt, *On Violence* (New York: Harcourt, Brace and World, 1969), pp. 39–45.

55 Cutler, *Lynch-Law*, p. 271; Wells, *Red Record*, pp. 147, 249.

56 Wells, *Red Record*, p. 150; Wells, *The Reason Why*, pp. 75, 77.

57 Charles Chesnutt, "The Sheriff's Children," in *The Wife of His Youth and Other Stories* (Ann Arbor: University of Michigan Press, 1968), pp. 66, 72–73, 74.

58 Wells, *Red Record*, pp. 166–170; Wells, *The Reason Why*, p. 85.

59 Dixon, *Spots*, p. 409.

60 Du Bois, *Black Reconstruction*, p. 700.

61 Quoted in Wells, *The Reason Why*, p. 55.

62 As white supremacist, lynching opponent Andrew Sledd put it in 1902, "As for 'teaching the niggers a lesson,' that catch phrase of the lynching mob betrays its whole attitude and temper. It would teach the negro the lesson of abject and eternal servility, would burn into his quivering flesh the consciousness that he has not, and cannot have, the rights of a free citizen or even of a fellow human creature." In this same *Atlantic Monthly* article, Sledd also indicates the level of pretense – as opposed to deception – involved in the defense of lynching:

No candid man who has seen the average lynching mob, or talked with the average lyncher, can deceive himself for a moment with the idea that this is the expression of a public sentiment righteously indignant over the violation of law and its impotence or delay. This, too, is a common Southern plea; but it is pure pretense.

See Sledd, "The Negro: Another View," *The Atlantic Monthly* 90 (1902), p. 70.

63 W. E. B. Du Bois, *The Souls of Black Folk* [1903] (New York: Signet, 1969) p. 224. Hereafter this edition is cited as *SBF*, with page references appearing in the text.

64 Priscilla Wald, *Constituting Americans: Cultural Anxiety and Narrative Form* (Durham and London: Duke University Press, 1995), pp. 182, 185.

65 *Ibid.*, pp. 185–186.

66 Eric J. Sundquist, *To Wake the Nations: Race in the Making of American Litera-ture,* (Cambridge, MA and London: Harvard University Press, 1993), pp. 578, 457–539.

67 Joseph Horowitz, *Wagner Nights: An American History* (Berkeley and Los Angeles: University of California Press, 1994), pp. 81, 90–95, 17.

68 *Ibid.,* pp. 110, 114.

69 Friedrich Nietzsche, *The Birth of Tragedy* and *The Case of Wagner,* trans Walter Kaufmann (New York: Vintage, 1967), pp. 171, 175–76.

70 *Ibid.,* pp. 161, 160, 191.

71 Theodor W. Adorno, *In Search of Wagner,* trans. Rodney Livingstone (London: Verso, 1984), pp. 115, 117, 118–119, 120–121.

72 Thomas Dixon Jr., *The Clansman: An Historical Romance of the Ku Klux Klan* (New York: Grosset and Dunlap, 1905), pp. 322, 324. When Dixon extols the "laws of our race, old before this Republic was born in the souls of white freemen," he offers a latter-day version of Wagner's mythic aesthetic, one which, as suggested earlier in this chapter, was too extreme to gain wide currency in United States race and immigration discourses, but which nevertheless sheds contrasting light on Du Bois's own aesthetic strategies in "Of the Coming of John." See Dixon, *The Clansman,* p. 388.

73 Herbert Lindenberger, *Opera: The Extravagant Art* (Ithaca and London: Cornell University Press, 1984), pp. 46, 199.

74 Russell A. Berman, "Du Bois and Wagner: Race, Nation, and Culture between the United States and Germany," *German Quarterly* 70 (1997), pp. 134, 127–128.

75 Dixon, *Spots,* pp. 79, 200, 297, 440–441. This is not to say that liberal democ-racy, as Du Bois's story's implicit alternative to a race-based politics, has utterly no truck with faith. Slavoj Zizek has pointed out that democracy's "underlying hypothesis that – in the long term, at least – the result [of elections, of relying on numeric contingency] will be in the best interest of society can never be proven." See Zizek, "'The Wound Is Healed Only by the Spear That Smote You': The Operatic Subject and Its Vicissitudes," in *Opera Through Other Eyes,* ed. David J. Levin (Stanford: Stanford University Press, 1993), p. 182. This kind of good faith effort to make good choices for the future is, more importantly in my view, predicated on a liberal faith in the human being's capacity to reason. As Rawls puts it, "the belief in freedom is more fundamental [than the belief in God and immortality]; it is a belief in the freedom, the absolute spontane-ity of reason itself. It is the belief that reason proceeds in accordance with its own principles that only it can identify and validate." See Rawls, *Lectures,* pp. 318–319.

76 Berman, "Du Bois and Wagner," p. 129.

77 *Ibid.,* p. 130.

78 Richard Wagner, *Lohengrin* (New York: Fred Rullman, 1900), p. 34, my trans-lation here and below.

79 *Ibid.,* p. 32, emphasis added.

80 For a similar reading of these scenes, see Ross Posnock's provocative and illu-minating *Color and Culture.* Emphasizing John's "lingering over the mesmeric

power of sheer speculation," Posnock sees affinities between Du Bois's commitment to an "autotelic" (as opposed to instrumental) mode of being a black intellectual and Hannah Arendt's ideas on "'[t]hinking as such.'" See Posnock, *Color and Culture: Black Writers and the Making of the Modern Intellectual* (Cambridge, MA and London: Harvard University Press, 1998), pp. 101–102.

81 Kate Chopin, *The Awakening*, ed. Nancy Walker (Boston and New York: Bedford Books, 1993), p. 136.

82 Friedrich Kittler, "World-Breath: On Wagner's Media Technology," in *Opera Through Other Eyes*, ed. David J. Levin (Stanford: Stanford University Press, 1993), pp. 217, 222–223.

83 Wagner, *Prose Works*, vol. 8, p. 236; quoted in Paul Rose's *Wagner: Race and Revolution*. This quotation is from Wagner's 1848, posthumously published platform piece, "The Revolution." As Rose comments, "Wagner's revolutionary experience was fundamentally religious in character" – to which one might also add aesthetic. See Rose, *Wagner: Race and Revolution* (New Haven and London: Yale University Press, 1992), pp. 50–51.

5 HARLEM, PRIMITIVISM, AND LARSEN

1 James Weldon Johnson, "Harlem: The Culture Capital," in *The New Negro*, ed. Alain Locke (New York: Atheneum 1970), p. 301. Charles Scruggs notes that Du Bois applied the phrase, "city within a city," to Philadelphia as well. See Scruggs, *Sweet Home: Invisible Cities in the Afro-American Novel* (Baltimore and London: Johns Hopkins University Press, 1993), p. 16.

2 James Weldon Johnson, *Black Manhattan* (New York: Atheneum, 1968), p. 3; Johnson, "Harlem," pp. 304, 306, emphasis added.

3 Adolph Reed, *W.E.B. Du Bois and American Political Thought: Fabianism and the Color Line* (Oxford and New York: Oxford University Press, 1997), p. 74.

4 Johnson, *Black Manhattan*, pp. 247, 143.

5 See chapter 3 for more detailed discussions of Rawls's formulation of the relation between the comprehensive doctrines comprising reasonable pluralism and the political-liberal conception.

6 Walter Benn Michaels, *Our America: Nativism, Modernism, and Pluralism* (Durham and London: Duke University Press, 1995), pp. 141, 15–16.

7 W. E. B. Du Bois, *Darkwater: Voices from within the Veil* (New York: AMS Press, 1969), pp. 158–159.

8 Nella Larsen, *Quicksand* and *Passing*, introd. Deborah McDowell (New Brunswick, NJ: Rutgers University Press, 1986), pp. 4–5. Hereafter this edition is cited as *Q*, with page references appearing in the text.

9 Lewis Alexander, "Streets," *Fire!!* 1 (1926), p. 23.

10 Johnson, "Harlem," p. 309.

11 Johnson, *Black Manhattan*, pp. 200–201.

12 Similarly, David Levering Lewis opens his history of the Harlem Renaissance with an account of the crowds gathered to witness in 1919 the return of the Fifteenth Regiment of New York's National Guard from World War I: "They

marched in the tight formation preferred by the French Army, a solid thirty-five-foot square of massed men." For Lewis, as for Johnson earlier, the public display of blacks *en masse* functions as a sign of Harlem's power and place. See Lewis, *When Harlem Was in Vogue* (New York: Vintage, 1982), p. 4.

13 Gabriel Tarde, *The Laws of Imitation*, trans. Elsie Clews Parsons (New York: Henry Holt, 1903), p. 85.

14 Quoted in Thadious Davis, *Nella Larsen: Novelist of the Harlem Renaissance* (Baton Rouge and London: Louisiana State University Press, 1994), p. 458.

15 Larsen was also among the minority of African Americans who praised Van Vechten's *Nigger Heaven*. Thadious Davis describes how she liked "what she called the 'mixedness of things, the savagery under the sophistication,' that Van Vechten captured." See Davis, *Nella Larsen*, p. 212.

16 T. J. Jackson Lears, *No Place of Grace: Antimodernism and the Transformation of American Culture 1880–1920* (Chicago and London: University of Chicago Press, 1994); Robert Nye, "Savage Crowds, Modernism, and Modern Politics," in *Prehistories of the Future: The Primitivist Project and the Culture of Modernism*, eds. Elazar Barkan and Ronald Bush (Stanford: Stanford University Press, 1995), pp. 42–55; Michael Tratner, *Modernism and Mass Politics: Joyce, Woolf, Eliot, Yeats* (Stanford: Stanford University Press, 1995), p. 4.

17 As noted in chapter 3, the distinction between a restrictive and a general economy is Derrida's. What the former disallows and the latter admits is "the sovereign operation, the *point of nonreserve*, [which] is neither positive nor negative. It cannot be inscribed in discourse, except by crossing out predicates or by practicing a contradictory superimpression that then exceeds the logic of philosophy." Derrida figures this excess as laughter, a "laughter that literally never *appears*, because it exceeds phenomenality in general, the absolute possibility of meaning." See Derrida, "From Restricted to General Economy: A Hegelianism without Reserve," in *Writing and Difference*, trans. Alan Bass (Chicago: University of Chicago Press, 1978), pp. 259, 256, all emphases in original. As we will see below, in *Quicksand* Helga's attacks of laughter figure similarly. While they, of course, phenomenally appear, in a sense they do not appear *to her*, since they erupt in an unpremeditated manner and overwhelm her conscious being.

18 Robert Park and Ernest Burgess, *The City: Suggestions for Investigation of Human Behavior in the Urban Environment* (Chicago and London: University of Chicago Press, 1967), pp. 40–41.

19 Georg Simmel, "The Adventure," in *Essays on Sociology, Philosophy, and Aesthetics*, ed. Kurt Wolff (New York: Harper Torchbooks, 1965), pp. 248–249, 243, 248, 253, 245–246.

20 Ann E. Hostetler, "The Aesthetics of Race and Gender in Nella Larsen's *Quicksand*," *PMLA* 105 (1990), p. 37.

21 Marmaduke Pickthall, *Saïd the Fisherman* (London: Methuen, 1903), p. 301. Pickthall's novel veritably swarms with images of crowds. Even when Damascus is not in the throes of rioting or massacre, it is teeming with crowds. Once

Saïd the protagonist arrives in "the great city," besides encountering a crowd at the khan where he stays, he winds in and out of streets "choked with a humming, gaily-colored crowd;" he negotiates "the busy throng," the "uproar of the crowded streets," the "noisy streams of wayfarers," and so forth, until he finds himself a dozen years later having to reckon with the "multitude of strangers," a "horde of ragged urchins," and "the dull roar of traffic" in London, then lastly with a riotous mob in Alexandria, pp. 46–47, 62, 63, 95, 279, 283, 285, 301.

22 In this manner Helga Crane enacts what Leo Bersani interprets as the self-shattering moment inhering in narcissism itself. For a sustained discussion of this event, see his book, *The Freudian Body: Psychoanalysis and Art* (New York: Columbia University Press, 1986).

23 Hazel Carby, *Reconstructing Womanhood: The Emergence of the Afro-American Woman Novelist* (New York and Oxford: Oxford University Press, 1987), p. 170.

24 Arthur Davis also equates Helga Crane and quicksand, but he limits the latter's signification to its potential to drown human beings: "The quicksand motif is used very skillfully in this work. The quicksand, of course, is Helga's own vacillating inner self, which the author renders with appropriate images of suffocation, sinking, drowning, and enclosure." See Davis, *From the Dark Tower: Afro-American Writers 1900–1960* (Washington, DC: Howard University Press, 1974), p. 96.

25 Edgar Allan Poe, *Poetry and Tales* (New York: Library of America, 1984), p. 827.

26 *Ibid.*, pp. 392–393, 396.

27 Charles Baudelaire, *Paris Spleen*, trans. Louise Varèse (New York: New Directions, 1970), p. 20. For differing accounts of the difficulty and rarity of women engaged in *flânerie*, see Janet Wolff, "The Invisible *Flâneuse*: Women and the Literature of Modernity," in *The Problems of Modernity: Adorno and Benjamin*, ed. Andrew Benjamin (London and New York: Routledge, 1989), pp. 86–111; and Elizabeth Wilson, "The Invisible *Flâneur*," *New Left Review* 191 (1992), pp. 90–110.

28 My analysis of this passage relies on a point asserted earlier, that Larsen's narrative consciousness intersects with but remains distinct from Helga's. Regarding this particular passage, my claim is buttressed by the fact that an excerpt from this crowd scene appeared in the program book of a posh benefit dance for the NAACP; it was entitled "Moving Mosaic or NAACP Dance, 1929." See Davis, *Nella Larsen*, p. 340.

29 Helga's conversion thus resembles what Julia Kristeva calls abjection. "The one by whom the abject exists is thus a *deject* who places (himself), *separates* (himself), situates (himself), and therefore *strays* instead of getting his bearings, desiring, belonging, or refusing. Situationist in a sense, and not without laughter... And the more he strays, the more he is saved." See Kristeva, *Powers of Horror: An Essay on Abjection*, trans. Leon S. Roudiez (New York: Columbia University Press, 1982), p. 8, emphasis in original.

30 Deborah McDowell, "Introduction," *Quicksand* and *Passing* (New Brunswick, NJ: Rutgers University Press), pp. xi, xii, emphasis added.
31 Quoted in Davis, *Nella Larsen*, p. 219.
32 Benjamin Elijah Mays and Joseph William Nicholson, *The Negro's Church* (New York: Institute for Social and Religious Research, 1933), p. 100.
33 Johnson, *Black Manhattan*, pp. 163, 164, 166.
34 Mays and Nicholson, *The Negro's Church*, pp. 200, 97–98, 225, 227.
35 Johnson, *Black Manhattan*, p. 165.
36 I am deliberately echoing and reversing Ann duCille's terms here. Where she claims that Helga Crane, in her move to Alabama is "[f]atally (as opposed to fatefully) married to a grandiloquent Baptist preacher," I want to suggest that the novel provides no grounds for such a conclusive interpretation. Other critics make similarly peremptory claims. Thadious Davis, for instance, calls Helga "symbolically dead" by the end of the novel; and Hazel Carby writes, "the novel ends with her fifth pregnancy which means her certain death." Instead of this fatalism, on my view Larsen dramatizes the self-dissolving but essentially life-confirming conditions of *amor fati*. Thus, to reverse the terms of another critic, Mary Lay, Helga Crane becomes a character not with whom to sympathize, but to admire – to admire, however, not as a possible role model, but as an impossible marvel. See Ann duCille, *The Coupling Convention: Sex, Text, and Tradition in Black Women's Fiction* (New York and Oxford: Oxford University Press, 1993, p. 96; Davis, *Nella Larsen*, p. 271; Carby, *Reconstructing Womanhood*, p. 169; Mary M. Lay, "Parallels: Henry James's *The Portrait of a Lady* and Nella Larsen's *Quicksand*," *CLA Journal* 20 (1977), p. 486.
37 Quoted in Davis, *Nella Larsen*, p. 358.

6 IMMIGRATION, TRAUMA, AND ETHNO-POLITICAL CONSCIOUSNESS

1 Henry Roth, *Call It Sleep* (New York: Noonday, 1991), p. 419. Hereafter this edition is cited as *CS*, with page references appearing in the text.
2 Peter Jukes, *A Shout in the Street: An Excursion into the Modern City* (New York: Farrar Straus Giroux, 1990), p. xvii.
3 As Bruce Robbins puts it, "[i]n his search for power and light, [David] mounts a sort of cult of public utilities; chasing telegraph poles into the distance or contemplating the world from behind the gas-works, he finds in the public face of power the sources and limits of his private tyranny." See Robbins, "Modernism in History, Modernism in Power," in *Modernism Reconsidered*, ed. Robert Kiely (Cambridge, MA: Harvard University Press, 1983), p. 245.
4 Randolph Bourne, "Trans-National America," in *The Radical Will: Randolph Bourne, Selected Writings 1911–1918*, ed. Olaf Hansen (New York: Urizen, 1977), p. 253.
5 For an extended meditation on "ethnic modernism's" debt to "hydrotropes" (energized liquid metaphors) of the immigrant crowd, see William Boelhower, "*Hic Sunt Pantherae*: Race, Ethnography and American Literature," in *The Future of American Modernism: Ethnic Writing between the Wars*, ed. William

Boelhower (Amsterdam: VU University Press, 1990), pp. viii–xliv. For an account of *Call It Sleep* as a text bridging modernism and ethnic writing, see Thomas Ferraro, "Avant-garde Ethnics," in *The Future of American Modernism: Ethnic Writing between the Wars*, ed. William Boelhower (Amsterdam: VU University Press, 1990), pp. 1–31.

6　Abraham Cahan, *Yekl* and *The Imported Bridegroom and Other Stories of Yiddish New York* (New York: Dover, 1970), pp. 13–14.

7　Anzia Yezierska, *Bread Givers: A Struggle between a Father of the Old World and a Daughter of the New* (New York: Persea, 1975), p. 129. Hereafter this edition is cited as *BG*, with page references appearing in the text.

8　John Higham, *Send These to Me: Immigrants in Urban America*, revised edition (Baltimore and London: Johns Hopkins University Press, 1984), p. 47.

9　For a most astute historical study of this resurgent psychoanalytic interest in trauma, to which I later return, see Ruth Leys, *Trauma: A Genealogy* (Chicago and London: Chicago University Press, 2000).

10　Alice Kessler Harris, "Introduction," *Bread Givers*, Anzia Yezierska (New York: Persea Books, 1975), p. xii; Jules Chametzky, *Our Decentralized Literature: Cultural Mediations in Selected Jewish and Southern Writers* (Amherst: University of Massachusetts Press, 1986), p. 47; William Boelhower, "Ethnic Trilogies: A Genealogical and Generational Poetics," in *The Invention of Ethnicity*, ed. Werner Sollors (New York and Oxford: Oxford University Press, 1989), p. 158.

11　The historical coincidence of a rising nativism and the emergence of trauma theory in the early decades of the twentieth century is intriguing, though at this point I am reluctant to draw any too firm conclusions about its significance.

12　Theodore Roosevelt, "True Americanism," in *American Ideals and Other Essays Social and Political*, second edition (New York and London: Putnam's Sons, 1898), p. 33.

13　Abraham Cahan, *The Rise of David Levinsky* (New York: Harper and Row, 1960), p. 291. Hereafter this edition is cited as *RDL*, with page references appearing in the text; Roosevelt, "True," p. 26.

14　Chametzky, *Decentralized*, p. 36.

15　Barrish writes: "Reading Cahan's work…points to how an intimate knowledge of Eastern European Jewish immigrant life could enable an immigrant intellectual to figure as an 'expert,' while, conversely, his status as expert could help him to seem safely distinct from the immigrant world his writing elaborated." See Barrish, "'The Genuine Article': Ethnicity, Capital, and *The Rise of David Levinsky*," *American Literary History* 5 (1993), p. 644.

16　Sigmund Freud, *Beyond the Pleasure Principle*, in *The Standard Edition of the Complete Psychological Works of Sigmund Freud*, vol. 18, ed. James Strachey (London: Hogarth, 1955), p. 18.

17　Isaac Rosenfeld, *An Age of Enormity* (Cleveland: World Pub., 1962), pp. 280, 278.

18　There are several valuable discussions of Kallen's argument, including John Higham, *Send These to Me*; David Hollinger, *Postethnic America: Beyond Multiculturalism* (New York: Basic Books, 1995); and Werner Sollors, "A Critique of Pure Pluralism," in *Reconstructing American Literary History*, ed. Sacvan Bercovitch (Cambridge, MA and London: Harvard University Press, 1986), pp. 250–279.

19 Roosevelt, "True," p. 29. For a fuller, more ominous interpretation of Roosevelt's phrase, see Priscilla Wald, *Constituting Americans: Cultural Anxiety and Narrative Form* (Durham and London: Duke University Press, 1995), pp. 243–260.

20 In *The New Covenant* Sam Girgus cites Sara Smolinsky's allusion to her father's "fanatical adherence to his traditions," and in the same breath argues that because she is "capable of internalizing and accepting responsibility for his model of authority," Smolinsky develops "the sort of independent personality essential for a democracy." But in light of liberal democracy's historical and theoretical repudiation of political authority based on tradition (such as monarchy, class or familial inheritance, and religion), it can be argued that her hewing to her father's dogmatic authority is deeply at odds with political independence. See Girgus, *The New Covenant: Jewish Writers and the American Idea* (Chapel Hill and London: University of North Carolina Press, 1984), p. 114.

21 Robert Westbrook, *John Dewey and American Democracy* (Ithaca and London: Cornell University Press, 1991), p. 145.

22 For an illuminating discussion of Cahan's critical use, in *The Rise of David Levinsky*, of frontier rhetoric to buttress a laissez-faire capitalist ideology, see William Gleason, *The Leisure Ethic: Work and Play in American Literature, 1840–1940* (Stanford: Stanford University Press, 1999), pp. 99–132.

23 Leslie Fiedler, "The Many Myths of Henry Roth," in *New Essays on Call It Sleep*, ed. Hana Wirth-Nesher (Cambridge, England: Cambridge University Press, 1996), p. 20.

24 David Hollinger, *Postethnic America*, p. 116.

25 In addition to the political-economic libertarians, Dewey pitted himself against those skeptical of a democratic public. As Westbrook explains, in the 1920s Dewey found himself opposed to social scientists such as William McDougall and Harold Lasswell, who were convinced of the democratic populace's psychopathological afflictions. He objected as well to the more moderate views of Walter Lippmann, who maintained that only an elite body of professional experts could manage the liberal democratic polity. See Westbrook, *John Dewey*, pp. 275–318.

26 Westbrook, *John Dewey*, pp. 440–41.

27 John Dewey, *The Public and Its Problems* (Athens, OH and Chicago: Swallow Press, n.d.), p. 8. Hereafter this edition is cited as *PP*, with page references appearing in the text.

28 For fuller analyses of Dewey's difficulty both accepting and rejecting Kantian principles and ethics, see James Kloppenberg, *Uncertain Victory: Social Democracy and Progressivism in European and American Thought, 1870–1920* (New York and Oxford: Oxford University Press, 1986); Westbrook, *John Dewey*; Matthew Festenstein, *Pragmatism and Political Theory: From Dewey to Rorty* (Chicago and London: University of Chicago Press, 1997); and William R.

Caspary, *Dewey on Democracy* (Ithaca and London: Cornell University Press, 2000).

29 John Dewey, *Liberalism and Social Action* (New York: Putnam's, 1935), pp. 82, 90, 57.

30 If nativism had its heyday in 1924, the year Dewey delivered (at Kenyon College) the lectures comprising *The Public and Its Problems* is the year John Higham cites as symbolically bringing 100 percent Americanism to a close: "Henry Pratt Fairchild's *The Melting-Pot Mistake* in 1926 proved as much an epitaph to this school of thought as a qualified summation of it." See Higham, *Strangers in the Land: Patterns of American Nativism, 1860–1925* (New Brunswick: Rutgers University Press, 1992), p. 327. From within this context, we can see how Dewey's and later Roth's willingness to address the situation of ethnic immigrants reflects their rejection of both Kallenesque pluralism and white middle-class quietism as adequate responses to lingering nativist sentiments. They neither assert the primacy of ethnic identity nor ignore the pressing public issue of ghetto poverty.

31 Despite their political affiliations via the Communist Party, it is unclear how influential, even negatively, Gold was on Roth. Morris Dickstein reports that in a 1987 interview Roth claimed not to have read *Jews without Money*, but had read Yezierska's *Bread Givers*. See Dickstein, "The Tenement and the World: Visions of Immigrant Life," in *The Future of American Modernism: Ethnic Writing between the Wars*, ed. William Boelhower (Amsterdam: VU University Press, 1990), p. 79.

32 Brian McHale, "Henry Roth in Nighttown, or, Containing *Ulysses*," in *New Essays on Call It Sleep*, ed. Hana Wirth-Nesher (Cambridge, England: Cambridge University Press, 1996), p. 79; quoted in Werner Sollors, " 'A world somewhere, somewhere else': Language, Nostalgic Mournfulness, and Urban Immigrant Family Romance in *Call It Sleep*," in *New Essays on Call It Sleep*, ed. Hana Wirth-Nesher (Cambridge, England: Cambridge University Press, 1996), p. 168.

33 Sollors, "A world somewhere," p. 141.

34 Hana Wirth-Nesher, "Between Mother Tongue and Native Language in *Call It Sleep*," Afterword, *Call It Sleep*, Henry Roth, introd. Alfred Kazin (New York: Noonday, 1991), p. 448.

35 Roth acknowledged his lay knowledge of Freud in an interview with Bonnie Lyons. See her biography, *Henry Roth: The Man and His Work* (New York: Cooper Square Pub., 1976).

36 Leys, *Trauma*, p. 27.

37 *Ibid.*, pp. 32, 33.

38 *Ibid.*, p. 33.

39 I have scanted the novel's richly textured and complicated thematics of memory, as it deserves an essay in itself. It is important to note, however, that David's seemingly immature ethnic-immigrant memory (which, if more fully developed, would articulate the remembered past to a present ethnic identity) does not preclude his possessing what his cheder rabbi calls his "iron

wit," furthermore associating it with "intellect" (*CS* 366, 233). He refers to David's talent for remembering the Yiddish rendering of the chad gadyaw, and for reciting Hebrew prayers "[a]s though, he knew what he read" (*CS* 367). For it is this latter kind of memory, this cerebral activity of pure, nonsensical repetition-remembering detached from self-knowledge, that transforms fragments of consciousness into dissociated, thing-like entities, such as hoarded calendar leaves. David most prominently enters this mode of consciousness, merging mind and matter, when he is on the wharf and under the "hypnotic" spell of the water's whiteness: "His spirit yielded, melted into light. In the molten sheen memories and objects overlapped" (*CS* 247). Susceptibility to this mental state is clearly behind his mother's frustration, which emerges when David fails to make basic social calculations regarding the advantages of having an American uncle. "'I really believe,' she continued in a scolding, bantering whisper, 'that you think of nothing. Now honest, isn't that so? Aren't you just a pair of eyes and ears! You see, you hear, you remember, but when will you know? If you didn't bring home those handsome report cards, I'd say you were a dunce'" (*CS* 173).

40 Mark Schoening, "T. S. Eliot Meets Michael Gold: Modernism and Radicalism in Depression-Era American Literature," *Modernism/Modernity* 3 (1996), pp. 67, 64, 63.

Bibliography

Abel, Darrel. *The Moral Picturesque: Studies in Hawthorne's Fiction*, West Lafayette, IN: Purdue University Press, 1988.

Adams, Henry. *The Education of Henry Adams* [1907/1918], ed. Ernest Samuels, Boston: Houghton Mifflin, 1973.

Adorno, Theodor W. *In Search of Wagner*, trans. Rodney Livingstone, London: Verso, 1984.

Prisms, trans. Samuel and Shierry Weber, Cambridge, MA: MIT Press, 1981.

Agnew, Jean-Christophe. "The Consuming Vision of Henry James," in *The Culture of Consumption: Critical Essays in American History, 1880–1980*, eds. Richard Wightman Fox and T. J. Jackson Lears, New York: Pantheon, 1983. 67–100.

Alexander, Lewis. "Streets," *Fire!!* 1 (1926): 23.

Angoff, Allan and Eric Dingwall, eds. *Abnormal Hypnotic Phenomena: A Survey of Nineteenth-Century Cases*, vol. 4, London: J. and A. Churchill, 1968.

Ankersmit, F. R. *Aesthetic Politics. Political Philosophy Beyond Fact and Value*, Stanford: Stanford University Press, 1996.

Appleby, Joyce. *Liberalism and Republicanism in the Historical Imagination*, Cambridge, MA and London: Harvard University Press, 1992.

Arendt, Hannah. *The Human Condition* [1958], introd. Margaret Cohen, Chicago and London: University of Chicago Press, 1998.

On Violence, New York: Harcourt, Brace and World, 1969.

Badger, Reid. *The Great American Fair: The World's Columbian Exposition and American Culture*, Chicago: Nelson Hall, 1979.

Barrish, Phillip. "'The Genuine Article': Ethnicity, Capital, and *The Rise of David Levinsky*," *American Literary History* 5 (1993): 643–662.

Barrows, Susanna. *Distorting Mirrors. Visions of the Crowd in Late Nineteenth-Century France*, New Haven and London: Yale University Press, 1981.

Barry, Norman. *An Introduction to Modern Political Theory*, second edition, Hampshire and London: Macmillan, 1989.

Baudelaire, Charles. *The Painter of Modern Life and Other Essays*, trans. Jonathan Mayne, London: Phaidon Press, 1964.

Paris Spleen, trans. Louise Varèse, New York: New Directions, 1970.

Bell, Ian. *Washington Square: Styles of Money*, New York: Twayne, 1993.

Bell, Millicent. "Style as Subject: *Washington Square*," *Sewanee Review* 83 (1975): 19–38.

Bellamy, Edward. *Looking Backward 2000–1887* [1888], ed. Robert C. Elliott, Boston: Houghton Mifflin, 1966.

Benfey, Christopher. *The Double Life of Stephen Crane: A Biography*, New York: Alfred E. Knopf, 1992.

Benhabib, Seyla. "Toward a Deliberative Model of Democratic Legitimacy," *Democracy and Difference*, ed. Seyla Benhabib, Princeton: Princeton University Press, 1996. 67–94.

Benjamin, Walter. *Illuminations*, ed. Hannah Arendt, New York: Schocken, 1969.

Berman, Marshall. *All That Is Solid Melts Into Air: The Experience of Modernity*, New York: Simon and Schuster, 1982.

Berman, Russell A. "Du Bois and Wagner: Race, Nation, and Culture between the United States and Germany," *German Quarterly* 70 (1997): 123–135.

Berryman, John. *Stephen Crane: A Critical Biography*, revised edition, New York: Farrar, Straus, Giroux, 1962.

Bersani, Leo. *The Freudian Body: Psychoanalysis and Art*, New York: Columbia University Press, 1986.

Blair, Sara. *Henry James and the Writing of Race and Nation*, Cambridge: Cambridge University Press, 1996.

Blood, Benjamin Paul. *The Anaesthetic Revelation and The Gist of Philosophy*, Amsterdam and New York: n.p., 1874.

Boelhower, William. "*Hinc Sunt Pantherae*: Race, Ethnography and Modern American Literature," in *The Future of American Modernism: Ethnic Writing between the Wars*, ed. William Boelhower, Amsterdam: VU University Press, 1990: viii–xliv.

"Ethnic Trilogies: A Genealogical and Generational Poetics," in *The Invention of Ethnicity*, ed. Werner Sollors, New York and Oxford: Oxford University Press, 1989. 158–175.

Borch-Jacobsen, Mikkel. *The Freudian Subject*, trans. Catherine Porter, Stanford: Stanford University Press, 1988.

Bourne, Randolph. "Trans-National America," in *The Radical Will: Randolph Bourne, Selected Writings 1911–1918*, ed. Olaf Hansen, New York: Urizen, 1977. 248–264.

Bowen, Francis. *The Principles of Metaphysical and Ethical Science Applied to the Evidences of Religion* [1852], Boston: Brewer & Tileston, revised edition, 1855.

Bowie, Andrew. *Aesthetics and Subjectivity: From Kant to Nietzsche*, Manchester and New York: Manchester University Press, 1990.

Bowman, Sylvia. *Edward Bellamy*, Boston: Twayne, 1986.

Boyer, Paul. *Urban Masses and Moral Order in America, 1820–1920*, Cambridge, MA and London: Harvard University Press, 1978.

Brand, Dana. *The Spectator and the City in Nineteenth-Century American Literature*, Cambridge, England: Cambridge University Press, 1991.

Brantlinger, Patrick. *Bread and Circuses: Theories of Mass Culture as Social Decay*, Ithaca and London: Cornell University Press, 1983.

Brewster, Henry. *The Theories of Anarchy and Law*, London: Williams and Norgate, 1887.

Brown, Bill. *The Material Unconscious: American Amusement, Stephen Crane, and the Economies of Play*, Cambridge, MA and London: Harvard University Press, 1996.

"Writing, Race, and Erasure: Michael Fried and the Scene of Reading," *Critical Inquiry* 18 (Winter 1992): 387–402.

Brown, Gillian. *Domestic Individualism: Imagining Self in Nineteenth-Century American Literature*, Berkeley and Los Angeles: University of California Press, 1990.

Brown, Julie K. *Contesting Images. Photography and the World's Columbian Exposition*, Tucson and London: University of Arizona Press, 1994.

Bruce, W. Cabell. "Lynch Law in the South," *North American Review* 155 (1892): 379–381.

Buel, James William. *The Magic City* [1894], New York: Arno Press, 1974.

Bush, Gregory. *Lord of Attention. Gerald Stanley Lee and the Crowd Metaphor in Industrializing America*, Amherst: University of Massachusetts Press, 1991.

Butler, Judith. *Bodies That Matter: On the Discursive Limits of "Sex"*, New York: Routledge, 1993.

Butwin, Joseph. "The Pacification of the Crowd: From 'Janet's Repentance' to *Felix Holt*," *Nineteenth Century Fiction* 35 (1980): 349–371.

Byer, Robert. "Mysteries of the City: A Reading of Poe's 'The Man of the Crowd,'" in *Ideology and Classic American Literature*, eds. Sacvan Bercovitch and Myra Jehlen. Cambridge, England: Cambridge University Press, 1986. 221–246.

Cadava, Eduardo. *Emerson and the Climates of History*, Stanford: Stanford University Press, 1997.

Cahan, Abraham. *The Rise of David Levinsky*, introd. John Higham, New York: Harper and Row, 1960.

Yekl [1896] and *The Imported Bridegroom and Other Stories of the New York Ghetto* [1898], introd. Bernard G. Richards, New York: Dover, 1970.

Calhoun, Craig, ed. *Habermas and the Public Sphere*, Cambridge, MA and London: MIT Press, 1993.

Calhoun, John. *A Disquisition on Government and Selections from the Discourse* [1853], ed. C. Gordon Post. New York and London: Macmillan, 1953.

Campbell, James, ed. *World's Columbian Exposition Illustrated* 3 Chicago: 1893–1894.

Carby, Hazel. *Reconstructing Womanhood: The Emergence of the Afro-American Woman Novelist*, New York and Oxford: Oxford University Press, 1987.

Cascardi, Anthony J. "Communication and Transformation: Aesthetics and Politics in Kant and Arendt," in *Hannah Arendt and the Meaning of Politics*, eds. Craig Calhoun and John McGowan, Minneapolis: University of Minnesota Press, 1997. 99–131.

Consequences of Enlightenment, Cambridge, England: Cambridge University Press, 1999.

Caspary, William R. *Dewey on Democracy*, Ithaca and London: Cornell University Press, 2000.

Chametzky, Jules. *Our Decentralized Literature: Cultural Mediations in Selected Jewish and Southern Writers*, Amherst: University of Massachusetts Press, 1986.

Chesnutt, Charles. *The Wife of His Youth and Other Stories* [1899], Ann Arbor: University of Michigan Press, 1968.

Child, Lydia Maria. *Letters from New York*, New York: Charles S. Francis and Co., 1843.

Chopin, Kate. *The Awakening* [1899], ed. Nancy Walker, Boston and New York: Bedford Books, 1993.

Chytry, Josef. *The Aesthetic State. A Quest in Modern German Thought*, Berkeley and Los Angeles: University of California Press, 1989.

Clark, Terry. "Introduction," *Gabriel Tarde: On Communication and Social Influence, Selected Papers*, ed. Terry Clark, Chicago and London: University of Chicago Press, 1969. 1–69.

Cocke, J. R. "The Power of the Mind as a Remedial Agent in the Cure of Disease," *The Arena* 9 (May 1894): 746–757.

Cole, Frank, ed. *Milestones in Anesthesia. Readings in the Development of Surgical Anesthesia, 1665–1940*, Lincoln, Nebraska: University of Nebraska Press, 1965.

Colton, Calvin. "Democracy." *Junius Tracts* no. 6 (Jan. 1844), New York: Greeley and McElrath, 1844.

Combe, Andrew. *Observations of Mental Derangement* [1834], ed. Anthony Walsh, Delmar, NY: Scholar's Facsimiles and Reprints, 1972.

Crane, Gregg. *Race, Citizenship, and Law in American Literature*, Cambridge, England: Cambridge University Press, 2002.

Crane, Stephen. *The Correspondence of Stephen Crane*, 2 vols., New York: Columbia University Press, 1988.

Prose and Poetry, New York: Library of America, 1984.

The Stephen Crane Reader, ed. R. W. Stallman. Glenview, Illinois: Scott, Foresman and Co., 1960.

The Works of Stephen Crane, 10 vols., Charlottesville: University Press of Virginia, 1969–1976.

Crary, Jonathan. *Techniques of the Observer: On Vision and Modernity in the Nineteenth Century*, Cambridge, MA: MIT Press, 1990.

Croly, Herbert. *The Promise of American Life* [1909], New York: Macmillan, 1919.

Curtis, Kimberly. "Aesthetic Foundations of Democratic Politics in the Work of Hannah Arendt," in *Hannah Arendt and the Meaning of Politics*, eds. Craig Calhoun and John McGowan. Minneapolis: University of Minnesota Press, 1997. 27–52.

Cutler, James Elbert. *Lynch-Law: An Investigation into the History of Lynching in the United States* [1905], New York: Negro Universities Press, 1969.

Dagger, Richard. *Civic Virtues: Rights, Citizenship, and Republican Liberalism*, New York and Oxford: Oxford University Press, 1997.

Davis, Arthur P. *From the Dark Tower: Afro-American Writers 1900–1960*, Washington D.C.: Howard University Press, 1974.

Davis, Thadious. *Nella Larsen: Novelist of the Harlem Renaissance*, Baton Rouge and London: Louisiana State University Press, 1994.

Dearborn, Mary. "Anzia Yezierska and the Making of an American Ethnic Self," in *The Invention of Ethnicity*. ed. Werner Sollors, New York and Oxford: Oxford University Press, 1989. 105–123.

Deleuze, Gilles. *Kant's Critical Philosophy. The Doctrine of the Faculties*, trans. Hugh Tomlinson and Barbara Habberjam, Minneapolis: University of Minnesota Press, 1984.

The Logic of Sense, trans. Mark Lester, New York: Columbia University Press, 1990.

Deleuze, Gilles, and Felix Guattari. *A Thousand Plateaus*, trans. Brian Massumi, Minneapolis: University of Minnesota Press, 1987.

Den Tandt, Christophe. *The Urban Sublime in American Literary Naturalism*, Urbana and Chicago: University of Illinois Press, 1998.

Derrida, Jacques. "From Restricted to General Economy: A Hegelianism without Reserve," in *Writing and Difference*, trans. Alan Bass, Chicago: University of Chicago Press, 1978. 251–277.

Dewey, John. "The Ethics of Democracy," in *The Political Writings*, eds. Debra Morris and Ian Shapiro, Indianapolis and Cambridge: Hackett, 1993. 59–65.

Liberalism and Social Action, New York: Putnam's, 1935.

The Public and Its Problems [1927], Athens, OH and Chicago: Swallow Press, n.d.

de Wit, Wim. "Building an Illusion: The Design of the World's Columbian Exposition," in *Grand Illusions: Chicago's World's Fair of 1893*, eds. Neil Harris et al., Chicago: Chicago Historical Society, 1993. 41–98.

Dickstein, Morris. "The Tenement and the World: Visions of Immigrant Life," in *The Future of American Modernism: Ethnic Writing between the Wars*, ed. William Boelhower, Amsterdam: VU University Press, 1990. 62–93.

Dimock, Wai Chee. *Residues of Justice: Literature, Law, Philosophy*, Berkeley and Los Angeles: University of California Press, 1996.

Dixon, Thomas, Jr. *The Clansman: An Historical Romance of the Ku Klux Klan*, New York: Grosset and Dunlap, 1905.

The Leopard's Spots: A Romance of the White Man's Burden 1865–1900, New York: Doubleday, Page and Co., 1902.

Douglass, Frederick. "The Lessons of the Hour," in *The Oxford Frederick Douglass Reader*, ed. William Andrews, New York and Oxford: Oxford University Press, 1996. 339–366.

"Lynch Law in the South," *North American Review* 155 (1892): 17–24.

"Inauguration of the World's Columbian Exposition," *World's Columbian Exposition Illustrated* 3 (1893): 300.

Dreiser, Theodore. *Sister Carrie* [1900], New York and London: Viking Penguin, 1990.

Du Bois, W. E. B. *Black Reconstruction in America 1860–1880* [1935], Cleveland and New York: Meridian, 1964.

Darkwater: Voices from within the Veil [1920], New York: AMS Press, 1969.

The Souls of Black Folk [1903], New York: Signet, 1969.

duCille, Ann. *The Coupling Convention: Sex, Text, and Tradition in Black Women's Fiction*, New York and Oxford: Oxford University Press, 1993.

Du Maurier, George. *Trilby*, [1894] Oxford and New York: Oxford University Press, 1995.

Dyer, Thomas G. *Theodore Roosevelt and the Idea of Race*, Baton Rouge and London: Louisiana State University Press, 1980.

Ellenberger, Henri F. *The Discovery of the Unconscious: The History and Evolution of Dynamic Psychiatry*, New York: Basic Books, 1970.

Elliott, Robert C. "Introduction," *Looking Backward*, Edward Bellamy, Boston: Houghton Mifflin, 1966. v–xii.

Elmer, Jonathan. *Reading at the Social Limit: Affect, Mass Culture, and Edgar Allan Poe*, Stanford: Stanford University Press, 1995.

Emerson, Ralph Waldo. *The Complete Works of Ralph Waldo Emerson*, 12 vols., New York: AMS, 1968.

Esdaile, James. *Mesmerism in India* [1846], Chicago: The Psychic Research Co., 1902.

Esteve, Mary. "William James's Onto-Physiology of Limits," *Genre* 29 (1996): 341–358.

Ferguson, Frances. *Solitude and the Sublime: Romanticism and the Aesthetics of Individuation*, New York and London: Routledge, 1992.

Ferraro, Thomas. "Avant-garde Ethnics," in *The Future of American Modernism: Ethnic Writing between the Wars*, ed. William Boelhower, Amsterdam: VU University Press, 1990. 1–31.

Ferry, Luc. *Homo Aestheticus: The Invention of Taste in the Democratic Age*, trans. Robert de Loaiza, Chicago and London: University of Chicago Press, 1993.

Festenstein, Matthew. *Pragmatism and Political Theory: From Dewey to Rorty*, Chicago: University of Chicago Press, 1997.

Fiedler, Leslie. "The Many Myths of Henry Roth," in *New Essays on Call It Sleep*, ed. Hana Wirth-Nesher, Cambridge, England: Cambridge University Press, 1996. 17–28.

Findling, John E. *Chicago's Great World's Fairs*, Manchester and New York: Manchester University Press, 1994.

Fine, William F. *Progressive Evolutionism and American Sociology, 1890–1920*, Ann Arbor: UMI Research Press, 1976.

Fisher, Philip. "Appearing and Disappearing in Public: Social Space in Late-Nineteenth Century Literature and Culture," in *Reconstructing American Literary History*, ed. Sacvan Bercovitch, Cambridge, MA and London: Harvard University Press, 1986. 155–188.

"Democratic Social Space: Whitman, Melville, and the Promise of American Transparency," *Representations* 24 (1988): 60–101.

Fitzhugh, George. *Cannibals All!* [1857], in *Antebellum: Writings of George Fitzhugh and Hinton Rowan Helper on Slavery*, ed. Harvey Wish, New York: G. P. Putnam's Sons, 1960.

Sociology for the South [1854], in *Antebellum*, ed. Harvey Wish, New York: G. P. Putnam's Sons, 1960.

Flower, B. O. "Hypnotism and Its Relation to Psychical Research," *The Arena* 5 (Feb. 1892): 316–334.

"Hypnotism and Mental Suggestion," *The Arena* 6 (July 1892): 208–218.

Foster, George G. *New York by Gas-Light and Other Urban Sketches* [1850], ed. Stuart Blumin, Berkeley and Los Angeles: University of California Press, 1990.

Foucault, Michel. *The History of Sexuality: An Introduction*, trans. Robert Hurley, New York: Vintage, 1978.

"Nietzsche, Genealogy, History," *Language, Counter-Memory, Practice*, ed. Donald Bouchard, Ithaca: Cornell University Press, 1977. 139–64.

"A Preface to Transgression," *Language, Counter-Memory, Practice*, ed. Donald Bouchard, Ithaca: Cornell University Press, 1977. 29–52.

Fraser, Nancy. "Rethinking the Public Sphere: A Contribution to the Critique of Actually Existing Democracy," in *Habermas and the Public Sphere*, ed. Craig Calhoun, Cambridge, MA and London: MIT Press, 1992. 109–142.

Freeman, Barbara Claire. *The Feminine Sublime: Gender and Excess in Women's Fiction*, Berkeley and Los Angeles: University of California Press, 1995.

Freud, Sigmund. *Beyond the Pleasure Principle*, in *The Standard Edition of the Complete Psychological Works of Sigmund Freud*, vol. 18, ed. James Strachey, London: Hogarth, 1955.

Group Psychology and the Analysis of the Ego, trans. James Strachey. New York: Bantam, 1960.

Fried, Michael. *Realism, Writing, Disfiguration: On Thomas Eakins and Stephen Crane*, Chicago: University of Chicago Press, 1987.

Fuller, Robert C. *Mesmerism and the American Cure of Souls*. Philadelphia: University of Pennsylvania Press, 1982.

Gandal, Keith. *The Virtues of the Vicious: Jacob Riis, Stephen Crane, and the Spectacle of the Slum*, New York and Oxford: Oxford University Press, 1997.

Gatell, Frank Otto and John M. McFaul, eds. *Jacksonian America 1815–1850: New Society, Changing Politics*, Englewood Cliffs, New Jersey: Prentice-Hall, 1970.

Gauchet, Marcel. *L'inconscient cérébral*, Paris: Édition Seuil, 1992.

Gelley, Alexander. "City Texts: Representation, Semiology, Urbanism," in *Politics, Theory, and Contemporary Culture*, ed. Mark Poster. New York: Columbia University Press, 1993. 237–260.

Gellner, Ernest. *Nations and Nationalism*, Ithaca and London: Cornell University Press, 1983.

Gernsheim, Helmut. *The Origins of Photography*, New York: Thames and Hudson, revised edition, 1982.

Girgus, Sam B. *The New Covenant: Jewish Writers and the American Idea*, Chapel Hill and London: University of North Carolina Press, 1984.

Gleason, William. *The Leisure Ethic: Work and Play in American Literature, 1840–1940*, Stanford: Stanford University Press, 1999.

Gold, Michael. *Jews without Money* [1930], New York: Carroll and Graf, 1984.

Gould, Philip. *Covenant and Republic: Historical Romance and the Politics of Puritanism*, Cambridge and New York: Cambridge University Press, 1996.

Gove (Nichols), Mary S. *Lectures to Ladies on Anatomy and Physiology*, Boston: Saxton and Pierce, 1842.

Grossman, Allen. "The Poetics of Union in Whitman and Lincoln: An Inquiry toward the Relationship of Art and Policy," in *The American Renaissance Reconsidered*, eds. Walter Benn Michaels and Donald Pease, Baltimore and London: Johns Hopkins University Press, 1985. 183–208.

Gunning, Sandra. *Race, Rape, and Lynching: The Red Record of American Literature, 1890–1912*, Oxford and New York: Oxford University Press, 1996.

Habermas, Jürgen. "Concluding Remarks," in *Habermas and the Public Sphere*, ed. Craig Calhoun, Cambridge, MA and London: MIT Press, 1992. 462–479.

"Further Reflections on the Public Sphere," in *Habermas and the Public Sphere*, ed. Craig Calhoun, Cambridge, MA and London: MIT Press, 1992. 421–461.

The Structural Transformation of the Public Sphere: An Inquiry into a Category of Bourgeois Society, trans. Thomas Burger, Cambridge, MA: MIT Press, 1991.

Hales, Peter B. *Silver Cities: The Photography of American Urbanization, 1839–1915*, Philadelphia: Temple University Press, 1984.

Halliburton, David. *The Color of the Sky. A Study of Stephen Crane*, Cambridge, England: Cambridge University Press, 1989.

Hanson, Russell L. *The Democratic Imagination in America*, Princeton: Princeton University Press, 1985.

Harris, Neil, et al. *Grand Illusions: Chicago's World's Fair of 1893*, Chicago: Chicago Historical Society, 1993.

Harris, Trudier. *Exorcising Blackness. Historical and Literary Lynching and Burning Rituals*, Bloomington: Indiana University Press, 1984.

Hawthorne, Nathaniel. *The House of Seven Gables* [1851], New York: Penguin, 1986. *Tales and Sketches*, ed. Roy Harvey Pearce, New York: Library of America, 1982. *Centenary Edition of the Works of Nathaniel Hawthorne*, 23 vols., eds. Thomas Woodson et al. Ohio State University Press, 1974.

Headley, Joel. *The Great Riots of New York, 1712–1873* [1873], Miami, FL: Mnemosyne Publishing Co., 1969.

Hegeman, Susan. *Patterns for America: Modernism and the Concept of Culture*, Princeton: Princeton University Press, 1999.

Henkin, David M. *City Reading: Written Words and Public Spaces in Antebellum New York*, New York: Columbia University Press, 1998.

Higham, John. *Send These to Me: Immigrants in Urban America*, Baltimore and London: Johns Hopkins University Press, revised edition, 1984. *Strangers in the Land: Patterns of American Nativism, 1860–1925* [1955], New Brunswick, NJ: Rutgers University Press, 1992.

Hollinger, David. *Postethnic America: Beyond Multiculturalism*, New York: Basic Books, 1995.

Holmes, Oliver Wendell. *The Guardian Angel*, Boston and New York: Houghton, Mifflin and Co. (Riverside Edition, vol. 6), 1895.

The Holy Bible: Authorized King James Version, London and New York: Collins' Clean-Type Press, 1975.

Horowitz, Joseph. *Wagner Nights: An American History*, Berkeley and Los Angeles: University of California Press, 1994.

Horwitz, Howard. "*Maggie* and the Sociological Paradigm," *American Literary History* 10 (1998): 606–638.

Hostetler, Ann E. "The Aesthetics of Race and Gender in Nella Larsen's *Quicksand*," *PMLA* 105 (1990): 35–47.

Hough, Robert. "Crane and Goethe: A Forgotten Relationship," *Nineteenth Century Fiction* 17 (1962): 135–148.

Howard, Lillie P. "'A Lack Somewhere': Nella Larsen's *Quicksand* and the Harlem Renaissance," in *The Harlem Renaissance Re-Examined*, ed. Victor Kramer, New York: AMS Press, 1987: 223–233.

Howe, Frederic C. *The City: The Hope of Democracy* [1905], introd. Otis A. Pease, Seattle and London: University of Washington Press, 1967.

Huxley, Thomas Henry. *Evolution and Ethics*, eds. James Paradis and George C. Williams, Princeton: Princeton University Press, 1989.

Ives, Halsey, ed. *The Dream City: A Portfolio of Photographic Views of the World's Columbian Exposition*, St. Louis: N.D. Thompson, 1893.

Jacobson, Matthew Frye. *Whiteness of a Different Color: European Immigrants and the Alchemy of Race*, Cambridge, MA and London: Harvard University Press, 1998.

James, Henry. *The American Scene* [1907], Bloomington: Indiana University Press, 1968.

The Complete Notebooks of Henry James, eds. Leon Edel and Lyall H. Powers, New York and Oxford: Oxford University Press, 1987.

The Complete Tales of Henry James, 12 vols., ed. Leon Edel, Philadelphia and New York: J. B. Lippincott, 1962–1965.

Hawthorne [1879], in *The Shock of Recognition*, ed. Edmund Wilson, Garden City and New York: Doubleday, 1943.

Henry James: Letters, 4 vols., ed. Leon Edel, Cambridge, MA and London: Harvard University Press, 1974–84.

Literary Reviews and Essays, ed. Albert Mordell, New York: Twayne, 1957.

The Question of Our Speech and *The Lesson of Balzac*, [1905] New York: Haskell House Pub., 1972 rept.

A Small Boy and Others, New York: Charles Scribner's Sons, 1913.

Washington Square [1881], London: Penguin Classics, 1984.

James, Henry and William James. *William and Henry James: Selected Letters*, eds. Ignas K. Skrupskelis and Elizabeth M. Berkeley, Charlottesville and London: University of Virginia Press, 1997.

James, William. *Collected Essays and Reviews*, London: Longmans Green and Co., 1920.

Essays, Comments, and Reviews, Cambridge, MA and London: Harvard University Press, 1987.

Essays in Radical Empiricism, Cambridge, MA and London: Harvard University Press, 1976.

The Letters of William James, 2 vols., Boston: Little, Brown, 1926.

"On a Certain Blindness," in *The James Family: A Group Biography*, F. O. Matthiessen, New York: Vintage, 1980. 397–403.

Pragmatism, Cambridge, MA and London: Harvard University Press, 1978.

The Principles of Psychology, 2 vols., New York: Henry Holt and Co., 1890.

"Social Psychology," *Psychological Review* 4 (1897): 313–315.

The Will to Believe and Other Essays in Popular Philosophy, New York: Dover, 1956.

Writings 1902–1910, ed. Bruce Kucklick. New York: Library of America, 1987.

Jay, Martin. "Reflective Judgments by a Spectator on a Conference that Is Now History," in *Hannah Arendt and the Meaning of Politics*, eds. Craig Calhoun and John McGowan, Minneapolis: University of Minnesota Press, 1997. 338–350.

Jewett, Sarah Orne. "Human Documents," *McClure's Magazine* 1 (June 1893): 16–18.

Johnson, James Weldon. *The Autobiography of an Ex-Colored Man*, [1912], in *Three Negro Classics*, ed. John Hope Franklin, New York: Avon, 1965.

Black Manhattan [1930], New York: Atheneum, 1968.

"Harlem: the Culture Capital," in *The New Negro* [1925], ed. Alain Locke. New York: Atheneum, 1970. 301–311.

Jukes, Peter. *A Shout in the Street: An Excursion into the Modern City*, New York: Farrar Straus Giroux, 1990.

Kant, Immanuel. *The Critique of Judgement*, trans. James Creed Meredith, Oxford: Oxford University Press, 1957.

Political Writings, ed. Hans Reiss, Cambridge, England: Cambridge University Press, 1970.

Karcher, Carolyn. *The First Woman in the Republic: A Cultural Biography of Lydia Maria Child*, Durham: Duke University Press, 1994.

Kasson, John F. *Amusing the Million: Coney Island at the Turn of the Century*, New York: Hill and Wang, 1978.

Kessler Harris, Alice. "Introduction," *Bread Givers*, Anzia Yezierska, New York: Persea Books, 1975.

Keys, Thomas E. *The History of Surgical Anesthesia*, New York: Schuman's, 1945.

King, Erika. "Democracy and the 'Sovereign Crowd' in Pre-World War I American Magazines," *Journal of American Culture* 15 (1992): 27–32.

Kittler, Friedrich. "World-Breath: On Wagner's Media Technology," in *Opera Through Other Eyes*, ed. David J. Levin. Stanford: Stanford University Press, 1993. 215–235.

Kloppenberg, James T. *Uncertain Victory: Social Democracy and Progressivism in European and American Thought, 1870–1920*, New York and Oxford: Oxford University Press, 1986.

The Virtues of Liberalism, New York and Oxford: Oxford University Press, 1998.

Knapp, Steven. *Literary Interest: The Limits of Anti-Formalism*, Cambridge, MA and London: Harvard University Press, 1993.

Kristeva, Julia. *Powers of Horror: An Essay on Abjection*, trans. Leon S. Roudiez, New York: Columbia University Press, 1982.

Larsen, Nella. *Quicksand* and *Passing*, introd. Deborah McDowell, New Brunswick, NJ: Rutgers University Press, 1986.

Larson, Kerry C. *Whitman's Drama of Consensus*, Chicago and London: University of Chicago Press, 1988.

Lay, Mary M. "Parallels: Henry James's *The Portrait of a Lady* and Nella Larsen's *Quicksand*," *CLA Journal* 20 (1977): 475–486.

Lears, T. J. Jackson. *No Place of Grace: Antimodernism and the Transformation of American Culture 1880–1920*, Chicago and London: University of Chicago Press, 1994.

Le Bon, Gustave. *The Crowd*, trans. anon., London: T. Fisher Unwin, 1896.

The Psychology of Peoples [1898], trans. anon., New York: G. E. Stechere, 1924.

Lefort, Claude. *Democracy and Political Theory*, trans. David Macey, Minneapolis: University of Minnesota Press, 1988.

Lewis, David Levering. *W.E.B. Du Bois: Biography of a Race 1868–1919*, New York: Henry Holt, 1993.

When Harlem Was in Vogue, New York: Vintage, 1982.

Leys, Ruth. *From Sympathy to Reflex: Marshall Hall and His Opponents*, New York: Garland, 1991.

"Mead's Voices: Imitation as Foundation, or, The Struggle against Mimesis," *Critical Inquiry* 19 (1993): 277–307.

Trauma: A Genealogy, Chicago and London: Chicago University Press, 2000.

Liebersohn, Harry. *Fate and Utopia in German Sociology, 1870–1923*, Cambridge, MA and London: MIT Press, 1988.

Lindenberger, Herbert. *Opera: The Extravagant Art*, Ithaca and London: Cornell University Press, 1984.

Livingston, James. *Pragmatism and the Political Economy of Cultural Revolution, 1850–1940*, Chapel Hill and London: University of North Carolina Press, 1994.

Lyons, Bonnie. *Henry Roth: The Man and His Work*, New York: Cooper Square Pub., 1976.

Lyotard, Jean-Francois. "*Sensus communis*: The Subject in *statu nascendi*," in *Who Comes After the Subject?*, eds. Eduardo Cadava, Peter Connor, Jean-Luc Nancy. New York and London: Routledge, 1991. 217–235.

Macy, John. "Mobs," *The Masses* (1916): 16.

Marshall, David. *The Surprising Effects of Sympathy: Marivaux, Diderot, Rousseau, and Mary Shelley*, Chicago: University of Chicago Press, 1988.

Matthews, Fred H. *Quest for an American Sociology: Robert E. Park and the Chicago School*, Montreal: McGill-Queen's University Press, 1977.

Matthiessen, F. O. *The James Family: A Group Biography*. New York: Vintage, 1980.

Mays, Benjamin Elijah and Joseph William Nicholson. *The Negro's Church*, New York: Institute for Social and Religious Research, 1933.

McClelland, J. S. *The Crowd and the Mob. From Plato to Canetti*, London: Unwin Hyman, 1989.

McDowell, Deborah. "Introduction," *Quicksand* and *Passing*, New Brunswick, NJ: Rutgers University Press, 1986.

McHale, Brian. "Henry Roth in Nighttown, or, Containing *Ulysses*," in *New Essays on Call It Sleep*, ed. Hana Wirth-Nesher. Cambridge, England: Cambridge University Press, 1996. 75–106.

Merwin, H[enry] C[hilds] "A National Vice," *The Atlantic Monthly* 71 (1893): 769–774.

Michaels, Walter Benn. "An American Tragedy, or the Promise of American Life," *Representations* 25 (1989): 71–98.

The Gold Standard and the Logic of Naturalism, Berkeley, Los Angeles, London: University of California Press, 1987.

Our America: Nativism, Modernism, and Pluralism, Durham and London: Duke University Press, 1995.

"The Souls of White Folk," in *Literature and the Body: Essays on Population and Persons*, ed. Elaine Scarry, Baltimore: Johns Hopkins University Press, 1988. 185–209.

Miles, George, ed. *The World's Fair from London 1851 to Chicago 1893*, Chicago: Midway Publ. Co., 1892.

Miller, Perry, ed. *The Transcendentalists: An Anthology*, Cambridge, MA: Harvard University Press, 1950.

Mills, Nicolaus. *The Crowd in American Literature*, Baton Rouge and London: Louisiana State University Press, 1986.

Mitchell, W. J. T., ed. *Against Theory: Literary Studies and the New Pragmatism*, Chicago and London: University of Chicago Press, 1985.

Mizruchi, Susan. *The Science of Sacrifice: American Literature and Modern Social Theory*, Princeton: Princeton University Press, 1998.

Moscovici, Serge. *The Age of the Crowd: A Historical Treatise on Mass Psychology*, trans. J. C. Whitehouse, Cambridge, England: Cambridge University Press, 1985.

Mouffe, Chantal. "Democracy, Power, and the 'Political,'" in *Democracy and Difference*, ed. Seyla Benhabib, Princeton: Princeton University Press, 1996. 245–256.

New York Times. August 13, 1896: 3.

Nietzsche, Friedrich. *Beyond Good and Evil*, trans. Walter Kaufmann, New York: Vintage, 1966.

The Birth of Tragedy and The Case of Wagner, trans. Walter Kaufmann, New York: Vintage, 1967.

"On the Uses and Disadvantages of History for Life," in *Untimely Meditations*, trans. R. J. Hollingdale, Cambridge, England: Cambridge University Press, 1983. 59–123.

Nye, Robert. *The Origins of Crowd Psychology: Gustave Le Bon and the Crisis of Mass Democracy in the Third Republic*, London: Sage Publications, 1975.

"Savage Crowds, Modernism, and Modern Politics," in *Prehistories of the Future: The Primitivist Project and the Culture of Modernism*, eds. Elazar Barkan and Ronald Bush, Stanford: Stanford University Press, 1995. 42–55.

Oppen, George. *Collected Poems*, New York: New Directions, 1975.

Park, Robert E. *The Crowd and the Public and Other Essays*, trans. Charlotte Elsner, Chicago: University of Chicago Press, 1972.

Park, Robert and Ernest Burgess. *The City. Suggestions for Investigation of Human Behavior in the Urban Environment* [1925], Chicago and London: University of Chicago Press, 1967.

Patrick, G. T. W. "The Psychology of Crazes," *Popular Science Monthly* 57 (1900): 285–94.

Pease, Donald. *Visionary Compacts: American Renaissance Writings in Cultural Context*, Madison: University of Wisconsin Press, 1987.

Pease, William and Jane Pease, eds. *The Antislavery Argument*, Indianapolis and New York: Bobbs-Merrill, 1965.

Peckham, Morse. "Darwinism and Darwinisticism," in *Darwin*, second edition, ed. Philip Appleman, New York: Norton, 1979. 297–304.

Perry, Ralph Barton. *The Thought and Character of William James*, 2 vols. Boston: Little, Brown and Co., 1935.

Pickthall, Marmaduke. *Saïd the Fisherman*, London: Methuen, 1903.

Pierce, James Wilson. *Photographic History of the World's Fair*, Baltimore: R. H. Woodward, 1893.

Pippin, Robert B. *Henry James and Modern Moral Life*, Cambridge: Cambridge University Press, 2000.

Plotz, John. *The Crowd: British Literature and Public Politics*, Berkeley and Los Angeles: University of California Press, 2000.

Poe, Edgar Allan. *Poetry and Tales*, New York: Library of America, 1984.

Posnock, Ross. *Color and Culture: Black Writers and the Making of the Modern Intellectual*, Cambridge, MA and London: Harvard University Press, 1998.

The Trial of Curiosity: Henry James, William James and the Challenge of Modernity, Oxford: Oxford University Press, 1991.

Pulzer, Peter G. J. *The Rise of Political Anti-Semitism in Germany and Austria*, New York: John Wiley and Sons, 1964.

Raper, Howard Riley. *Man against Pain: The Epic of Anesthesia*, New York: Prentice-Hall, 1945.

Raushenbush, Winifred. *Robert E. Park: Biography of a Sociologist*, Durham: Duke University Press, 1979.

Rawls, John. *Lectures on the History of Moral Philosophy*, ed. Barbara Herman, Cambridge, MA and London: Harvard University Press, 2000.

Political Liberalism, New York: Columbia University Press, 1993.

"Themes in Kant's Moral Philosophy," in *Kant and Political Philosophy: The Contemporary Legacy*, eds. Ronald Beiner and William James Booth, New Haven and London: Yale University Press, 1993. 291–319.

A Theory of Justice, Cambridge, MA: Harvard University Press, 1971.

Reed, Adolph L., Jr. *W.E.B. Du Bois and American Political Thought: Fabianism and the Color Line*, Oxford and New York: Oxford University Press, 1997.

Robbins, Bruce. "Modernism in History, Modernism in Power," in *Modernism Reconsidered*, ed. Robert Kiely, Cambridge, MA: Harvard University Press, 1983. 229–245.

ed. *The Phantom Public Sphere*, Minneapolis and London: University of Minnesota Press, 1993.

Robertson, Michael. *Stephen Crane, Journalism, and the Making of Modern American Literature*, New York: Columbia University Press, 1997.

Robinson, Victor. *Victory over Pain: A History of Anesthesia*, New York: Henry Schuman, 1946.

Rogin, Michael Paul. *Subversive Genealogy: The Politics and Art of Herman Melville*, Berkeley and Los Angeles: University of California Press, 1985.

" 'The Sword Became a Flashing Vision': D. W. Griffith's *The Birth of a Nation*," *Representations* 9 (1985): 150–195.

Roosevelt, Theodore. "True Americanism," in *American Ideals and Other Essays Social and Political*, second edition, New York and London: Putnam's Sons, 1898. 15–34.

The Writings of Theodore Roosevelt, ed. William H. Harbaugh, Indianapolis and New York: Bobbs-Merrill, 1967.

Rose, Paul Lawrence. *Wagner: Race and Revolution*, New Haven and London: Yale University Press, 1992.

Rosenfeld, Isaac. *An Age of Enormity*, Cleveland: World Pub. Co., 1962.

Ross, Edward. "The Mob Mind," *Popular Science Monthly* 51 (1897): 390–398.

Roth, Henry. *Call It Sleep*, introd. Alfred Kazin. New York: Noonday, 1991.

Rotman, Brian. *Signifying Nothing: The Semiotics of Zero*, London: Macmillan, 1987.

Rudé, George. *The Crowd in History, 1730–1848*, New York and London: John Wiley and Sons, 1964.

Ruttenburg, Nancy. *Democratic Personality: Popular Voice and the Trial of American Authorship*, Stanford: Stanford University Press, 1998.

Ryan, Mary. "Gender and Public Access: Women's Politics in Nineteenth-Century America," in *Habermas and the Public Sphere*, ed. Craig Calhoun, Cambridge, MA and London: MIT Press, 1992. 259–288.

Rydell, Robert. *All the World's a Fair*, Chicago: University of Chicago Press, 1984.

Salmon, Richard. *Henry James and the Culture of Publicity*, Cambridge, England: Cambridge University Press, 1997.

Scheiber, Andrew. "The Doctor's Order: Eugenic Anxiety in Henry James's *Washington Square*," *Literature and Medicine* 15 (1996): 244–62.

Schivelbusch, Wolfgang. *The Railway Journey: Trains and Travel in the Nineteenth Century*, trans. Anselm Hollo, New York: Urizen Books, 1979.

Schlesinger, Arthur M., Jr. *The Age of Jackson*, Boston and Toronto: Little, Brown, 1945.

Schoening, Mark: "T. S. Eliot Meets Michael Gold: Modernism and Radicalism in Depression-Era American Literature," *Modernism/Modernity* 3 (1996): 51–68.

Schudson, Michael. *The Good Citizen: A History of American Civic Life*, Cambridge, MA and London: Harvard University Press, 1998.

Scruggs, Charles. *Sweet Home: Invisible Cities in the Afro-American Novel*, Baltimore and London: Johns Hopkins University Press, 1993.

Seltzer, Mark. "Statistical Persons," *diacritics* 17 (Fall, 1987): 82–98.

Sherard, R. H. "The Hypnotic Experiments of Doctor Luys," *McClure's Magazine* 1 (November 1893): 547–554.

Sidis, Boris. *The Psychology of Suggestion*, New York: Appleton, 1898.

"A Study of the Mob," *The Atlantic Monthly* (Feb. 1895): 188–197.

Simmel, Georg. *The Sociology of Georg Simmel*, trans. Kurt Wolff. London: Free Press of Glencoe, 1950.

"The Adventure." in *Essays on Sociology, Philosophy, and Aesthetics*, ed. Kurt Wolff, New York: Harper Torchbooks, 1965.

"Massenpsychologie," *Die Zeit*, vol. 5 (23 November 1895): 119–120 (Vienna).

Sledd, Andrew. "The Negro: Another View," *The Atlantic Monthly* 90 (1902): 65–73.

Sollors, Werner. "A Critique of Pure Pluralism," in *Reconstructing American Literary History*, ed. Sacvan Bercovitch, Cambridge, MA and London: Harvard University Press, 1986. 250–279.

" 'A world somewhere, somewhere else': Language, Nostalgic Mournfulness, and Urban Immigrant Family Romance in *Call It Sleep*," in *New Essays on Call It Sleep*, ed. Hana Wirth-Nesher, Cambridge: Cambridge University Press, 1996. 127–188.

Stallman, R. W. *Stephen Crane. A Biography*, New York: George Braziller, 1968.

ed. *The Stephen Crane Reader*, Glenview, IL: Scott, Foresman and Co., 1972.

Stoehr, Taylor. *Hawthorne's Mad Scientists: Pseudoscience and Social Science in Nineteenth-Century Life and Letters*, Hamden, CT: Archon Books, 1978.

"Words and Deeds in *The Princess Casamassima*," *ELH* 37 (1970): 95–135.

Stowe, Harriet Beecher. *Uncle Tom's Cabin: Or Life Among the Lowly*, ed. Elizabeth Ammons, New York: Norton, 1994.

Sullivan, Louis H. *The Autobiography of an Idea* [1924], New York: Dover, 1956.

Sundquist, Eric. J. *To Wake the Nations: Race in the Making of American Literature*, Cambridge, MA and London: Harvard University Press, 1993.

ed. *American Realism. New Essays*, Baltimore and London: Johns Hopkins University Press, 1982.

Tarde, Gabriel. *The Laws of Imitation*, trans. Elsie Clews Parsons, New York: Henry Holt, 1903.

L'opinion et la foule [1901], Paris: Presses Universitaires de France, 1989.

"Opinion and Conversation" [1901], in *Gabriel Tarde: On Communication and Social Influence, Selected Papers*, ed. Terry Clark. Chicago and London: University of Chicago Press, 1969. 297–318.

"The Public and the Crowd" [1901], in *Gabriel Tarde: On Communication and Social Influence, Selected Papers*, ed. Terry Clark. Chicago and London: University of Chicago Press, 1969. 277–293.

Taylor, Bayard. *Diversions of the Echo Club*, in *The Shock of Recognition*, ed. Edmund Wilson, Garden City and New York: Doubleday, 1943.

Thomas, Brook. "Citizen Hester: *The Scarlet Letter* as Civic Myth," *American Literary History* 13 (2001): 181–211.

ed. *Plessy v. Ferguson: A Brief History with Documents*, Boston and New York: Bedford Books, 1997.

Tocqueville, Alexis de. *Democracy in America*, trans. George Lawrence, ed. J. P. Mayer, New York: HarperPerennial, 1988.

Trachtenberg, Alan. "Experiments in Another Country: Stephen Crane's City Sketches," in *American Realism: New Essays*, ed. Eric J. Sundquist. Baltimore and London: Johns Hopkins University Press, 1982. 138–154.

   The Incorporation of America: Culture and Society in the Gilded Age, New York: Hill and Wang, 1982.

Tratner, Michael. *Modernism and Mass Politics: Joyce, Woolf, Eliot, Yeats*, Stanford: Stanford University Press, 1995.

Tumber, Catherine. "Edward Bellamy, the Erosion of Public Life, and the Gnostic Revival," *American Literary History* 11 (1999): 610–641.

Van Ginneken, Jaap. *Crowds, Psychology, Politics 1871–1899*, Cambridge, England: Cambridge University Press, 1992.

Wagner, Richard. *Lohengrin* [1850], New York: Fred Rullman, 1900.

   Richard Wagner's Prose Works, 8 vols., trans. William Ashton Ellis, New York: Broude Bros., 1966.

Wald, Priscilla. *Constituting Americans: Cultural Anxiety and Narrative Form*, Durham and London: Duke University Press, 1995.

Warner, Michael. "The Mass Public and the Mass Subject," in *Habermas and the Public Sphere*, ed. Craig Calhoun, Cambridge, MA and London: MIT Press, 1992. 377–401.

Welch, Margaret. "Is Newspaper Work Healthful for Women?" *Journal of Social Science* 32 (1894): 110–116.

Welling, William. *Photography in America: The Formative Years 1839–1900*, New York: Thomas Y. Crowell, 1978.

Wells, Ida B. *Selected Works of Ida B. Wells-Barnett*, introd. Trudier Harris, New York and Oxford: Oxford University Press, 1991.

Westbrook, Robert B. *John Dewey and American Democracy*, Ithaca and London: Cornell University Press, 1991.

Whalen, Terence. *Edgar Allan Poe and the Masses*, Princeton: Princeton University Press, 1999.

Wheeler, Candace. "A Dream City," *Harper's New Monthly Magazine* 86 (1893): 830–846.

Whitman, Walt. *Leaves of Grass*, New York: Library of America, 1992.

   Complete Poetry and Collected Prose, New York: Library of America, 1982.

Wild, John. *The Radical Empiricism of William James*. Garden City, New York: Doubleday, 1969.

Wilson, Elizabeth. "The Invisible *Flâneur*," *New Left Review* 191 (1992): 90–110.

Wirth, Louis. *On Cities and Social Life*, ed. Albert Reiss Jr., Chicago and London: University of Chicago Press, 1964.

Wirth-Nesher, Hana. "Between Mother Tongue and Native Language in *Call It Sleep*," Afterword, *Call It Sleep*, Henry Roth, introd. Alfred Kazin, New York: Noonday, 1991. 443–462.

Wittgenstein, Ludwig. *Philosophical Investigations*, trans. G. E. M. Anscombe, New York: Macmillan, 1958.

Wolff, Janet. "The Invisible *Flâneuse*: Women and the Literature of Modernity," in *The Problems of Modernity: Adorno and Benjamin*, ed. Andrew Benjamin, London and New York: Routledge, 1989. 86–111.

Yezierska, Anzia. *Bread Givers: A Struggle between a Father of the Old World and a Daughter of the New*, introd. Alice Kessler Harris, New York: Persea Books, 1975.

Ziff, Larzer. *Literary Democracy: The Declaration of Cultural Independence in America*, Middlesex, England and New York: Penguin, 1982.

"Whitman and the Crowd," *Critical Inquiry* 10 (1984): 579–591.

Zizek, Slavoj. "'The Wound Is Healed Only by the Spear That Smote You': The Operatic Subject and Its Vicissitudes," in *Opera Through Other Eyes*, ed. David J. Levin, Stanford: Stanford University Press, 1993. 177–214.

Index